Management for Professionals

The Springer series "Management for Professionals" comprises high-level business and management books for executives, MBA students, and practice-oriented business researchers. The topics cover all themes relevant to businesses and the business ecosystem. The authors are experienced business professionals and renowned professors who combine scientific backgrounds, best practices, and entrepreneurial vision to provide powerful insights into achieving business excellence.

The Series is SCOPUS-indexed.

Martin A. Bader • Oliver Gassmann
Mark James Thompson

Patent Management

Protecting Intellectual Property and Innovation

Second Edition

Springer

Martin A. Bader
THI Business School
Technische Hochschule Ingolstadt
Ingolstadt, Germany

School of Continuing Studies
McGill University
Montréal, QC, Canada

Oliver Gassmann
Institute of Technology Management
University of St. Gallen
St. Gallen, Switzerland

Mark James Thompson
Zurich University of Applied Sciences
Winterthur, Switzerland

ISSN 2192-8096 ISSN 2192-810X (electronic)
Management for Professionals
ISBN 978-3-032-12029-8 ISBN 978-3-032-12030-4 (eBook)
https://doi.org/10.1007/978-3-032-12030-4

This Springer imprint is published by the registered company Springer Nature Switzerland AG
The registered company address is: Gewerbestrasse 11, 6330 Cham, Switzerland

Preface

Innovation is paramount to competitive advantage because it both creates and captures value. The CoViD-19 crisis in 2020 underscored this reality: Companies had to innovate rapidly—often by adopting remote work supported by new information technologies. Today, the advent of artificial intelligence (AI) is accelerating innovation cycles in unprecedented ways; for example, new compounds can be discovered, simulated, and positioned for patenting with minimal human intervention. While AI can make invention cheaper and faster, commercial viability does not automatically follow. There is no longer a natural moat in the difficulty of the innovation process itself. Only organizations that appropriate the results of innovation effectively can sustain profitability.

In global competition, managing intellectual property (IP)—especially patents—has become at least as important as managing factories. Control over key technologies and platforms is not easily substituted, whereas suppliers of physical production can be. At the same time, the locus of IP generation has shifted eastward, with China and Korea now ranking alongside the USA, Japan, and Europe. China's patenting surge—led by firms such as *Huawei* (telecom), *Oppo* (smartphones), *BOE* (LCD panels), *Lenovo* (computers), *Tencent* (gaming), and *ZTE* (telecom)—has changed the center of gravity of IP, even as U.S. companies continue to dominate foreign filings.

Beyond this quantitative growth, the legal effectiveness and strategic use of patents have gained importance. On one side, organizations need experts who work closely with research and development (R&D) to secure and defend patents. On the other, the sheer volume of IP raises the bar for portfolio management in complex competitive environments. Comprehensive patent management, adapted to a firm's strategy and context, is essential to avoid being blindsided technologically. Patents also increasingly influence mergers and acquisitions—traditionally in pharmaceuticals, and now more widely in information and communications technology and computer science.

Despite the rising importance of patent management for corporate competitiveness, management-oriented literature remains limited. Our German book, *Patentmanagement*, has been very successful—now in its fifth edition—and this encouraged us to produce an English version. Rather than a direct translation, we present illustrative examples, cases, and anecdotes that reflect the international dimension of patents. We also look more deeply at current industries and practices, and we consider emerging technologies such as AI and distributed ledger technologies in the context of patents.

Our research has been anchored at the *Institute of Technology Management (ITEM-HSG)* at the *University of St. Gallen (HSG)*, Switzerland, and increasingly conducted with collaborators and in joint projects including, for example, the *THI Business School* at the *University of Applied Sciences Ingolstadt (THI)*, *Zurich University of Applied Sciences*, *Technical University of Applied Sciences Regensburg*, the *Stiftungsfonds Deutsche Bank Chair of Innovation Management and Entrepreneurship at HHL Leipzig Graduate School of Management*, the *Institute Business and Innovation (IBUS)* at *IMC Krems University of Applied Sciences*, *Management Center Innsbruck (MCI)*, *Goldsmiths, University of London*, the *Dickson Poon School of Law, King's College London*, the *Center for Intellectual Property at Universidad Austral*, Buenos Aires, Argentina, and the *Centre for Intellectual Property Policy at McGill University*, Montréal, Canada.

Our work—conducted with companies and organizations across Europe, China, Japan, Korea, India, Canada, and the USA—encompasses:

- Global benchmarking of strategic technology and IP management, and research/transfer projects on patent management across industries.
- Doctoral research on patent management, patent aggregators, and value capture with patents.
- In-depth studies on patent management, generation, licensing, and trading with the *European Commission (EC)*, *Audi/Volkswagen*, *Dennemeyer*, *PricewaterhouseCoopers (PwC)*, the *Swiss Federal Institute of Intellectual Property (IPI)*, the *European Patent Office (EPO)*, and the *World Intellectual Property Organization (WIPO)*.
- Public-sector projects informing IP and innovation policy—such as creating frameworks for markets in IP and mapping regional innovation activity—for the *Commission for Technology and Innovation (CTI, Switzerland)*, the *Austrian Federal Ministry of Economy, Family and Youth (BMWFJ)*, and the *Argentinian Ministry of Science, Technology and Productive Innovation (MinCyT)*.
- Extensive collaboration with industry partners on real-world IP strategy and management challenges.

A key element of this book is our leadership and consulting experience in managing innovation and IP. True to our motto—from insight to impact—we have learned as much from engaging with partners and clients across industries and regions as we have from our own research.

The first edition of Patent Management received recognition as "patent book of the year" from the IPKat blog. Many fundamentals remain stable: Top patent assignees and markets are broadly similar to 5 years ago from an IP perspective. In this second edition, we have incorporated developments since CoViD-19: Technologies such as blockchain, once novel, now being implemented in IP management; AI-enabled services are reshaping economies of scale; and we include material aimed at start-ups, including valuation, and explain how corporate patent departments and small and medium-sized enterprises (SMEs) can ensure compliance under the principal-agent dilemma when governing their external legal advisors and service providers.

We thank Ashkan Fredström (University of St. Gallen, Switzerland), Sylvain Roy (SRA, Montréal, Canada) and Todd Bailey (Scale AI, Canada) for their contributions to this edition. Special thanks go to the THI Business School at Technische Hochschule Ingolstadt and the Free State of Bavaria, Germany, to the University of St. Gallen and its ITEM-HSG Foundation, and to the School of Continuing Studies and the Centre for Intellectual Property Policy at McGill University, Montréal, for their support. We are grateful to Dr. Prashanth Mahagaonkar, Ruth Milewski, Ramya Prakash, and Martina Himberger at Springer for guiding the publication process. Last but not least, we thank our donors and partners, project collaborators, interview partners, PhD researchers, and students, whose commitment has been essential to this book.

We wish you success in creating and capturing value through innovation—using intellectual property as a strategic asset for your company or institution.

Montréal, Canada & Ingolstadt, Germany — Martin A. Bader
St. Gallen, Switzerland — Oliver Gassmann
Winterthur, Switzerland — Mark James Thompson
September 2025

Competing Interests The authors have no competing interests to declare that are relevant to the content of this manuscript.

Endorsements

"Not only a must-read for every IP specialist but also an exciting introduction for the non-professional with great examples and insights into the business world and its use of the patent system."

—Dr. jur. Catherine Chammartin, *Director General, Swiss Federal Institute of Intellectual Property (IPI), Bern, Switzerland*

"The reader will learn about all aspects of successful patent management: Protection, defense, as well as exploitation, valuation, and organization. A key feature of the book, which should be part of every innovation and IP management reference library, are the practical examples from different industries."

—Dr. Beat Weibel, *former Chief IP Counsel, Siemens*

"An absolute complete overview on the topic with very tangible and practical examples in industry and covering the latest technology trends."

—Dr. Erich Ruetsche, *Technology & IP Leader, IBM Research Europe*

"A must-read for every technology and innovation manager, who is active in the patent race. The international author team provides valuable insights, many examples, and strong managerial recommendations."

—Dr. Amir Bonakdar, *Senior Director Customer Innovation, SAP Labs Palo Alto*

"IPR is not limited to 'intellectual property rights'; it is more about 'innovation,' 'patents,' and 'relationship'. This book provides in-depth studies on patent management in all respects, to highlight the core value of IPR by the art of management."

—Dr. Li Tian, *Director of IPR & Standardization Department, ZTE Corporation*

"This book not only provides a comprehensive guide and best practices for all aspects of enterprise patent management but also highlights several interesting opportunities for patent practitioners, such as a patent protection scheme for artificial intelligence-based business method and a blockchain solution for patent transactions. Overall an excellent read."

—He Sidan, *Managing Director of Strategy, HiSilicon, Huawei*

"The book gives very good and structured insights into the crucial topic of patent management; especially helpful are the numerous examples."

—Prof. Dr. Thomas Kropf, *President of Corporate Research and Advanced Engineering, Bosch*

"Essential reading on patent management. A comprehensive and practical overview covering everything from the fundamentals to the development of a corporate patent strategy."

—Stephen Albrecht, *Director Corporate Technology, Liebherr International*

"A comprehensive overview of IP management, with a focus on patents. A must-read for anyone involved in creating and managing IP for competitive advantage."

—Dr. Matthias Kaiserswerth, *President of the Board, Abraxas*

"Well-written introduction to IP management for business and innovation managers."
—Dr. Hermann Bach, *SVP, Innovation Management & Commercial Services, Covestro*

"A structured overview of IP strategy considerations, along with a comprehensive teaching of the fundamental principles, terminologies, and processes relating to the world of IP."
—Charles Jeffries, *Group Intellectual Property, Novartis*

"An outstanding textbook on intellectual property protection in innovation management. Explanations are immediately understood. Examples confirm the closeness to daily practice. Perfect for use in industry and academia. I wish all textbooks were as great as this one."
—Prof. Dr. Thomas Müller-Kirschbaum, *Senior VP Innovation & Sustainability, Henkel*

"The book provides an easy-to-use framework, how to develop and implement a holistic IP strategy. Insights into different industries as well as on the impact of disruptive technologies (e.g., blockchain) make it a great guide and reference."
—Dr. Thorsten Mueller, *former CTO of Osram*

"*Intellectual Property Management for Professionals* is a great book for engineers to leverage and implement their IP strategy and learn about best practices."
—Dr. Oliver Mayer, *former Senior Principal at General Electric Research Center*

"A value-driven IP strategy is the key to effectively protect the business of the future. Many companies are struggling to implement the appropriate strategy. This book provides the right tools to implement the necessary processes."
—Dr. Thomas Jetzfellner, *Lead IP Counsel Blockchain, Siemens*

"A great book for IP professionals to leverage and implement their IP strategy and learn about best practices. An experienced handling of IP challenges is essential presently. This book supports all IP professionals to improve their IP strategy and to learn about best practices."
—Dr. Jörg Friedhofen, *Co-Head Patent Department, Vorwerk*

"*Intellectual Property Management for Professionals* is a good book that supports IP specialists both in their training and during their work. But also experienced readers will benefit from the book, as they find overviews and best practices that help them optimize IP strategy and IP processes."
—Alexander Poledna, *Head of Intellectual Property Rights, Standards & Journals, voestalpine stahl, Linz, Austria*

"The patent strategy reference book for patent managers, CTOs, CIOs and CEOs in innovation-intensive sectors. Bader, Gassmann, and Thompson provide a comprehensive guide to effectively build and strategically manage patent portfolios across a variety of sectors and technologies. The ultimate guide in patent tactics to create and extract value from R&D efforts and to stay ahead in the innovation game, including a wide array of compelling business cases."
—Josep Maria Pujals, *Licensing Director, Fractus, Sant Cugat del Vallès, Spain*

"Very comprehensively written, well-illustrated with examples, and directly applicable for real-life business. A must-read for every innovator who is in patent-intensive industries."
—Nicolas Durville, *CEO & Partner, Zühlke*

"One of those rare combinations of the practical with the cutting-edge academic that manages to condense it all into best practice for managing a sophisticated patent portfolio inside a business. The book does not assume knowledge and works as an excellent introduction, but it quickly moves on to show the best practices for different industries, from crop sciences to fintech, and technologies ranging from biotech to AI for how to build, commercialise, and maintain your patent portfolio. The book is packed with great examples, and invites the reader to explore beyond your own immediate sphere, and always with a mind to assisting with how to manage what is a business-critical asset—intellectual property."

—Benjamin Mitra-Kahn, *Assistant Commissioner, Productivity Commission, Melbourne, Australia*

"We live in an age of ever-increasing pressure to 'innovate or die,' to balance the need for collaborative knowledge production and dissemination with the need to thrive in a competitive global economy. This book offers an accessible guide to the complex world of intellectual property rights and patents—whether you are a student or practitioner of innovative practices, supply chain management, digital transformation, or knowledge entrepreneurship."

—Prof. Dr. Carola Weil, *Dean of Continuing Studies, McGill University/ Université McGill, Montréal, Canada*

"A comprehensive practical guide to effective patent management that takes into account the rapidly changing technological environment of companies and the increasing complexity of the patent system. This book offers a great match between general insights and practical implications."

—Prof. Dr. Martin Woerter, *KOF Swiss Economic Institute, ETH Zürich, Switzerland*

"A great book that does fill a niche on the market. Its value lies in combining theory and practice of patent management. The book does provide a comprehensive overview of patenting trends. Its clear structure in combination with many practical examples is of great help for both practitioners and scientific scholars alike."

—Dr. Nikolaus Thumm, *Senior Consultant, OECD, Paris*

"Whether you are an executive who wants to understand the business logic of patenting, an IP consultant who wants to provide legal advice better tailored to your clients' strategies, or a student of business and technology, this book offers in-depth and timely answers to your questions about patent management. It is packed with real-world examples, from all major industries as well as from new and emerging technologies."

—Prof. Dr. Marcus Holgersson, *Professor of Industrial Management and Economics, Chalmers University of Technology, Gothenburg, Sweden*

"This is a very timely book with IP management gaining increasing importance among executives. The book goes beyond an overview of protection strategies, providing valuable insights into commercialization practices, how to successfully organize patent management followed by important considerations of how patent management varies across industries. Given the applied perspective the authors take, this book will be of particular value to practitioners."

—Prof. Dr. Frank Tietze, *Professor of Innovation Engineering, University of Cambridge, Great Britain*

"Managing intellectual property as the core values of a firm is much more than IP protection. This book addresses the importance and relevance of IP topics for business success. In addition, up-to-date examples and benchmarks, presented tools, and frameworks are very useful for IP professionals and applicants."

—Prof. Dr. Sevim Süzeroglu-Melchiors, *OTH Regensburg, Germany, former Global Head of Consulting, Dennemeyer Group*

"This comprehensive book is the perfect mix between theory and practice and the ultimate reading for anyone interested in a real-world picture of patent management. Definitely a must-read."

—Prof. Dr. Massimiliano Granieri, *Professor of Law, University of Brescia, Italy*

"An engaging and useful book, rich in examples that help illustrate the protection of innovation to a wide audience, including postgraduate students, innovation scholars, and practitioners. Besides explaining the fundamentals of patent management in plain words, the book introduces the reader to the nuances of patent strategy in different industries and technological fields."

—Prof. Dr. Salvatore Torrisi, *Professor of Strategic Management, University of Milano-Bicocca, Italy*

"The book is a very good resource for the managers of companies and other innovative organizations, so that they can properly manage the results of the R&D processes. It illustrates the theoretical structure on the management of intangible assets using numerous practical cases, more from a business perspective than from legal practice. It helps to understand how decisions on innovation and protection of intellectual property rights are made."

—Prof. Gustavo Schötz, *Universidad Austral, Intellectual Property Center, Buenos Aires, Argentina*

"This is an excellent book for professionals working in the field of the intellectual property management. It provides a practical and comprehensive guide for generating, evaluating, managing, and monetizing intellectual property rights (patents). Professionals can use information from this book in a wide variety of industry and technology sectors."

—Michael Kucher, *Attorney at Law, Partner at Slater & Matsil, Dallas, USA*

"A must-read for all those involved with transforming innovation into intangible company assets, for its comprehensive coverage of all industry sectors and its didactic approach to managing and exploiting these assets."

—Philippe Therias, *Avocat au Barreau de Paris, BCF Global, France*

"A comprehensive and accessible book on patent fundamentals and practice, from a practical management perspective. It offers both a comprehensive and deep analysis of the most important current industries and technologies, its important implications, and specific practices. I recommend it both as a reference manual, to clarify basic concepts on the subject, and for consultation in professional practice related to the protection of specific inventions and technology."

—Reyes Campello Estebaranz, *Managing Partner, CEALAW, Alicante, Spain*

"A great overview of how to manage and protect patent and intellectual property. This book will serve as a very important tool to encourage those who dedicate their time to innovation in every field. I am looking forward to be delighted with this book, which I will certainly use in my routine."

—Ramon Fernandez Aracil Filho, *Partner at Mourão Campos, São Paulo, Brazil*

"A practical yet comprehensive handbook on patent management. It is the reference text I wish I had, when starting out in research commercialization!"

—Dr. Luke Krieg, *Digital Innovation Lead, GHD, Auckland, New Zealand*

"Which patent specialist is not familiar with the successful patent management series by Martin A. Bader and Oliver Gassmann? With five editions in German and, since 2021, also in English? Overall, the work provides an excellent foundation for familiarizing oneself with the topics of 'patent strategy' and 'patent management.' Supported by numerous graphics and case studies, the book is easy to read. Despite its scientific depth, it is also practice-oriented. This is no surprise given the authors' backgrounds: Before embarking on an academic career, Gassmann was head of research at the elevator manufacturer Schindler, while Bader was vice president and chief IP officer at Infineon Technologies. In keeping with this, they have added Mark James Thomson, a native English speaker who [worked as assistant director of the center for data excellence at the Australian patent office, was chief economist at the Austrian patent office and economist at the Swiss office, and] is also a specialist in patent valuation, to the team of authors."

—Dr. Peter Kurz, *Stuttgart, Germany*, in *Mitteilungen der deutschen Patentanwälte*

"It must have been a Herculean task to write a book on patent management, as the practice area is wide and covers a lot of different subjects. One of the first major tasks of the authors must have been to overcome the bias that 'patent management' is just about filing patent applications when, where, and at what costs and paying maintenance fees to keep the patents alive. They did well, as can be expected from authors with a deep knowledge of intellectual property. [...] Impressive is the way the authors have managed to clarify the specifics of patent management in very different corporate and market conditions by going into company-specific examples for each of the industry groups they cite. [...] An excellent book that anyone dealing with patent management can enjoy exploring, albeit that it is often quite heavy stuff and not suited for a weekend read. However, the thoroughness of the book is amazing and unique in its form and will provide the patent practitioner a vast amount of knowledge and insights for which we need to be grateful to the authors."

—Severin de Wit, *The Hague, the Netherlands*, in *World Patent Information*

"A well-structured set of valuable managerial insights into patent management from a practical perspective while analyzing the most important current industry sectors and new technologies across the world. They provide an overview of the common concepts and building blocks of patent management."

—*IPKat Book Review*

Contents

1 Fundamentals of Intellectual Property Rights 1
1.1 Creating Value by Generating Innovation 1
1.2 Capturing Value by Protecting Innovation 4
1.3 Types of Intellectual Property Rights 15
References 23

2 Protection Strategies 27
2.1 Patent Strategies in General 27
2.2 Offensive and Defensive Patent Strategies 30
2.3 Core Dimensions of Patent Strategies 32
2.4 Cost of Patents 40
2.5 Complementary Strategies to Patenting 43
References 50

3 Evaluating and Valuing Patents 51
3.1 Evaluating Patents 52
3.2 Valuing Patents 61
3.3 Managing the Patent Portfolio 81
References 96

4 Successful Practices in Commercializing Patents 99
4.1 Licensing 100
4.2 Cross-Licensing 101
4.3 Sale 103
4.4 Strategic Alliance 104
4.5 Spin-Off and Call-Back 105
4.6 Joint Venture 106
4.7 Patenting for Access to Finance 107
4.8 Litigation for Value 110
4.9 Complex Strategies 112
4.10 Commercialization Concepts and Conclusions 114
References 118

5 Organizing Patent Management . . . 121
5.1 Corporate Governance vs. Service Department . . . 121
5.2 Governing Outsourcing and Compliance . . . 123
5.3 Costs and Benefits of a Patent Department . . . 128
5.4 Core Processes of Patent Management . . . 133
5.5 Generative Artificial Intelligence in Patent Management . . . 139
5.6 Blockchain and DLTs in Patent Management . . . 147
References . . . 155

6 Patent Management by Industry . . . 157
6.1 Pharma . . . 157
6.2 Chemistry . . . 160
6.3 Crop Science . . . 162
6.4 Life Sciences . . . 164
6.5 Consumer Goods . . . 167
6.6 Retail . . . 169
6.7 Machinery . . . 172
6.8 Electronics and Electrical Equipment . . . 176
6.9 Automotive and Connectivity . . . 182
6.10 Information and Communication Technology . . . 188
6.11 Financial Services and Fintech . . . 195
6.12 Transport and Logistics . . . 198
References . . . 201

7 Patent Management in New Technology Environments . . . 205
7.1 Biotechnology . . . 206
7.2 Nanotechnology . . . 215
7.3 Industry 4.0 and Internet of Things . . . 220
7.4 Software and Business Methods . . . 225
7.5 Artificial-Intelligence-Based Business Models . . . 237
References . . . 251

8 Patent Management in VUCA Environments . . . 257
8.1 Inventor Culture as a Catalyst . . . 257
8.2 Need for Action at SMEs . . . 265
8.3 Challenges for Start-Ups . . . 267
8.4 Measures Against Product Piracy . . . 274
References . . . 278

9 Useful Information for Practitioners . . . 281
9.1 Patent Growth Worldwide . . . 281
9.2 Structure of a Patent . . . 282
9.3 Patent Document Codes . . . 284
9.4 Patent Classification . . . 285
9.5 Notes on Patent Search . . . 286
9.6 Member States of the European Patent Organisation . . . 288
9.7 EUIPO/Unitary Patent/Unified Patent Court . . . 288

9.8 IP Tax Regimes 290
9.9 Brief Comparison of Patent Legislations 292
9.10 The World Intellectual Property Day 294
References 295

Glossary 297

References 301

Index 317

About the Authors

Martin A. Bader is a European and Swiss Patent Attorney as well as a European Patent Litigator. He is Founder and Partner of BGW IP GmbH in St. Gallen, Switzerland, a firm specializing in intellectual property management advisory services. Martin is Professor of Technology Management and Entrepreneurship at the Technical University of Ingolstadt (THI), Germany, and Adjunct Professor at the School of Continuing Studies at McGill University in Montréal, Canada. He also serves as an Associate Member of the McGill Centre for Intellectual Property Policy.

Martin previously founded and led the Competence Center for Intellectual Property Management at the Institute of Technology Management at the University of St. Gallen (HSG) and held senior industry roles including Vice President and Chief Intellectual Property Officer at Infineon Technologies. He is a certified mediator with the WIPO Mediation Center for Alternative Dispute Resolution and has been recognized for many years among the world's leading IP strategists in the IAM Strategy 300 Global Leaders. Martin is the author of numerous specialist publications and an internationally sought-after speaker on intellectual property management and innovation policy.

Oliver Gassmann is Professor of Technology and Innovation Management at the University of St. Gallen (HSG) and also Chairman of the Board of the Institute of Technology Management there. He is a keynote speaker for several Executive MBA programs aside from being the author and editor of 20 books and of over 800 international papers in technology and innovation management. Oliver is a member of the board of the Swiss Federal Institute of Intellectual Property, a board member of several international companies, as well as co-founder of several spin-offs. Until 2002, he was the head of research and pre-development at Schindler. His research focuses on success factors for innovation and business models.

Oliver has received numerous awards and honors for his work, including the RADMA Prize (1998, Manchester), and in 2013 was ranked the Top Economist of Germany (2013, FAZ). Also listed as being among the Top 50 Researchers (2014, IAMOT), he became the recipient of the prestigious Scholarly Impact Award (2014, *Journal of Management*). According to Google Scholar, he is the most frequently cited authority in the field of "R&D Management" worldwide (2020).

Mark James Thompson is Docent at the ZHAW, and former Assistant Director of the Center for Data Excellence at the Australian patent office (IP Australia) and CEO of Arêté Statistics AG, an inferential statistical consultancy. He was Chief Economist of the Austrian Patent office and worked for several years at the Swiss office as an economist on patent reform legislation.

Mark did his PhD specifically on statistical and econometric patent valuation and competition and uses that knowledge to price drugs and assess clinical trials at the European Medicines Agency at the Lithuanian State Medicines Control Agency.

Fundamentals of Intellectual Property Rights 1

1.1 Creating Value by Generating Innovation

Since the beginning of the twenty-first century, innovation has had unique conditions: The entrepreneurial environment has been characterized by a high degree of dynamism, complexity, and competition due to globalization, which has reduced the probability of success—or has finally enabled it through new niches that continually emerge. Only 0.6% of all innovations are commercially successful (Stevens & Burley, 1997). In pharmaceuticals, the probability of success is even lower at 1:10,000 (Gassmann et al., 2018; Schuhmacher et al., 2018). This high rate of failure tends to be at the idea or concept stage, embodied in a patent, other studies indicate a lower failure of around 45% once an innovation can make it to the product stage (Castellion & Markham, 2012). The demands placed on innovation management have thus compounded: globalized competition, an explosion of technical knowledge, rapid and accelerating technological diffusion, decentralization of knowledge, the escalation of innovation costs, business model innovations, and shorter innovation cycles.

Globalization of Competition

The power of economies of scale in production, combined with dramatically declining transport and information costs, is forcing companies into global activities. This became particularly clear in 2009 after the economic crisis. Despite the protectionist actions of nations, like the trade war between *China* and the *USA* in 2020, overall competition has become global. Companies like *Amazon* and *Alibaba* have brought globalization into the consumers' living rooms. At the beginning of the new decade, important transformations and global power shifts are on the horizon.

M. A. Bader et al., *Patent Management*, Management for Professionals,
https://doi.org/10.1007/978-3-032-12030-4_1

Explosion of Technical Knowledge

The amount of available knowledge doubles every 13 months (Buckminster Fuller, 1982) and the growth and expansion of the "internet of things" might soon reach a point from where on knowledge doubles every 12 h (IBM, 2006). While the number of scientific journals at the beginning of the nineteenth century was still 100, it grew to 1000 in 1850, to 10,000 around the year 1900, and to approximately 300,000 in 2010. Approximately 80% of the technical knowledge has been published in the form of patent specifications. Over 90% of the information disclosed in patent documents is unprotected because it has either expired, or been rejected, or withdrawn, or not renewed (Ehrat, 1997). Most of the technical knowledge from patent specifications is thus not only openly accessible but can even be used freely. Indeed, there is a large gap between the available knowledge and that knowledge embedded in physical technologies—constrained by the market and physical real growth usable technology, which is much slower. The recombinant nature of patents and technologies is a major driver of the strong growth in patents (Youn et al., 2015).

Technological Fusion

The major breakthroughs in mapping and identifying the human genome are the result of a close cooperation between computer science and genetic engineering. *IBM* already ranks seventh in the world in terms of the number of patents in the field of biotechnology. "Software eats the world" as was boldly proclaimed in the *Wall Street Journal* in 2011. Software and algorithms are entering every industry—from healthcare and machinery to the automotive industry.With these developments, a new innovation and patent protection behavior is also entering into these industries. For example, the automotive industry has made 2020 the year of the connected car, since this has been defined as one of their three main focal areas of innovation. As a result, it has entered into the complex and dynamic patent wars over connectivity, traditionally the realm of major information and communication technology (ICT) players.

Decentralization of Knowledge

Information technology, free global movement of highly skilled labor, regional research specializations, and wage arbitrage have led to integrated network structures with clearly defined research and development (R&D) competence centers: European businesses spend 30% of their R&D budget abroad; for *Swiss* firms, the portion is even higher, namely at over 50%, despite being innovation champions. New innovation hotspots are all located in economically emerging countries such as *China* and *India*.

Increase in the Cost of Innovation

Due to the dynamic technology and its increased research requirements, R&D costs are rising dramatically. An increasingly large share of the R&D budget is spent on intellectual property rights (IPRs). In technology-intensive industries, up to 5% of the R&D budget is spent on generating and maintaining industrial property rights and on the costs of enforcing or defending one's own IPRs. Some industries are challenging this model of IPRs because of the very high costs involved.

Innovation in Business Models

Over the past 15 years, increasingly systematic approaches to developing new business models have emerged. These models are designed to generate more sustainable and profitable competitive advantages than can be achieved through product, technology, or process innovations alone (e.g., Gassmann & Frankenberger, 2025; Winterhalter et al., 2017). *Skype* became the world's largest telecommunications provider without needing its own network infrastructure. *Amazon* is the largest bookseller even without running a single physical bookstore. *Alibaba*, *TenCent*, and *WeChat* are *Chinese* business model innovators, which have not just imitated *Silicon Valley* companies, but radically developed their own business models (Bonakdar et al., 2017). What does this mean for IPRs? Business models as such used to be patentable only in the *USA* (if "concrete" and "useful"), but the products and technologies relevant to the business model can be protected very well (e.g., *Nespresso's* capsule principle; see Fig. 1.1):

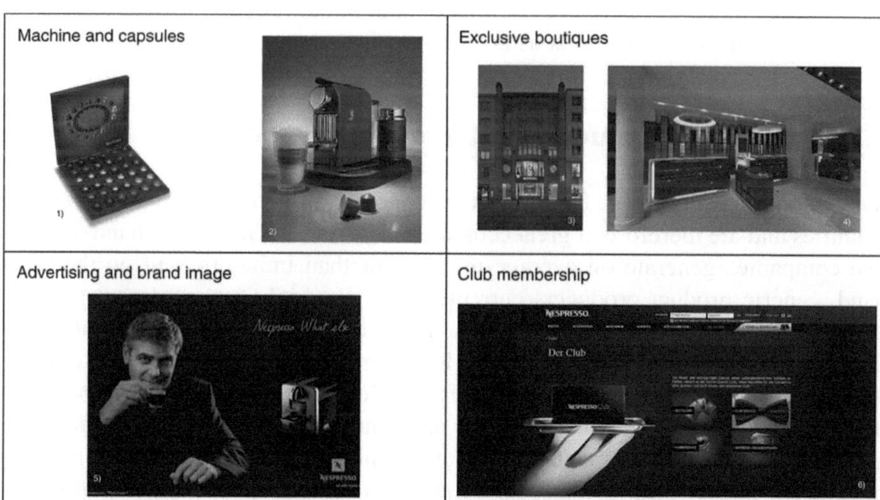

Fig. 1.1 Nespresso business model protection through a holistic approach (Brem et al., 2016) (Used with kind permission by Emerald Publishing Limited. All rights reserved.)

- Machine and capsules (patents, trademarks, and designs);
- Exclusive boutiques (direct sales concept);
- Advertising and brand image (branding); and
- Club membership (service).

Shorter Innovation Cycles and Faster Diffusion

The diffusion of innovation has accelerated as a result of globalized competition, shorter innovation cycles, and the constant tightening of cost constraints. The innovation cycle of a mechanical typewriter, for example, was 25 years, while today that of a microprocessor-controlled typewriter is 5 years. In the electronics industry, it now takes a few months for *Chinese* competitors, for example, to launch a product innovation on the market as a low-cost imitation. In the toy industry, this time span can be brought down to just a few weeks. Innovation and technology leadership, despite rising R&D costs, have become the decisive competitive factor. This means that protecting innovation is becoming increasingly important for technology-intensive companies to amortize investments in product development, as lead time is no longer an entry threshold. The risks of a delayed market launch are increasing.

The main challenges for the management of innovation in companies can be summarized in terms of complexity, dynamics, and costs. After the intensive restructuring waves of recent years, forward-looking companies are now trying to get a head start through innovation. In order to escape fierce cost competition, their aim is to differentiate themselves to their customers. New products in the electrical, telecommunications, and software industries are usually associated with performance increases and cost reductions at the same time. An essential part of innovation management is therefore to make continued product differentiation as sustainable as possible and to constantly renew it.

1.2 Capturing Value by Protecting Innovation

Innovations are responsible for half of the economic growth in highly industrialized countries and are therefore of great economic importance. On the one hand, innovative companies generate on average more profit than imitators, and on the other hand, generic product producers currently show the highest annual growth rates, 10%, in the pharmaceutical industry (Gassmann et al., 2018). This highlights a distinction between margins and revenues. Profits go to innovators; sales go to imitators. An important aspect of innovating is therefore not just creating an innovation but also how its value is captured (Bader & Stummeyer, 2019, 2024). In order to be able to afford high investments in the future, monopoly profits achieved must be maintained in the form of temporary competitive advantages. Suitable, situation-appropriate protection strategies for one's own innovation are therefore necessary. *De facto* protection strategies are increasingly being supplemented by *de jure* ones (see Fig. 1.2).

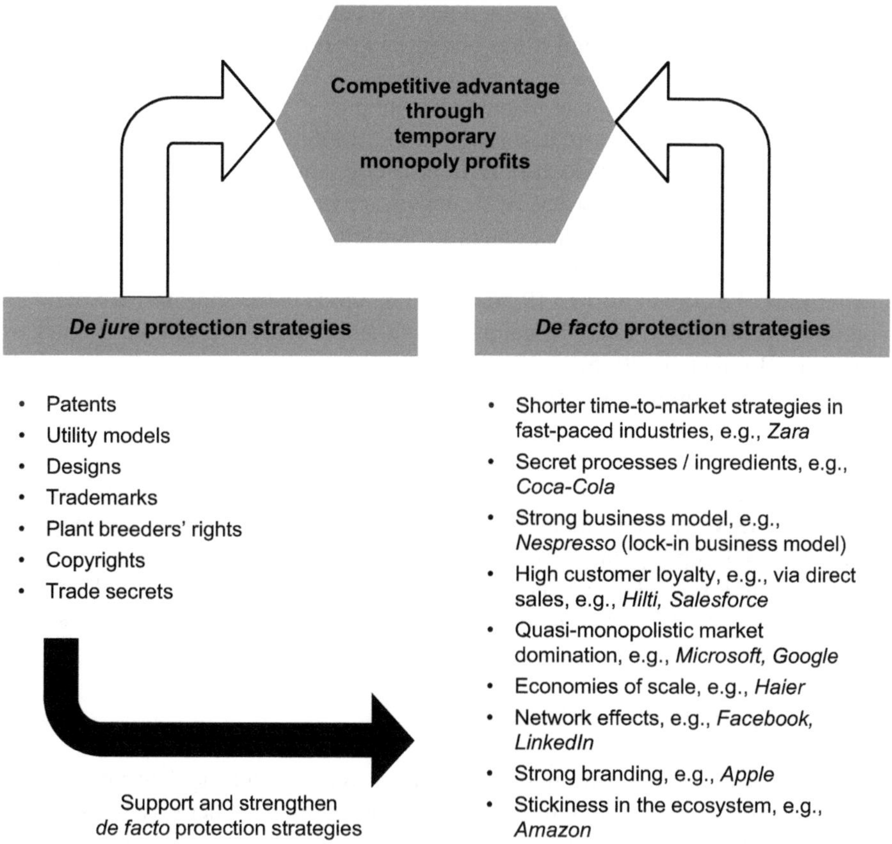

Fig. 1.2 *De jure* (formal) and *de facto* (informal) protection strategies can complement one another (authors' own figure)

There has been an evolution in research, starting with Teece (1986), who is considered to be one of the first to describe the mechanisms of value capture in the context of technological innovation. Other researchers have also included product and process innovation (Chesbrough & Rosenbloom, 2002) and have discussed the protection of intellectual property (IP) in the economic context (Cohen et al., 2000; Dosi et al., 2006). For example, the knowledge-intensive business service firms protect their inventions through a joint use of informal and formal protection strategies (Amara et al., 2008; Bader, 2008). In general, *formal* (i.e., *de jure*, legal) and *informal* (i.e., *de facto*) protection mechanisms have to complement each another and are both fundamental for capturing value from innovation (Arora & Ceccagnoli, 2006; Hall & Ziedonis, 2001; McGahan & Silverman, 2006; Pisano, 2006; Rivette & Kline, 2000).

Also, with regard to business models, value capturing has been discovered as being key to the sustainable profitability of companies (Chesbrough, 2007; Teece, 2010; Zott et al., 2011). There are two main reasons for this (Lepak et al., 2007):

First, value creation is no longer limited just to a company and the industry boundaries (Amit & Zott, 2001), and it has become important for the individual market player to understand where value creation takes place (Gassmann & Frankenberger, 2025). Second, the question has arisen on how to protect the created value. Profiting from innovation framework (Chesbrough et al., 2006; Teece, 2006) Desyllas and Sako (2013) indicates that formal IP right protection methods and strategies should be complementary. While formal IP strategies are mainly effective for short-term purposes, specific complementary assets are needed to capture long-term value. For example, the fast-moving consumer goods giant *Nestlé* applied, for its coffee capsule business *Nespresso,* formal IP protection methods in the short term to build up a premium position and today is mainly relying on informal IP protection strategies long term (Brem et al., 2016).

Legal, de jure, protection strategies are *formal* strategies, while *de facto* protection strategies are *informal* (Bader, 2023). Which protection strategy to choose also depends on factors such as the type of innovation, the size and market share of the firm, and the firm's R&D activities. In that context, Gallié and Legros (2012) evaluated seven forms of formal and informal protection strategies: patents, design rights, trademarks and copyrights as *formal* protection strategies and trade secrets, and then the complexity of products and the manufacturing process, and lead-time advantage—as an *informal* protection mechanism. They define the protection strategies as follows:

Formal (De Jure) Protection Strategies

1. *Patents:* An inventor, who registers a patent, receives the right to prohibit the imitation or use (apart from his/her own use or selling it) of her invention by others for a limited period of time. This allows the inventor to realize monopolistic prices when exploiting the innovation. However, when registering a patent, the inventor must disclose the information pertaining to the innovation and hence enables competitors to "invent around" the patent. This drawback may well overshadow the benefits of being able to implement monopolistic prices for an innovation.
2. *Design rights:* Design rights protect the visual appearance of objects such as the shape, the colors, and the materials. To register a design, two requirements must be met. First, it has to be new, which means that no identical design was published before the registration. Second, it has to be unique, which means that the overall appearance must differ from other designs.
3. *Trademarks:* A trademark is a sign, a symbol, a design, or expression that distinguishes the products or services of a company from those of other companies. Although a trademark is not limited in time, the registering company needs to renew it periodically.
4. *Copyrights:* A firm that registers copyright receives exclusive rights for original work and hence obtains the power to determine who may financially benefit from it.

5. *Trade secrets*[1]*:* Trade secrets are sensitive, non-public information that is commercially valuable and that helps companies get ahead of other companies because those do not have the same information (Aplin et al., 2023). This includes formulas, methods, techniques, processes, and instruments. Companies must take steps to identify, manage, and protect this information accordingly to establish statutory rights (Radauer et al., 2022, 2023, 2025).

Informal (De Facto) Protection Strategies

1. *The complexity of products and manufacturing processes:* The complexity of products and manufacturing processes constitutes an instrument to capture value from innovation. If a product or a service consists of complex processes, technologies, or components that are necessary to build and distribute it, this complexity grants the firm a competitive advantage, since the offerings are made more difficult to imitate.
2. *Lead-time advantage:* In this context, the lead-time advantage is established if firms innovate faster than their competitors. This leads to competitive advantages that enable them to capture value from their innovation.
3. *Secrecy:* Secrecy is an effective intellectual property protection mechanism (IPPM), particularly for firms seeking to protect know-how, processes, or technologies that are difficult to reverse engineer and that do not qualify for legal protection, i.e., fulfill the abovementioned requirements, as trade secrets (Searle et al., 2026). This also applies in legislations where there are no specific trade secret laws in place, like in *Canada.* Unlike patents or design rights, which require public disclosure, secrecy enables firms to retain exclusive control over valuable knowledge without revealing it to competitors. This makes secrecy attractive in uncertain or costly environments. Moreover, secrecy can be less resource-intensive than sustaining a first-mover or lead-time advantage. Empirical research shows that secrecy is preferred to formal protection strategies, especially in fast moving or competitive industries (Cohen et al., 2000; Fedorenko et al., 2023; Hannah et al., 2018; Ottoz & Cugno, 2008). Recent literature reviews highlight the strategic role of secrecy in firms' IP portfolios and its complementarity with other IPPMs (Fedorenko et al., 2023; Hall et al., 2014; Ozcan et al., 2023).

The complementary use of intellectual property rights is also increasingly affecting small and medium-sized enterprises (SMEs). Seventy percent of all patent applicants at the *European Patent Office (EPO)* hold only one patent. In the furniture supply

[1] Although Gallié and Legros (2012) considered trade secrets to be informal protection strategies, trade secrets are considered statutory rights under legal terms. Therefore, it is advisable to reclassify them as formal protection strategies. However, "secrecy" in general, when a secret does not qualify as a "trade secret," would be an informal protection strategy.

industry, which is dominated by SMEs, a new competitive component has established itself: Since the beginning of the 1990s, patents and utility models have seen an increase in being applied for. The industry is under high price and performance pressure. Design alone is no longer enough to survive in the longer run and certainly not anymore if in the form of prototypes manufactured shortly before the trade fair. Today, the timely identification of trends and the development of corresponding technical solutions each play an important role in the furniture and furniture supply industry. This raises the problem of how to prevent complex and sales-relevant technical functionalities from being taken over directly by the competition.

Looking beyond just creating high-performance R&D organization, protecting the outcomes of those innovation processes legally with intellectual property has thus become a central part of innovation management. Only those firms that can effectively protect their innovations from competitors can retain their competitive advantage; and the costs of acquiring and managing those rights are minimal compared to the opportunity cost of not maintaining them.

Patents and the Economy

According to *Joseph Schumpeter*, the purpose of patents for innovative companies is the attainment of temporary monopoly power, through which incentives for inventions and technical development are created. These in turn lead to economic growth and the wealth of an economy (Schumpeter, 1934). From a macroeconomic, perspective, patents foster innovation (Landes & Posner, 2003). In a study, the Organisation for Economic Co-operation and Development (OECD) finds that the effects of patents on the innovativeness and on the economic capacity of companies are not that clear and have therefore to be viewed in a more nuanced way (OECD, 2004).

Studies find that *biotechnology*, *pharmaceuticals* and the *chemical industry* benefit the most in that patent protection plays a strong role in securing their comparative advantage. To a certain extent, this is also the case for the computer and machinery industries. Companies from other industries often primarily use other protection mechanisms, for example, the use of secrecy, market leadership, technical complexity, and control over complementary advantages (Cohen et al., 2000). Protection strategies can also be based on credibility as it is often the case in *consumer electronics*, or use stronger customer ties by controlling distribution channels, like *Hilti* does with direct distribution.

However, patent protection can also hinder innovation by making access to important knowledge more difficult. This is particularly the case with emergent technologies, if basic patents exist, on which further developments are dependent, and the patent holders refuse licenses on reasonable terms. This type of a situation exists partly in genetic engineering (Bar-Shalom & Cook-Deegan, 2002; OECD, 2003) and also in the software sector (Jaffe & Lerner, 2004).

However, patents have a *positive effect on competition* and company start-ups by giving small and young companies the opportunity to penetrate existing markets

Table 1.1 Economic advantages and disadvantages of the patent system

Effect	Advantages	Disadvantages
Innovation	Incentive for R&D activity through a reward	Higher transaction costs for subsequent innovations
Competition	Reduction of barriers to entry especially for small and young firms	Temporary monopolies, in networks often with a long-term effect Danger of cartel formation
Diffusion of knowledge	Revealing of technical information	Insecurity whether and which published knowledge is available for reasonable conditions

Source: Based on Hall (2003)

through using their own patents, to assert themselves against larger companies, and to persuade financial investors (Gans et al., 2002). *Gore-Tex*™ is so successful because their breathable textile products have been protected by patents and trademarks. The patent portfolio has traditionally been one of *Gore*'s strongest competitive factors. In the biotechnology sector, patents represent the largest, secured share of the company value for most start-ups.

A *positive effect on the dissemination of knowledge* through patents can be seen in the intensive use of patent documents to obtain technical information: 80% of the technical knowledge published worldwide is only published in patent specifications. By far the largest part of this knowledge is no longer covered by patent protection, since the patents have already been dropped or have already expired. On the other hand, a common reason for companies to not apply for a patent is its subsequent publication (Sheehan et al., 2003).

Table 1.1 summarizes the advantages and disadvantages of the patent system with regard to innovation competition and the use of knowledge.

Patents Leverage Competitive Advantage

Numerous studies have found a positive influence of patent protection on the company's success (see Fig. 1.3). This has shown that patent protection and thus patent management are of great importance for the company's success, with the quality of patents and patent portfolios in particular being decisive for success (Gassmann & Bader, 2024; Granstrand, 2018; Thumm & Blind, 2025).

Thus, a company's patents and frequently cited patents have a positive influence on its market value (Deng et al., 1999). Patents with a broad technological patent claim also increase company valuation (Lerner, 1994). Companies with systematic patenting behavior have proven more successful than companies with unsystematic patenting behavior (Ernst, 1996), with significant sales increases based on this showing after a delay of 2–3 years (Ernst, 2001). The probability of commercialization in the form of business start-ups or licensing agreements increases with the quality of the underlying patents. The quality can be determined on the basis of the breadth of claims and the citation frequency (Shane, 2001).

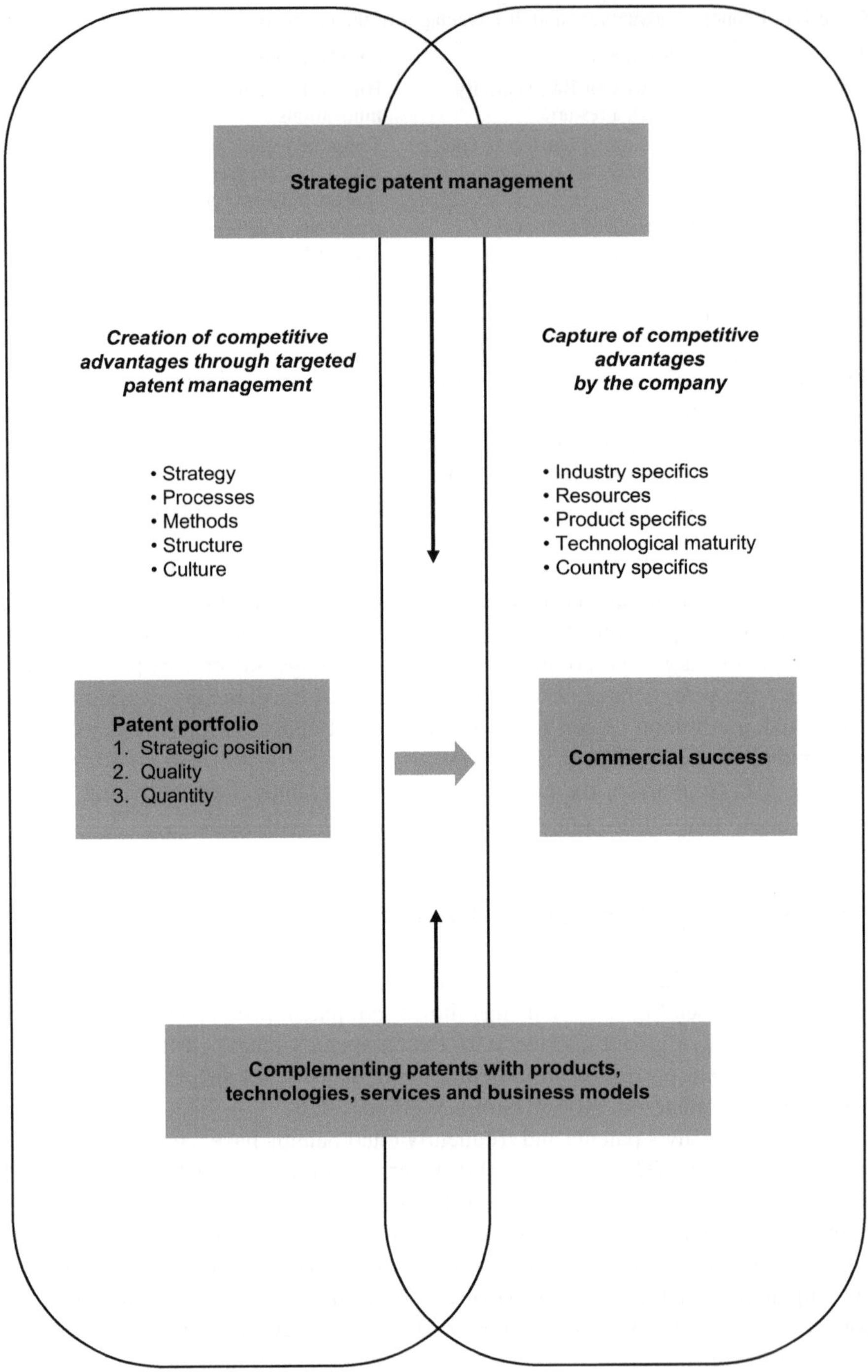

Fig. 1.3 Direct influence of patent portfolio on business success (authors' own figure)

Among patents, the following trends are discernible:

- The number of patents continues to increase.
- The quality of patents is likely decreasing over time (Squicciarini et al., 2013), due to patent office backlogs under ever larger patent documents, and a relative erosion of fees in real terms (Thompson, 2017).
- Individual patents are attaining astronomical values, e.g., *RIM* for *BlackBerry* and *NTP* at US$612.5 million.
- Individual regions, like *China*, still exhibit specific characteristics (Prud'homme et al., 2018; Thraen & Bader, 2026; Zeschky et al., 2014).
- Patents are becoming increasingly like commodities through pricing.

The goal of patent management is to contribute to the company's success by optimizing not only the simple number of patents but also their quality and effectiveness—and to attain the strongest possible patent position.

There are many ways by which to influence the success of a company with patents. Patents can have the following effects on companies:

- *Securing market revenues for the invention:* In practice, patent applications are often derived from inventions that arise as a "by-product" from in-house development. In this context, the desired legal protection through patents often concentrates primarily on securing market revenues: Its own products are protected against counterfeiting, as in the example of *Aventis*, whose patents are often valid in more than a hundred countries. The fields of activity of competitors then play a secondary role in the invention generation phase. Nevertheless, companies are generally interested in achieving the broadest possible scope of protection for inventions in order to make it more difficult for competitors to circumvent them.
- *Access technologies by trade:* A company can also gain access to technology patent pools by owning patents that are relevant to them. This is playing an increasingly important role in cross-licensing negotiations and technical standardization procedures. In the late 1980s, *Siemens* cleverly used its own patent portfolio to make the leap ahead at a relatively late stage to the already established Global System for Mobile Communications (GSM) standard, which was protected by numerous patents.
- *Comparative competitive advantages by blocking competitive technology:* From a policy perspective economically questionable, but often sensible from a business perspective, intellectual property rights are filed with the intent purely to block others. The Rhine-Valley-based company *Leica Geosystems*, today part of the *Hexagon Group*, is active in the field of geomatics in about 25 fields of technology (e.g., laser distance measurement, Global Positioning System (GPS) surveying, and microsystems). The international competitive environment is also active on a similar scale. Leica Geosystems must, therefore, monitor and analyze more and more carefully so that its own products are not blocked by the intellectual property rights of competitors having perhaps only a very small market share, thus hindering its own further technological development.

- *Direct revenue from external technology commercialization:* In this context, own research shows that the thrust of legal protection strategies is directed not only at protecting intellectual property against counterfeiting but also at generating licensing revenue through external marketing. *Schindler* has applied for over 20 patents during its development of an aramid rope for elevators. The total pre-development project costs of several million Swiss francs have already been refinanced through the granting of licenses and the sale of patents in non-elevator areas. Today, one in two companies already markets intellectual property rights externally. Pioneer *IBM* generates over US$1 billion in annual licensing revenue.
- *Image enhancement and marketing of innovation:* Patents are often also used for marketing purposes. This is especially the case in the Swiss watch industry, where technology and marketing represent the core of the product appeal. In the mechanical engineering industry, for example, patents are also used to emphasize the innovativeness of products or that of the company. The textile fiber manufacturer *Gore* pursues a consistent brand and patent policy in order to retain customers.

Strategic Management of Patents

The generation, evaluation, and commercial exploitation of patents are part of strategic technology and innovation management. In recent years, there has been a strong, so far unbroken trend toward open innovation processes and external technology commercialization. Open innovation has meanwhile developed into an established business model, which is actively used not only by multinational corporations but also by SMEs (Gassmann et al., 2025).

Generation

The generation of a company's own patent portfolio can take place internally through its own patent applications. In addition, a company can also obtain external industrial property rights or the corresponding rights through purchase or in-licensing. Joint ventures and cooperation in which internal and external generation merge are a special case.

Valuation

An essential part of patent management is the evaluation of patents and patent portfolios. Already in the generation phase, an evaluation provides the basis for necessary decision-making. The question is whether a patent should be filed for an invention, or whether the renewal fees for an existing patent should continue to be paid, or whether the license should be priced for an external patent portfolio. Due to their information function, evaluation methods can also be used for the early detection of technology in order to pursue competitive activities.

Exploitation

The company's own patent portfolio can be exploited internally by directly supporting the company's primary business, i.e., products, technologies, and processes. On the other hand, external exploitation aims at generating value through second parties' capacities rather through an own business model, since an additional financial value creation arises. These include the sale and out-licensing of intellectual property; in the *USA*, tax benefits can even be claimed (donation) by donating patents and other property rights to nonprofit organizations such as universities; another example would be *IBM's* donations to the open-source community. In addition, patents are often used by companies as trading goods to "buy" their way into comparable or other technologies. When designing technology standards, it is often even necessary for companies to contribute their own relevant intellectual property (IP), such as trademarks or patents, in order to be able to participate in the standard without license payments.

Creation of Competitive Advantages

With the help of patent management, competitive advantages are aimed to be attained by optimizing the patent portfolio. The way in which companies can systematize and implement patent management can be analyzed using five categories, namely: strategy, processes, methods, structure, and culture.

Strategy

Does a company's management and do its employees use intellectual property as protection or to gain access to new business domains? Are actual property rights strategies systematically combined with patent and trademark protection? Are alternative ways of securing freedom to operate being examined under cost–benefit considerations? Are patents actively commercialized externally? Is there an intellectual property strategy that is closely linked to the business and innovation strategy?

Processes

Does a company rely on only a few singletons or is it able to use its full network for patent management? Does a systematic idea and knowledge management take place, which is joined with the patent management? Are there clear milestones for drafting invention announcements? Do inventors and engineers systematically coordinate with patent attorneys? What other interfaces exist, for example, to the marketing department, and are these kept up?

Methods

Are systematic methods used to generate patents? According to which evaluation criteria are patents selected? How is the value of patents determined? Which software is used to manage patents? Which portfolio technology is used to evaluate patents?

Structure

Are patent applications handled by a separate patent department or outsourced to external patent attorneys? Where is the patent department organizationally located? Is the organization of the patent management system structured top-down or bottom-up? Does the broad organization have access to relevant information regarding patents? Is the creative potential used in the company?

Culture
How are routine processes and change processes handled? What degree of willingness to share knowledge early and to file strategic patents is there? What is the interaction between the inventor and the patent department? How much does the company value intellectual property?

> **Competitive Advantages**
> Companies can gain enormous competitive advantages through active patent management, which addresses the five categories already mentioned: Strategy, processes, methods, structure, and culture.

Capture of Competitive Advantages

The realization and utilization of competitive advantages are subject to numerous business conditions specific to the respective companies. In this context, the following characteristics of patent management must be taken into account.

Industry Specifics
In which industry does the company operate? How fast is the rate of change in the industry in question? Is temporary monopolization through intellectual property rights feasible or is there a high degree of standardization? How mature is the industry? What are the barriers to entry in this industry? What is the competitive structure of this industry (duopolistic, oligopolistic, polypolistic), and what are the power and market share ratios?

Resources
Is the company a global corporation or a small or medium-sized company with a strong niche focus? What resources are available within the company? What is the degree of complexity? Can a patent also be defended in a dispute if the legal costs, as in the *USA*, have to be borne by the patent holder?

Product Specifics
The type of products affected plays an important role, especially the question in which stages of the value chain the company is active. Is the product highly diversifiable? Which technological alternatives exist? How attractive is the product at the moment (fashion, trend products)?

Technological Maturity
Depending on the maturity of a technology, a product, or a service, the so-called first-mover or second-mover advantages are decisive when it comes to taking advantage of emerging trends. How many basic technologies are already protected by patent rights held by competitors? Does the company have technological core competencies in the potential area?

Country Specifics

The scope within which the company and its competitors operate or intend to operate is crucial for the necessary preventive and relevant measures to be taken. Is there a market, and if yes, is it perhaps a key market? Do the competitors have production capacities in the respective country? How strong is the enforcement of patent law, for example, in *China*?

Aligning with Products, Technologies, Services, and Business Models

Without aligning the intellectual property generated to real products, technologies, services, and business models that create direct value for a company, the best patent portfolio is a toothless tiger. In other words, the competitive advantages created by patent management must also be used by the company.

This is only possible if the patent strategy is consistently aligned with the corporate strategy and actively supports it. In innovative companies, intellectual property must be consistently integrated into R&D and marketing strategies. *Gore* demonstrates this particularly well, as IP is the company's core value driver. A portfolio of lucky hits may be successful in individual cases; however, this is usually cost-intensive and less effective. The patent strategy must be aligned with the strategic directions and existing core competencies of the company. Especially, R&D-intensive companies typically achieve major competitive advantages via patents.

1.3 Types of Intellectual Property Rights

A general overview of various types of intellectual protection rights (IPRs) is given in Table 1.2, which will be elucidated further.

Patents

What Is a Patent?

A patent grants its owner the right to prevent others from:

- *Commercially* producing, using, offering, storing, importing, or selling the invention;
- For a given jurisdiction; and
- For a limited period of time.

Table 1.2 Overview of the main types of intellectual property rights

IPR	Subject	Application	Examination	Max duration
Patent	Technical invention	Yes	Yes	20
Supplementary protection certificate	Pharmaceuticals or regulated chemicals	Yes	No	5/5.5 years
Utility model	Technical invention (no processes)	Yes	No	10 years
Design patent	Visual arrangements, smells	Yes	No	25 years
Topography	Semiconductor circuits	Yes	No	10 years
Plant breeders'/ plant variety right	Plant varieties	Yes	Yes	25/30 years
Trademark	Brand, acoustic sign, color, scent, 3D-shape	Yes	Yes	Extendable every 10 years
	Business name	No		
	Origin	No		
Geographic designation of origin	Local goods, foods, and products	No	No	Indefinite (typically legislated)
Trade dress	Packaging	No	No	During life of product
Copyright	Software/writing, architecture, art, music	No	No	50 years/70 years after death of author
Trade secret	Proprietary processes and information	No	No	Indefinite

Source: Table compiled by authors

In *Europe*, an invention in the legal sense solves a technical problem with technology. However, a granted patent does not necessarily confer on its owner the right of unlimited use for the invention. For example, other *industrial property rights* or other regulations may prevent the use of the invention by the inventor or the patent holder. Patents are therefore also referred to as exclusionary rights or prohibitive rights. The other types of industrial property rights also have this characteristic.

The European Patent Office (EPO), for example, grants patents for inventions that (EPC, Art. 52) are:

- New;
- Based on an inventive step; and
- Are commercially applicable.

The criteria for novelty and for what is inventive are "absolute" and apply worldwide, i.e., they are independent of the territorial origin of the knowledge available at the time of the priority date, the so-called *state of the art*. The *priority date* is usually the date of the first filing of the invention application at a patent office. Historically, the USA followed the principle of the invention date *(first-to-invent)*, distinguishing it from most other countries. However, with the enactment of the *Leahy–Smith America Invents Act (AIA)*, which took full effect in 2013, the USA transitioned to a *first-to-file* system, aligning its patent law more closely with international standards.

Prior Art
Anything published prior to the filing date in written or oral form, through overt usage, or otherwise made known. There are no restrictions with regard to object, language, space, or time.

During the patent application procedure, the patent applicant must determine for which countries he needs patent protection. The decision on the subsequent application must be made within 1 year of the priority date. Since there are various official and translation fees for each country/region named, the selection of countries or regions is typically based on the expected economic benefit that patent protection can potentially achieve in that country. The duration of patents is controlled by the patent applicant through the payment of annual fees, which are usually collected by the patent offices on an annual basis (not in the *USA*). In most countries, the maximum term of a patent is 20 years after the filing date. In the *USA*, patents filed after June 8, 1995, also have a term of 20 years.

If patent protection is intended in several countries, patent application procedures can be bundled internationally via the Patent Cooperation Treaty (PCT), and grant procedures for numerous European states via the European Patent Convention (EPC).

Patents Are Exclusionary Rights
Patents are not permissive rights—unfortunately, a still widespread misconception, which often leads to erroneous investments in the millions. Patents are exclusionary rights that prohibit the imitation of the protected invention by third partics.

When it comes to the question of what is ultimately accessible to patent protection—products, systems, processes, procedures, software, or even business models—regional legal areas play a major role.

Supplementary Protection Certificates for Pharmaceuticals (SPCs)

The marketing of medicinal products, and of some chemicals, can only take place after relatively lengthy approval procedures, which severely restrict the effective patent term, have been completed. After the statutory term of the basic patent has expired, the supplementary protection certificate provides the possibility of extending the effectiveness of patent protection by a maximum of 5 years with a maximum remaining term of 14 years after approval (EC Regulation No. 1768/92; 35 U.S.C. §§ 155, 156).

Utility Models

Utility models or innovation patents are also sometimes called *petty patents* because they have a shorter duration and also cover a more limited range of inventions. The exact legal definition and scope of the utility model vary by jurisdiction more than for that of patents, which have been more harmonized internationally. This makes utility models and patents more of a national legal instrument. In *Germany*, the "*Gebrauchsmuster*" are technical inventions based on an inventive step and its industrial application, and not on processes. The 8-year *Australian* innovation patent requires an "*innovative step*" rather than an "*inventive step.*" Utility models, typically have a 10-year term, like in *Austria*, and can nevertheless serve as priority applications in order to file subsequent patent applications in other countries.

However, compared to patent protection, there are lower requirements for the required inventive step of a utility model. Utility model applications can, e.g., be filed in *Austria, Australia, Brazil, China*, the *Czech Republic, Denmark, Finland, France, Germany, Hungary, Italy, Japan, Mexico, Poland, Russia, Spain*, and *South Korea*. Not every jurisdiction offers a utility model: *Switzerland* and the *USA* do not have a national utility model, and *Australia* is rethinking whether to convert their "innovation patent."

Design Patents

Two- or three-dimensional manifestations of a product or parts thereof may be protected as designs (Sec. 1 (1) GeschmMG). In the *fashion industry*, for example, fabric samples are often protected, while in the consumer goods industry, packaging, such as beverage bottle shapes, is often protected. A protectable design must be new, and it must exhibit a sufficient degree of peculiarity. The maximum term of protection is 25 years, starting from the filing date.

Example—Legal Dispute About Design: Apple Versus Samsung

In 2012, there were numerous legal disputes between the technology groups *Apple* and *Samsung* over the alleged infringement of protected designs.

The iPad manufacturer Apple, for example, sued Samsung, a competitor, before the Düsseldorf Regional Court with an application for an injunction for infringement of a registered European Community design. According to Apple, Samsung infringed Apple's registered Community design No. 000.181.607–0001 with its tablet "Galaxy Tablet 10.1." The Düsseldorf court ruled in favor of Apple on the ground that the design of the Galaxy Tablet gives the same overall impression even to informed users and is therefore worthy of protection. Samsung filed an appeal, but the appeal was rejected because the Higher Regional Court found that Samsung's tablet was an imitation of the *iPad* (see Fig. 1.4).

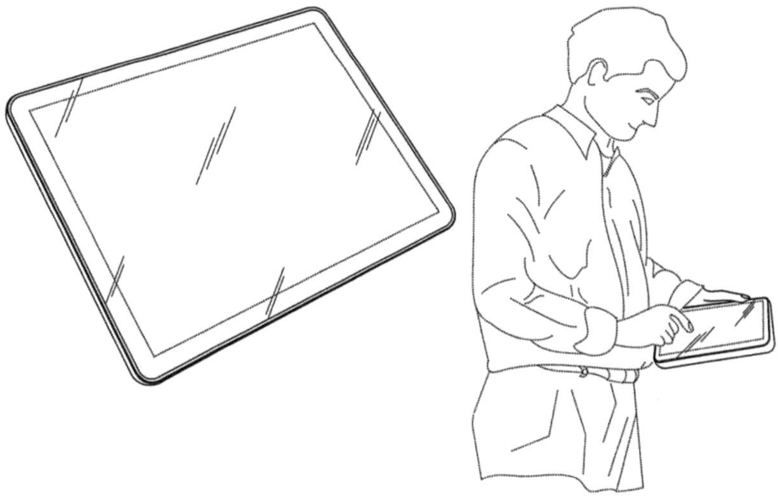

Fig. 1.4 Excerpt from Apple US-Design Patent US D504,889 S

In response, Samsung published a successor model, which, with a different design, differed from its predecessor model and thus also from the iPad. Apple reacted with a renewed application for an injunction and again claimed infringement of its Community design. The Düsseldorf court rejected this claim on the grounds that the design of the successor model left the user with a different overall impression and was therefore outside the scope of protection (Bartenbach et al., 2013). ◀

In addition to the national procedure, there is the possibility of depositing designs internationally in more than 50 member countries of the Hague Agreement, including *Germany* and *Switzerland*, via the *Hague Model Convention (HMA)*.

If design protection is to be obtained exclusively in *European Union (EU)* countries such as *Germany* or *Austria*, an EU Community design, valid for the entire Community territory, can also be registered. In contrast to German law, it is irrelevant whether the design has an aesthetic content or is functional.

Design protection is also possible in the *USA* and *Japan*. In both countries, a cost- and time-intensive, computer-aided novelty examination is carried out, whereby in principle, no protection against infringers exists until a grant has been given. In the USA, however, the enforcement of designs has generally proved to be difficult in practice, as more than 70% of designs have so far been declared invalid in infringement proceedings.

Topography

Topographies are three-dimensional structures of microelectronic semiconductor products and are protectable similarly to inventions. However, a topography can only be protected if it has a "peculiarity." Similar to utility models, topography registration does not involve any substantive examination by the patent office. Although numerous topographies have been registered to date, this type of property right has not yet had any significant effect in the practice of law enforcement.

Plant Breeders' Rights (PBRs)/Plant Variety Rights (PVRs)

Plant variety protection rights are exclusionary rights comparable to patent protection, with the aim of protecting intellectual property rights in new plant varieties in order to aid progress in breeding in agriculture and horticulture. Breeders or discoverers of new plant varieties can apply for protection for varieties of the entire plant kingdom at the respective national plant variety protection offices. A plant variety is in principle eligible for protection if it is distinct, homogeneous, stable, and new, and if it is also designated by a registrable variety denomination. Plant variety protection has the effect that only the owner of the plant variety protection or his legal successor is entitled to market, produce, or import propagating material (plants and parts of plants, including seeds) of a protected variety for commercial purposes.

Trademarks and Similar Rights

A trademark is a registered right, which is suitable for distinguishing the products or services of one entity from those of other entities, and which fulfills the purpose of indicating origin. Trademarks can be registered at the national, regional (e.g., the European Union Intellectual Property Office EUIPO), or international level (the World Intellectual Property Organization WIPO). The most relevant criterion in practice is the distinctiveness from other trademarks, and it should also not be descriptive; the word *"Apple"* can be trademarked for computers, but not for a type of apple. The term of protection can then be extended as often as desired. Trademarks can be protected as:

- Words, e.g., Persil (*Henkel*).
- Letter combinations, e.g., *ABB*.
- Number combinations, e.g., 501 (*Levis*).
- Pictorial representations and logos, e.g., the *Mercedes* star (*Daimler*).
- Three-dimensional shapes, e.g., *Coca-Cola* bottle.
- Slogans, e.g., "Vorsprung durch Technik" (*AUDI*).
- Combinations of these elements as word/picture marks, e.g., *Continental*.
- Contourless colors and color combinations as visually perceptible signs, e.g., magenta/gray of *Deutsche Telekom*.
- Acoustic signs, e.g., *twentieth Century Studios* melody.
- Position mark, e.g., red stripe in *Lloyds* men's shoe heel.

In addition to classic trademarks, there are a number of other similar rights meant for protecting the symbols of organizations, groups, or for enabling special protection (discussed below).

Trademarks: Some Special Cases

Established Trademarks. Descriptive signs can obtain protection if they become generally known on the market for goods or services of a certain company, if they have "prevailed" in technical jargon, in *Switzerland*, e.g., *Valser* for mineral water.

Public Domains. Due to their presence over many years, trademarks can mutate into designations for entire product categories, make their way into the general vocabulary, and lose their defensibility—no American today says "paper facial tissue," the expected term is "*Kleenex*"; in *Great Britain*, people say "*to hoover*" when they mean "to vacuum." The legal test for this entry into the public domain is whether general reference works have the term (MSchG 231.11 Art. 16).

Famous Brands. Brands like *Nestlé* or *Nike* enjoy, as an example, in case there is a risk of exploitation by third parties, protection as well for goods and services for which they were not even registered.

Internet Domain Names. The official registry *Switch* under a mandate from the Swiss Federal Office of Communications (OFCOM) is responsible for the registration of domain names with the country code CH. Domain names can also be registered as trademarks in accordance with the usual principles.

Declaration of Origin. Declarations of Origin distinguish certain goods or services from each other, but not with regard to the manufacturer of the goods, instead rather with reference to a particular geographical origin. A distinction is made between direct indications of source, e.g., *Swiss chocolate*, indirect indications of source, e.g., *William Tell chocolate*, and qualified geographical indications, e.g., *Geneva* for watches.

Protected Appellations of Origin (AOP)/Protected Geographical Indications (IGP). Protected appellations of origin, e.g., *Tête de Moine AOP*, and protected geographical indications, e.g., *St. Gallen Kalbsbratwurst IGP*, are registered in *Switzerland* in the *Register of Agriculture*. They can only be registered as a trademark or as a trademark component under certain conditions.

Source: IPI (2024).

Domain Names

The *Domain Name System (DNS)* is coordinated by the *Internet Assigned Numbers Authority* (IANA—www.iana.org/) and the *Internet Corporation for Assigned Names and Numbers* (ICANN—www.icann.org/). Allocation and registrations take place via the respective national, central registries for top-level domain names, as is exemplified below:

- Germany (.de): www.denic.de;
- Austria (.at): www.nic.at;
- Switzerland (.ch): www.nic.ch; and,
- Generic top-level domains (e.g.,.com,.net): www.verisign.com.

Trade Dress

Trade dress is a narrower intellectual property right than trademarks in that it typically applies to packaging, boxes, and the visual appearance. The visual elements combine in such a way as to evoke a feeling of knowing the source in the consumer's perception.

Copyrights

The only condition is that the intellectual property has to be detectable by the senses. Direct embodiment or publication is not required. Software as such is also protected by copyright. However, the protection only applies to the software as such, not to the ideas.

Copyright Law

The legal prerequisite of copyright law is that a personal creative achievement is present. No official procedures or other formal requirements are typically required for the creation and enforcement of protection.[2] Works in the copyright sense are creations that have a unique character. These include in particular:

- Literary works of any kind, e.g., novels, scientific treatises, newspaper articles, advertising brochures.
- Works of music and other acoustic works.
- Works of fine art, e.g., painting, sculpture, graphics as well as applied art, e.g., objects with a utility value, whereby the deposit as a design patent does not exclude copyright protection.
- Source code or programming text.

Works of personal intellectual creation may be marked with a copyright notice. The © label should then be used in conjunction with the name of the copyright holder and the year of the first publication.

[2] In addition, a voluntary registration of the protected work with the United States Copyright Office—The Library of Congress—makes sense. This makes the work public on the one hand and the Office issues a certificate of registration on the other. In the context of the judicial enforcement of copyrights, registration is even a prerequisite for being able to assert a flat-rate claim for damages provided for by law and for being able to demand reimbursement of lawyer's fees in the event of success.

Trade Secrets

Trade Secrets cover any confidential business information that provide an enterprise with a competitive edge. Trade secrets encompass manufacturing or industrial secrets and commercial secrets. The unauthorized use of such information by persons other than the holder is regarded as an unfair practice and a violation of the trade secret. Depending on the legal system, the protection of trade secrets forms part of the general concept of protection against unfair competition or is based on specific provisions or case law on the protection of confidential information (Radauer et al., 2022, 2023, 2025). The subject matter of trade secrets is usually defined in broad terms and includes sales methods, distribution methods, consumer profiles, advertising strategies, lists of suppliers and clients, and manufacturing processes. While a final determination of which information it is that specifically constitutes a trade secret will depend on the circumstances of each individual case, practices that are clearly unfair in respect of secret information include industrial or commercial espionage, breach of contract, and breach of confidence (WIPO, 2025).

References

Amara, N., Landry, R., & Traoré, N. (2008). Managing the protection of innovations in knowledge intensive business services. *Research Policy, 37*(9), 1530–1547.

Amit, R., & Zott, C. (2001). Value creation in e-business. *Strategic Management Journal, 22*(6/7), 493.

Aplin, T., Radauer, A., Bader, M. A., & Searle, N. (2023). The role of EU trade secrets law in the data economy: An empirical analysis. *International Review of Intellectual Property and Competition Law, 54*, 826–858. https://doi.org/10.1007/s40319-023-01325-8

Arora, A., & Ceccagnoli, M. (2006). Patent protection, complementary assets, and firms incentives for technology licensing. *Management Science, 52*(2), 293–308.

Bader, M. A. (2008). Managing intellectual property in the financial services industry sector: Learning from Swiss Re. *Technovation, 28*, 196–207.

Bader, M. A. (2023). An introduction to intellectual property rights and formal and informal protection strategies. In M. A. Bader & S. Süzeroglu-Melchiors (Eds.), *Intellectual property management for start-ups—Value-enhancing approaches and practices for leveraging the potential*. Springer Nature.

Bader, M. A., & Stummeyer, C. (2019). The role of innovation and IP in AI-based business models. In R. Baierl, J. Behrens, & A. Brem (Eds.), *Digital entrepreneurship—Interfaces between digital technologies and entrepreneurship* (pp. 23–56). Springer.

Bader, M. A., & Stummeyer, C. (2024). Innovation und geistiges Eigentum in KI-basierten Geschäftsmodellen. In L. Fend & J. Hofmann (Eds.), *Digitalisierung in Industrie-, Handels- und Dienstleistungsunternehmen* (4th ed.). Springer Gabler.

Bar-Shalom, A., & Cook-Deegan, R. (2002). Patents and innovation in cancer therapeutics: Lessons from CellPro. *The Milbank Quaterly, 80*(4), 637–676.

Bartenbach, K., Jung, I., & Renvert, A. (2013). Apple vs. Samsung—Zu den Grenzen von Geschmacksmusterschutz und ergänzendem wettbewerbsrechtlichen Leistungsschutz. *Mitteilungen der deutschen Patentanwälte, 104*(1), 18–24.

Bonakdar, A., Frankenberger, K., Bader, M. A., & Gassmann, O. (2017). Capturing value from business models: The role of formal and informal protection strategies. *International Journal of Technology Management, 73*(4), 151–175.

Brem, A., Maier, M., & Wimschneider, C. (2016). Competitive advantage through innovation: The case of Nespresso. *European Journal of Innovation Management, 19*(1), 133–148.

Buckminster Fuller, R. (1982). *Critical path*. St. Martin's Press.

Castellion, G., & Markham, S. K. (2012). Business model innovation: It's not just about technology anymore. *Journal of Product Innovation Management, 30*(5), 976–979.

Chesbrough, H. (2007). Business model innovation: It's not just about technology anymore. *Strategy and Leadership, 35*(6), 12–17.

Chesbrough, H., Birkinshaw, J., & Teubal, M. (2006). Introduction to the research policy 20th anniversary special issue of the publication of 'profiting from innovation by David J. Teece'. *Research Policy, 35*(8), 1091–1099.

Chesbrough, H., & Rosenbloom, R. S. (2002). The role of the business model in capturing value from innovation: Evidence from Xerox Corporation's technology spin-off companies. *Industrial and Corporate Change, 11*(3), 529–555.

Cohen, W. M., Nelson, R. R., & Walsh, J. P. (2000). *Protecting their intellectual assets: Appropriability conditions and why US manufacturing firms patent or not*. NBER Working Paper, No. 7552.

Deng, Z., Lev, B., & Narin, F. (1999). Science and technology as predictors of stock performance. *Financial Analysts Journal, 55*(5), 20–32.

Desyllas, P., & Sako, M. (2013). Profiting from business model innovation: Evidence from pay-as-you-drive auto insurance. *Research Policy, 42*(1), 101–116.

Dosi, G., Marengo, L., & Pasquali, C. (2006). How much should society fuel the greed of innovators? On the relations between appropriability, opportunities and rates of innovation. *Research Policy, 35*(8), 1110–1121.

Ehrat, M. (1997). *Kompetenzorientierte, analysegestützte Technologiestrategieerarbeitung*. Dissertation University of St. Gallen (HSG), St. Gallen, No. 1981.

Ernst, H. (1996). *Patentinformationen für die strategische Planung von Forschung und Entwicklung*. Gabler.

Ernst, H. (2001). Patent applications and subsequent changes of performance: Evidence from time-series cross-section analyses on the firm level. *Research Policy, 30*, 143–157.

Fedorenko, I., Berthon, P., & Edelman, L. (2023). Top secret: Integrating 20 years of research on secrecy. *Technovation, 123*, 102691. https://doi.org/10.1016/j.technovation.2023.102691

Gallié, E. P., & Legros, D. (2012). French firms' strategies for protecting their intellectual property. *Research Policy, 41*(4), 780–794.

Gans, J., Hsu, D. H., & Stern, S. (2002). When does start-up innovation spur the gale of creative destruction? *RAND Journal of Economics, 33*(4), 571–586.

Gassmann, O., & Bader, M. A. (2024). *Patentmanagement: Innovationen erfolgreich nutzen und schützen* (5th ed.). Springer Gabler.

Gassmann, O., & Frankenberger, K. (2025). *The business model navigator* (3rd ed.). FT Publishing.

Gassmann, O., Schuhmacher, A., Reepmeyer, G., & von Zedtwitz, M. (2018). *Leading pharmaceutical innovation—How to win the life science race* (3rd ed.). Springer.

Granstrand, O. (2018). *Evolving properties of intellectual capitalism: Patents and innovations for growth and welfare*. Edward Elgar.

Hall, B. H. (2003). *Business method patents, innovation and policy*. NBER Working Paper, No. 9717.

Hall, B., Helmers, C., Rogers, M., & Sena, V. (2014). The choice between formal and informal intellectual property: A review. *Journal of Economic Literature, 52*, 375–423.

Hall, B. H., & Ziedonis, R. H. (2001). The patent paradox revisited: An empirical study of patenting in the US semiconductor industry 1979–1995. *RAND Journal of Economics, 32*(1), 101–128.

Hannah, D., Parent, M., Pitt, L., & Berthon, P. (2018). Secrets and knowledge management strategy: The role of secrecy appropriation mechanisms in realizing value from firm innovations. *Journal of Knowledge Management, 23*, 297–312.

IBM. (2006). *The toxic terabyte: How data-dumping threatens business efficiency*. IBM Global Technical Services white paper. Retrieved June 6, 2025, from https://archive.org/stream/TheToxicTerabyte/The%20Toxic%20Terabyte_djvu.txt

IPI. (2024). *Envisioned. Created. Protected. A concise guide to trade marks, patents and co* (13th ed.). IPI Swiss Federal Institute of Intellectual Property.

Jaffe, A. B., & Lerner, J. (2004). *Innovation and its discontents: How our broken patent system is endangering innovation and progress, and what to do about it*. Princeton University Press.

Landes, W. M., & Posner, R. A. (2003). *The economic structure of intellectual property law*. Belknap Press of Harvard University Press.

Lepak, D. P., Smith, K. G., & Taylor, M. S. (2007). Value creation and value capture: A multilevel perspective. *Academy of Management Review, 32*(1), 180–194.

Lerner, J. (1994). The importance of patent scope: An empirical analysis. *RAND Journal of Economics, 25*(2), 319–332.

McGahan, A. M., & Silverman, B. S. (2006). Profiting from technological innovation by others: The effect of competitor patenting on firm value. *Research Policy, 35*(8), 1222–1242.

OECD. (2003). *Genetic inventions, IPRs and licensing practices: Evidence and policies*. OECD.

OECD. (2004). *Patents and innovation: Trends and policy challenges*. OECD.

Ottoz, E., & Cugno, F. (2008). Patent–secret mix in complex product firms. *American Law and Economics Review, 10*, 142–158.

Ozcan, O., Pickernell, D., & Trott, P. (2023). A trade secrets framework and strategic approaches. *IEEE Transactions on Engineering Management*, 1–17. https://doi.org/10.1109/TEM.2023.3285292

Pisano, G. (2006). Profiting from innovation and the intellectual property revolution. *Research Policy, 35*(8), 1122–1130.

Prud'homme, D., von Zedwitz, M., Thraen, J. J., & Bader, M. A. (2018). Forced technology transfer policies: Workings in China and strategic implications. *Technological Forecasting and Social Change, 134*, 150–168.

Radauer, A., Bader, M. A., Aplin, T., Konopka, U., Searle, N., Altenburger, R., & Bachner, C. (2022). *Study on the legal protection of trade secrets in the context of the data economy.* European Innovation Council and SMEs Executive Agency (European Commission). Retrieved July 1, 2025, from https://op.europa.eu/publication-detail/-/publication/c0335fd8-33db-11ed-8b77-01aa75ed71a1

Radauer, A., Bader, M. A., Aplin, T., Konopka, U., Searle, N., Altenburger, R., & Bachner, C. (2025). Trade secrets as a complementary tool to patenting in the data economy of the 21st century. In N. Thumm & K. Blind (Eds.), *A modern guide to patenting: Challenges of patenting in the 21st century*. Elgar Publishing.

Radauer, A., Searle, N., & Bader, M. A. (2023). The possibilities and limits of trade secrets to protect data shared between firms in agricultural and food sectors. *World Patent Information, 73*, 102183. https://doi.org/10.1016/j.wpi.2023.102183

Rivette, K. G., & Kline, D. (2000). Discovering new value in intellectual property. *Harvard Business Review, 79*(1), 54–66.

Schuhmacher, A., Gassmann, O., McCracken, N., & Hinder, M. (2018). Open innovation and external sources of innovation. An opportunity to fuel the R&D pipeline and enhance decision making? *Journal of Translational Medicine, 119*(16), 1–14.

Schumpeter, J. A. (1934). *Theorie der wirtschaftlichen Entwicklung* (8th ed.). Dunker und Humblot.

Searle, N., Bader, M. A., Radauer, A., & Aplin, T. (2026). *Intellectual property protection mechanisms and secrecy.* Based on: Searle, N., Bader, M. A., Radauer, A, Aplin, T. (2024). Degrees of Secrecy: Factual Secrets and Trade Secrets in Data; EPIP 2024 (European Policy for Intellectual Property); 09/2024. Forthcoming.

Shane, S. (2001). Technological opportunities and new firm creation. *Management Science, 47*(2), 205–220.

Sheehan, J., Guellec, D., & Martinez, C. (2003). Business patenting and licensing: Results from the OECD/BIAC survey. In: *Proceedings of the OECD Conference on IPR, Innovation and Economic Performance*, 28–29. Paris: OECD.

Squicciarini, M., Dernis, H., & Criscuolo, C. (2013). *Measuring patent quality*. OECD.

Stevens, G. A., & Burley, J. (1997). 3000 raw ideas = 1 commercial success! *Research-Technology Management, 40*(3), 16–27.

Teece, D. J. (1986). Profiting from technological innovation: Implications for integration, collaboration, licensing and public policy. *Research Policy, 15*(6), 285–305.

Teece, D. J. (2006). Reflections on "profiting from innovation". *Research Policy, 35*(8), 1131–1146.

Teece, D. J. (2010). Business models, business strategy and innovation. *Long Range Planning, 43*(2), 172–194.

Thompson, M. (2017). The cost of patent protection: Renewal propensity. *World Patent Information, 49*, 22.

Thraen, J. J., & Bader, M. A. (2026). Key success factors in nurturing and sustaining 21st-century technology clusters. In J. J. Thraen, & C. H. Hoffmann (Eds.), *Successful technology clusters in the 21st century.* Berlin: Walter de Gruyter. Forthcoming.

Thumm, N., & Blind, K. (2025). *A modern guide to patenting; challenges of patenting in the 21st century*. Elgar Publishing.

Winterhalter, S., Zeschky, M., Neumann, L., & Gassmann, O. (2017). Business models for frugal innovation in emerging markets: The case of the medical device and laboratory equipment industry. *Technovation, 66–67*, 3.

WIPO. (2025). *What is a trade secret?* Geneva: WIPO. Retrieved June 6, 2025, from https://www.wipo.int/en/web/trade-secrets

Youn, H., Strumsky, D., Bettencourt, L. M. A., & Lobo, J. (2015). Invention as combinatorial process: Evidence from US patents. *J. R. Soc. Interface, 12*(20150272), 1–15.

Zeschky, M., Widenmayer, B., & Gassmann, O. (2014). Organizing for reverse innovation in Western MNCs: The role of frugal product innovation capabilities. *International Journal of Technology Management, 64*(2–4), 255–275.

Zott, C., Amit, R., & Massa, L. (2011). The business model: Recent developments and future research. *Journal of Management, 37*(4), 1019–1042.

Protection Strategies

2

2.1 Patent Strategies in General

Industrial property rights make it possible to influence, if not control, to a greater extent one's own corporate strategic position and affect the activities of competitors. The guidelines for patent strategy must be determined by corporate strategy so that the contribution to the whole is thereby ensured. A strategy should explicitly address, in particular, the existing and desired products, technologies, and applications.

> **Strategy**
> A *strategy* sets out the guidelines within which a company operates. It outlines the company's goals and objectives and indicates the possible ways of achieving them.
>
> A *patent strategy* sets out the guidelines for generating business value through patents. It answers questions such as: Which areas of invention should be patented for what business purpose; which market and production areas should be covered by patent protection; and what resources, expenses, and willingness to invest and to take risks are required to defend this protection.

Positioning of the firm happens in relation to:

- Products, technologies, and services.
- Markets.
- Financial framework and business model.

It is often the case in small and medium enterprises (SMEs) that the strategy is made implicit by the running of the company. According to Mintzberg et al. (2005), five ways of exercising strategy can be distinguished:

M. A. Bader et al., *Patent Management*, Management for Professionals,
https://doi.org/10.1007/978-3-032-12030-4_2

- *Plan:* Path/goal description—What is to be achieved and how is the goal to be achieved?
- *Chess move:* Presentation of the strategy as a game move in competition with and against competitors.
- *Patterns:* Decision and action patterns typical of a company.
- *Position:* Market and competitive position of a company in relation to its environment.
- *Perspective:* Perception and reconstruction of the environment.

Implementing a strategy requires management, which itself requires feedback ("You can't manage what you can't measure"). A patent strategy must not only consider the company as a whole but also see the individual business areas and be at the same time production- and product-oriented, setting a financial framework. In doing so, the following questions arise:

- What specifications do I need from other areas of strategy, for example, from the corporate, technology, product, or innovation strategy?
- What minimum requirements or minimum statements are required for intellectual property portfolio management to be carried out?
- What are the target figures for which statements must be made, for example, whether there is a general willingness to license, and to what extent, and also by what means, license revenues should be generated?

The reformulation of a patent strategy can be set in motion by a general strategic business reorientation or an internal restructuring.

Preconditions for a Patent Strategy

For a well-embedded patent strategy, clear statements on the corporate strategy are a prerequisite. How do we create and capture value for customers? What are our core competencies? What is it that creates a comparative competitive advantage? In which countries are we active, in which of these do we want to be active in the near future, and also: In which countries are our core competitors active? What is the core of the business model of the company?

The main question here is: "How should the company create and capture value by means of the patent strategy?"

However, external pressure leading to the initiation of a patent strategy is often caused by resource and budget adjustments requiring a realignment and optimization of the existing approach. On the one hand, this raises the question of which technologies and products should be protected while on the other hand asking what this protection should look like. Which characteristics should be protected and for how long a time in which countries? When developing a new product generation, a successful approach lies in defining the desired patent protection of certain technology, and defining also the product characteristics as a concrete goal, and lastly, to measure this continuously in accordance with the progress of the project.

The requirement for a successful patent strategy and, in particular, the value of *freedom-to-operate* or even the *freedom-of-action* as a strategic asset of the company generally becomes very clear when it is lacking. This is the case, for example, when disputes related to or caused by patents cause a blockade and obstruct current business activities. This can result in a decline in sales or profits (*Siemens*, pacemakers) or a severe impairment of market capitalization (*Adobe* vs. *Macromedia*).

When initiating a patent strategy, coordination between the Intellectual Property, R&D, and Corporate Development departments is important, whereby consistency and ultimately maintaining consensus are critical success factors. While the patent department should be the process owner for the initiation of the patent strategy, clear support by management is required.

Endress + Hauser, a medium-sized Swiss manufacturer of measurement instruments and automation solutions, has attached particular importance to the invention and the protection of inventions through patents since the end of the 1990s. It only arrived there after successfully defending itself against a patent infringement suit filed by an American competitor.

Critical success factors are having sufficient resources, a common understanding of the necessity for a patent strategy, the support of middle management, and having made a sufficient analysis of the current situation. The preferred tools for bringing this about are good communication and visualization, such as meaningful patent statistics, possibly with the aid of external patent databases. Important stakeholders who should be involved in the initiation phase of a patent strategy are a company's management, inventors, technical experts, and patent attorneys or patent managers.

Patent Strategy

The initiation of a patent strategy is essential when starting a technology-based venture. In many companies, such a patent strategy is only initiated when its own freedom of action has been blocked by a competitor's patent or when the company has experienced patent infringement.

Important factors for a patent strategy proving successful are:

- Consistency with corporate and business strategy;
- A clear market view;
- Thinking in terms of competitive advantages;
- Technological competence in-house;
- Patenting expertise in the team;
- Managerial commitment.

2.2 Offensive and Defensive Patent Strategies

Depending on their orientation and aggressiveness, patent strategies can be subdivided into offensive and defensive patent ones. This should not be confused with patent tactics. While a *strategy* is the overall plan or direction a business or organization takes to achieve its long-term goals, *tactics* are the specific actions or steps taken to execute that strategy and achieve short-term objectives. In essence, strategy is the "what and why," and tactics are the "how."

Patent Strategy vs. Patent Tactics

Tactics are the means by which the strategy is executed. A successful strategy requires effective tactics to achieve its goals:

Strategy:

- Aims to set the overall direction of an organization;
- Involves long-term planning and decision-making;
- Focuses on the big picture, including the vision, mission, and long-term goals;
- Is more flexible and adaptable to changes in the external environment.

Tactics:

- Are the specific actions taken to implement the strategy;
- Involve short-term planning and decision-making;
- Focus on day-to-day operations and the execution of the strategy;
- Are more concrete and detailed than strategy.

Offensive Patent Strategies

This orientation is based on the strategic planning of intellectual property use within the framework of corporate and business activities, in addition to which patent rights are then proactively and aggressively enforced. This strategy is rounded off by active participation in various interest groups in the legal development of intellectual property legislation.

For years, the American semiconductor memory company *Rambus* has pursued an aggressive marketing strategy for its patent portfolio with licensing requirements for a specific clock and bus process for SDRAM memory chips. For several years, numerous patent infringement cases have been pending in the *USA* and *Europe*, causing irritations within the semiconductor memory industry. Rambus, one example, reached a settlement with *Samsung*, which secured for the company a large compensation payment.

As a tactical maneuver, some companies also apply for patents to lure their competitors down the wrong path. These patents involve little effort, and the examination fees are also not paid. The only desired effect of this measure is to deliberately mislead competitors as to the technological direction being taken. However, the value of this maneuver should not be overestimated, especially if used too frequently.

US-based patent assertion companies (PAEs), also known as NPEs (Non-Practicing Entities), having no products of their own, which business leaders often characterize as "patent trolls," are companies characterized by the most aggressive use of patent strategies, since defending patents *is* the business model. These strategies also make sense for the reason that most patent litigations end in a settlement (Krech et al., 2015). Trolling is most practicable where the cost of litigation is enormous, especially in the USA or where legal discovery is part of the legal action (Thompson, 2013).

Defensive Patent Strategies

This strategy aims to minimize the impact of third-party patent strategies on your business. The medium-sized furniture supplier *Hettich* pursues an aggressive defense strategy. The company engages in numerous confrontational proceedings against competitors' patents and leverages their attacks with state-of-the-art information handling.

Offensive/Defensive Patent Strategies

Large companies in particular often pursue hybrid patent strategies with both offensive and defensive components. Though, *Siemens* and *Microsoft* both pursue offensive strategies in the abovementioned sense. One particular tactic is always directed at minimizing the effects of third parties on their own companies. At *Siemens*, this is driven by the broad diversity of its products and services. For example, competitors of one division are often customers of another. *Microsoft*, on the other hand, is very sensitive to attacks coming from third parties; this is due to the company's high global market share based on a comparatively limited product and service offering.

Companies characterized by such an activity and competition configuration therefore increasingly conclude exchange contracts for patent licenses in order to reduce their own exposure. As a result, lighting manufacturer *Osram* and electronics manufacturer *Sharp* concluded a far-reaching agreement on the reciprocal licensing of patents in 2013. This agreement covers patents of both companies in the field of optoelectronic semiconductor components as well as products in which these are contained. It thus encompasses LED and laser diode chips and modules, as well as luminaires. Osram had previously to this entered into patent exchange agreements with other major opto-semiconductor manufacturers such as *Nichia*, *Philips*, *Toyoda Gosei* , *Cree*, *Samsung*, and *LG* to reduce the risk of unintentionally using the intellectual property rights of other companies (Osram, 2013).

Example—The 10 Patent Management Principles of Geberit

Geberit is active in sanitary technology and has over 32 subsidiaries and 10,000 employees worldwide; the tenets of its patent policy are:

1. *Application policy:* Geberit applies for protectable inventions consciously and in a targeted manner. Before applying, the positioning of the patents is decided upon.
2. *Collision avoidance:* For each development project, a patent analysis is conducted.
3. *Portfolio review:* The Geberit patent portfolio is evaluated annually in terms of cost–benefit. The application criteria serve as a decision basis for dropping or maintaining each individual patent.
4. *Invention offerings:* Geberit examines inventions made by other companies in terms of their technical and commercial viability. The patent legal analysis becomes part of the corporate decision process.
5. *Competitor surveillance:* Geberit follows a strict publication policy in its own domain and also for adjacent technical ones; this is to prevent competitors from being able to ease in on their territory.
6. *Competitive and technology analyses:* For specifically defined competitors, systematic patent and technology analyses are conducted.
7. *Licensing:* Through an internal Geberit licensing system, R&D activities are financed, but Geberit does not actively license its patents to third parties.
8. *Enforcement:* Geberit robustly enforces its patents against all possible infringers.
9. *Information systems:* Geberit ensures the necessary flow of information for its own patents using a periodic report, suited for its level and business units.
10. *Organization:* The patent activities are centrally led and coordinated; the decentralized R&D units protect their own market-specific developments themselves. ◀

2.3 Core Dimensions of Patent Strategies

Most leading international technology companies pursue a patent strategy aimed at securing their own freedom-of-operate, such as *Siemens* or *IBM*. A further aspect of this strategy is wanting to prevent the imitation of their own products and to thereby sustainably strengthen their competitive differentiation. Especially, in the pharmaceutical and chemical industries, the development of new active ingredients would not be affordable without effective patent protection. Some companies successfully defend their own products with patents, for example, *Bayer* versus *Barr Laboratories*, *Ruby,* and *Hoechst-Marion-Roussel*. Relatively, few companies still focus their patent strategy on generating licensing revenues, such as is done by *Philips*.

A patent strategy aimed at the protection of innovations demonstrates the following core dimensions (Gassmann & Bader, 2024; see Fig. 2.1):

- Goal I: Ensuring Freedom-to-Operate (FTO).
- Goal II: Differentiation by applying one's own intellectual property.
- Goal III: Multiplier effect by generating licensing revenues.

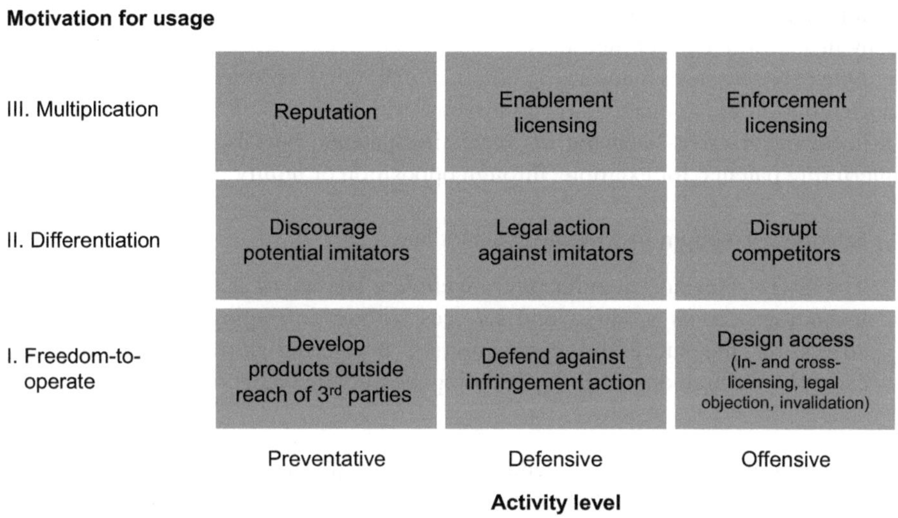

Fig. 2.1 The core dimensions of a patent strategy (authors' own figure)

A comprehensive patent strategy already in itself provides for an initial situation in which the company can be attacked as little as possible by third parties. The less vulnerable a company is, the greater its *freedom-to-operate* vis-à-vis patents of third parties, and the stronger its own products can be defended, and have intellectual property rights enforced vis-à-vis competitors. Three types of activities can be distinguished:

- *Preventative* measures for prevention;
- *Defensive* measures to defend one's own competitive position; and
- *Offensive* measures for the self-initiated attack on competition.

Goal I: Ensuring Freedom-to-Operate

Here, the focus is on securing one's own freedom to operate vis-à-vis third parties. As a rule, European companies attach great importance to this dimension and try to develop products and technologies that do not collide with the intellectual property rights of third parties. The own freedom of action can already be underpinned by the quantity of own patents and patent applications. On the one hand, competitors can be deterred and on the other, products can potentially get covered by potential attackers.

Freedom-to-operate (FTO) can thus be achieved through *preventative*, prophylactic measures in the development of one's own products and technologies.

Defensive measures must be initiated if one company is attacked by another on the grounds of patent infringement. In practice, the attacked company tries to use its own protective rights against products and business activities of the attacking company in addition to other measures.

Offensive measures that serve to obtain or maintain freedom of action can also be carried out on the company's own initiative. This includes, in particular, proactive in-licensing or cross-licensing of interesting patents, but also the destruction of interfering patents, for example, through opposition or nullity proceedings.

Example—Freedom-to-Operate at Schindler

The Swiss elevator manufacturer *Schindler* strives to use the best possible technology for its products and services without infringing on them and also strives for the successful destruction of interfering third-party patents, for example, through opposition proceedings before the patent offices. ◀

Freedom-of-Action (FOA) vs. Freedom-to-Operate (FTO)

"Freedom of action" and "freedom to operate" are distinct concepts, though related, especially in the context of intellectual property (see also London, 2023).

Freedom-of-action (*FOA*) refers to the ability to act freely, without external constraints, whether physical, social, or legal.

Freedom-to-operate (*FTO*), particularly in the context of IP, refers to the ability to develop, make, and sell a product or service without infringing on the existing intellectual property rights of others. It is about ensuring that a company's actions are legal and won't lead to infringement claims.

Key Differences:

- *Scope:* FOA is broader, encompassing any constraints on a company's ability to act, while FTO is more specific to the IP landscape, focusing on potential infringement risks.
- *Focus:* FOA is about the freedom to act, while FTO is about the freedom to act legally without infringing on others' IP rights.

Develop Products Outside Reach of Third Parties

This objective should be pursued by companies in general. In practice, this means that the IP activities of third parties must be monitored and analyzed, and if necessary, specific circumvention solutions have to be developed.

This process, known as *Product Clearing* or *Patent Clearing*, is often associated with a high expenditure of time and money as well as a continuous qualification of employees. A disregard or negligence can be punished in the USA in patent infringement proceedings by a trebling of damages. In general, intellectual property rights are monitored with regard to the specifics and granularity of the relevant markets.

Example—Information Monitoring at Alcatel

For example, the telecommunications equipment manufacturer Alcatel (now *Alcatel-Lucent*) monitored different sources of information: Publications and disclosures were used to prepare the technical information. Patents were mainly monitored for risk assessment with reference to the USA, Europe, and Germany. Patent searches were carried out by Alcatel using contract services, proprietary data profiles, and statistical evaluation methods. Typically, *Derwent's WPIDS*, *Inpadoc*, *EUROPatfull,* and *USPatfull* were queried, and the data were further analyzed. Furthermore, the patent administration system *Memotech* of *CPA* was available. Further processing of the data, including statistical processing, was carried out using Excel and structured according to business areas, keywords, and other criteria. The results were released by the Senior IP Counsels and made available via the internal intranet site *Quick-Place*. *Alcatel* used a specially configured *Lotus Notes* database. Alcatel had by then found that the own preparation of the data was ultimately more cost-effective than purchasing evaluations via information service providers. In addition, researchers and developers were able to conduct patent searches themselves via the intranet. ◀

Defend Against Infringement Action

An earlier OECD study on Business Patenting and Licensing showed that 70% of the companies surveyed reported growing involvement in patent infringement proceedings. The following applies to those affected: "Attack is the best defense." The basic strategy of defense against attacks by third parties is based on four pillars:

- Counter-attack on the legal validity of the action patents, for example, through nullity actions.
- Counter-determination as to whether an infringement of property rights exists at all, for example, through negative declaratory relief.
- Counter-attack on the product, technology, and service range of the aggressor with his own intellectual property rights.
- Further procedural, legal, and possibly even political steps to influence the infringement proceedings in one's own sense.

Nevertheless, the high costs that can generally arise in the enforcement of intellectual property rights should be taken into account: The costs of patent litigation in the USA amount to a median of US$4 million—in most cases, this is a zero-sum game (AIPLA, 2024; Cotropia et al., 2017). In the end, most litigation ends up with a settlement in order to prevent massive litigation costs. Furthermore, innovative SMEs have to consider in particular the consequential costs and resource commitment in a possible legal dispute; this applies in particular to the USA. In this respect, legal protection strategies must always be based not only on legal but also on financial and political considerations.

Example—Cultural Aspects

Cultural aspects have also changed. While pharmaceutical companies such as *Bayer Pharma* or *Sanofi* were generally able to reach an out-of-court agreement with third parties in the past, there has now been an increase in court-supported disputes, not least due to the influence of American companies. ◀

Design Access

Anyone wishing to avoid the latent risk of knowingly infringing third-party patents must proactively seek access to these rights or at least attempt to nullify them.

In-Licensing

In many cases, the complete development of workarounds is not possible, too costly, or undesirable for other reasons, reasons such as required adherence to technical standards. Then licensing or the acquisition of the IP right offers a solution for the exploitation of the rights.

Many companies, such as *IBM*, are already pursuing an open licensing strategy and offering licenses to third parties on fair, reasonable, and non-discriminatory terms. However, as a rule, there is no general obligation for a company to license to third parties. Especially, for large companies, the granting of licenses to third parties is often additionally tied to security being offered in return, for example, in the form of back-licenses. The in-licensing company is to be prevented from later being able to approach the licensing company for patent infringement. The licensing company could then only defend itself with great difficulty because the relevant patents have already been licensed and can no longer be used for a counter-attack.

Example—Licensing Practices at Google and Qualcomm

The foundations of *Google's* search technology were developed by the founders Page and Brin in 1998 during their studies at *Stanford University* (California). The patent rights have been held by the university ever since. However, Google was able to acquire the exclusive license rights until 2011.

In 2002, Google was sued in the USA by *Yahoo!* subsidiary *Overture* for patent infringement. The core patent (U.S. Patent US 6,269,361) protects a process that affects an essential function for the advertising market—Google's main source of income: The process allows the order of automatically generated search results to be subsequently changed and ads to be placed. The patent dispute was settled shortly before the Initial Public Offering (IPO) in 2004: Google received a license. In return, Google paid 2.7 million shares with an issue value of around 100 US dollars and also paid license fees to Yahoo! subsidiary Overture for permission to use it.

One of the more controversial decisions is when the *US Federal Trade Commission (FTC)* sued *Qualcomm* for its unfair licensing practices. The US circuit court ruled that the company's infamous "no license, no chips policy" was anti-competitive. The company had essentially forced companies, which needed its hardware in the form of specialized modem chips for mobile networks, to license its technology. Qualcomm's biggest profit center had been patent licensing rather than manufacturing. Judge Koh ruled that the royalty agreement, which was 5% of the value of the phone, had to be assessed off the price of the chips instead. *Apple* had been battling Qualcomm in court over the same issue for years before (Wallstreet Journal, 2019). ◀

Cross-Licensing

If back-licenses are granted in return for the in-licensing of industrial property rights, a cross-licensing exists. In particular, companies with large market shares have the problem of high vulnerability in the respective market segments due to third-party patents. In addition, if there is a high level of competition and innovation in these segments with a high volume of intellectual property rights, many companies try to increase their degrees of freedom by gaining access to other intellectual property right portfolios, as *Siemens* and *Microsoft* do, which two companies have concluded a patent license exchange. Whereas in the past, there were often pure barter transactions of reciprocal rights of use, in recent years, a balancing out of the mutual benefits has increasingly been compensated by monetary compensation.

The technology group *OC Oerlikon* has so far primarily used cross-licensing agreements to settle disputes. According to the head of the *Emch* legal department, however, in the future, these procedures will increasingly also be used for the economically viable procurement of intellectual property, for example, as a substitute for the pure acquisition of property rights, for company acquisitions, or for the precautionary safeguarding of access to certain property rights.

Example—Patent License Exchange Between SAP and Microsoft

During negotiations with *Microsoft* on a joint partnership to develop Internet services, *SAP* confirmed that it had already been approached in 2003 regarding a possible merger with Microsoft. The preliminary discussions stalled, but in 2004, both parties entered into a joint collaboration to develop Internet services. The agreement also included a patent license exchange agreement to improve the development framework of the two companies. ◀

Opposition and Invalidation Actions

The opposition procedure gives the public not previously involved in the patent grant procedure the opportunity to have the patent reexamined by the patent office. The adversary is involved in the opposition procedure. If the opposition is successful, the patent is either restricted or revoked. The effect of the patent is accordingly retroactive. In the European and German proceedings, a period of 9 months is available for filing an opposition. In the *USA*, the one-party procedure *Ex Parte Reexamination* and the two-party procedure Inter Partes *Reexamination* for examination of the patent are available. After that, only the usually expensive and costly nullity proceedings are available at the national level in many legislations.[1]

With these legal instruments, the emergence of new protective rights can thus be restricted or even prevented at an early stage. In practice, the legal uncertainty existing until the conclusion of the proceedings is usually problematic. If the European procedure involves two instances, it will take about 4 years before the final decision is reached. In addition, the patent owner is made aware by the opponent that he is disturbed by the patent; otherwise, the costs for the procedure would not be invested. The proportion of patents challenged by oppositions before the European Patent Office has been at a low level for years, 2.4% in 2024 (2018, 3.2%, 2014, 4.7%) (EPO, 2019, 2024). In many sectors, however, such as the consumer goods industry or the furniture supply industry, a real culture of objection is still lived. The consumer goods manufacturer *Henkel* alone lodges around 80 appeals a year in Europe.

Goal II: Differentiation by Applying Own Intellectual Property

Deterrence requires credibility: A legal protection strategy only retains its deterring effect vis-à-vis third parties if the fundamental willingness to enforce property rights is also believable. The real value of patents decreases if competitors infringe them and the patent holder knowingly or unknowingly tolerates this. In addition to the purely prophylactic deterrent effect of a patent portfolio, it is therefore important for companies to take offensive measures and also to use their own intellectual property rights to block infringers.

This behavior, which is questionable from an economic point of view because it can lead to legal battles, makes sense if companies in duopolistic or oligopolistic markets want to gain comparative advantages over competitors or gain access to other third-party technologies. The extension of the disruption option, therefore, consists of building up intellectual property rights whose restricted area is primarily geared to competitors' products, technologies, and services—irrespective of the focus of the notifying company itself. Competitors can be approached in an even more focused manner, or future markets can be opened up if corresponding competitive products are analyzed within the framework of systematic reverse engineering and potential improvements are then patented themselves—this makes it possible to sustainably improve one's own starting and negotiating position. In this way, leverage can be gained over competitors, for example, to gain access to other technologies or to control substitution technologies.

From the customer's point of view also, products get better if the competitor has to technologically circumvent the other's products in the same area. Comparative

[1] While the opposition procedure also exists at the national and regional European levels, the nullity procedure is only possible at the national level. Furthermore, nullity proceedings are not possible in many legislations as independent proceedings, but only in connection with infringement proceedings.

competitive advantages in *Porter's* sense not only aim to improve relative customer benefits but are also deliberately directed against competitors.

Example—Gore

The *Gore* company, known by the *Gore-Tex*™ brand, is unique, and it consistently secures its products and technologies based on fluoropolymers through patents and brands against imitation and substitutes. In this way, prices and margins can be maintained and further developments made possible. However, Gore verifies that the cost of legal protection is economically justified. ◀

However, the motivation to disrupt the market reaches its limits when companies achieve outstanding market dominance. It can then happen that the public sector is required to "open up" patents to competitors within the framework of compulsory licenses. In the relevant areas, the question arises as to whether patents should be granted at all or not. However, it is not only US companies that are affected by such a stalemate:

Example—Swisscom

The telecommunications group *Swisscom*, for example, suffers from its dominant market position in Switzerland and the resulting "deregulation activities" of the Swiss regulatory authority. The then *Swisscom* CEO Jens Alder already warned: "As a result of this uncertainty, investments in innovation are at risk!" ◀

Goal III: Multiplier Effect Through Licensing Revenues

The commercialization of intellectual property rights via licenses takes place under profit/loss aspects. The licensing policy, therefore, exerts a strong influence on the desired patent generation: If exclusivity is the sole objective, or if the company's own patents are generally available to third parties for an appropriate licensing fee, for example, to avoid conflicts with competition and trade administrations due to the company's positioning.

The formation of alliances also has a major influence on the generation of patents. In the case of standardization alliances or competitive alliances, the alliance participants usually have a looser arrangement for dealing with the specific intellectual property among themselves than for third parties who are not members of the alliance. The latter are either excluded altogether or have to pay (higher) license fees.

Therefore, the reputation of a company in this area plays an important role in generating license revenues; reputation especially with regard to technical, financial, and procedural experience in the licensing business and the assertiveness achieved in this respect vis-à-vis third parties. In principle, a distinction is made between enablement and enforcement licensing in the generation of licensing income.

Example—Case Study: Julius Blum GmbH

The example of the Austrian kitchen and furniture fittings manufacturer *Julius Blum* shows the importance of a functioning patent strategy. The Austrian company generated sales of nearly 2 billion euros and employed over 6500 people at production sites close to the headquarter, the USA, Poland, and Brazil. Blum holds over 1000 patents and attaches great importance to patent management after the company had a negative experience in the 1960s when a competitor's patent prevented it from entering the market. One example of this: The success of the innovative "Blumotion®" damping system, which was introduced at the turn of the millennium and is now the standard in the furniture industry, was secured. ◀

Blum's patent strategy focuses on preserving freedom of action, i.e., ensuring unrestricted market access regarding the main European markets and their competitors. Thanks to this strategic focus and the active management of the patent portfolio, patent disputes with Asian patent infringers were also successfully resolved (BMWFJ, 2013).

2.4 Cost of Patents

Patents legally preclude the imitation of an innovation only in those countries in which the patent has been granted and is maintained (*Territoriality principle*). With the international *Patent Cooperation Treaty (PCT)* procedure, patent protection can be sought in over 148 countries with a single patent application. Additional regional patent offices include the *European Patent Office (EPO)* as well as the *Eurasian Patent Organization (EAPO)*. The inter-governmental *African Regional Intellectual Property Organization (ARIPO)* and the *Organisation Africaine de la Propriété Intellectuelle (OAPI)* cover Africa.

Central criteria for the selection of the jurisdictions to maintain a patent are:

- Location of the company's markets and competitors;
- Production location of the company and those of the competitors;
- Country-specific legislation, for example, enforceability; and
- Cost aspects, for example, translation and maintenance.

The optimal selection of countries depends on the industry and company-specific configuration and flexibility of the value chain. The guidelines for the selection of countries are derived from the competitive strategy. Important criteria are the locations of the competitors and the current and potential markets.

The acquisition and maintenance of a patent family in Europe cost about 25,000 € for a multi-country portfolio for 10 years. These costs arise over the course of the proceedings and show peaks mainly when there are transfers of proceedings, as lawyers and translation costs are incurred. This is particularly the case when the international Patent Cooperation Treaty patent application procedure (PCT procedure) passes into the regional or national phase and whenever the

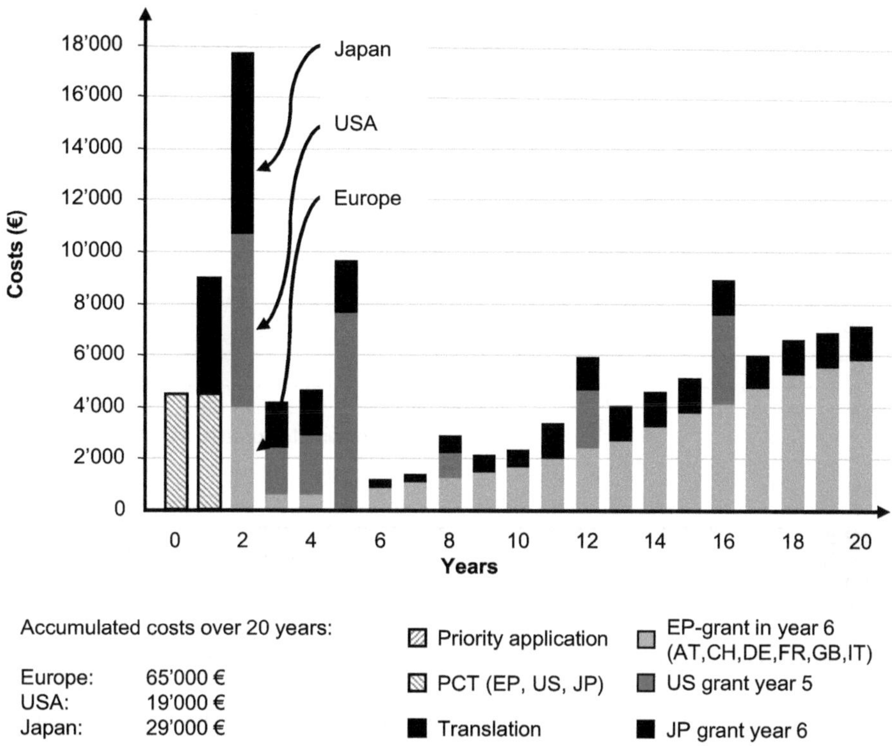

Fig. 2.2 Cost development of an international patent application (authors' own figure)

European patent application procedure passes into the national phase (Gassmann & Bader, 2024).

In the case of granted patents, the annual fees increase depending on the term of the protection (see Fig. 2.2). With this regulation, the legislator intends to increase the opportunity costs for the non-use of a patent. However, many companies still neglect a regular review of the existing patent portfolio and overlook the creeping increase in expenses due to patents no longer required. These are hidden costs that do not create a competitive advantage.

Since the fees and costs also depend on the specificities of the respective countries, a company must carefully consider in which countries patent protection will later become valid. Although the bundled international PCT procedure is usually more expensive and takes longer than an individual procedure, total costs can be saved with large patent portfolios. Due to the longer international application and search procedure, more time is available for the selection of those procedures that should be continued in the first place due to the state of the art as well as due to the company's and the competition's activities. The "international" phase of the procedure enables the applicant to initially conduct a formally relatively manageable and bundled application procedure and to use this time for the final country selection before further translation and legal costs are incurred. Expensive wrong decisions

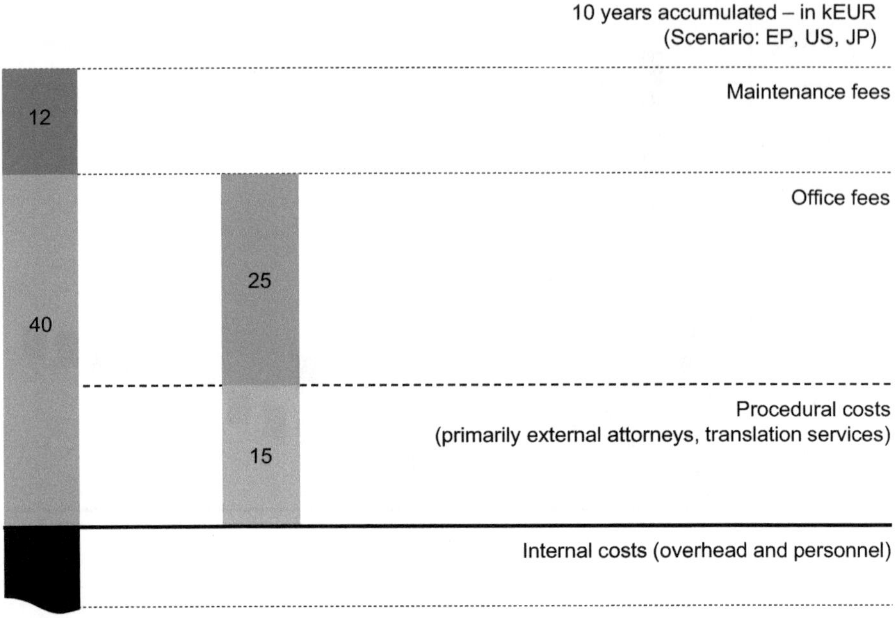

Fig. 2.3 Average patent costs for a patent family over 10 years (authors' own figure)

for unnecessary patent applications can thus be avoided, and the portfolio can be optimized at a very early stage at low cost.

Covering a period of 10 years, a larger patent portfolio in North America (USA, Canada) will cost around 15,000 € per invention, in Europe (Germany, Austria, Switzerland, Great Britain, France, and Italy) around 25,000 €, and in Asia (Japan, South Korea, China, and Taiwan) around 25,000 €. This sum results from the costs of obtaining a granted patent on the one hand and from the costs of maintaining patent protection on the other (see Fig. 2.3):

- The costs for obtaining a patent grant consist of internal costs, such as those for personnel in the patent department, as well as external costs. The latter include costs for external patent attorneys, translations, and official fees.
- The costs for maintaining patent protection are essentially the annual fees. Many companies also use the services of external organizations or law firms to pay annual fees worldwide. As a rule, a lump sum per country and annual fee are charged as a retainer.

The costs for obtaining the granted patent and thus for obtaining patent protection, excluding internal expenses, amount to approximately 75% of the accumulated total costs. It is therefore an expensive error, if it turns out only after the grant that the originally applied for patent protection is actually no longer needed.

If the patents are enforced at a later date, further high costs may arise. For example, the average cost of an infringement suit in the USA is US$3.5 million median to the end of the discovery phase and US$6 million to the end of the proceedings

(AIPLA, 2024) for amounts in dispute in excess of US$25 million at risk. It should be noted, however, that each party must bear its own cost.

IP outsourcing partners are often used to save costs in patent management and at the same time reduce the risks of global applications. In the early 1960s, the Luxembourg company *Dennemeyer* specialized in paying patent fees for its customers. Today, Dennemeyer is one of the world's largest IP service providers with over 180 employees and offers comprehensive IP services such as portfolio management, IP software solutions, and legal IP consulting.

Cost–Benefit Ratio

Cost–benefit consideration should also include robustness of patent enforcement: A large block of costs often goes back to pay for the defense in patent infringement proceedings. As a golden rule of thumb: If you do not have the budget for a fight in court, the patent has only half the value claimed. It is important that potential patent violators believe that you will always take violators to court.

2.5 Complementary Strategies to Patenting

Although this book focuses mainly on patents, we must stress that using IP alone, in most cases, is not the best strategy. In some cases, IP-based strategies are even the wrong choice to make. One of the better studies done on a basically firm choice was conducted by the Intellectual Property Office of the UK (UKIPO, Athreye & Fassio, 2018). In a large survey, it found that some of the strategic reasons for why it may be wise *not* to patent are:

- The innovation is not new to the market.
- The cost of a patent application was too high.
- A patent would have disclosed too much.
- Patent infringement cannot be well detected.
- A patent would be difficult to enforce.

More essential than perhaps lording an innovation over competitors is ensuring that the core business model can operate. A company's own patent is a method of ensuring the firm's own freedom to operate, though being not the only one or even necessarily the best. In addition to filing patents, there are four other alternatives—or better—*complementary techniques* to patenting:

- Defensive publication (Prior Art publications);
- Secrecy;
- Speed and time to market; and
- Designed complexity.

Table 2.1 presents an overview of protection strategies with five typical strategies that firms use to protect innovation. Patenting and IP are the obviously known ones.

Table 2.1 Innovation protection strategies: Capturing value (table compiled by authors)

	Patenting	Defensive publication	Secrecy	Speed	Designed complexity
Exclusivity	Max 20 years	Until publication	Until the secret is made known	Until being copied	Limited
Defense against others' protection rights	Unlimited once disclosed (latest after 18 months)	Unlimited	Sometimes internal grandfathering of usage	Unlimited	Depends on level of public disclosure
	Limited from day of application		Illicit usage remains unknown		
Defense against previous protection rights	Identification through official or internal search enables early defense possible	No	No protection	No	No
			Illicit usage remains unknown		
Possibility for cooperation	Cross-licensing	No	Exchange of know-how	Product specific possibility to influence standards	Strong (through use of licensing)
	Patent pools				
	Reduction of licensing royalties or unit price				
	Influence over standards				
Applicability	Guarantee of temporary monopoly profits through exclusivity of the products	Ensuring freedom to operate for a very low cost	Procedures, processes, based on internal knowledge	Highly attractive products, e.g., trendy products with short life-cycles or highly dynamic technical fields	Good for products where there is a large amount of complementary knowledge or IP (like design and trademarks)
	Possibility to prohibit competitors and new market entrants	SMEs with a small war chest	Inventions for which patent violation is hardly provable, algorithms and production processes		
		Establishing standards through the diffusion of knowledge			

Sometimes used are defense publications, which can permit the firm the freedom-to-operate quickly. Secrecy is often used by smaller firms. Speed and first-mover advantage are classic strategies that are used for innovations where economies of scale and network effects can create their own monopolistic rent. Designed complexity includes a collective set of strategies like black box technologies, knowledge-intensive applications, process know-how, or a strong brand.

Defensive Publication

In order to minimize the risk of "unwanted" patent applications by third parties, and to ensure future freedom of action, publications of all kinds, which in this context are also referred to as "*defensive publications*" or "*defensive disclosures*," are helpful.[2] Once published, the competitor can no longer patent at least the invention described. In addition, the company's image as a technology leader is promoted. *Swisscom* publishes inventions that cannot be patented, for example, on the Internet at *ip.com* and in technical journals. *Roche Diagnostics* takes a very differentiated approach: Where appropriate, publication may take the form of a special publication sheet published every 2 weeks.

Example—Microsoft and Siemens

Microsoft and *Siemens* use technical reports or conference papers that reach numerous interest groups. Special publication media can be used to conceal the originator, but are still available to patent offices for examination and finding prior art—an example is *priorartpublishing.com*. Publications are safeguards against possible later patenting and blocking attempts by competitors. ◀

Prior art publications can be overt, for example, in a journal, and sometimes even covert. Swiss pharma firms occasionally take out advertisements in regional papers and publish formulae—thus ensuring the freedom to operate without tipping off competitors! Today, publishing in paper form would be a good way of doing this since it would not then be searchable via the Internet.

Loss of Novelty

The flip side is that the premature revelation of an invention jeopardizes its patentability. Publications, trade-fair appearances, and the construction of pilot plants must, therefore, be strategically managed and coordinated with patent application activities. The legal validity of patents has more than once been vitiated because pilot plants were installed in publicly accessible buildings or because some extroverted project manager presented technical innovations in a public lecture before these had been patented.

[2] Pre-emptive publication must also be developed and thought through. There are some costs associated with it, and there is a certain level of dependence on the publisher's discretion.

Example—"Guerilla Strategy" for Freedom-to-Operate (FTO)

Publications in specialist media also make sense in terms of technological progress. The disadvantage, however, is that this procedure often enables the competitor to draw helpful conclusions regarding patent and product strategy as well as current R&D activities. There are more creative alternatives, especially for SMEs:

The Swiss company Kern, now part of the Swedish company *Hexagon*, used the *Swiss Aarau Cone* magazine as a publication medium for inventions. These were special inventions that were not strong enough for cost-intensive patents but were in danger of potentially appearing in the form of competitive patents.

Their guerilla strategy to guarantee their freedom-to-operate was: Publish in such a way that nobody reads it! The main competitor was unlikely to find them. The publication is then stored in the company's own archives, constituting a cheap insurance against unwanted patents by third parties. Swiss pharmaceuticals used to do the same thing by publishing their formulae in the local penny-saver papers. ◀

Secrecy

An important alternative to patent applications in the protection of one's own technology and products is secrecy. Indeed, a solid and sophisticated econometric study found that "The results of these analyses show that a higher percentage of R&D-performing firms in all size classes find secrecy to be a more effective means of appropriation than patents" (Arundel, 2001).

Secrecy is particularly useful if it is difficult or impossible to determine whether the subject matter of the IP right has been used or if the enforceability of the IP rights is generally questioned.

Many manufacturing companies, therefore, keep production processes secret and apply for patents for invention objects that can be easily proven only on the product or on the technology. *Coca-Cola* keeps the recipe of the well-known Coca-Cola lemonade secret in order to avoid imitations. Looking back, it can be said that this was the more effective protection strategy because patents would have expired long ago. There is still no identical imitation of Coca-Cola, despite numerous attempts having been made by competitors.

The elevator manufacturer *Schindler* keeps the control algorithms of its elevator systems secret. It would be difficult to prove patent infringement because the source code of elevator control algorithms is generally not accessible to competitors, which is why the company opted for secrecy as a protective measure.

If secrecy is to be maintained, supplementary measures are advisable to avoid the outflow of knowledge via other channels. The most frequently used methods for keeping technical innovations secret are, in particular, the following:

- Implementation of internal confidentiality guidelines[3];

[3] These should, in particular, provide for the use of confidentiality agreements, which are agreed before the start of a conversation with external parties. Supplementary minutes of the discussion are useful.

- Control over presentations and publications given and written by researchers and employees;
- Absolute IT security control over critical documents and plans so that no employee can take them; and
- Decentralized access to innovation by keeping data, teams, and personnel segregated from the entire development (most applicable to larger firms).

Trade secrets, or tacitness, is a common tactic used to prevent imitation. A core technological advantage may even be protected this way and effectively so. Even with perfect formal knowledge of some technology, it may not be operationalized without highly specific knowledge or impossible to transfer. Tacit knowledge can and does move between companies through the transfer of key personnel with intimate knowledge of the technology. In this sense, non-compete agreements and various legal and contractual measures have to be taken to safeguard secrets. Filing patents immediately alert competitors to new products. Tacitness is especially effective for highly specialized installed, non-mass-market products. For example, building specialized forklift attachments—filing a patent would immediately make competitors worldwide aware of a new invention.

Speed and Time to Market

The faster innovation cycles move, the more difficult it is to achieve sustainable competitive advantages through intellectual property rights, since patent protection only provides effective protection against imitation after a certain time delay. A CEO of a consumer electronics company put it succinctly: "Our innovation competition is 'blitzkrieg'—realizing it faster is the match-deciding factor. Strategy is important, but patents only help us in a few platform and key technologies."

The effect that patents can have also depends on the range of manufacture that a company aims to achieve and the position and share that the company occupies in the entire value chain. The more a company succeeds in influencing, not only its own but also other stages of the value chain via patents, the stronger their effect will be. Conversely, dependency and risk increase if a company is directly or indirectly dependent on other value chains to develop and market its own products.

Example—Patent Challenge: System Integration and Customer IP

At the transitions from semiconductor to electrical engineering products, semiconductor companies are expanding their value chains due to the continuously progressing integration of functionalities on the integrated circuits and are coming into collision with the value creation stage of their current customers. Often, cross-licensing agreements are common between companies like, e.g., *IBM*, *Siemens*, and *Infineon Technologies* in order not to block each other. ◀

Designed Complexity

The natural goal of engineers is to design something in as simple a way as possible. Simplicity goes with creating lean products that are easy to be manufactured. All simultaneous engineering and design-for-manufacturing philosophies subscribe to simplicity. However, adding an artificially designed complexity to a product or its related processes prevents products from being imitated. Keeping complex technology in a black box within one critical module is what enables this strategy. Often the black box module is designed and manufactured in the central R&D lab close to the headquarters. In the international R&D literature, it is therefore also called the "national treasure strategy" (von Zedtwitz & Gassmann, 2002). Complexity can be also achieved through highly specific maintenance requirements. Elevator companies such as Otis, Thyssen, and Schindler earn most of their revenues by maintenance and services. This is especially true when it comes to high-rise elevators. Here the maintenance of an elevator is highly specific, the investments in the installation of the elevator are mostly monetized by the maintenance business following it.

In the machinery industry, it has become more difficult to patent. Chinese low-cost competitors have often caught up to European companies. However, one way to protect the intellectual property is the tacit knowledge regarding the application and parametrization of the product.

Example—Buehler: Complexity as Protection Means

The Swiss food processing company *Buehler*, a world market leader and hidden champion of the industry, keeps the process as the real differentiating factor inside its walls. The complexity of system optimization and parametrization lies in a deep knowledge about how to process food. This process know-how is much more difficult to imitate than the machine itself where reverse engineering makes it easy to manufacture the components. ◀

Complexity

Firms often use the design of complexity as a source of protection from imitation. Complexity can be designed in:

- *Products*, e.g., high-tech modules as a black box, typically developed and manufactured in a secure location;
- *Processes*, e.g., service integration, cryptographic protocols;
- *Systems*, e.g., IT security on all levels, firewalls, segmented IT network; and
- *Organization*, e.g., highly integrated patterns of job rotation, loyalty programs, decentralized R&D teams with the critical technologies located close to the headquarter (von Zedtwitz & Gassmann, 2002).

These measures of creating complexity by design are typically applied in countries with a weak appropriability regime, such as in China, India, or Russia (Gassmann et al., 2012; Prud'homme et al., 2018; Thraen & Bader, 2026).

Complementary Alternatives of Value Appropriation

Aside from the major techniques listed above, there are further complementary alternatives to appropriate value and ensure freedom-to-operate. In a comprehensive survey of firms in two technologically advanced and innovative countries with strong IP regimes, the USA and Japan, researchers found that only about 36% of companies find patents effective in protecting and appropriating innovation (Cohen et al., 2002). Lead time/first-mover advantage was more important, with secrecy being especially important to US firms.

There are other motives, more ancillary in importance:

- *Control over complementary assets:* There may be some strategic resources necessary to produce an invention. Perhaps, a common example is *Tesla's* high-capacity lithium–cobalt battery technology, which allows for higher discharge rates. Tesla has moved to secure a lot of the supply, making it more difficult for competitors wanting to use the same-known technology.
- *Retention of strategic personnel:* Keeping loyal personnel is perhaps the most critical aspect of IP protection. There is an old saying: "*Know-how travels with people.*" The diffusion of technology among firms takes place mostly through this channel. Disclosures concerning a patent are strategic and intentionally opaque; any astute patent attorney only discloses as much as is necessary when having to circumscribe the invention. However, critical R&D personnel know much more details about how to use and implement the invention, and thus, much of the knowledge resides in employees; important are incentive systems and, most important, a strong corporate culture.
- *NDAs (Non-Disclosure Agreements) and traditional licensing contracts:* Are often much more enforceable in court than intellectual property. This means starting every critical meeting with an NDA, which is too often this is neglected.
- *Open source:* One alternative in the software and hardware spaces has been to open up the key technologies and build the business model off of services and specialized applications; if the technology is attractive enough, people will use it, thus growing it to the very market size the business intends to target.
- *Service contracts* that tie into the technology.
- *Branding, naming, and advertising:* A strong brand can be stronger than a patented technology; see, e.g., *Red Bull.*
- *Strict control over distribution channels:* Build your own distribution channels, e.g., through direct sales, as is done by *Hilti*, *Vorwerk*, or *Nespresso*.
- *Complementary manufacturing:* It is an important technique whereby certain bits of the technology are kept in-house so that no supplier and no other manufacturer can replicate the product without having the core manufacturing technology.

References

AIPLA. (2024). *Report of the economic survey*. Arlington, Virginia: AIPLA American Intellectual Property Law Association.

Arundel, A. (2001). The relative effectiveness of patents and secrecy for appropriation. *Research Policy, 30*(4), 611–624.

Athreye, S., & Fassio, C. (2018). *When do firms not use patents and trademarks to protect valuable innovations? Evidence from the SIPU 2015 survey*. UK Intellectual Property Office.

BMWFJ. (2013). *Immaterielle Vermögenswerte—geistiges Eigentum als Wachstumstreiber*. Vienna: Bundesministerium für Wirtschaft, Familie und Jugend.

Cohen, W. M., Goto, A., Nagata, A., Nelson, R. R., & Walsh, J. P. (2002). R&D spillovers, patents and the incentives to innovate in Japan and the United States. *Research Policy, 31*(8–9), 1349–1367.

Cotropia, C. A., Kesan, J. P., Rozema, K., & Schwartz, D. L. (2017). *Endogenous litigation costs: An empirical analysis of patent disputes*. Northwestern Law & Econ Research Paper 17–01; University of Illinois College of Law Legal Studies Research Paper No. 17–14. Available at SSRN: Retrieved January 3, 2017, from https://ssrn.com/abstract=2893503, https://doi.org/10.2139/ssrn.2893503

EPO. (2019). *Annual report 2018*. Munich: European Patent Office.

EPO. (2024). *Statistics reported to the administrative council (CA/F 5)*. Munich: European Patent Office.

Gassmann, O., & Bader, M. A. (2024). *Patentmanagement: Innovationen erfolgreich nutzen und schützen* (5th ed.). Springer Gabler.

Gassmann, O., Beckenbauer, A., & Friesike, S. (2012). *Profiting from innovation in China*. Springer.

Krech, C.-A., Rüther, F., & Gassmann, O. (2015). Profiting from invention: Business models of patent aggregating companies. *International Journal of Innovation Management, 19*(3), 1–26.

London, S. (2023). Strategic uses of IP: Applying learnings from large companies to start-ups. In M. A. Bader & S. Süzeroglu-Melchiors (Eds.), *Intellectual property management for start-ups—Value-enhancing approaches and practices for leveraging the potential*. Cham.

Mintzberg, H., Ahlstrand, B., & Lampel, J. (2005). *Strategy safari: A guided tour through the wilds of strategic management*. Simon and Schuster.

Osram. (2013). *Osram GmbH und Sharp Corporation schließen Patentlizenzaustauschvertrag*. Munich: Osram. http://www.osram.ch/osram_ch/de/presse/pressemeldungen/_fachpresse/2013/osram-gmbh-und-sharp-corporation-schliessen-patentlizenzaustauschvertrag/index.jsp

Prud'homme, D., von Zedwitz, M., Thraen, J. J., & Bader, M. A. (2018). Forced technology transfer policies: Workings in China and strategic implications. *Technological Forecasting and Social Change, 134*, 150–168.

Thompson, M. (2013). Costs of Swiss patent litigation. *Sic!* Retrieved June, 6, 2013, 332–345.

Thraen, J. J., & Bader, M. A. (2026). Key success factors in nurturing and sustaining 21st-century technology clusters. In J. J. Thraen & C. H. Hoffmann (Eds.), *Successful technology clusters in the 21st century*. Walter de Gruyter. Forthcoming.

von Zedtwitz, M., & Gassmann, O. (2002). Market versus technology drive in R&D internationalization: Four different patterns of managing research and development. *Research Policy, 31*(4), 569–588.

Wallstreet Journal. (2019). *Qualcomm's practices violate antitrust law, judge rules*, Retrieved May 22, 2019.

Evaluating and Valuing Patents 3

A basic problem of patent management in most companies is that there are more ideas than a patent can be applied for operationally. Getting and maintaining a patent are associated with high costs, and so firms are required to both *evaluate* their patents and to *value* their patents. We use *evaluation* to refer to the business logic and strategic impact of the patent, and the term *valuation* to refer to the monetary number assigned to a patent. Therefore, a solid evaluation and valuation of ideas worth patenting, along with the regular supervision of existing patent applications and patents, are essential. Hence, an important goal of both evaluation and valuation is to help focus on internal firm resources.

An important objective of an evaluation is to provide assistance in focusing resources on activities that are expected to make the greatest contribution to the market success. On the one hand, this can be done anticipatively and top-down by applying standardization strategies to build and optimize patent portfolios, while on the other hand, retrospectively and bottom-up by applying valuation methods to existing patent portfolios. An evaluation can be *qualitative*, i.e., strengths and weaknesses of a patent are evaluated on the basis of business-relevancy, and/or valued *quantitatively* by assigning a monetary value to patents or patent portfolios.

The following dimensions influence the value of a patent and are therefore more or less taken into account in the portfolio and valuation method:

- Market factors (market potential, market volume, and market growth);
- Competition (intensity of competition, product life cycle, and products of other market players);
- Research and Development (R&D) criteria (technical risks, resources, investments, and time);
- Production criteria (capacity and manufacturing costs);
- Overlap criteria (synergies with other products, probability of follow-up projects, effects on infrastructure and organization, and learning effects); and
- Legal criteria (validity, scope of protection, dependency, and remaining patent life).

M. A. Bader et al., *Patent Management*, Management for Professionals,
https://doi.org/10.1007/978-3-032-12030-4_3

Due to the strong time reference of the evaluation, several evaluations have to be carried out in the patent process. Ideally, the times at which cost-effective decisions are to be made in the patenting process are suitable for this:

- Selection of the invention disclosures that are to be pursued as industrial property rights;
- Decision on subsequent applications (within priority year period);
- Transition from international or regional examination phase to national phases; and
- Maturity of annual fees.

Different Purposes—Different Methods

- *Evaluation:* Finding the qualitative value of the protection right using different levels.
- *Valuation:* Finding the quantitative value of the protection right using recognized valuation methods.
- *Portfolio management:* Values the right from the point of view of the market and technology positions, and normative action in relation to the entire portfolio.

3.1 Evaluating Patents

The qualitative evaluation of patents, also called patent evaluation, analyzes the strengths and weaknesses of a patent. This evaluation is carried out on the basis of criteria, each of which is assigned a specific value number. The result of a qualitative evaluation is usually a statement from which direct recommendations for action can be derived. A qualitative evaluation of a patent could, for example, be formulated as follows: "The patent protects a technology of strategic importance in a semi-attractive market. It can be enforced efficiently."

A qualitative evaluation, therefore, supports patenting decisions, allows for portfolio comparisons to be made, and supports patent management decisions.

Valuation methods can be classified (see Fig. 3.1).

Monovariate Patent Evaluation

For one-dimensional patent evaluation, criteria are defined on the basis of which the quality and value of a patent are assessed. These criteria can be both *subjective* (e.g., difficulty in circumventing a patent for competitors and the attractiveness of use for competitors), and *objective* (e.g., frequency of citation and geographical scope).

With the patent value number method, the criteria are assigned a value number, e.g., from 0 to 6 or from A to E. The criteria are then used to calculate the patent value. Table 3.1 gives an overview of criteria that are frequently used in practice for

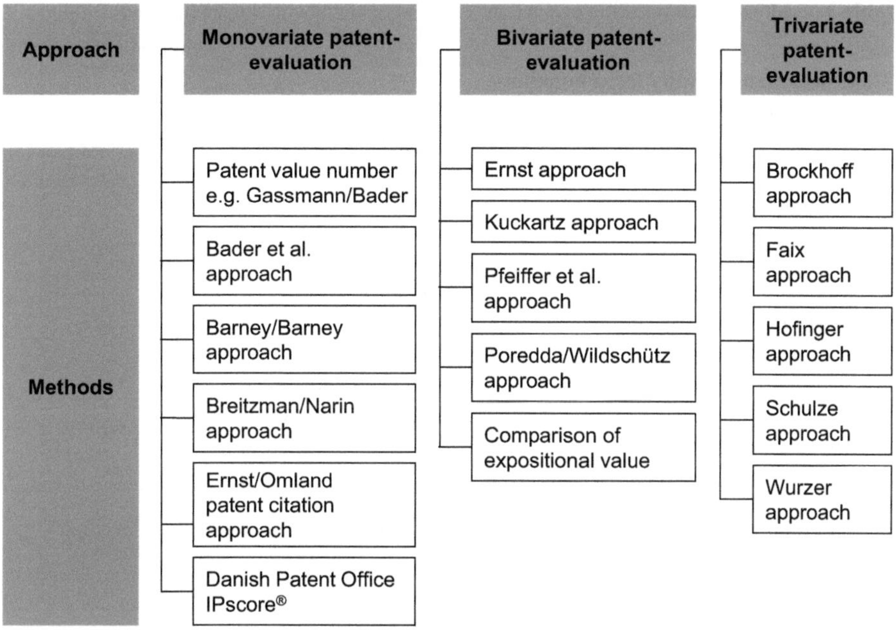

Fig. 3.1 Qualitative patent evaluation methods (authors' own figure)

the qualitative evaluation of inventions, patent applications, and patents. For each criterion, a value number is defined between "0" (worthless) and "6" (excellent). The overall result can be obtained either by averaging or by a weighted evaluation of the individual results.

Objective Evaluation methods are often used for ratings. These objective criteria are so-called empirical indicators (Reitzig (2002) provides an overview of empirical indicators). Statistical studies confirm a correlation between patent value and these indicators. The advantage of these indicators is that they can be easily determined from databases.

Ratings are often carried out by professional providers. One rating provider, for example, is *PatentRatings*, which was part of *Ocean Tomo* for some time, which patented its rating process (US 6,556,992). Another patent for a rating method was filed by *1790 Analytics* (US 6,175,824). Patent ratings are also offered in German-speaking countries. According to Ernst and Omland (2010), the approach evaluates the current extent of worldwide patent protection and the relevance of the patent for subsequent developments.

The *St. Gallen Patent Index (SGPI)* developed by Bader et al. (2012) evaluates both the relevance of the patent and the strength of the markets in which the patent is applied for (see also US 2012/0303537). A particular advantage is that not only individual patents are evaluated, but also the strength of the portfolio, taking into account that the value of a portfolio is more than the sum of its individual patents.

Statements about the patent value are made by one-dimensional valuation methods over previously defined ranges or the direct comparison of several patents.

Table 3.1 Monovariate portfolio evaluation: Patent value number (table compiled by authors)

Criterion		Value number (0…6)
Circumvention difficulty for competitors:		…
Direct substitutes	Practically impossible	5…6
	Requires effort	2…4
	Easily achieved	0…1
Attractiveness for competitors:		…
Competitive interest	Strong	5…6
	Average	2…4
	Minimal	0…1
Discovery of competitive usage:		…
Proof	Easily obtained	5…6
	Difficult to obtain	2…4
	Impossible to obtain	0…1
Direct usage in production:		…
	Probable	5…6
	Possible	2…4
	Improbable	0…1
Size of respective patent portfolio segment:		…
	Too small	5…6
	Appropriate	2…4
	Too big	0…1
Additional criteria:		…
Future technology or future products	…	
Ensuring important R&D results	…	
Supporting sales	…	
Strengthening negotiation position	…	
Public funding for project	…	
Contributes to a standard	…	
Other	…	
Total value number:		…

Example—Patent Evaluation at Eastman Kodak

Kodak evaluates patents in connection with acquisitions, maintenance, and licensing. It recognizes the value of intellectual property primarily in terms of the market advantages of protection and for licensing purposes. Kodak uses the following criteria:

- Proven or expected internal use;
- Proven or expected external use;
- Breadth of patent claims; and
- Identification of the use of proprietary technologies or products.

The review for internal purposes is based on a qualitative evaluation and does not include a financial one. ◀

Example—Patent Evaluation at Schindler

Schindler has outsourced the management of intellectual property to a subsidiary, Inventio. The latter uses an internally developed IP database as the basis for evaluating patents. The patents are classified within the database. The classification is carried out by the R&D team, the sales team, and Inventio itself. The keywords of the classifications are defined by all of these deciding together, which takes place about every 2 years.

The evaluation of individual property rights and bundles of property rights is also carried out by *Inventio* after consultation with the product managers. The patents are evaluated qualitatively with the help of a uniform evaluation sheet making use of a point system. The evaluation sheet takes into account both the economic perspective (market success) and the legal perspective (sustainability). In addition, an evaluation is carried out according to technical aspects. Inventio's patent evaluation criteria guiding the technology process consist of the creative phase, the development phase, and the maturity phase (see Fig. 3.2).

The addressees of the evaluation are indicated in the phases above. Below the process, evaluation criteria are assigned to each phase. Market success is assessed on the basis of cost advantage, customer benefit, and turnover. The demands on the technology reveal the *strength of the patent claims*, *clarity*, *completeness*, and the *scope of protection*. The criteria for evaluating sustainability are *chances of being granted*, *circumventability*, *territorial scope of the protection* as well as *validity* and *enforceability* of the patent. ◄

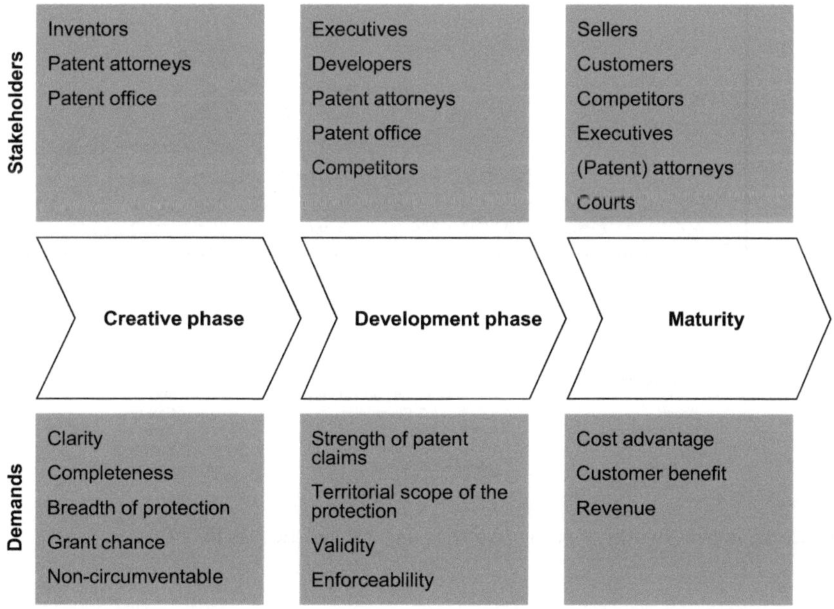

Fig. 3.2 Database concept for patent evaluation at *Schindler* (authors' own figure)

Bibliometric Patent Quality

The value of a patent can be inferred by its apparent quality. Patent quality indicators are, for example, citation rate, international scope, i.e., foreign applications file, duration, and opposition rate against the patent. While none of these causes patent value, high-value patents often have more family members, get cited, and are legally attacked (see Figs. 3.3 and 3.4).

Bivariate Patent Evaluation

Within the framework of patent license negotiations or in preparation for them, risk and reward assessments between companies are often conducted. A proven practical concept is a comparison of the respective *exposure* of one company with the other and vice versa.

Exposure is determined on the basis of two variables: the turnover of one enterprise and the number of patents and patent applications of the other enterprise relevant to its turnover.[1] In the simplest case, exposure is the product of the two variable

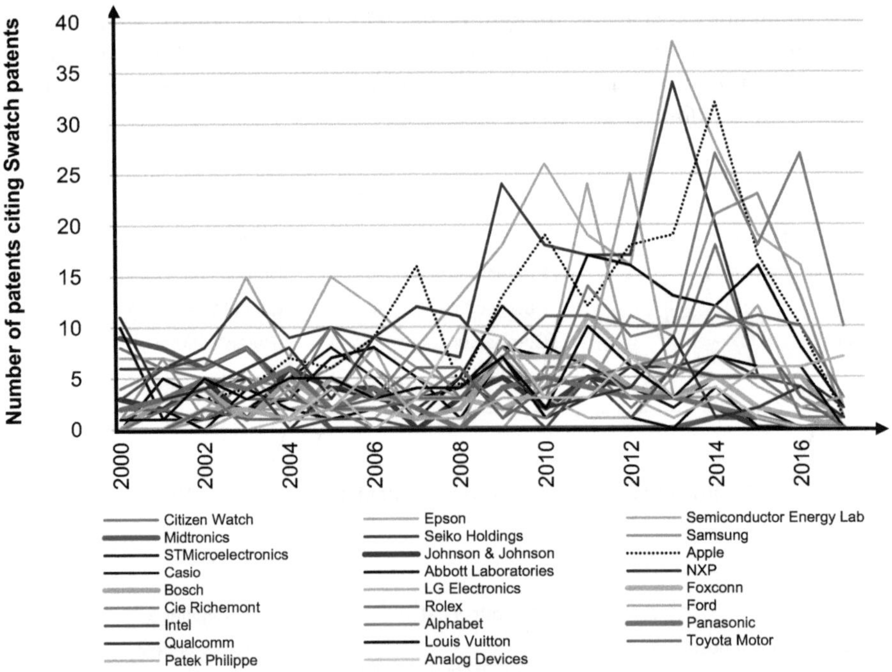

Fig. 3.3 Example: Number of patents citing *Swatch* patents (Econsight, 2020)

[1] There may be other types of protection rights, like utility models, that can be incorporated into this analysis.

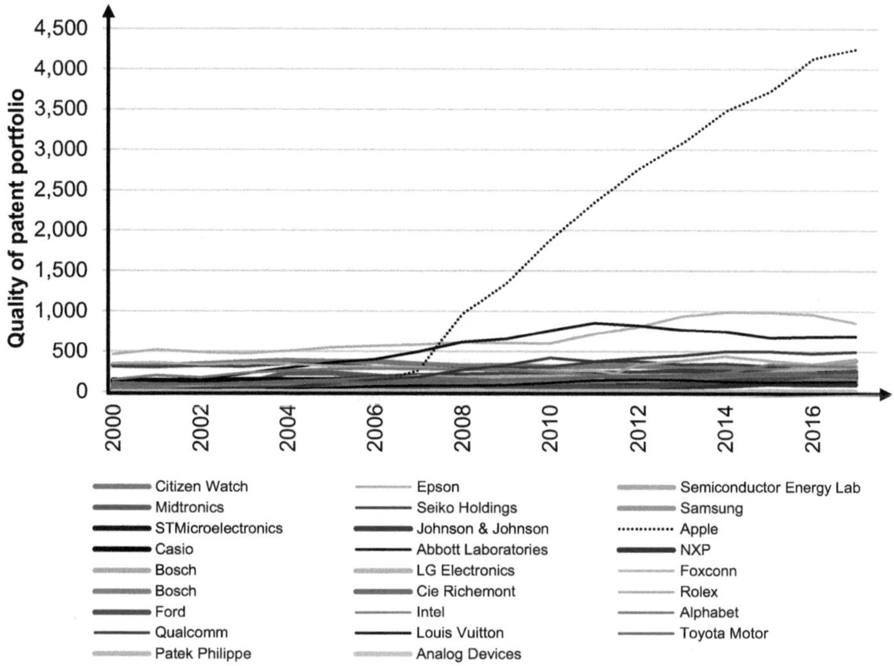

Fig. 3.4 Example (cont.): Comparison of the same patent portfolios on the basis of a patent- quality approach (Econsight, 2020)

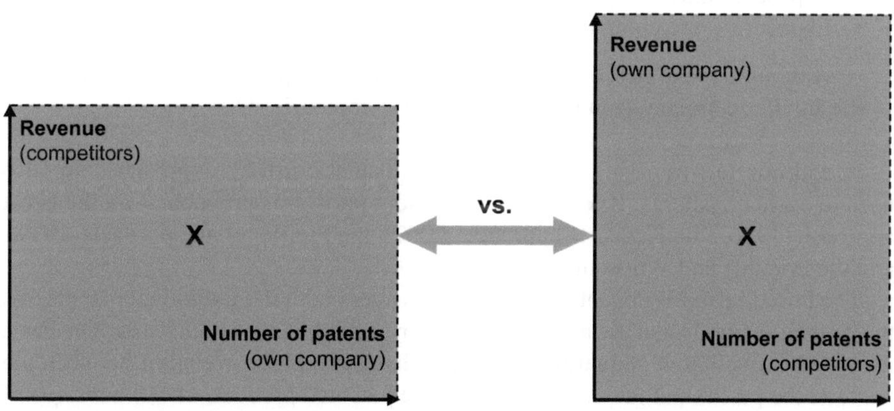

Fig. 3.5 Bivariate portfolio evaluation: exposure comparison (authors' own figure)

values. In comparison, it can then be determined whether *risks* and *opportunities* are evenly balanced or whether one of the companies has a higher exposure value and is therefore disadvantaged compared to the other (see Fig. 3.5).

If, for example, a *cross-licensing agreement* is to be concluded between two companies, the agreement could be concluded in a financially neutral manner due to the balance out. In the latter case, the company with the lower exposure could additionally demand financial recompense or some other form of compensation to make up for the imbalance. The advantage is that, especially in the case of very large patent portfolios, the values of the variables can initially be determined without information from the negotiating partner, and the exposure values can be qualitatively estimated: sales can be determined through market studies, and the number of patents can be found out through patent searches. If the valuation method is accepted by both partners as a basis for negotiation, the values can be discussed in a mutually comprehensible manner. The disadvantage of this method, however, is that it is generally assumed that one company's sales will at first be evenly covered by the intellectual property of the other company and vice versa. This is therefore only plausibly justifiable in the case of large patent portfolios.

An important supplementary criterion is therefore the hit rate. This is the proportion of intellectual property rights that are ultimately also used by the products and technologies of the negotiating partner and can, therefore, be introduced into patent infringement proceedings. A comparison of the exposure values only makes sense if both parties assume a balanced hit rate and can prove this credibly. For smaller portfolios, it is advisable to calculate and compare exposure values for each patent or clearly defined portfolio. A total exposure value can then be determined for each company by summing up the exposure values.

Example—Calculation Example for Exposure Values

For example, a company A has a turnover of 150 million euros and 20 patents. Company B, on the other hand, has a turnover of 20 billion euros and 1000 patents:

- Exposure value company A: 150 × 1000 = 150,000.
- Exposure value company B: 20,000 × 20 = 400,000.

Although the larger company B holds many more patents, it is subordinate to the smaller company A in the exposure value comparison. ◀

In addition to comparing exposure values, patent portfolio approaches are also used to evaluate patents. Known bivariate patent portfolio approaches are the Ernst approach (1996), the Kuckartz approach (2007), the Pfeiffer et al. approach (1989), and the Poredda and Wildschütz approach (2004).

The Poredda and Wildschütz approach considers both the individual patents and the patent portfolios that are assigned to a defined product or product area. The basic idea of this qualitative valuation method is that there is a correlation between the value of the patent and the market share of the patented product. The dimensions of patent valuation are:

- Market value of the patent; and
- Legal value of the patent.

Starting from the consideration of individual patents, a two-dimensional patent portfolio representation can be generated (see Fig. 3.6). In addition, recommendations for action can be derived for individual patents.

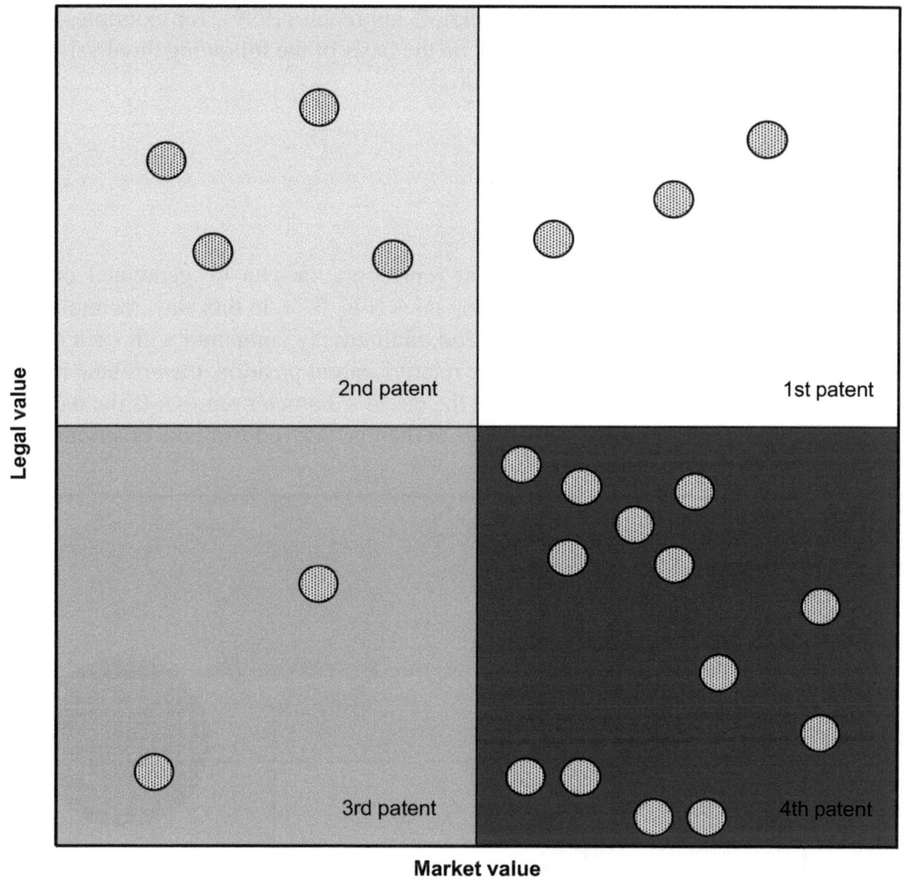

Fig. 3.6 Bivariate portfolio evaluation according to Poredda and Wildschütz

Market Value of the Patent

Indicators for the market value of a patent are the relative attractiveness of patented technical solution, the total profit of the product category, and its effective blocking duration.

Legal Value of the Patent

Indicators for the legal value are patentability, ease in identifying patent violation, the dependency of other protection rights, and territorial coverage. These indicators are established in cooperation with patent, market, and technology experts.

Trivariate Patent Evaluation

Well-known trivariate approaches are the Brockhoff approach (1999); the Faix approach (2001); the Hofinger approach (1997); the Schulze approach (2005); and the Wurzer approach (2005). The Brockhoff approach (1999), for example, compares technologies and patent portfolios on the basis of the following three variables (Brockhoff, 1999; Ernst, 1998, 1999, 2002):

- Relative patent position;
- Technological attractiveness; and
- Technological significance.

A three-dimensional patent portfolio representation can be generated on the basis of certain technology fields of companies (Fig. 3.7). In this way, technologies or technology groups can be classified and qualitatively compared with each other. For example, the abscissa represents the relative patent position, the ordinate represents the technology attractiveness, and the circle's diameter represents the technological significance. Standard strategies can then be derived from the positions.

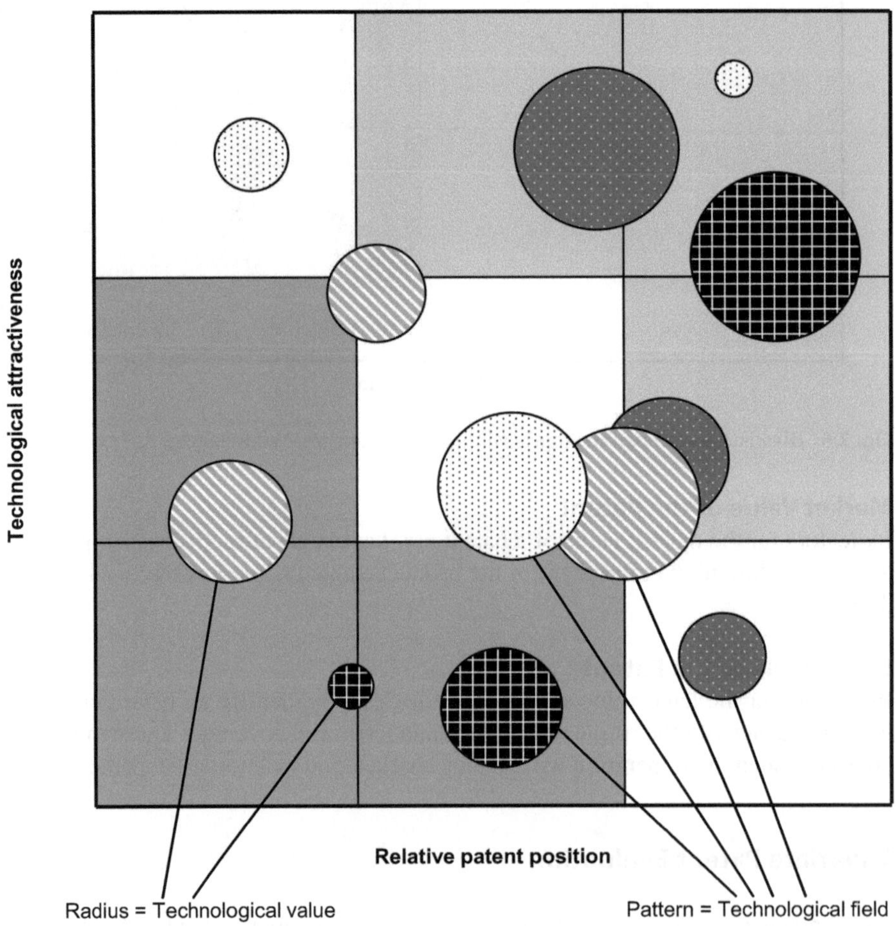

Fig. 3.7 Trivariate portfolio evaluation according to Brockhoff

Relative Patent Position
Calculation of the relative patent position of a company in relation to other companies. For example, the ratio of a company's own patents to the *(quality-adjusted)* total number of patents relating to the field of technology under investigation is calculated. The maximum value is therefore 1.

Technological Attractiveness
Technological attractiveness is calculated, for example, out of the relationship between the growth in the patent applications of the respective technological field and the growth of patent applications of all observed technological fields.

Technological Significance
The significance of a technology for a company is calculated out of the relation of the number of patents of a technological field of a company and the entire number of patents of the company.

Evaluation of Patents
Qualitative patent evaluation is a suitable tool to support patent management decisions. The following points have to be considered:

- *Strategic recommendations for action:* To identify strategic recommendations for action and to support decisions, there is a multitude of analytic methods.
- *Communicability of the results:* A good communicability is given by systematized scales or graphical preparation of the results.
- *Subjective value indicators:* These help to depict the value more realistically, but also make the assessment dependent on the person making the assessment.

3.2 Valuing Patents

While the evaluation aims to analyze the strengths and weaknesses of a patent and to make a statement about the quality of the patent on the basis of certain criteria along with subsequent options for action, valuation determines the monetary value of a patent.

However, no strategic recommendations for action can be derived directly from the valuation (Bader et al., 2008).

In spite of a diverse set of methods, the determination of a patent's value is complex because the term "value" does not have a clear definition. Depending on the point of view and the perception, the value can take on the following forms:

- *Value in the sense of meaning*: A thing having meaning for a certain person;
- *Value in the sense of price*: The monetary amount that a seller demands for the good offered; and
- *Value in the sense of transaction*: The monetary amount actually realized in a transaction.

If one explains this by using as an example an invention, it is evident that the product is often of great importance to the inventor because they have invested a lot of time, including some of their leisure time, into it. So, if the invention is then to be sold, the inventor might demand, say, € 50,000 for it. The company that is willing to buy the invention assesses the invention differently from the inventor, and eventually, both agree on a transaction price of € 25,000. Patents are always context-specific due to their dependence on their use in and for the company, their age, and other factors. Therefore, there is no such thing as objective patent value.

However, in order to estimate the value of a patent, the future benefit of the patent can be taken into account. The economic benefit results in particular from the products for which the patent is granted or on the basis of which these are manufactured. The influencing variables of the patent value are divided into technical, economic, and legal factors (Moser & Goddar, 2007).

Technological factors are, for example, the uniqueness of the technology, its degree of novelty, the status of R&D relating to it, the level of innovation, or the life cycle of the technology. The technology of the underlying invention influences the positioning of a product in different ways. For example, a product can be differentiated by patents. The manufacturer can charge a surcharge for the product. The development of a new technology can result in lower production costs and competitive advantages. A patent can also enable exclusive production or guarantee freedom of production.

The market factor reflects the economic dimension and is described, for example, by market potential, market volume, market growth, industry structure, or product life cycle.

However, only legal protection enables the various forms of use of patents, and therefore, it has a great influence on the value of a patent. The legal protection is influenced by the factors: validity, scope of protection, dependencies with other patents, or the remaining patent life. If the patent is not valid, or if it is unenforceable, the property right has no value, even if the market grows exponentially or the product can be produced particularly cost-effectively. On the other hand, a patent that blocks competitors can guarantee high sales.

In contrast to patent evaluation, which is mainly conducted in order to optimally control the strategic management of patents, patent valuation is carried out for a large number of different business transactions. The general conditions determine whether a valuation is done voluntarily or due to external compulsion, for example, in the case of company takeovers. In M&A, patents are evaluated more extensively than in purely internal considerations. This is one more reason why valuation plays an important role.

Reasons for a monetary patent evaluation are:

- *Management-oriented events:* Patent portfolio maintenance, budget allocation, monitoring of R&D, inventor remuneration, risk analyses, patenting decisions;
- *Corporate actions:* Due diligence, joint venture, initial public offering, company sale, company valuation;
- *Financing and balance-sheet-oriented events:* Patent as loan collateral, accounting, debt and equity financing, voluntary capital market information;
- *Transfer-oriented events:* Licensing, cross-licensing, strategic alliances, technology transfer; and
- *Conflict-oriented events:* Liquidation, insolvency, transfer prices, determination of damages.

More than 100 quantitative patent valuation methods are now discussed in the literature. For this reason, it is often assumed that the valuation methods can be divided into three main valuation methods (including Smith & Parr, 2019; DIN 77100, 2011; IDW S 5, 2013), namely:

- Cost-oriented procedures;
- Market-oriented procedures; and
- Income-oriented procedures.

Figure 3.8 (see also Table 3.5) shows an overview of this trichotomy and the most frequently cited patent evaluation methods in the literature. Smith and Parr are probably the most frequently cited representatives of this trichotomy. They argue that any method they have identified in their extensive literature research can basically be traced back to one of the above methods (Smith & Parr, 2019). In order to

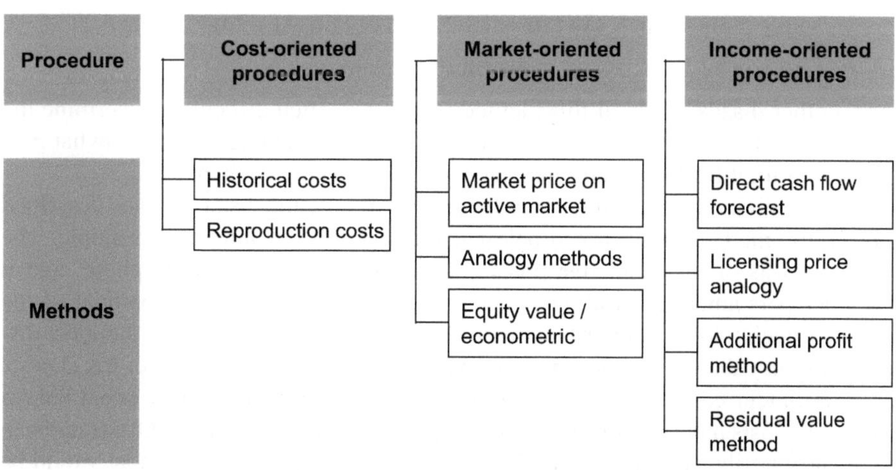

Fig. 3.8 The trichotomy of quantitative patent valuation procedures (authors' own figure)

do justice to their complexity or their use in practice, further methods are explained at the end of this section in addition to the methods of the three methods mentioned here.

Cost-Oriented Procedures

The basic assumption of the cost-oriented procedure is that the value of a patent is best represented by the costs incurred during the lifetime of the patent. The two most commonly used methods are the historical cost method and the replacement cost method.

(1) Historical Costs

In practice, the historical cost method is often used when the amount of information available is still relatively small. This is often the case in the R&D phase of a patented technology (Turner, 2000) because an R&D project undergoes a constant stream of cash outlays. Using a theoretical example, Turner shows that the *historical costs* [*C*] (for example, the costs involved in creating and filing a patent) can be derived from the corporate *cost of capital* [*r*]:

$$\text{Value} \cong \text{Cost } (C) = \text{Investment } (I) + \text{total cost of carry } (R)$$

The total time cost of money is the carry cost of the amount spent up until time (t).

$$R = I_1 * r + (I_1 * r + I_2 * r) + (I_1 * r + * * + I_t * r)$$

So, for a three-million-dollar project (I = 3 m) over 3 years (I_1 = 1 m; I_2 = 1 m; I_3 = 1 m) with a 10% corporate cost of capital (r = 0.1), we would compute the approximate patent value as:

$$\begin{aligned}\text{Value} &\cong 3\text{m} + (1\text{m} * .1) + (1\text{m} * .1 + 2\text{m} * .1) + (1\text{m} * .1 + 2\text{m} * .1 + 3\text{m} * .1) \\ &= 4 \text{ million dollars}\end{aligned}$$

Another disadvantage of this method is that it is often difficult to determine the start and end times of R&D for a particular technology and to determine what proportion of total R&D expenditure is attributable to a single patent.

As this method is used relatively frequently despite the disadvantages described above, the method is illustrated below using a simplified numerical example. The example was divided into five phases. The first phase is the R&D phase, and it includes personnel, material, and search costs incurred in the development of the patented technology and attributable to the patent. This attribution is the most difficult to carry through because it is strongly based on estimates. Further R&D costs were not incurred in later phases. Defining the costs in the later subsequent phases is easier. Costs incurred for the application are defined by the Patent Office and can be clearly attributed to the patent. The same applies to possible costs that would be incurred in patent disputes. In Table 3.2, these costs were waived. By simply adding up all costs incurred, a patent value of € 965,100 is obtained.

Table 3.2 Simplified example of method of historical costs (in Euro)

Type of cost	t_4[a]	t_3[b]	t_2	t_1	t_0[c]
R&D costs					
Personnel costs	750,000				
Material costs	150,000				
Research costs	50,000				
Sum R&D costs	950,000	0	0	0	0
Patent prosecution costs					
Application fee		100	0	0	0
Examination fee		1565	0	0	0
Search fee		1035	0	0	0
Translation(s)		0	0	0	4000
Annual fees		0	0	0	400
Monitoring		600	600	600	600
Opposition procedure		0	0	0	0
Nullity procedures		0	0	0	0
Searches		300	250	300	250
Patent litigation		0	0	0	0
Patent attorney costs		3000	500	500	500
Sum prosecution costs	0	6600	1350	1400	5750
Sum of patent costs	950,000	6600	1350	1400	5750
Patent value	**965,100**				

Source: Table compiled by authors
[a]R&D phase
[b]Time of patent application
[c]Time of valuation

(2) Reproduction Costs

In this method, the patent value is calculated by adding all the costs that would be incurred if the existing patent were recovered. Replacement does not mean the exact reproduction of the existing patent, but the development of a patent with exactly the same functionalities as the existing one (Smith & Parr, 2019). It may happen that the new patent is more advantageous than the existing one in some respects. Although the development and methods used to create the new patent may differ greatly from those used for the present patent, the basic functions of both patented technologies are the same. It should be noted that the costs used are virtual costs.

Pros and Cons of Cost-Oriented Procedures

The biggest advantage of the cost-oriented method is its ease of use. To obtain a patent value, only the costs have to be added. In addition, relatively little information is required, which can often be queried by *R&D controlling*. On the other hand, information is required that is very specific and often cannot be generated at the push of a button (Ensthaler & Strübbe, 2006).

The cost-oriented procedure is based on the assumption that costs are equal to value. This is classified as problematic (Smith & Parr, 2019; Wurzer & Reinhardt, 2010). There is also no empirical evidence that there is a correlation between the value of a patent and its costs (Bertolotti, 1996; Dressler, 2006). Patents that do not generate any economic added value but have cost a lot of money in R&D (e.g., classic undesirable developments) are categorized here as very valuable. On the other hand, patents that have low development costs but generate high market returns could then be classified as worthless.

Application of Cost-Oriented Procedures

The cost-oriented method is a *simple tool* to calculate the ranges of prices for patent sales or *licensing negotiations*. It is also used by cost-based accounting or in cases where *taxation* is necessary. In technology and patent management, this approach is particularly suitable for *make-or-buy decisions*. However, strategic decisions in which the future utility of the patent plays a central role should not be made on the basis of this procedure since it is largely an *accounting technique*.

Market-Oriented Procedures

The market-based methods rely on the assumption that the precise value of a patent is the value that the market would be willing to pay for a similar patent in similar circumstances. There are two methods in this procedure. The patent value can be determined either by the market price in an active market or by analogy.

(3) Market Price on Active Market

The simplest way of a market-price-oriented patent valuation is to offer the patent on the open market and thereby find out what price potential buyers would be willing to pay. This simple description also includes the most important condition for the application of market-price-oriented procedures. In order to obtain a precise value, the existence of a market must be guaranteed. *ICAP Patent Brokerage* offers auctions of patents and patent portfolios (formerly *Ocean Tomo*).

(4) Analogy Method

Another valuation method is to collect information on comparable transactions (comparable patent, technology, situation of participants, etc.) and to determine the value of one's own patent through a detailed comparison.

Using a simplified numerical example, Table 3.3 shows how a patent was evaluated using the analogy method. The comparator patent should be comparable to your own patent and should be reviewed for relevant product and market sizes. These variables can include the actual and possible *scope of use* of the patent, *extent of the innovation*, *property right situation* (e.g., nullity actions), *territorial scope* of protection, achieved and achievable *competitive advantages* through the patent, remaining *useful life*, *market growth*, *size*, *potential*, *share*, possibilities of *subsequent inventions*, *industry specifics*, etc. (Rings, 2000). In the example below, the settlement patent transaction implies a licensing *royalty rate* of 3%. This 3% is applied then used. The patent value is now determined by forecasting the turnover

Table 3.3 Simplified example of the analogy method (in Euro)

	t_1	t_2	t_3
Comparable patent			
Revenue	100,000	100,000	
Licensing: 3% per year (patent protection: 2 years)			
Patent to value			
Revenue	80,000	80,000	80,000
Licensing: 3% per year (patent protection: 3 years)	2400	2400	2400
Discount rate: 8%/year	2222	2058	1905
Patent value	**6185**		

Source: Table compiled by authors

for the next 3 years (the previously determined remaining useful life). The license rate is calculated based on the revenue and the royalty. The fictitious license payments are discounted to reflect the *time value of money*. The patent value then results from the addition of all potential discounted license payments. As can be seen from the example, only the license rate of the comparable patent is used. Remaining useful life and possible revenues are based on the estimate of the own patent.

(5) Equity Value/Econometric

Most of the valuation approaches here employ on a business perspective. Yet, it is worth mentioning that there is also an econometric way of valuing patents. The basic premise of the market value approach is to predict the excess value of a firm beyond its book value using the company's patents as a regressor. This approach, first pioneered by Griliches, 1981, uses *Tobin's q* as a dependent variable and past patenting to predict the value of a company in excess of its book value.

A series of articles refining and extending the same basic approach in that pilot study were conducted using *Bayesian methods* (Connolly & Hirschey, 1988), incorporating appropriability (Cockburn & Griliches, 1987); addressing technological opportunity (Connolly & Hirschey, 1988). Hall et al. (2005) further refined this approach adding patent quality to the mix. In addition to these variants on the same basic approach, the technique has been applied to specific industries like those of semiconductors (Megna & Klock, 1993), as well as local markets like the United Kingdom (Otto Toivanen & Bosworth, 2002), Malaysia (Ghapar et al., 2014), Australia (Bosworth & Rogers, 2001), and Europe (Hall & Mairesse, 2007). This technique has likely been so appealing because it is intuitive and uses public market pricing requiring, in its simplest form, only three variables: *market capitalization*, *book value*, and *patents*.

Thompson (2016) then extends this approach by incorporating all global stocks in order to assess the local market valuation of patents—different investors pay different amounts for technological growth firms; he finds that patenting stocks tends to outperform the market by about 83 bps beyond the *standard risk-adjust 4-factor equity model*. Using this technique, he estimates the median patent to be worth about US$123,000 and the average value to be higher at US$316,000.

Pros and Cons of Market-Oriented Procedures

There are four basic conditions for an efficient patent valuation based on market pricing methods (Smith & Parr, 2019): The most important condition is that an active market exists in the first place. In addition to this, the transaction partners must act according to the arm's length principle. This means that they must not allow themselves to go for political transfer prices but must instead negotiate prices as between neutral market participants. Sufficient information from a sufficiently large number of past comparable transactions is also necessary. This condition implies that access to the information must be available. If one assesses the conditions listed here on the basis of the current situation on the patent transfer market, it can be seen that not even the first condition is fulfilled. Compared to stocks or commodities, there is still no active market for patents. Most patent deals are bilateral transactions and are thus in direct opposition to the concept of perfect markets without transaction costs, high liquidity, no arbitrage opportunities, and many market participants. Even though an active market is a central prerequisite for the application of market-based approaches, the most important requirement for these approaches is the comparability of transactions and the availability of information. Due to the bilateral nature of patent transactions mentioned above, information on details or prices of patent deals is often not publicly available. Comparability is also often difficult to achieve, as patents are already, by definition, IP rights for new and often unique inventions. Since there are still relatively few transactions at present, this quantity is severely limited by the requirement that the information must be publicly accessible and the transferred patents must be comparable. One method used extensively in the academic literature is using stock-market price changes to evaluate the value of a patent, either using key events like publish date or grant or as stock variables. Econometric inferences from real-world equity data are a good thing when wanting to capture the IP value at the level of the economy, but not necessarily just as good for explaining the value of any particular patent.

Market-based approaches are often used to determine price estimates for sales or licensing negotiations. Tax authorities, in particular, prefer these methods, as the inherent concept has already been established by their application to other assets. In the case of patents, it is difficult to determine a meaningful value due to unknown transaction values.

Income-Oriented Procedures

The income-based method relies on the concept of *Discounted Cash Flows (DCF)*. In this method, the value is determined by the economic benefit associated with the internal or external commercialization of the patent (cash flow). In addition, the cash flows are discounted using an appropriate interest rate. This interest rate also reflects the risk associated with generating the cash flows. By discounting the cash flows, the fair value of the money is taken into account, and the final value of the patent corresponds to the present value concept.

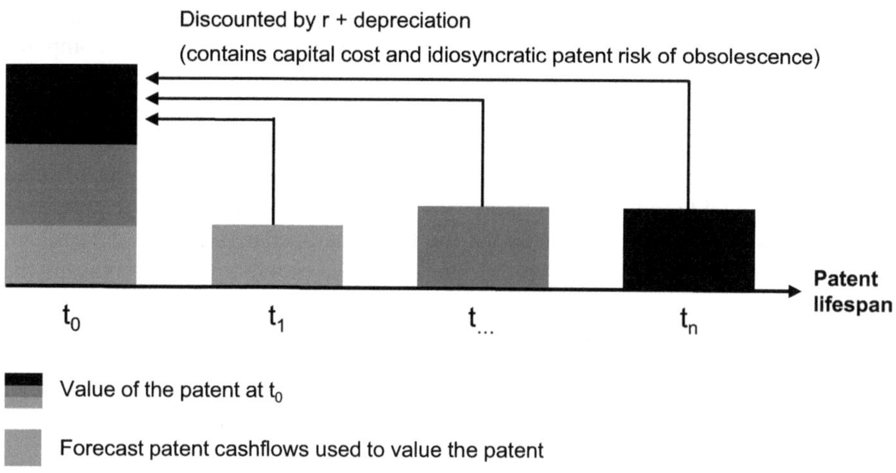

Fig. 3.9 The basic concept of discounted cash flows (DCFs) (authors' own figure)

Figure 3.9 describes the basic concept of discounted cash flows graphically. The first step is to predict how high the cash flows resulting from the patent are and how long they will last. Then an interest rate is determined, which reflects the capital costs of the company, possible capital costs of the patent or product, and the risk associated with the patent (consisting of legal risks, technical risks, and economic risks). To obtain the patent value, each cash flow per period of time is discounted using the discount rate. In the end, the sum of all discounted cash flows results in the patent value.

The method of *direct cash flow forecasting* is described below, the method of *license price analogy*, the *surplus profit method*, and the *residual value method* are all based on this concept (see Fig. 3.9). They differ above all in the way in which cash flows are determined.

(6) Direct Cash Flow Forecast

The direct cash flow forecasting method assumes that the cash flow generated by a patented product can be attributed to certain value drivers, such as the business model, marketing, or patent protection. In order to calculate the patent value, the cash flows directly attributable to the patent are discounted using the patent-specific, risk-adjusted discount rate. The main prerequisite for this is that the cash flows directly attributable to the patent can be determined.

(7) Licensing Price Analogy

With the license price analogy method (also known as *Relief From Royalty* method), the payment flows of a patent are approximated by means of license fees using an analogous patent or invention. These license fees are fees that the owner of the patent does not have to pay because he owns the patent and does not have to license it in. It is, therefore, determined which royalty payments would fictitiously have to be paid if the patent in question had been owned by a third party. These notional royalty payments are derived on the basis of normal market royalty rates for comparable patents, which relate, for example, to sales revenues. Here, too, comparable license rates are chosen that have been negotiated according to the arm's length principle. Reference values for license rates are also published (for example, in Hellebrand et al., 2007). The license rate must then be multiplied by the planned revenues attributable to the patent to be valued. After the deduction of the corporate taxes that have to be taken into account, the fictitious license payments determined are to be discounted to the valuation date using the patent-specific risk-adjusted discount rate.

Table 3.4 shows a simplified example of a patent valuation using the license price analogy method. A comparable patent was identified that was licensed out at a license rate of 3%. In order to determine the economic benefit of the patent to be valued, patent-specific revenues are forecast for 3 years. The license rate of 3% is calculated using these revenues. Since it is its own patent, the company can save between € 3000 and € 3600 in license fees. These saved royalties are now used to calculate the patent value. First, taxes are deducted. The license savings are then discounted at 8% and then added. There are several ways the discount rate can be estimated. For example, a basic component is the inter-temporal risk-free rate, usually proxied by a government bond. Patent risk comprises both the legal risk and technical risk. These can both be expressed by an annualized probability that the patented invention is obsoleted or the patent is invalidated in any given year (Köllner, 2009). We could also take various factors, such as the firm's *opportunity costs* into account.

(8) Additional Profit Method

Under the additional profit method, the expected *future cash flows* from the company including the patent to be valued are compared with the corresponding cash flows from a fictitious peer company excluding the corresponding patent. It is assumed that the comparable company either does not own this patent or waives its use completely. The additional cash flows can result from additional payments that were realized through the patent or from saved payments and/or costs from the utilization of the patent. The difference between the cash flows of the two companies

Table 3.4 Simplified example of the license price analogy method (in Euro)

	t_1	t_2	t_3
Patent-specific revenue	100,000	110,000	120,000
Licensing fee: 3% per year			
Licensing savings before taxes	3000	3300	3600
Tax: 25%	750	825	900
Licensing savings after taxes	2250	2475	2700
Discount: 8% per year (1% risk-free rate + 7% legal risk and technical risk)			
Cash value	2083	2122	2143
Patent value	**6348**		

Source: Table compiled by authors

shows the additional cash flow attributable to the patent being valued. To determine the value, these additional cash flows are discounted to the valuation date using the patent-specific risk-adjusted discount rate.

(9) Residual Value Method

As a rule, patents only generate cash flows in combination with other tangible or intangible assets. Under the residual value method, fictitious payments for these supporting assets are deducted from the total cash flow when determining the cash flows generated by the patent. These payments can be regarded as fictitious usage fees for the supporting assets.

The remaining cash flows, which can now be attributed to the patent, are discounted to the valuation date using the patent-specific risk-adjusted discount rate.

The residual value method is generally reserved for the patents with the greatest influence on the overall cash flow of the company, so that the assets for which usage fees are deducted are actually only supportive. If the residual value method is used for several patents, it must be ensured that multiple allocations of the same cash flows to different assets are excluded.

Identification of the Value-Determining Parameter

The problem in the application of income-oriented methods lies in determining the basic idea itself, since the three essential input parameters (level of cash flows, duration of cash flows, and risk associated with the patent) are crucial for a correct calculation of the patent value.

The first challenge of income-oriented methods is to quantify the amount of cash flows and to consider all exploitation possibilities that make sense from a business point of view. There are direct and indirect methods of calculating income flows. If sufficient information about specific economic benefits that can be generated by the patent is available, the direct method can be used. Price premiums through higher customer benefits or cost savings through greater efficiency are typical examples of such specific economic benefits. The indirect method tries to quantify the economic benefits through general economic or financial information. To calculate cash flows using the indirect method, the difference between the turnover of companies with and without the legal protection of the patent under assessment is often determined (Smith & Parr, 2019).

In order to obtain an adequate patent value, it is also necessary to determine the trajectory of the economic benefits. The determination of a realistic time frame is just as important as the level of the cash flows themselves (Parr, 1999). Since the legal patent life is often much longer than the economic patent life, the estimation is complex. The economic patent life ends either when it becomes unprofitable to maintain the patent or when another patent becomes more profitable and replaces the old one. The economically useful existence can be terminated for a variety of reasons: One of the most important reasons is the speed of technological change. The duration of payment flows is therefore of great importance for the income-oriented process, as younger patents have more time to generate economic benefits.

Another central element of the income-based method is that the risk associated with the patent is included in the calculation of the patent value. The risk results from the fact that information about the future can only be estimated. The longer the time frame in which forecasts are made, the higher the risk due to insufficient information. The literature distinguishes three types of risk that are important when using a patent: Economic risks, technical risks, and legal risks. In order to take these risks into account in the income-oriented procedure, they are estimated and transformed into a percentage value. The application of the risk-specific percentage then depends on the design of the valuation model. Either the risk-specific percentage discounts the determined cash flows directly or the risk-specific percentage is added as a premium to the company's standard cost of capital. In their search for an appropriate discount rate, most companies choose either *Capital Asset Pricing Model* (*CAPM*) or *Weighted Average Cost of Capital* (*WACC*).

Pros and Cons of Income-Oriented Procedures

Due to the well-founded concept and the general acceptance of the concept of value, the income-oriented procedure can be applied to most valuation problems. In theory, they are very useful for patent management, as the use of future economic benefits can well support patent management decisions. However, the method is error-prone in the context of patents, and one should not be underestimating the numerous parameters that need to be determined and assumptions that need to be made.

Further Methods of Patent Valuation

All the patent evaluation methods listed below can be traced back to one of the methods already mentioned. They are listed separately due to their being of high practical importance:

(10) 25% Rule

The royalty rate is 25% of the gross profit before or after taxes of the company using the intellectual property rights (*25% rule*).

This procedure has the advantage that it can be applied as a simple "rule of thumb." Therefore, it is particularly suitable if fundamental estimates are to be made, if only a small amount of data is available, or if it is to be disclosed. The disadvantage is that neither future profitability nor the relationship between the opportunities and risks of the license business model is included in the valuation. The method is therefore only suitable for stable industries having low growth.

(11) Profit Share

The valuation takes place in the form of the determination of a certain license rate in relation to the profit. Valuation by pro rata profit can be applied if the future revenue to be expected on the basis of the underlying industrial property rights can be easily estimated.

Despite the simple calculation method, however, the proportional factor must be negotiated. For this reason, a threshold value is often agreed upon which the expected turnover must reach as minimum. The valuation result thus depends on the respective negotiating partner.

(12) Technology Factor

This valuation method was developed by the management consultants *Arthur D. Little* and the chemical company *Dow Chemical*. The cash flow is determined using a technology factor. The technology factor is based on the contribution of the protected technology to the total revenue of the technology.

In addition to the business risk, the technology factor is derived from application, competitive, and legal positions and can, therefore, be used for internal valuations and combined with other valuation methods.

At the same time, agreement on the technology valuation is reached within the framework of the valuation. However, numerous experts from various disciplines must work together on the basis of detailed knowledge of the competitive environment and the underlying business plans.

In recent years, evaluation methods based on possible future events have become increasingly important. From the basic idea, the new methods are based on the idea that the patent value can best be determined by future economic benefits (cash flows). Compared to the simple income-oriented valuation method, however, real options and decision tree analyses in particular have the advantage that they take into account the patent owner's options for action when exploiting a patent (Rudolf & Witt, 2002).

(13) Real Options Method

This method is also based on the basic idea of discounted cash flows. However, it takes into account the fact that if the *net present value (NPV)* is negative, the owner has the option of abandoning the patent or postponing a project. Therefore, the ownership of a patent can also be compared with an option that includes the monopoly to exploit a patent. The value of such an option basically results from the inherent asymmetric peculiarity, which protects against the risk of a price drop and at the same time offers the possibility to benefit from larger price increases (Wu & Tseng, 2006).

The real options method assumes that there is a constant timeline between the time of valuation and the expiration of the patent; it is based on the concept used for financial options. The parameters used to value a patent are the present value of cash flows resulting from the exploitation of the patent, investment costs, economic patent life, standard deviation of project value due to technical, economic, and legal risks, and risk-free interest. If one of these parameters changes, it has a direct influence on the value of the option (Pitkethly, 1997). The real options method is often used in the pharmaceutical industry (Bogdan & Villiger, 2010, see Sects. 6.1 and 6.2).

The specific advantage of the real options method lies in the fact that both initially weak cash flows and high risks can be taken into account as well as future decisions, such as further investments in business conditions.

(14) Decision-Tree Analysis

Another possibility of taking into account the flexibility of the patent owner with regard to decisions about patent valuation is the so-called decision-tree analysis. Decision-tree analysis recognizes the possibility of postponing decisions beyond the future of a project until the end of a certain period is reached. The owner can wait until a defined milestone has been reached before postponing, exercising, or discontinuing a project (in the pharmaceutical industry, for example, a milestone can be the result of clinical phases). However, only a limited number of possibilities can be included in the model. In addition, decisions must be made at specific, predefined points in time. The decision tree is determined by all significant occasions and possible decisions en route to commercializing a patent (Razgaitis, 2003b).

As with all methods of the income-oriented procedure, however, the determination of the parameters cannot be objectified in decision-tree analysis. The required probabilities of occurrence even add another estimated parameter.

(15) Monte Carlo Method

Monte Carlo simulation is a technique to simulate the behavior of stochastic systems (Howell et al., 2001). Many random experiments are carried out. The outcome of each random experiment is observed and summarized in a distribution. To obtain a large number of possible future patent values, a sequence of random numbers is first generated, which forms the basis for the uncertainty. In addition, for each variable (remaining patent life, turnover, costs), both upper and lower limits as well as distributions within these limits are defined.

Based on this, the computer program simulates individual cash values for thousands of combinations of variables and summarizes them in a distribution. This type of patent evaluation does not calculate a patent value but gives out a range of possible values and the probability with which they occur (Razgaitis, 2003a).

This distribution is an advantage of the Monte Carlo method because in reality it is unlikely that the future will occur exactly as it was modeled with discount factor and input parameters. The output of a distribution also gives one a feeling for the respective project, because the range gives values for the best possible and worst possible project developments (Brealey & Myers, 2003).

Even though the Monte Carlo method is more realistic in that it generates a distribution, it is also very dependent on the input parameters. Since the Monte Carlo method is very complex and correct input parameters are prerequisites for determining a correct distribution, this method is even more prone to errors. Due to the high complexity, the calculation effort is enormous and relatively expensive, even in the case of perfect information. Therefore, it is rarely appropriate to use it in most enterprises. The importance of patent evaluation also lies in its practicality.

While it does not apply in many situations, it certainly does apply very well in the pharmaceutical sector because the parameters are well known and are also repeatedly measured. Perhaps it is best use is to simulate patient outcomes where the parameters and costs can easily be ascertained from healthcare records—simulations using those data can then be used to value alternate courses of treatment and thereby very directly value the patent that covers the new treatment.

Business Valuation Methods and Their Relevance to Patent Valuation[2]

Business valuation serves as the backbone of day-to-day financial markets, corporate finance, and commercial lending. Investment decisions, M&A transactions, credit assessments, and equity valuations all rely on established business valuation methodologies that have been refined through decades of market practice. Banks use these methods for loan underwriting, investors apply them for portfolio decisions, and corporate development teams depend on them for strategic planning. The methods provide standardized frameworks that allow different stakeholders to assess company worth using common metrics and assumptions.

Business valuation proves substantially easier than patent valuation because of readily available data from public companies, standardized financial statements, and comprehensive credit reporting systems. Public markets generate continuous pricing data, regulatory filings provide detailed financial information, and accounting standards ensure consistency across companies and jurisdictions. Credit bureaus, financial databases, and market data providers supply updated information that allows for real-time benchmarking and analysis. Patent valuation, by contrast, operates with limited comparable data, inconsistent disclosure practices, and subjective assessments that make reliable benchmarking difficult.

The use of benchmarking and established accounting methods facilitates objective analysis by correlating valuation assumptions with verified market data. Financial benchmarks include indexes of listed companies, currencies, and interest rates, while financial ratios assess performance across liquidity, solvency, profitability, and market metrics. No single indicator works alone; credible valuation conclusions draw on multiple benchmark methods interpreted together. This systematic approach provides the transparency and defensibility that patent valuation often lacks (Table 3.6).

Berkus Method

Created by venture capitalist Dave Berkus (1996), this method assigns fixed monetary values to five qualitative factors: (1) sound idea, (2) prototype, (3) management team, (4) strategic relationships, and (5) product rollout or sales. The method specifically targets pre-revenue start-ups where traditional financial metrics prove inadequate for meaningful valuation analysis. *Relevance to patent valuation:* Not relevant. The method does not isolate or value IP assets. It provides a general framework for start-up potential and is not designed for use in stand-alone patent or IP asset valuations.

[2] This section has been authored by Sylvain Roy, Canadian attorney and IP valuation advisor, founder and CEO of SRV (SR Valuation Inc.) and at SRA (Sylvain Roy Avocat), at 407 McGill St., Suite 700.6, Montréal QC Canada H2Y 2G3 (srvaluation.com; sroy.ca).

Book Value/Asset-Based Method

This traditional accounting method calculates the equity value of a company based on the net value of its tangible and intangible assets, minus liabilities, as stated on the balance sheet. Book value essentially represents the liquidation value or net worth recorded on the balance sheet. *Relevance to patent valuation:* Not relevant for patent valuation since the method excludes intangible assets by design and relies solely on tangible assets that appear on financial statements. Patents and intellectual property typically do not appear on balance sheets at meaningful values, making this approach unsuitable for IP-intensive businesses.

BVM—Backward Valuation Method

Developed by IP valuation advisor Sylvain Roy in the 2020s, the Backward Valuation Method (BVM) is a two-step methodology that estimates early-stage company or projects value based on the funding trajectory of comparable ventures. At Level 1, BVM establishes a reference valuation range by inferring historical pre-money valuations at defined funding stages (Seed, Series A, etc.) and estimating the company's current value (NOW) based on the time to next expected round. All values are normalized for sector, funding stage, macroeconomic cycle, and geography. At Level 2, BVM provides a fixed point estimate by scoring the company's position within the reference range using four weighted dimensions: (1) product–market fit and positioning, (2) team and execution, (3) traction and milestones, and (4) moat or IP strength. *Relevance to patent valuation:* Not applicable. The method requires company-level funding data and comparables that individual patents do not generate.

Checklist Method

The checklist method applies a structured scoring framework covering both qualitative and quantitative criteria determined by the valuation professional. Points are assigned to defined factors including product maturity, market validation, intellectual property protection, financial controls, team capability, and strategic partnerships. These scores are compared to industry benchmarks or weighted to produce a valuation adjustment or category assignment. *Relevance to patent valuation* Directly relevant, as IP-specific attributes such as patent breadth, freedom-to-operate, and commercialization readiness can be incorporated into the scoring system.

First Chicago Method

Originating from valuation practice at First Chicago Corporation in the 1980s, the First Chicago Method models a company's value using three core financial scenarios—optimistic, base case, and pessimistic—each assigned a probability weighting. These scenarios project potential exit values, which are then discounted to present value and aggregated to yield a weighted average valuation. The method is particularly suited to ventures where outcomes are highly sensitive to strategic, regulatory, or commercial inflection points. *Relevance to patent valuation:* Moderately relevant when patent-driven uncertainty materially affects commercialization outcomes. The method enables modeling of divergent IP-related scenarios—such as regulatory approval, market adoption, or competitive blocking value. However, it requires structured forecasts that are rarely available for early-stage or stand-alone IP assets.

Future Valuation Multiple Approach

This approach projects the company's financial performance to a defined future event horizon (typically 3–7 years), applies an industry-specific exit multiple (such as EV/EBITDA or EV/Revenue), and discounts the projected enterprise value back to the present using a risk-adjusted discount rate. Effectiveness depends on the quality of forward-looking assumptions and the stability of comparable market multiples. *Relevance to patent valuation:* Partially relevant when IP contributes significantly to projected revenue streams or exit value. However, the method captures IP value only indirectly through financial forecasts and cannot isolate the distinct contribution of patents or proprietary rights to enterprise value.

Precedent Transactions

This method derives valuation by referencing prices and deal terms from comparable market transactions involving similar companies or assets. It is widely used in investment banking and M&A contexts but depends heavily on the availability of detailed, recent, and relevant transactional data. *Relevance to patent valuation:* Conditionally relevant when comparable licensing deals, IP sales, or IP-rich company acquisitions are accessible. In practice, confidentiality and lack of granularity in disclosed deals often limit the method's applicability to stand-alone patent valuation.

Public Comps (Multiples)

The Public Comps method benchmarks a private company's value against publicly listed peers using valuation multiples such as EV/Revenue or EV/EBITDA. Adjustments are made for growth, size, liquidity, and capital structure. The approach is best suited to later-stage companies with stable revenues and operating profiles analogous to public comparable. *Relevance to patent valuation:* Limited relevance unless the target operates in a patent-intensive sector with transparent, comparable peers. While the method can indirectly reflect IP value embedded in company multiples, it is not designed to isolate or quantify individual patent contributions.

Risk Factor Summation Method

This method starts with a base valuation—often derived from regional averages or comparables—and systematically adjusts it based on qualitative and quantitative assessments of defined risk factors. Each category, such as team strength, technology development, legal or regulatory exposure, and market timing, receives a score that translates into monetary adjustments. *Relevance to patent valuation:* Highly relevant, as the framework allows direct integration of IP-specific risks such as enforceability, litigation threat, claim strength, design-around risk, and regulatory hurdles, with reference to at least one known comparable. The method's structure complements technical patent assessments and provides a bridge between legal risk and monetary value.

Scorecard Method (Ranking and Scoring)

Developed by angel investor Bill Payne in the early 2000s, the Scorecard Method begins with a regional average pre-money valuation for start-ups, then applies weighted adjustments across standard categories including team, product, market size, competitive position, and funding environment. The output is a scored, modified valuation that reflects qualitative differences from the baseline. *Relevance to patent valuation:* Limited in its original form, which does not account for IP or patents as stand-alone criteria. However, the structure is adaptable, and with modification, the method could include IP-related metrics such as claim breadth, FTO status, or portfolio competitiveness.

Sum-of-the-Parts (SOTP)

The SOTP method disaggregates a company into its constituent business units, product lines, or tangible/intangible assets and values each component independently, before aggregating them into a total enterprise value. It is commonly used in conglomerates or businesses with distinct, separable operations. *Relevance to patent valuation:* Highly relevant when a patent portfolio represents a discrete asset class or when IP-centric business lines can be individually modeled. This method allows targeted valuation of IP assets apart from the operational business and is frequently used in M&A and divestiture contexts.

VC Benchmark Multiples

The VC Benchmark Multiples method aggregates historical venture capital deal data to infer valuation ranges by stage (e.g., Seed, Series A), sector, and geography. Values are typically expressed as median or average pre-money valuations and are updated periodically to reflect changing market conditions. The method tracks broad shifts in market sentiment—for instance, contraction from 2021 peak multiples (15–20x revenue) to 2024 medians (3–7x). *Relevance to patent valuation:* Not relevant for valuing individual IP assets, as VC benchmarks focus on company-level investment patterns and omit asset-specific considerations. IP may be embedded in the valuation logic but is not isolated or scored directly.

Venture Capital (VC) Method

First formalized by Harvard Business School's Bill Sahlman in the 1980s, the VC Method estimates a company's present value by applying a target ROI to a projected exit valuation, then adjusting for investor dilution. The method is widely used in early-stage venture financing where exit events are prioritized over long-term cash flows. *Relevance to patent valuation:* Applicable only when patents or IP forms a strategic part of a venture's business model and exit planning. The method presumes the presence of a venture vehicle and investor roadmap, making it unsuitable for stand-alone patent portfolios or early-stage IP assets without defined commercialization models.

Valuation of Patents

The following must be considered when using quantitative patent valuation methods for patent management (overview see Tables 3.5 and 3.6):

- *Patent value:* The value of a patent is idiosyncratic, i.e., it strongly depends on who owns the patent, uses it, and in what context this happens. So, there is no "one" or absolute patent value.
- *Valuation method:* The chosen valuation approach and the valuation method to be used strongly depend on the reason for the valuation.
- *Subjective value:* Especially in patent management, not only objective but also subjective values of a patent or subjective input parameters are important. However, this subjectivity makes the evaluation susceptible to misjudgments.

Table 3.5 Overview of quantitative patent valuation methods

Method	Description
Cost-oriented:	
(1) Historical costs	Sum of costs needed to generate the patent.
(2) Reproduction costs	All costs needed to reproduce it.
Market-oriented:	
(3) Market price on active market	Valuation of patents based exclusively on how much would be willing to be paid on an open market.
(4) Analogy methods	Value of the patent of an analogous known in the market.
(5) Equity value/econometric	Marginal contribution to equity market value of the patent, usually ascertained econometrically.
Income-oriented:	
(6) Direct cash flow forecast	Cash value based on directly calculable cash flows.
(7) Licensing price analogy	Cash value based on licensing (analogous) payments.
(8) Additional profit method	Cash value based on the difference compared to a fictional company without patent protection.
(9) Residual value method	Cash value based on payments after subtracting pro forma costs of firm.
Further methods of patent valuation:	
Profit-oriented:	
(10) 25% rule	25% of gross profit before or after taxes.
(11) Profit share	Value in the form of licensing as a fraction (%) of profit.
Future-value-oriented:	
(12) Technology factor	Cash value in assessing the technology's contribution to cash flow.
(13) Real options method	Cash value based on the value of potential business options over time.
(14) Decision-tree analysis	Cash value incorporating future decisions at pre-defined milestones.
(15) Monte Carlo method	Simulation of a patent's value based on random draws.

Source: Table compiled by authors

Table 3.6 Business valuation methods in alphabetical order, indicating their relevance to patent valuation contexts

Method	Primary Inputs	Relevance to Patent Valuation
Berkus method	Assigns fixed amounts to qualitative factors (team, product, market)	Not relevant
Book value/asset-based method	Accounting value of tangible assets minus liabilities	Not relevant
BVM—Backward valuation method™	Comparable companies, funding history, inferred dilution, NOW-time adjustment	Not relevant
Checklist method	Structured criteria for qualitative and quantitative assessment	Relevant
Cost-to-duplicate method	Rebuild cost for team, technology, IP, and other resources	Partially relevant, discussed in Sect. 3.2 (2) (Table 3.2)
Discounted cash flow (DCF)	Projected revenues, costs, discount rate, terminal value	Relevant, discussed in Sect. 3.2 (6) (Fig. 3.9)
First Chicago method	Multiple scenario-based projections with probability weights	Relevant
Future valuation multiple approach	Forecasted metrics × expected exit multiples	Partially relevant
Monte Carlo simulation	Probability-distributed financial projections	Relevant, discussed in Sect. 3.2 (15)
Precedent transactions	Valuation multiples or terms from M&A or venture rounds	Partially relevant
Public comps (multiples)	EV/revenue, EV/EBITDA, or sector-specific ratios from public peers	Partially relevant
Real options analysis (ROA)	Strategic flexibility modeled as financial options	Relevant, discussed in Sect. 3.2 (13)
Residual income valuation (RIV)	Net income minus cost of equity capital	Partially relevant, discussed in Sect. 3.2 (9)
Risk factor summation method	Base valuation adjusted by scored risk categories	Relevant
Scorecard method	Regional average adjusted by weighted comparative factors	Not relevant
Sum-of-the-parts (SOTP)	Separate valuation of business segments or product lines	Relevant
VC benchmark multiples	Aggregated VC valuations by round, geography, sector	Not relevant
Venture capital (VC) method	Exit value, required return, dilution assumptions	Partially relevant

Source: Table compiled by author

3.3 Managing the Patent Portfolio

Portfolios are instruments for the analysis and visualization of strategic positioning and thrust directions. The variety of the portfolio techniques is immense, each technique has its own weakness when it comes to the selection of the dimensions. The *St. Gallen Approach to Managing Technologies and Patents* from Gassmann and Bader (2024) goes back to a method developed at the Institute of Technology Management (ITEM-HSG) at the *University of St. Gallen (HSG)*, Switzerland, in the early 1990s (Boutellier et al., 1995). It has been continuously refined through numerous practical projects and introduced in numerous European and international companies (Boutellier et al., 2008).

We developed the *St. Gallen Patent Portfolio Management Model* further to strategically manage patents. It derives the patent strategy per core dimension from the corporate strategy or from the technology and innovation strategy.

Via portfolio management, action measures are derived from evaluated market and technology positions, which serve to implement the corporate strategy. The vision and mission of the corporate strategy form the basis for evaluating the challenges posed by customers, the market, competitors, and substitutable technologies. The company's competencies, technology, and product fields are evaluated and positioned, taking into account the company's resource strength. This forms the basis for deriving standardization strategies. On the basis of the strategies developed, the necessary measures for dealing with intellectual property rights in these areas to build up and secure potential are finally derived (see Fig. 3.10).

Step 1: Vision and Mission

Vision and mission reflect the normative framework of the corporate strategy; they are supplemented by medium-term objectives and general corporate values. Such a guiding corridor is necessary in order to be able to assess the challenges that arise in relation to corporate competencies. It is important that the vision and mission are concrete and thus groundbreaking. Exchangeable statements such as "No. 1 in the market," "Customer orientation," or "Employee development" are generally not sufficient.

A *vision* answers the question "Where do we want to go by when?" and is based on the following elements:

- The central idea of the desired development;
- Feasible utopia;
- Future orientation; and
- Time reference with regard to realization.

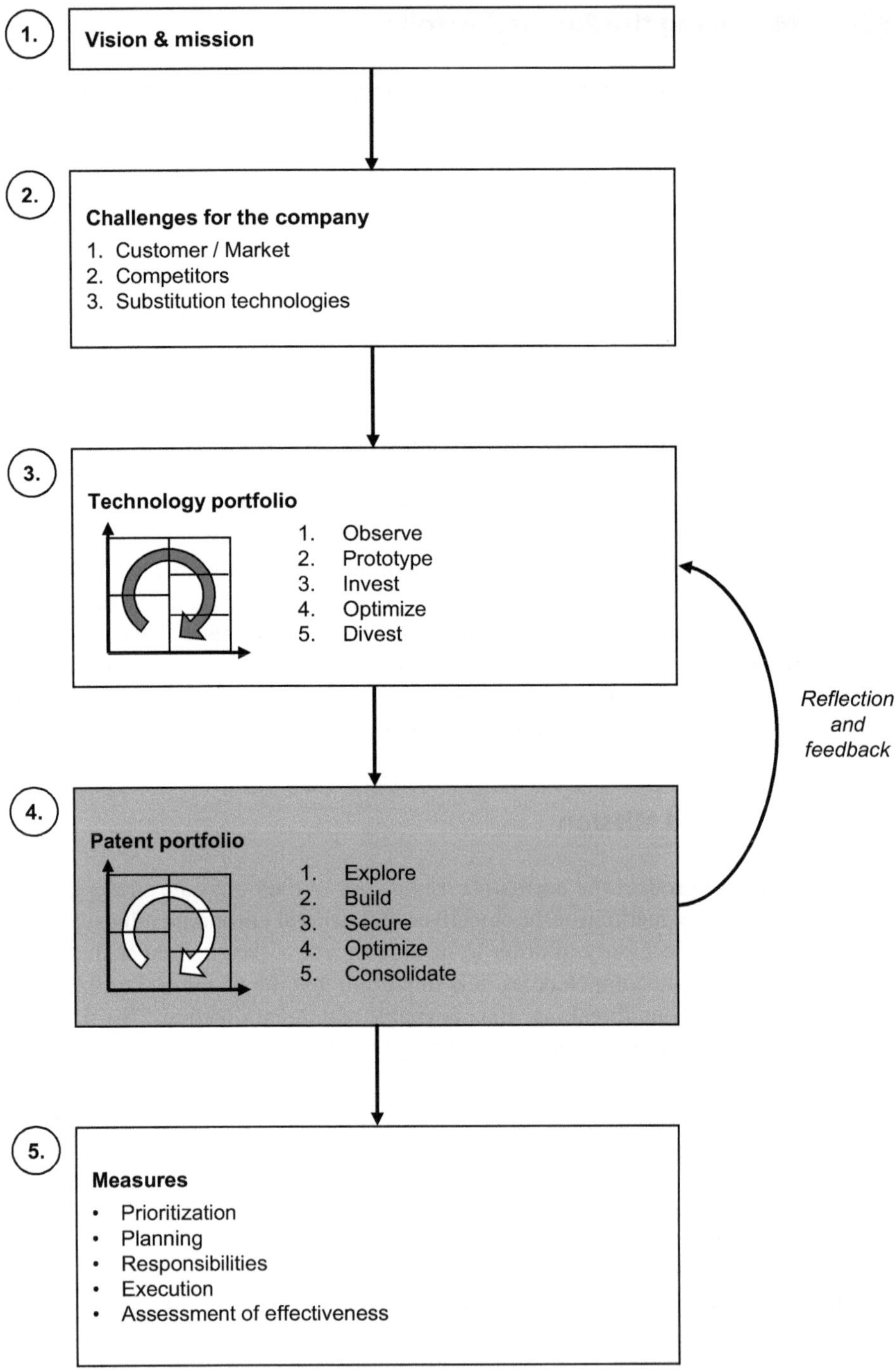

Fig. 3.10 Deriving the patent portfolio from the overarching strategy (authors' own figure)

A *mission* addresses the question “How and with what do we want to achieve the vision” and considers the following aspects:

- Guard rails of the desired development;
- Instrumental focus on implementation: task at the center; and
- Orientation to the present.

Step 2: Challenges for the Company

In this step, the technological challenges that the company has to face are determined. Three perspectives have to be considered with regard to corporate competencies:

- Customer/market;
- Competitors; and,
- Substitution technologies.

Customer/Market

The customer and market perspectives take the requirements placed by customers and markets on the competencies, skills, technologies, products, and services available from the company into account. A distinction must be made between the requirements of individual lead users and broad market trends.

Competitors

The competitive perspective makes relativize the comparison to the activities of the competition and takes into account the comparative advantages and disadvantages, strengths, and weaknesses. If, for example, the company is not a technology or competence leader in one area, the question arises as to whether the company should adopt a fast follower or better a differentiation position.

Substitution Technologies

On the one hand, the importance of in-house competences in terms of substitutability with new, external technologies, products, or services must be assessed. On the other hand, the question of replacing existing technologies with new internal technologies arises. Even if the introduction of new technologies does not bring new advantages to the market or even should it provide additional functions that are not required, the introduction of substitution technologies makes sense if internal costs can be saved or internal logistics processes can be optimized. Taiwanese light-emitting diode manufacturer *Huga Optotech*, for example, is replacing conventional neon tube lighting in offices with light-emitting diodes.

Step 3: Technology Portfolio

The basic orientation of the technology portfolio can be derived from a two-dimensional portfolio representation. Based on the competencies to be classified, their strategic significance is determined on the basis of the challenges posed by customers, the market, competition, and substitution technologies, and then mapped on the vertical axis. For each competence, the relative resource strength of the company is determined as well, which is mapped on the horizontal axis: The technological capabilities of the company, such as infrastructure, employees, available knowledge, and experience, are also taken into account and evaluated in comparison to the competition.

The *St. Gallen Approach* distinguishes between five technology portfolio sectors and the resulting norm strategies, which correspond, in chronological order, to a typical product development life cycle (see Fig. 3.11): *Observe*, *prototype*, *invest, optimize,* and *divest* (Boutellier et al., 2008).

Observe

Competencies in this segment are characterized by a strategic importance that is still perceived as low. The corresponding competence, technology, product, or service fields should be actively monitored, for example, by attending exhibitions and congresses, by studying magazines, journals, and the Internet, and cooperating with universities.

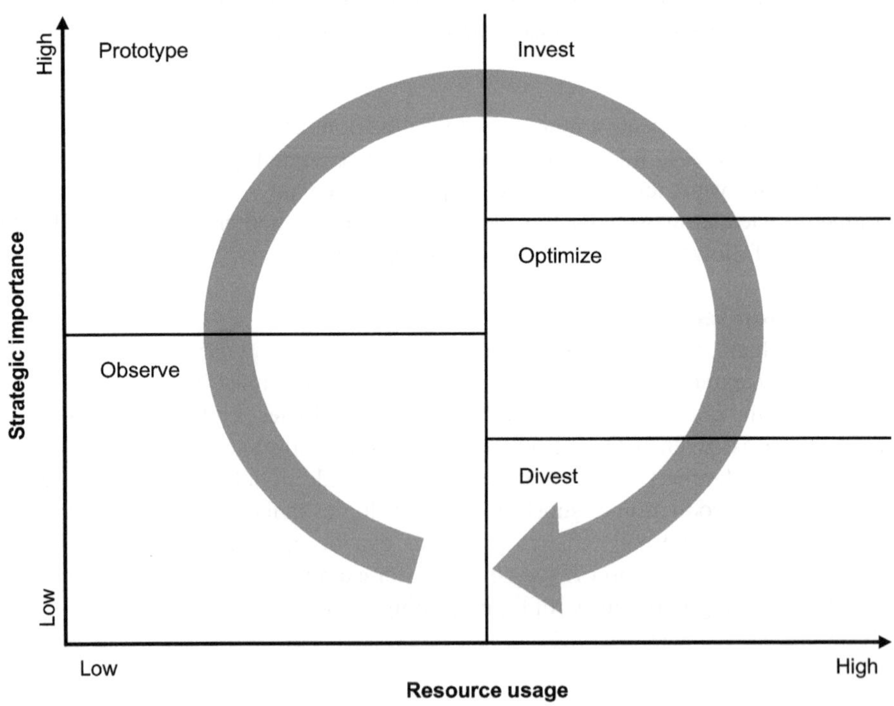

Fig. 3.11 Normative strategies for strategic technology portfolio management. Source: Boutellier et al. (2008)

Prototype

If the strategic importance grows from the perspective of customers, markets, competitors, or substitution technologies, the initial trials must be conducted and skills have to be built up, for example, through prototypes. In addition, external partners are sought and integrated in order to thereby develop internal competencies as efficiently as possible.

Invest

High internal resource strength contrasts with high long-term strategic importance. Long-term investments in the core competence area are therefore necessary and reasonable in order to secure existing technologies and investments and to further expand competitive advantages.

Optimize

If, despite high internal resource strength, there is only medium strategic importance or if it is foreseeable that this will even decrease, no larger investments are meaningful any more, but an optimization becomes necessary.

Divest

If no competitive advantage becomes visible over the next 5–10 years, resources previously tied up must be reduced in good time to make it available for realizing new technology potential. A continuation of the technologies and products only makes sense as long as revenues can still be generated. However, further investments in the expansion of competencies are not expected.

Step 4: Patent Portfolio

The patent strategy to be derived from the business or corporate strategy should serve both to create business opportunities and to capture realized potential. Accordingly, it makes sense to derive appropriate *standardized* patent strategies on the basis of the technology portfolio structure already described.

The *patent standardization strategies* make general statements about the control of the development as well as the dismantling of intellectual property rights under corporate strategic aspects. The portfolio can be expanded, for example, by filing its own patent applications, purchasing or acquiring intellectual property rights, or taking out a license. The portfolio is reduced by dropping patents, selling them, or selling them in the context of spin-offs.

The scope of protection can often already be derived from the claim categories. For example, the chemical industry differentiates between claims relating to processes for the manufacture from the claims relating to substance compositions. While infringing manufacturing processes are usually difficult to prove, infringing substance compositions can be proven relatively easily.

By categorizing products and countries, country-specific legal requirements can later be taken into account. Furthermore, a strategic evaluation of the countries must be incorporated into the portfolio management, for example, determining which countries are relevant for the market and production—not only from the point of view of the own company but also from the point of view of the competitors.

A further criterion in portfolio management is the potential for own use and use by third parties, an important prerequisite for licensing projects.

Particularly in the *pharmaceutical industry*, *life cycle management* plays an important role, one in which attempts are made to build up product-related succession protection rights beyond the basic patents; this is often the only way to maintain an effective blocking effect even after the basic active ingredient patent has expired. This is of great importance due to the rapidly growing generics market.

The phases of the technology portfolio serve as the basis for the respective measures of the patent strategy along the technology life cycle. The *St. Gallen Patent Portfolio Management Model* therefore has five phases (see Fig. 3.12):

- Explore;
- Build;
- Secure;
- Optimize; and
- Consolidate.

The norm strategies address the three core dimensions of the patent strategy.[3] In the portfolio presentation, the dimension of *strategic impact* also reflects the *external perspective* (customers/competitors/substitution technologies) just as the dimension of *resource intensity* indicates the *internal perspective* (capabilities/competencies).

In the first phase, i.e., *Explore*, patent scanning can be used to identify potential across industries. Based on the technology portfolio and the technology roadmap, for example, a decision must be made in this phase as to whether broad conceptual patents should be applied for. In the development phase of the patent portfolio life cycle, i.e., *Build*, targeted patent searches are then initiated. Selected competitors are analyzed in order to be able to take strategic competitive advantages into account when filing patent applications. In the further phase, i.e., *Secure*, patent clusters should be formed systematically in order to provide the best possible protection. On the basis of the technology portfolio and the technology roadmap, broad basic patents and patents on specific design variants (*growing and pruning*) can be considered for better protection. Out-licensing potential to secure long-term financial returns may be conceivable in other application areas and should be reviewed. In order to optimize the patent portfolio, i.e., during the phase *Optimize*, licensing opportunities in one's own field can also be considered for short-term financial returns. Furthermore, the patent clusters should be reviewed in particular on the basis of cost–benefit considerations. Depending on the competitive situation, blocking patents can protect against substitutions. In the final phase of the patent portfolio life cycle, i.e., the phase *Consolidate*, the abandonment or exclusive exploitation of patents may be considered (sale, exclusive out-licensing, and possibly donations).

[3] For the core dimensions of patent strategy, see Chap. 2

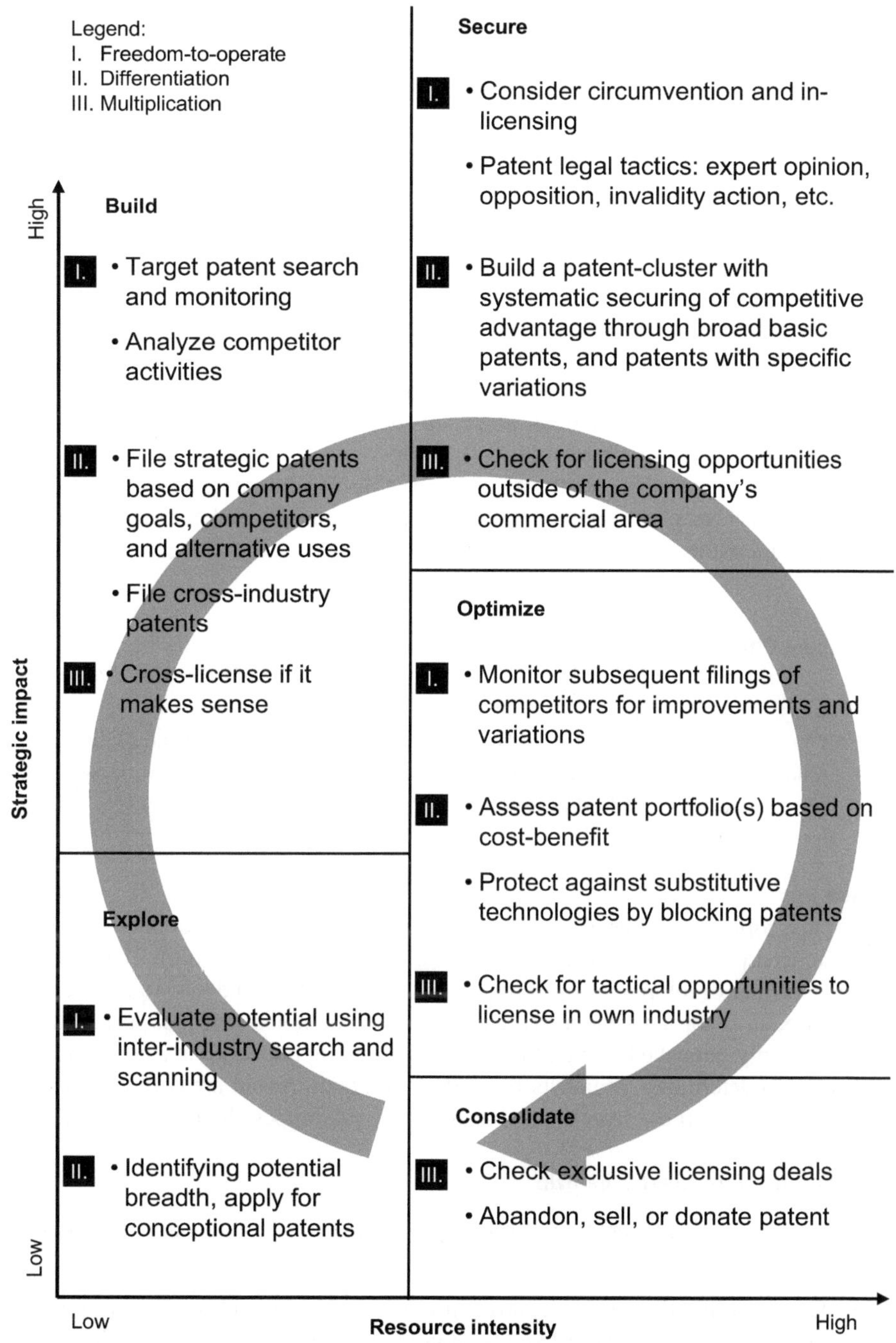

Fig. 3.12 Normative strategies for strategic patent portfolio management (authors' own figure)

Explore

The contribution of a patent strategy in this phase of the technology life cycle, therefore, focuses primarily on broadly based searches, which are intended to examine whether earlier inventions exist (*patent scanning*).

The underlying inventions should be continuously further developed, and the protection of improvements and variants should also be considered.

Example—DSM Nutrition

DSM Nutrition (formerly Roche Vitamins) systematically uses patent searches to identify trends in manufacturing process technologies and also to identify efficient substitution technologies in good time. With researchers and marketing specialists, search profiles are defined on the basis of keywords in order to narrow down relevant areas of interest. A special focus of the trend analyses are the life cycle curves. The time horizon is 5–10 years.

Publicly accessible platforms are available for initial research. Relatively quick overviews can be obtained, individual documents can be downloaded, and simple questions can be answered. ◀

Explore Checklist

- Evaluating risks and potential by means of cross-industry patent searches *(patent scanning);*
- Using further analysis methods, e.g., scenario techniques or road mapping;
- Understanding trends and future markets, for example, service innovations; and
- In the case of identified potentials, filing broad, conceptual patents.

Build

As soon as topics and areas of competence of growing strategic importance are identified, focused patent searches must be carried out (patent monitoring). The aim is to monitor further developments in certain fields of technology and also to monitor certain competitors through patent searches. It should be noted that most patent documents are only published 18 months after the priority application. In a company, it is advisable to determine specialists for certain competitors and areas of competence who will carry out these searches and analyze any prototypes already available.

Example—Erbe Elektromedizin

The medium-sized company *Erbe Elektromedizin* systematically monitors its competitors:

- Every month, the patent department receives the new publications of the previous month from the IP rights monitoring department. The monitoring of intellectual property rights is largely carried out by the search department of an external patent attorney, who prepares these on the basis of a defined filter. In urgent cases, it is also possible to conduct searches yourself.

- The patent department checks and pre-selects the documents. The documents are then sent to the respective R&D experts. An engineer receives precisely those documents that relate to his technical areas.
- The technical experts prepare short presentations of the publications submitted to them. Three minutes are available for this purpose.
- Within the framework of a monthly patent round, the short presentations of the technical experts are shown. A short discussion is held afterward, and the next steps are decided upon, for example, a decision to file an opposition or to be included in the monitoring of publications. Since the patent round meets once a month, there is in principle the possibility of an opposition for all documents discussed there.[4]
- The patent department draws up minutes that are distributed to the participants of the patent round. ◀

Advantages of this procedure: The fixed date of the patent round guarantees a high degree of regularity, which in turn ensures that the specialist engineers have constant knowledge of the intellectual property rights situation. The obligation to give short presentations guarantees that the engineers deal with the patent specifications on time (opposition deadline), while the direct feedback to the patent department and colleagues brings a lively discussion of the documents, concrete suggestions to each R&D working group, and it also avoids having duplicate developments and applications.

Example—Phonak

The highly innovative Swiss hearing aid manufacturer *Phonak (today: Sonova)* makes intensive use of patent information to support its internal technology early warning system. The patent disclosure documents of all relevant competitors, such as Siemens Audiology, are collected, broken down by technology and core competence fields, and analyzed under the responsibility of the head of the research department. A time horizon of 3–5 years is achieved for the identification of trends. ◀

The focus should not only be on the company's own activities but also on the expected directions of existing and potential competitors. This is the only way to build up an effective blocking potential through intellectual property rights in good time.

Patent claims should aim for the broadest possible protection corridor, address solution architectures, and concepts and be formulated in a cross-sectoral manner. In this phase, the foundations are laid for later patent license exchange options. Even if a direct confrontation with competitors only takes place after a further maturity phase of the competencies, groundbreaking intellectual property rights generally date back to this technology phase. *Endress+Hauser* specifically develops intellectual property rights in order to avoid later disputes with major competitors.

[4] The German and European opposition deadline is 9 months after publication of the intent to grant.

If R&D activities are carried out with external partners, it is necessary to weigh up which exploitation and commercialization requirements will be sought later. Accordingly, cooperation negotiations must be conducted appropriately.

Example—CeramTec

CeramTec, a group of companies within the *Dynamit Nobel Group*, developed a cylinder head for engines in cooperation with an automotive supplier. Negotiations on the handling of the resulting industrial property rights were conducted carefully. While joint use was agreed on for the engine area, CeramTec received the exclusive rights for the ceramics area. ◀

Build Checklist

- Conduct targeted patent search (patent monitoring);
- Analysis of competitors' activities;
- Applying for patents of strategic importance;
- Flesh out patent families;
- Targeted patent to block competitors;
- Alternative areas outside of the field of activity;
- Application for patents applicable to multiple industries; and
- Investigate cross-licensing possibilities.

Secure

In this phase, a company has already built up its own resources in a field of competence of high strategic importance. At the same time, however, one's own activities increase the risk of conflict with competitors' patents. Securing one's own freedom to operate is therefore of great importance in this phase. If, however, signs of disruptive patents from third parties become more frequent, these should be investigated as quickly as possible and with high priority. Only in this way can suitable countermeasures be introduced in good time and investment decisions be made accordingly:

- Disturbing patent applications can be monitored and, if necessary, expert opinions prepared or opposition proceedings considered when granting a patent.
- Technical circumvention solutions can still be developed.
- Make-or-buy decisions can be made on the basis of cost–benefit considerations and in- or cross-licensing and cooperation options can be examined and tackled if necessary.

The potential for applying for broad basic patents is declining, since public knowledge, the *state of the art*, has grown considerably in all areas. The focus of patent applications is increasingly on more detailed, very concrete forms of execution. It is therefore important to systematically examine the subject areas for solution and execution variants or for workarounds.

Within the framework of patent portfolio optimization, companies increasingly endeavor to create *patent clusters* in strategically important technology fields. This approach comprises two steps. First, broad covering patent portfolios are built up *(growing)*. At a later point in time, when it is easier to assess which ideas are technically and commercially relevant, these broad portfolios are thinned out *(pruning)*. It is advantageous to make cost-effective decisions according to the benefit aspect already in the current patent application procedure.

Example—Henkel

The German consumer goods manufacturer *Henkel* successfully uses this method to protect as many variants as possible at an early stage and to avoid excessive costs for the patent portfolio later on (see Fig. 3.13). ◀

Particularly in the case of competences that have been developed with external cooperation partners, it should be examined to what extent out-licensing possibilities are possible in other technical areas or other markets in order to be able to generate licensing income in the long term.

Example—BMW

BMW cooperated with the small Californian software company *Immersion* in the cooperative development of the central, multifunctional control element "iDrive." This company had already developed relevant competencies in the field of force feedback technology, a technology used in joysticks, operating devices in the design sector, and medical technology. It was agreed that BMW would be granted limited, exclusive rights to the development results for the automotive sector, but that *Immersion* would be entitled to independent use and marketing outside the automotive sector. ◀

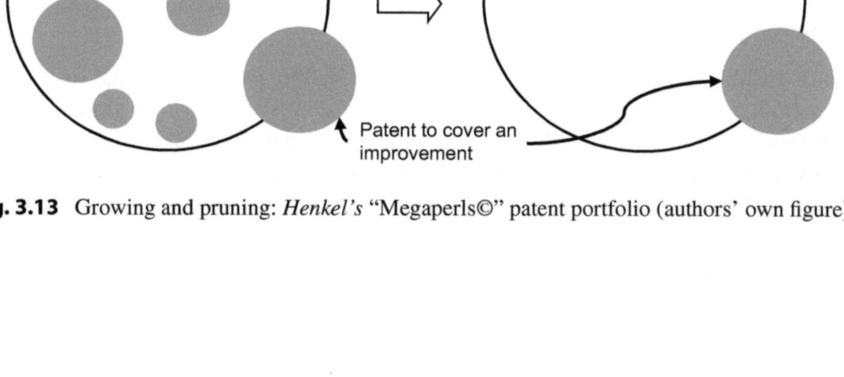

Fig. 3.13 Growing and pruning: *Henkel's* "Megaperls©" patent portfolio (authors' own figure)

Secure Checklist

- When there are signs of disruptive third-party IP rights:
  - Check for ways of circumventing, in-licensing, and cross-licensing;
  - Patent procedural measures (opinions and opposition);
- Development of patent thickets to systematically protect strategic advantage:
  - Wide scope, basic patents;
  - Patents for specific refinements and features;
- Check licensing to other domains and industries:
  - Long-term return on investment (ROI).

Optimize

In this case, the company has high competencies in these fields, but its strategic importance is declining from the customer, market, competitive, or technological point of view. Now at the latest, existing *patent clusters* must be thoroughly reviewed for cost–benefit considerations. This includes the monitoring of competition activities with regard to the (re-)registration of improvements and variants. If there is possibly even the danger that competences could be replaced at an early stage by substitution technologies, consideration should be given to using patents of one's own, patents relating to these areas as blocking protection rights, in order to prevent a one-sided decline in the value of the existing core technologies.

Example—Porsche

The sports car manufacturer, *Porsche*, for example, uses intellectual property rights on substitution technologies in a targeted manner in order to avoid a premature decline in value and a dilution of existing technologies. If necessary, exclusive licenses are even taken and kept in stock for this purpose. ◀

In addition to this, out-licensing opportunities must be examined, which, unlike potential protection, also encompass the Group's own technical areas or markets in order to generate licensing income in the short term. Sometimes, even a market segment can be stimulated by means of a greater openness to such an extent that substitution tendencies can be further delayed by greater standardization and price reductions.

Example—ReSound

For example, after a patent dispute with *3M*, the Danish hearing instrument manufacturer *ReSound* was able to purchase a strong patent portfolio that ReSound contributed to the hearing instrument patent pool *HIMPP (Hearing Instrument Manufacturers Patent Partnership)*. This pool, which was formed with other companies such as *Danavox*, *Oticon*, *Phonak*, *Starkley,* and *Widex*, can now be joined by companies willing to pay a membership fee. In practice, this creates barriers to entry for potential new competitors. ◀

Optimize Checklist

- Competition monitoring by means of patent searches;
- Review patent clusters according to cost-benefit considerations;
- Protection against substitution technologies through blocking patents; and
- Investigate out-licensing possibilities also in own field; short-term return on investment (ROI).

Consolidate

If the strategic importance of a technology or competence has decreased considerably, it must be examined whether the patent claim versions permit a reassessment with an allocation to other fields of competence or competition. The possibility of an *exclusive* out-licensing should be considered, as far as this is possible due to other, already existing license agreements. Otherwise, a low benefit can be assumed, which is offset by high costs. If there are no other reasons, such as the necessity of a large patent portfolio, such patents can be abandoned, sold, surrendered, or donated.[5]

Example—Endress+Hauser

Endress + Hauser, for example, segregates or sells all patents if the subject areas concerned are not incorporated into its own products or manufacturing processes within a period of about 7 years. ◀

Consolidate Checklist

- Check exclusive licensing to an active firm;
- Investigate partial licensing to a patent pool; and
- Resign patent, sell, or sell/donate.

Step 5: Measures

Once the technology and patent strategies have been derived, the final step is to implement the portfolio measures. In order to implement the developed strategies in the over-burdened patent departments, the first step is to prioritize the directions of action. The most important measures (*vital few actions*) must be planned in detail with the business units or developers and implemented with them.

Example—Patent Portfolio Management at Daimler

With its intellectual property strategy, the *Daimler Automotive Group* pursues the following two main objectives:

1. Securing its own monopoly positions; and
2. Protecting against monopoly positions of third parties. ◀

[5] In the USA, donating patents to universities or charitable organizations can be taken as a tax deduction.

According to Mr. Einsele, the former Head of Intellectual Property, Daimler is committed to project-integrated patent work in order to achieve these goals: "At the beginning of development projects, the relevant state of the art and external property rights are searched for, and the respective property right status is recorded and evaluated."

A separate patent strategy is defined for each development project. During the course of the project, the assessment of the property right situation is regularly updated, and project-related information on third-party property rights is made available. This reduces the chance of duplicate developments and of possible collisions. Additionally, this phase is used to determine protectable results. During projects, the acquisition of intellectual property rights of third parties is an increasingly important aspect, but the marketing and licensing of one's own know-how are also gaining in importance. In the case of cooperation or R&D partnerships, the search for suitable partners also begins with patent portfolio analyses. The Intellectual property department later accompanies the drafting of cooperation and development agreements as well as bringing about confidentiality agreements to safeguard know-how. At the end of the project, final project reviews are carried out, in which final statements about the state of the art, third-party property rights, own property right position, contractual situation, and standards are recorded.

Patent management at Daimler consists of nine elements:

- Early involvement of the Intellectual Property department in the innovation process;
- Accompanying support of the R&D projects by the intellectual property department, in particular also important project reviews;
- Definition of strategic priorities;
- Support of the developers on site;
- Monitoring competitor activities;
- Avoidance and minimization of risks;
- Protection of protectable results;
- Checking the transferability and marketability of development results; and
- Enforcement of own intellectual property rights against third parties.

The importance of proactive patent management was demonstrated with the introduction of the "BAS" brake assistant. Daimler, then *Daimler-Benz*, began developing its own brake assist system in 1989. Based on a German basic patent application, over 30 further patent applications in the areas of BAS function, on/off criteria, brake system, and vehicle properties were generated in succession thanks to the intensive support provided by the intellectual property department during the project.

Almost a decade later, the decisive importance of these early patent applications for Daimler became apparent: In 1997, *Toyota* approached Daimler and applied for a license for Daimler's basic patent for the series introduction of a brake assist system. It besides this turned out that Toyota had also filed a basic patent application for a brake assistance system in Japan in 1990—albeit 5 days later. Daimler agreed to the granting of the license: Toyota paid licenses for the basic patent for Germany and the USA and for the subsequent patents in France, Italy, Great Britain, and even Japan. In return, however, Daimler also received a license to Toyota's basic patent for the Japanese market.

Managing the Patent Portfolio

Finally, the three core dimensions of patent strategy (see Sect. 2.3) and their connection with the five patent management process phases of the *St. Gallen Patent Portfolio Management Model* are summarized below. It is of great importance that the company is aware of the five standard strategies Exploring, Constructing, Securing, Optimizing, and Divestment. More important than the perfect classification, which can hardly exist in practice, are the regularity of the implementation and the consistency with the corporate strategy.

Checklist for Managing the Patent Portfolio

Measures for freedom-to-operate:

- Patent searches (patent scanning and patent monitoring);
- Development of circumvention solutions;
- In-licensing, exchange of patent licenses, design access; and
- Patent law measures (e.g., expert opinions, oppositions, reexaminations, nullity proceedings).

Measures against imitators:

- Establishment of patent clusters to systematically secure competitive advantages;
- Registration of broad, conceptual basic patents;
- Protection of specific design variants;
- Analysis of competitive products or processes, and registration of improvement solutions based on them;
- Patenting or in-licensing of substitution technologies; and
- Consistent legal action against piracy.

Measures for commercialization:

- Treatment of patents as a "real material product" (including a business model);
- Development of the company's own patent portfolio from the point of view of competitive attractiveness, i.e., the potential for use or infringement by third parties;
- Examination of out-licensing possibilities depending on the technology life cycle (long-term or short-term orientation in other fields or in one's own field); and
- Consideration of exchange transactions as an alternative or supplement to cash license payments (e.g., exchange license agreements, purchase or sales obligations, and design access).

References

Bader, M. A., Beckenbauer, A., Gassmann, O., König, T., Lohwasser, E., & Menninger, J. (2008). *One valuation fits all?—How Europe's most innovative companies valuate technologies and patents*. PricewaterhouseCoopers.

Bader, M. A., Vogel, H., Tobias, M., Rüther, F., & Gassmann, O. (2012). Intellectual property right valuation index and a method and a system for creating such an index. US 2012/0303537 A1.

Bertolotti, N. (1996). *The valuation of intellectual property*. World Intellectual Property Organization (WIPO).

Bogdan, B., & Villiger, R. (2010). *Valuation in life sciences*. Springer.

Bosworth, D., & Rogers, M. (2001). Market value, r&d and intellectual property: An empirical analysis of large Australian firms. *The Economic Record, 77*(239), 323–337.

Boutellier, R., Gassmann, O., & von Zedtwitz, M. (2008). *Managing global innovation* (3rd ed.). Springer.

Boutellier, R., Hallbauer, S., & Locker, A. (1995). *Technologiestrategie für kleinere und mittlere Unternehmen*. University of St. Gallen (HSG).

Brealey, R. A., & Myers, S. C. (2003). *Principles of corporate finance* (7th ed.). McGraw-Hill.

Brockhoff, K. (1999). *Forschung und Entwicklung: Planung und Kontrolle* (5th ed.). Oldenburg.

Cockburn, I., & Griliches, Z. (1987). Industry effects and appropriability measures in the stock market's valuation of r&d and patents. *American Economic Review, 78*, 419–423.

Connolly, R. A., & Hirschey, M. (1988). Market value and patents: A Bayesian approach. *Economics Letters, 27*, 83–87.

DIN 77100. (2011). *Patentbewertung—Grundsätze der monetären Patentbewertung*. DIN Deutsches Institut für Normung e.V..

Dressler, A. (2006). *Patente in technologieorientierten Mergers & Acquisitions. Nutzen, Prozessmodell, Entwicklung und Interpretation semantischer Patentlandkarten*. DUV.

Econsight. (2020). Difference between quantitative and qualitative patent analysis—Citation of Swatch patents by third parties (number of cited patents vs. cumulative value of cited patents), 2000-2017. In: *Green technologies—A new approach for investment strategies*, Basel.

Ensthaler, J., & Strübbe, K. (2006). *Patentbewertung. Ein Praxisleitfaden zum Patentmanagement*. Springer.

Ernst, H. (1996). *Patentinformationen für die strategische Planung von Forschung und Entwicklung*. Gabler.

Ernst, H. (1998). Patent portfolios for strategic R&D planning. *Journal of Engineering and Technology Management, 15*(4), 279–308.

Ernst, H. (1999). Evaluation of dynamic technological developments by means of patent data. In K. Brockhoff, A. K. Chakrabarti, & J. Hauschildt (Eds.), *The dynamics of innovation. Strategic and managerial implications* (pp. 107–132). Springer.

Ernst, H. (2002). Patentmanagement. In D. Specht & M. G. Möhrle (Eds.), *Lexikon Technologiemanagement* (pp. 214–218). Gabler.

Ernst, H., & Omland, N. (2010). The patent asset index—A new approach to benchmark patent portfolios. *World Patent Information, 33*(1), 34–41.

Faix, A. (2001). Die Patentportfolio-Analyse—Methodische Konzeption und Anwendung im Rahmen der strategischen Patentpolitik. *Zeitschrift für Planung, 2*, 185–208.

Gassmann, O., & Bader, M. A. (2024). *Patentmanagement: Innovationen erfolgreich nutzen und schützen* (5th ed.). Springer Gabler.

Ghapar, F., Brooks, R., & Smyth, R. (2014). The impact of patenting activity on the financial performance of malaysian firms. *Journal of the Asia Pacific Economy, 19*(3), 445–463.

Griliches, Z. (1981). Market value, R&D, and patents. *Economic Letters, 7*, 183–187.

Hall, B., Jaffe, A., & Trajtenberg, M. (2005). Market value and patent citations. *RAND Journal of Economics, 36*(1), 16–38.

Hall, B. H., & Mairesse, J. (2007). Empirical studies of innovation in the knowledge-driven economy. *Economics of Innovation and New Technology, 15*(4-5), 289–299.

Hellebrand, O., Kaube, G., & Falckenstein, R. (2007). *Lizenzsätze für technische Erfindungen* (3rd ed.). Carl Heymanns.

Hofinger, S. (1997). Portfolio-Analyse als Instrument unternehmerischer Patentpolitik. *epi Information, 4*, 100–104.

Howell, S., Stark, A., Newton, D., Paxson, D., Cavus, M., Pereira, J., & Patel, K. (2001). *Realoptions. Evaluating corporate investment opportunities in a dynamic world.* Financial Times Prentice Hall.

IDW S 5. (2013). *IDW standard: Principles of the valuation of intangible assets (IDW S 5) (5/2011)*. IDW.

Köllner, M. (2009). Due diligence or discount monetary effect of legal aspects in patent valuation. *LES Nouvelles*, March 2009, 24–37.

Kuckartz, M. (2007). *IPC-Patentportfolio-Bewertung: Patentmanagement speziell für den Mittelstand.* 5. Patentforum Nordbayern 2007.

Megna, P., & Klock, M. (1993). The impact of intangible capital on Tobin's q in the semiconductor industry. *The American Economic Review, 83*(2), 265–269.

Moser, U., & Goddar, H. (2007). Grundlagen der Bewertung immaterieller Vermögenswerte am Beispiel der Bewertung patentgeschützter Technologien. *Finanzbetrieb, 10*, 594–609.

Otto Toivanen, P. S., & Bosworth, D. (2002). Innovation and the market value of UK firms, 1989-1995. *Oxford Bulletin of Economics and Statistics, 64*(39), 0305–9049.

Parr, R. L. (1999). *IP valuation issues and strategies*. World Intellectual Property Organization (WIPO).

Pfeiffer, W., Schäffner, G. J., Schneider, W., & Schneider, H. (1989). *Studie zur Anwendung der Portfolio-Methode auf die strategische Analyse und Bewertung von Patentinformationen.* Nürnberg.

Pitkethly, R. (1997). *The valuation of patents.* Working paper, University of Oxford, Said Business School.

Poredda, A., & Wildschütz, S. (2004). Patent valuation—A controlled market share approach. *Les Nouvelles—Journal of the Licensing Executives Society, 34*(2), 77–85.

Razgaitis, R. (2003a). *Dealmaking using real options and Monte Carlo analysis*. Wiley Finance.

Razgaitis, R. (2003b). *Valuation and pricing of technology-based intellectual property*. Wiley.

Reitzig, M. (2002). *Die Bewertung von Patentrechten. Eine theoretische und empirische Analyse aus Unternehmenssicht.* DUV.

Rings, R. (2000). Patentbewertung—Methoden und Faktoren zur Wertermittlung technischer Schutzrechte. *GRUR, 10*, 839–848.

Rudolf, M., & Witt, P. (2002). *Bewertung von Wachstumsunternehmen: Traditionelle und innovative Methoden im Vergleich.* Gabler.

Schulze, A. (2005). Patent-Portfoliomanagement für große Unternehmen. *Mitteilung der deutschen Patentanwälte, 9*(10), 416–421.

Smith, G. V., & Parr, R. L. (2019). *Intellectual property. Valuation, exploitation and infringement damages* (5th ed.). Wiley.

Thompson, M. (2016). Estimating global patent rents from public market data. Paper presented *IP Statistics for Decision Makers*, OECD, Sydney 2016.

Turner, J. (2000). *Valuation of intellectual property assets; valuation techniques: Parameters, methodologies and limitations*. World Intellectual Property Organization (WIPO).

Wu, M., & Tseng, C. (2006). Valuation of patent—A real options perspective. *Applied Economics Letters, 13*(5), 313–318.

Wurzer, A. (2005). Wertorientiertes Patentportfolio. *Mitteilung der deutschen Patentanwälte, 9*(10), 430–439.

Wurzer, A., & Reinhardt, D. F. (2010). *Handbuch der Patentbewertung* (2nd ed.). Carl Heymanns.

Successful Practices in Commercializing Patents

4

When it comes to patenting, much of the strategic focus is on protecting the products and processes from imitation and on ensuring one's own freedom of action. This enables companies to create quasi-monopolies on the market and generate returns. This chapter shows another side to patents, which is generating value through proactive commercialization rather than building up a static defense against technological and commercial encroachment. When patents are exploited commercially, the focus shifts away from simply protecting the product to generating added value through the patent in a myriad of manners.

Patents have traditionally been embedded in a product that a company sells. Increasingly complex supply chains, cross-border trade, tax rules, and a competitive landscape have led to many different ways of exploiting a patent commercially. This chapter presents an overview of these techniques to give the IP manager a toolbox. Exactly how firms go about deriving value is quite idiosyncratic since technologies and competitive environments are often highly specific. Yet there are a host of common strategies: sale, licensing, cross-licensing, etc. Cross-licensing, which works well in the semiconductor industry, may not work well in the pharmaceutical industry. So rather than be prescriptive, we hope to show the essential techniques for a successful commercialization of patents.

In broad strokes, there are two main motives for commercialization. A distinction can be made between *monetary* and *strategic* motives. Monetary motives refer to directly measurable financial income. Monetary motives include the generation of income, the increase of returns, and the reduction of costs. The strategic motives are more diverse. They can be divided into motives with a focus outside the company, i.e., with external effects, and motives with focus and effects within the company. Commercialization often involves deep strategic questions about the business model and what it means to "give away" acquired knowledge and patents.

The most common form of patent exploitation is licensing. Other types of patent exploitation include cross-licensing, selling patents, setting up spin-offs or joint ventures, and forming strategic alliances for joint research, and also the

M. A. Bader et al., *Patent Management*, Management for Professionals,
https://doi.org/10.1007/978-3-032-12030-4_4

development and marketing of an innovation (Parr & Sullivan, 1996; Ziegler et al., 2011; Bader & Liegler, 2013). While "patenting to protect" typically does not change the core business model, commercialization has broad implications since (cross-)licensing, financing, spinning-off often touch on the core business model.

In the following, different forms of patent commercialization are elaborated:

- Licensing;
- Cross-licensing;
- Sale;
- Strategic alliance;
- Spin-off and call-back;
- Joint venture;
- Patenting for access to finance;
- Litigation for value; and
- Complex strategies.

Rather than discuss implications theoretically, we present a series of case studies illustrating how exactly firms go about balancing deriving value from patents without destroying the original business model.

4.1 Licensing

In principle, licensing means that the patent holder grants one or more parties permission to use the technology described by the patent. In return, the licensee pays the patent holder (licensor) a license fee. The patent remains in the possession of the licensor. However, licenses differ in various characteristics. Three important characteristics of licenses are described below.

First, a license differs in its degree of exclusivity: An exclusive license means that the patentee licenses out the right to use the patent to only one licensee. If licenses of a patent are granted to several licensees, it is called a nonexclusive license.

Second, licenses differ in the scope and content of the transaction. If only the patent is transferred in the form of the patent specification, it is a license without knowledge transfer. In the case of a license with knowledge transfer, know-how and technical expertise are transferred in addition to the patent specification:

- License agreements without know-how include patents or patent applications, worldwide or regional, exclusive or nonexclusive use, and the term of the license.
- License agreements with know-how include research and test reports, samples, prototypes, market studies, and competitive analyses; and they may even include cooperation partners and customers. In addition, technical experts are often made available to support the transfer of knowledge and for further developments. This raises the question of which components can be commercialized in which way: On the one hand, a complete business model can be externally out-licensed,

while on the other hand, an in-house spin-up could deliver faster and more sustainable profits. Although some patents could be out-licensed, they would have to be aggressively enforced in other markets at great expense.

A *third* characteristic is the type of licensing, i.e., *enablement* vs. *enforcement* licensing:

- *Enablement* licensing, also known as opportunity or carrot licensing: It seeks a licensee who is interested in using the subject matter of the license. Since use only begins after the license has been taken, negotiations are usually characterized by the design of a joint business model.
- *Enforcement* licensing, also known as assertion or stick licensing: A potential infringer of the intellectual property to be licensed is sought. It is therefore assumed that intellectual property rights are used by third parties before the actual licensing. Since the potential infringer has usually already invested and become active on the market, negotiations usually focus on clarifying whether an infringement has occurred, whether the intellectual property rights are legally valid, and if so, how high the license payments should be.

In the USA, and increasingly in Europe as well, a new business model already exists here, according to which patent attorneys track down patent infringements, buy up the patent in question, sue the infringer, and demand license payments. In economic terms, however, these models must be strongly questioned.

Example—Licensing Master Qualcomm

The American mobile technology company *Qualcomm* generates a substantial part of its revenues from license revenues. One of the three business units is exclusively engaged in the marketing of intellectual property. One hundred and thirty patents alone relate to the American mobile communications standard *CDMA*. In addition, obvious users of the patent portfolio are convinced of the "necessity" of taking out a license. The patent portfolio is also open to potential licensees. ◀

4.2 Cross-Licensing

Cross-licensing is a licensing agreement in which the consideration of the cooperation partner is not the license fee but a reciprocal license. The partners grant each other the right to use their respective patents, enabling further development or product marketing. Depending on the agreement, additional license fees may still be payable. Cross-licensing agreements primarily serve to ensure freedom to operate, reduce litigation risks, and secure access to complementary knowledge or technologies.

In principle, cross-licensing agreements can be categorized into two types:

- *Perpetual agreements:* Intellectual property rights remain mutually licensed for the lifetime of the patent; and
- *Fixed-term agreements:* Rights are licensed for a defined period. Upon expiration, licenses may lapse, triggering renegotiation (so-called *guillotine approach*).

Cross-licensing arrangements are particularly relevant in sectors characterized by dense patent landscapes or standard-dependent innovation, such as information and communication technology (ICT), semiconductors, automotive, and even the biomedical sector (Grindley & Teece, 1997; Heller & Eisenberg, 1998). Recent studies confirm that cross-licensing is increasingly used not just to avoid litigation but also as a strategic coordination mechanism in cumulative innovation settings (UKIPO, 2013; Hall et al., 2021).

Cross-licensing can serve both competitive and cooperative purposes. On the one hand, it allows firms to circumvent blocking positions in overlapping patent portfolios, enabling broader innovation. On the other hand, cross-licensing—especially when combined with exclusivity clauses or standard-setting influence—can potentially restrict market competition, attracting antitrust scrutiny (OECD, 2019).

Empirical studies show that cross-licensing positively influences firm performance when used selectively and strategically. For instance, Grindley and Teece (1997) identify its use in enabling freedom to operate in high-tech industries, while Lerner et al. (2007) discuss its role in building patent pools[1] for overcoming fragmented IP rights.

Technologically dominant firms may also use cross-licensing to consolidate their leadership by entering into asymmetric agreements, where smaller players receive access but pay supplemental fees or grant more limited rights.

[1] Patent pools can be defined as (Lerner et al. 2007): "Cases where either (i) two or more firms combine to license patents to third parties ("open" pools), or (ii) three or more firms come together to license patents among themselves ("closed" pools), or both. This definition excludes several other types of arrangements:

- Cross-license arrangements between two firms, where there was no clearly stated intention of engaging in future licensing transactions;
- New operating companies that were established to manufacture products based on intellectual property of a number of firms (e.g., Radio Corporation of America);
- Firms that acquired large numbers of patents and then licensed them to other concerns (e.g., American Steel and Wire Company, American Tobacco Company, and other "patent consolidators");
- Pools that are dominated by non-profit entities (e.g., universities), where profit maximization may not be paramount."

Example—Cross-Licensing: Siemens and Microsoft

In 2004, *Siemens* and *Microsoft* entered into a patent license exchange agreement by which they gave each other extended access to their respective patent portfolios (Microsoft, 2004). This also gave both companies the opportunity to expand their offerings to their customers and provide them with comprehensive solutions. Although the companies spent a similarly large research and development budget of about 5 billion euros, Microsoft had to pay Siemens an additional license fee. ◀

Example—Cross-Licensing in Sustainable Technologies: Hyundai and Audi

A notable case of strategic cross-licensing in the field of hydrogen mobility is the agreement between *Hyundai Motor Company* and *Audi AG*, signed in 2018. Both companies committed to sharing patent licenses covering a broad range of fuel cell electric vehicle (FCEV) technologies, including components, systems, and manufacturing processes (Hyunday, 2018).

The agreement enabled Audi and its parent company *Volkswagen Group* to gain access to Hyundai's robust patent portfolio, developed over two decades of fuel cell R&D. Hyundai, in turn, secured reciprocal access to Audi's relevant fuel cell technologies. Importantly, the deal also extended to affiliated suppliers, reflecting a growing trend toward ecosystem-level collaboration rather than firm-centric exclusivity.

The cross-licensing agreement was not only technologically significant but also strategically motivated: It aimed to accelerate the commercial deployment of FCEVs, reduce duplicative R&D investments, and lay the groundwork for industry-wide scale-up of hydrogen-based mobility solutions.

By pooling intellectual assets, Hyundai and Audi sought to jointly overcome common barriers, such as high production costs, limited fueling infrastructure, and fragmented regulatory frameworks. The collaboration highlighted how cross-licensing can be leveraged as a mechanism for advancing sustainable innovation, particularly in industries characterized by long innovation cycles and high capital intensity. ◀

4.3 Sale

When a patent is sold, all rights are transferred to the buyer, who also becomes the new owner of the patent. The sale of a patent may be appropriate if the developed technology is outside the business area of a company. If there are no plans to develop the new business area, it is still possible to generate added value by selling the patent portfolio. The sale process is usually completed when the contract is signed, which means that the seller does not incur any further expenses in the form of know-how transfer or—as in the case of licenses—fee monitoring or enforcement activities.

Example—A Market for IP: IPXI

The example of *Intellectual Patent Exchange International (IPXI)* shows the obstacles that have to be overcome in establishing IP marketplaces. The marketplace founded by *Ocean Tomo* in 2008, according to its own statement, was the first worldwide marketplace for licensing and trading intellectual property rights. It saw itself as a market-based alternative for private licensing and IP commercialization. By introducing the concept of a Unit License Rights (ULR), IPXI wanted to ensure nonexclusive licensing with market-based prices and standardized terms that could be traded on an electronic trading platform. IPXI's goal was to provide patent owners with an efficient and transparent monetization opportunity. For investors, the added value of this marketplace was the ability to speculate on future technologies and invest directly in IP rights rather than in the proprietary companies. The marketplace was to be financed by an annual membership fee and a 20% share of the transactions to cover running costs (Bader et al., 2012a, b).

Following approval by the U.S. Department of Justice in 2013, the marketplace opened for the first time in 2014 with the trading of *JP Morgan Chase* patents. After 1 year, however, IPXI ceased trading in March 2015. In a press release, IPXI blamed various market obstacles, such as requirements from potential licensees, and complained that the time was not yet ripe for its idea (IPXI, 2015). The high number of high-ranking companies that have been part of the IP marketplace until recently, including numerous companies from technology sectors as well as universities and research institutions, shows that there is a great deal of interest in such an institutionalized IP marketplace. In the end, IPXI had over 70 members, including ones such as *JP Morgan Chase*, *Philips*, *Hewlett-Packard*, and *Sony*. ◄

4.4 Strategic Alliance

Especially for early developments and technologies that are not yet ready for the market, strategic alliances between companies and/or research institutions can be beneficial for all parties involved. The alliance partners contribute complementary know-how and patents to the alliance in order to advance research and development activities more efficiently and achieve the goal of market entry or market share expansion. At the same time, risks and costs are shared. In contrast to joint ventures, the alliance partners remain legally independent, i.e., there is no capital commitment underlying the contracts.

Example—Strategic Alliance: IBM and Philips

IBM began formulating licensing strategies in the 1980s. Today, IBM has an established licensing program that pursues a strategy of issuing nonexclusive licenses to third parties. In addition, a complementary relationship with the licensee is to be established. Over the past few years, the company, which holds over 40,000 active patents, has generated annual license revenues of approximately US$1 billion.

Philips has defined its most important strategic goal in licensing to be: setting standards. Philips' intellectual property has been organized into a holding company, *Philips Intellectual Property and Standards (IP&S)*, since 1924. Today, IP&S has about 450 employees and holds over 55,000 patents. In its licensing program, the company offers patents, technologies, and services and grants nonexclusive licenses to a broad target group.

Until a few years ago, *Microsoft* focused its licensing activities on the enforcement of intellectual property rights through stick licensing. Following a change in strategy, Microsoft is now focusing on a cooperative approach through cross-licensing. In addition, the IP exploitation program *Microsoft Intellectual Property Ventures* was born; the company expects the new approach to strengthen the network and reduce risk. ◀

4.5 Spin-Off and Call-Back

Spin-offs are another way of exploiting research and development results. The formation of spin-offs also allows the company to further develop innovations that meet with little interest from existing business units and to also generate income from them through equity investments or licensing income. This is also illustrated by two examples from *Roche* and *Novartis*.

Example—Spin-off: Roche and Actelion

As part of restructuring measures in the mid-1990s, *Roche* decided not to pursue the research and development of the substance "Bosentan" after Phase II trials. Despite this decision, the spin-off *Actelion*, which included four former Roche managers, was set up to exploit the potential of the substance, which was traded as a potential active ingredient for the treatment of heart defects. In 1998, Roche licensed the substance Bosentan to Actelion, but reserved a call-back option. During the Phase III trials, Actelion changed the original indication of Bosentan. Instead of treating congestive heart failure, Actelion focused on pulmonary hypertension. This change increased the potential for an approved drug. Finally, *Actelion* successfully launched the product under the Tracleer® brand. After Phase III, Roche decided not to use the call-back option in exchange for ca. 10% of revenues (see Fig. 4.1).

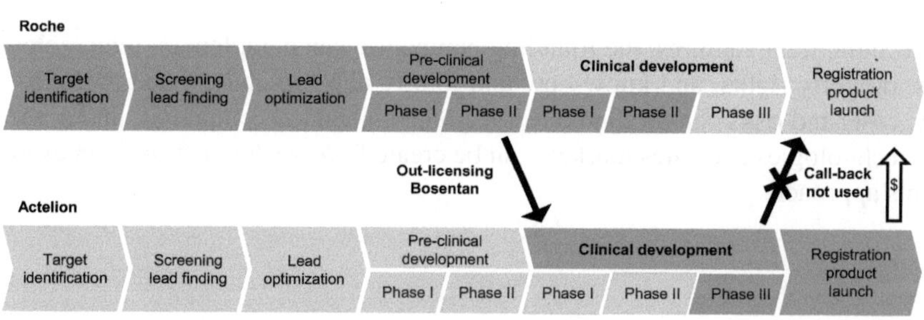

Fig. 4.1 Licensing agreement between *Roche* and *Actelion* (Gassmann et al., 2016) (Used with kind permission by Wiley-VCH, Weinheim. All rights reserved.)

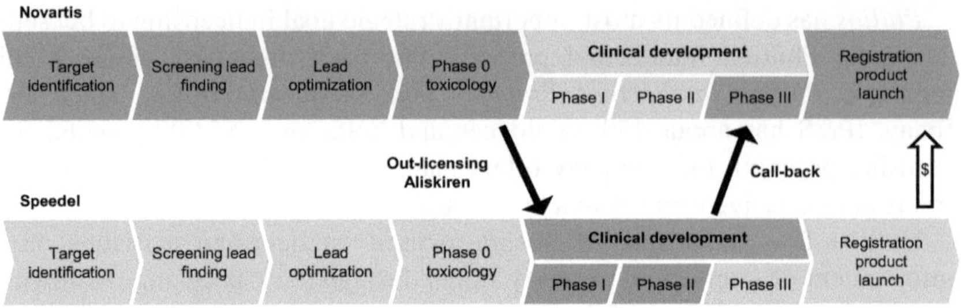

Fig. 4.2 Licensing agreement between *Novartis* and *Speedel* (Gassmann et al., 2016) (Used with kind permission from Wiley-VCH, Weinheim. All rights reserved.)

Roche was able to generate income from an originally abandoned project through the spin-off. The risk of the Phase III trials and market launch was transferred to Actelion. Actelion was given the opportunity to launch a new product without taking the risk in the early stages of development (Gassmann et al., 2016, 2018; Gassmann & Bader, 2024). b ◄

Example—Call-Back: Novartis and Speedel

To further develop a project that did not fit into the portfolio, *Novartis* founded the spin-off *Speedel* in 1998. Novartis had stopped a project involving the substance "Aliskiren" for the treatment of hypertension after the preclinical phase. By out-licensing to Speedel, Novartis offloaded the Phase I and Phase II clinical trials to Speedel (see Fig. 4.2). In 2002, following the successful completion of the Phase I and II trials, Novartis used its call-back option to move the compound into Phase III trials and, finally, launched the product. Both Novartis and Speedel received revenues from sales of the drug. The spin-off allowed Novartis to launch a new drug without bearing the cost and risk of the Phase I and II trials. Speedel was able to generate revenues from a project without early development risks and production and marketing expenses (Gassmann et al., 2016, 2018; Gassmann & Bader, 2024). ◄

4.6 Joint Venture

By forming joint ventures, the founding companies can complement their technologies, property rights, and know-how and jointly develop and expand them. In this way, costs and risks can be shared between the associated companies, and access to new technologies and sales markets can be created. *Bayer Innovation* is an example of this approach.

Example—Joint Venture: Bayer Innovation

Bayer Innovation used to be a part of *Bayer's* innovation strategy and worked with the aim of identifying and developing new growth areas for Bayer and thereby preparing its entry into new high-growth markets. The strength of Bayer Innovation lied in developing innovative solutions beyond the boundaries of the subgroups and developing new products and businesses together with external partners. The technologies developed by Bayer Innovation were sold to interested Bayer subgroups for commercial integration. Technologies that were not integrated into the Bayer Group were commercialized externally by Bayer Innovation. The company still pursues a venture capital approach, i.e., industrial property rights are used as tradable assets with the aim of forming joint ventures or similar partnerships and thus maximizing the return on research and development. ◄

4.7 Patenting for Access to Finance

In addition to the exploitation possibilities already mentioned, patents are now also used in the context of corporate financing. They can be financed through equity or debt, or in debt-equity hybrid forms of financing (Bessler et al., 2003). The following possibilities of a patent-based financing are among others available:

- Credit security through patents;
- Issue of equity securities based on core competencies monopolized by patents;
- Sale-and-lease-back transactions through the sale of patents;
- Securitization of future cash flows generated from patents on the capital market; and
- Patent funds as a means of financing the further development of embryonic technologies.

Example—Patenting for Access to Finance: Uber!

Aside from being well-known, *Uber* presents an interesting case in that its patents likely played a major role in the company's ability to access capital, which eventually led to its stock market debut in May of 2019. It is also illustrative from a commercialization perspective, in that Uber acquired components of its patent portfolio that were essentially unexploited by their inventors.

Legend has it that Uber began with a simple idea by two guys trying to hail a cab in wintry Paris while attending the 2008 *LeWeb*, a major tech conference. A year later, those same two guys (*Garrett Camp* and *Travis Kalanick*) had filed a patent for "System and method for operating a service to arrange transport amongst parties through use of mobile devices" (US 9,959,512 B2) and a patent for "Providing user feedback for transport services through use of mobile devices" (US 2013/0246301 A1). The idea and patents (along with the fact that both of them had already sold tech 10m+ start-ups before) were enough to secure financing. In October 2010, Uber received its first major funding, a US$1.25 million round led by *First Round Capital*. At that same LeWeb conference where it had all started, the CEO announced that Uber had raised US$37 million in Series B funding from *Menlo Ventures*, *Jeff Bezos* (CEO of *Amazon*), and *Goldman Sachs*. It was then able to secure another US$11 million in series A funding a San Francisco VC firm, *Benchmark Capital*, in February of 2012. The company took some of that money and filed 14 more utility and design patents at the USPTO just a few months later over the course of 2012, and by June 2016, Uber was able to raise a US$3.5 billion investment from Saudi Arabia's *Wealth Fund* and had filed about 163 patents and designs.

The company used its cash pipeline to make a number of IP acquisitions. In an interview, Kurt Brash, head of Uber's patent transactions team, said "With patents taking on average four years to grant, we hadn't had enough time to build up our own portfolio. [A]nd we knew we needed some way to protect our business." Seeing the future in robotic rather than human drivers with pesky wages, benefits, and demands that started to plague management, Uber acquired *Otto*, a self-driving company founded by a former *Google* employee, for an estimated US$680 million.

That was a bridge too far into big player's technology portfolios, and Google's self-driving subsidiary *Waymo* sued Otto/Uber for violation of trade secrecy. Uber promptly then bought up some of *AT&T's* portfolio in February of 2017 to give it priority over *Lyft* and others.

To facilitate the acquisition, Uber developed its "own acquisition portal to directly solicit assets, speed our team's analysis and provide Uber with protection against third party patent threats cloaked as purchase opportunities" (Lloyd, 2018). They have a "quality" acquisition strategy. "For *Uber*, a quality patent is one that has applicability in an identified area of technology, reasonably broad claim scope, and an early priority date as compared to known technologies. By whittling down the number of patents at the outset, the group can concentrate on applying their sector expertise to thoroughly scrutinize claim breadth, validity, patent term, assignment information, sale price expectation, etc."

Ironically, all this IP acquisition to defend its business model put the company in the legal crosshairs of Google when it acquired Waymo, whose technology came from a former Google engineer who had allegedly stolen trade secrets for self-driving cars. Reuters reported Uber had to settle with Google for US$245 million ("Waymo accepts US$245 million and Uber's 'regret' to settle self-driving car dispute," Reuters, 2018)—nearly 20 times the total value of all their patents in 2018! Rather than buying technological value, Uber inadvertently bought a legal grenade with its Waymo acquisition.

In its Initial Public Offering(IPO) prospectus, Uber stated to the US Securities and Exchange Commission (SEC) that:

> As of December 31, 2018, we have 904 issued patents (of which 323 are international) and 1297 pending patent applications (of which 486 are international), many of which relate to our core technology such as match optimization, pricing, routing, traffic, navigation, mapping, safety, and telematics. ◀

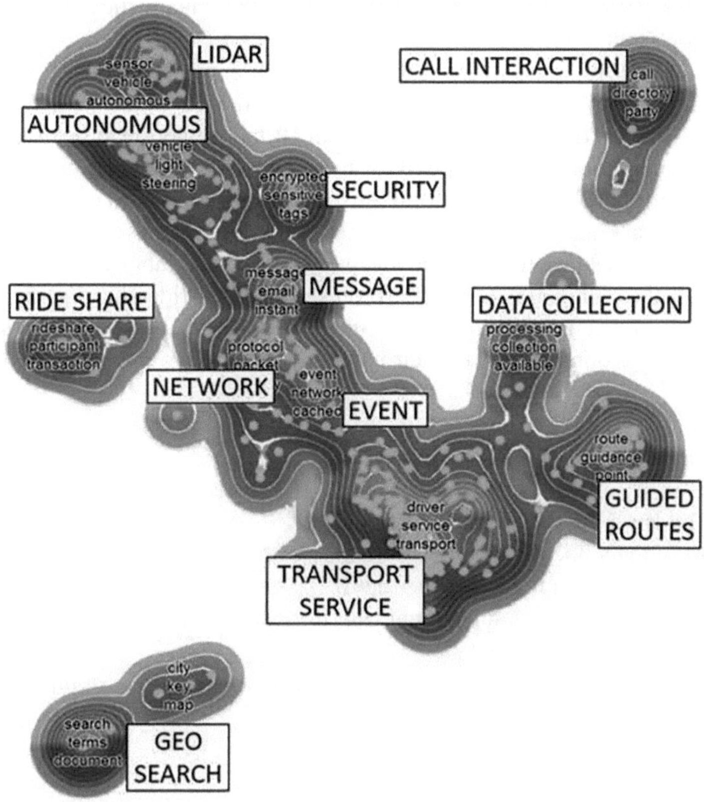

Fig. 4.3 Patent landscape: *Uber* US grants and applications (TechInsights, 2018)

Figure 4.3 shows the landscape of patents Uber has.

That same SEC IPO prospectus valued the patent portfolio at US$12 million versus the US$70 million in "developed technology." Meaning, the software and setup are worth more than the patents, which perhaps are only 5–13,000 a piece, depending on how they are counted. On the back of this prospectus, Uber raised another ca. US$8 billion in May of 2019 through its IPO, bringing the total of capital raised to US$16.2 billion. The company came public at around an 80-billion-dollar valuation. IP acquisitions may have been part of the "window-dressing" underwriters do before taking it public.

Ironically, the patents do not protect the core business; protection of the business model comes from economies of scale and self-reinforcing network effects. Many of the "inventions" are not patentable outside of the USA. Hence, valuing Uber's technology portfolio at US$82 million seems a bit over the top considering that an Estonian high-school student and his code-savvy friends were able to re-create a similar platform, copied from the Ukraine, within about 9 months and with minimal investment. Their company, *Bolt* (formerly *Taxify*), is the go-to ride-sharing app in the Baltics—not Uber (Treija, 2016). *Yandex* was active in the East Bloc countries, another Uber clone, and had to be bought out by Uber, again showing the limits of IP protection for the business model.

Uber continues to hemorrhage cash at US$1 billion per year and is coming under pressure from competing services such as Bolt, Lyft, and others with similar technology; this may indicate that reliance on an IP moat may have been a bad idea. *Tesla* and the major automakers are likely to be far ahead in the self-driving technology race—and the Waymo litigation is just a taste of what is to come if any company should crack the self-driving nut, unleashing billions in idle capital sitting in driveways and obviating the demand swathes of unskilled labor to pilot vehicles. If anything, all the companies with idle IP on self-driving, ride-sharing, and adjacent technology have been the ones to profit most from Uber's patent buying spree and are finally able to commercialize their patents.

Takeaways Patenting for Access to Finance

- Patents signal to investors that a CEO is serious and that the technology can be appropriated;
- Most of the value accrued to companies with fragments of the ride-sharing technology could not monetize them;
- IP portfolio played a substantial role in raising capital and was a motivation for acquisitions; and
- Portfolio size and foray into self-driving tech opened the company up to litigation.

4.8 Litigation for Value

In addition, new companies are entering the market with increasing frequency, no longer commercializing their patents through products but using them primarily to generate licensing income. Such non-operating companies are therefore also referred to as *Non-Practicing Entities (NPEs)* and include universities, research institutes, and research companies such as *ETH Zurich*, *Fraunhofer Society,* and *InterDigital.*

Among the NPEs, the so-called *Patent Assertion Entities (PAEs)*, which acquire patents from third parties for later exploitation, deserve special mention. Their main business purpose is to generate licensing income through patent infringement suits. They are often indiscriminately labeled as *Patent Trolls*.[2] However, PAEs often also represent individual inventors or small companies on a commission basis. They,

[2] The term "troll" is also frequently used to refer to patent assertion entities (PAEs) in a tongue-in-cheek manner. PAEs are companies that do not practice their patents themselves.

therefore, play an important role for those inventors and companies, who do not have the competence, resources, or means to fight the protracted patent legal battles, requisite to enforce them. In this sense, NPEs fill an ecological niche in the complex and competitive IP/inventor ecosystem.

PAEs can be divided into four different groups based on the type of value they added (Krech et al., 2015):

- **Guarders**, for example, *Golden Rice, MPEG LA*;
- **Shielders**, such as *Intellectual Discovery*;
- **Funders**, e.g., *Pete Invest, Patent Select*; and
- **Earners**, for example, *Acacia Research, Allied Security Trust, Intellectual Ventures*.

For exploitation, PAEs usually resort to a very aggressive exploitation strategy, specifically searching for potential patent infringements and taking action against them (Ewing & Feldman, 2012). The aim is usually not a court ruling but a settlement. This litigation-focused strategy can be lucrative since the median award is about US$6 million according to *PricewaterhouseCoopers*; Fig. 4.4 reveals this figure having been relatively stable, even if the variance of damage awards in the USA is high.

It is estimated that the damage payments to PAEs now exceed those to manufacturing companies (Bessen & Meurer, 2013). Even *IBM* faced an aggressive exploitation attack in the 1990s when *TechSearch*, a PAE, threatened the company with an injunction for infringement of a patent and asked IBM to pay a large license fee (Hess-Blumer, 2009; IP Watchdogs, 2013).

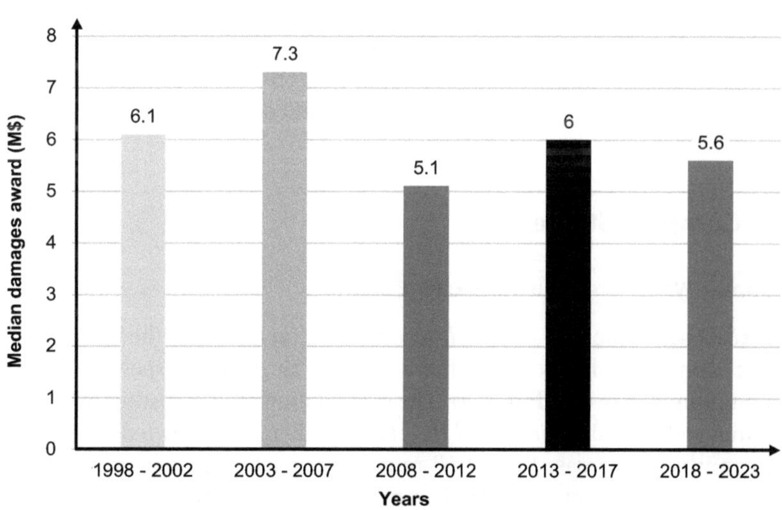

Fig. 4.4 Median damage award (based on Marcum, 2024; PwC, 2018)

These new exploitation strategies received particular attention, among other things, due to the bidding competition for the patents of the Canadian telecommunications provider *Nortel* (see also Ziegler et al., 2011). When Nortel filed for bankruptcy in 2011, *Google* and *Rockstar Bidco*, a consortium of originally five mobile phone companies, including *Apple* and *Microsoft*, competed intensively for the 6000 patents of the telecommunications provider. Ultimately, the patents were auctioned for US$4.5 billion by the Rockstar consortium. The consortium used the acquired patents to conduct licensing negotiations for patent infringement with *Android* developer Google and device manufacturers such as *HTC* and *Samsung*. At the end of 2014, it became known that Rockstar had fulfilled its purpose and the 2000 most valuable patents had been transferred to its owners, while in 2015, the remaining 4000 patents had been taken over by *RPX*, a so-called defensive patent exploiter, for US$900 million (Reuters, 2014). In 2018, *HGGC*, a private equity firm, ended up taking RPX with its patent portfolio private in an all-cash transaction worth US$555 million, implying a potential massive loss on the 2014 Rockstar purchases!

Example—Patent Assertion Entity: Acacia Research

Picture archival and communications systems store medical images from CT scans, MRIs, ultrasounds, and similar images. A medical engineering team in Florida filed a patent for distributing medical imagery via communications networks. Not having the capacity to market the technology, they sold the patent to the *Acacia Research Corporation* in 2005. Acacia is a non-practicing entity (NPE). *Acacia* claimed a wider scope of coverage for its newly acquired patents, arguing that the patents covered any system that could "enable multiple, remote users to simultaneously access image data from remote display terminals over common phone and data networks, such as the Internet." This description obviously applies to a much wider range of industries and technologies than the original patent had covered. Acacia then launched multiple suits against some of the biggest players: *GE*, *Siemens*, and *Philips*. This had an immediate chilling effect on those companies imaging software sales, freezing millions in R&D dollars. ◀

4.9 Complex Strategies

Example—Value Creation Matrix: BT Exact

The R&D department of *British Telecom (BT Exact)* defines the nature and scope of the commercialization of internal research from a specially developed exploitation matrix (see Fig. 4.5). The exploitation matrix distinguishes between informal and formal IP: *informal IP* refers to intangible knowledge, such as skills and expertise; whereas, *formal IP* refers to legal IPRs, such as copyrights and patents (see also Sect. 1.3). With regard to licenses, BT Exact is prepared to license patents, copyright, and knowledge to external companies. Such an agreement usually involves the transfer of knowledge and technology. However, if there is a specific market for formal intellectual property, BT Exact prefers to

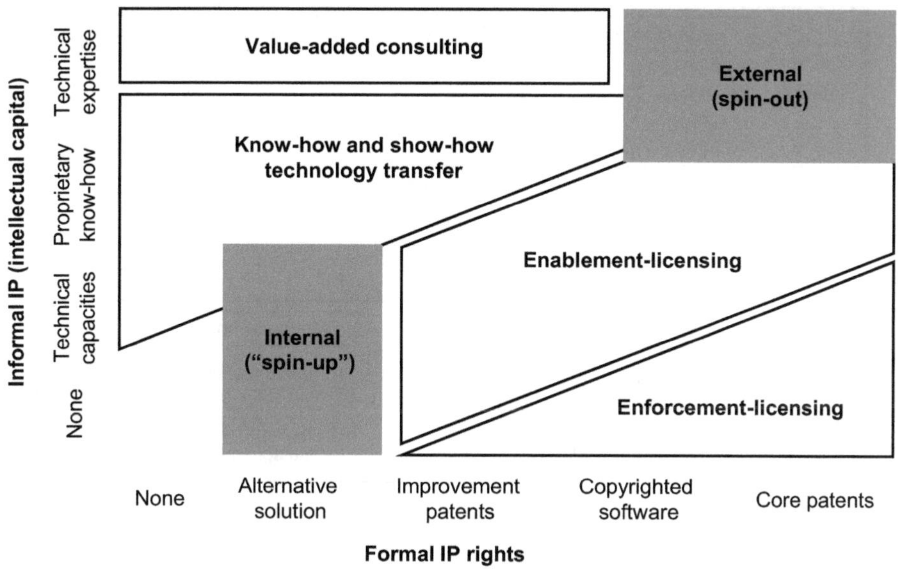

Fig. 4.5 Intellectual property usage and value creation matrix of *BT Exact* (authors' own figure)

outsource it as a separate business. BT Exact normally holds less than 100% of the equity. Another option is to invest IP into existing businesses, such as start-ups. Licensing and "spin-ups" (company-internal start-ups) are not mutually exclusive and can even stimulate each other. In markets that are already well developed, licenses often can generate immediate profits. If a technology cannot be sufficiently patented, internal spin-up activities are preferred to licensing. If good patents meet high technical expertise, a spin-out offers the greatest benefit but is also associated with increased risk. Sharing these risks with other partners can help to reduce costs and risks. Spin-outs also have the advantage of stimulating entrepreneurial and intrapreneurial opportunities. ◀

Example—Make or Buy: Bayer

The *Bayer* chemicals and pharmaceuticals group has established a life cycle process for intellectual property consisting of three phases: knowledge acquisition; knowledge assurance; and knowledge exploitation (see Fig. 4.6). Knowledge is acquired either internally through its own knowledge generation or externally through contract research, cooperation, and joint ventures, in-licensing, purchase, or via acquisition (*make or buy*). Knowledge can be exploited internally, for example, through proprietary applications, products, processes, or services. Externally, the stored knowledge can be used in research cooperation and joint ventures, licensed or sold to third parties, or used as part of outsourcing or benchmarking (*keep or sell*). ◀

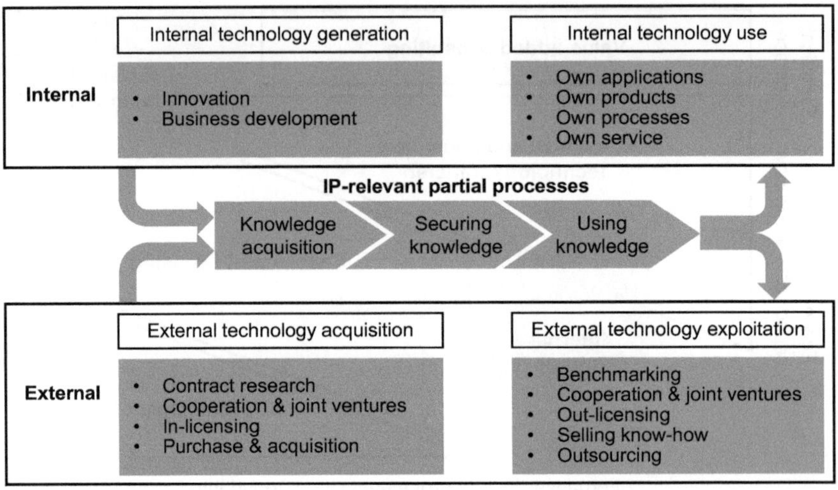

Fig. 4.6 Commercialization cycle of intellectual property at *Bayer* (authors' own figure)

4.10 Commercialization Concepts and Conclusions

Despite the growing trend to use patents as strategic levers in management and to exploit patents and create additional value by using them internally in products and processes, companies face several challenges. The technology markets in which patents can be traded are often not transparent. In addition, there is still a need for uniform and recognized valuation methods for patents (Kamiyama et al., 2006). Negotiations on a licensing agreement often fail because the financial and non-financial terms are not agreed upon. High transaction costs, the identification of an exploitation partner, and a lack of resources also represent barriers to patent exploitation (Gambardella et al., 2007; Gassmann et al., 2010).

Within the framework of an industry consortium project, a guideline for patent exploitation was therefore coordinated by the *Competence Center for Intellectual Property Management at the University of St. Gallen (HSG)* (Ziegler et al., 2011).

The guideline for the successful exploitation of patents consists of four phases (see Fig. 4.7):

1. Identification of potential patents for exploitation;
2. Evaluation of these patents and pricing;
3. Search for suitable transaction partners; and
4. Implementation of the transaction.

Each of the phases is associated with specific challenges, issues to be clarified, and decisions to be taken. The key to patent exploitation is: which decisions are made and how, and what challenges these decisions entail. In the following, the individual phases of the exploitation process are therefore presented in more detail, and the aspects already mentioned are addressed.

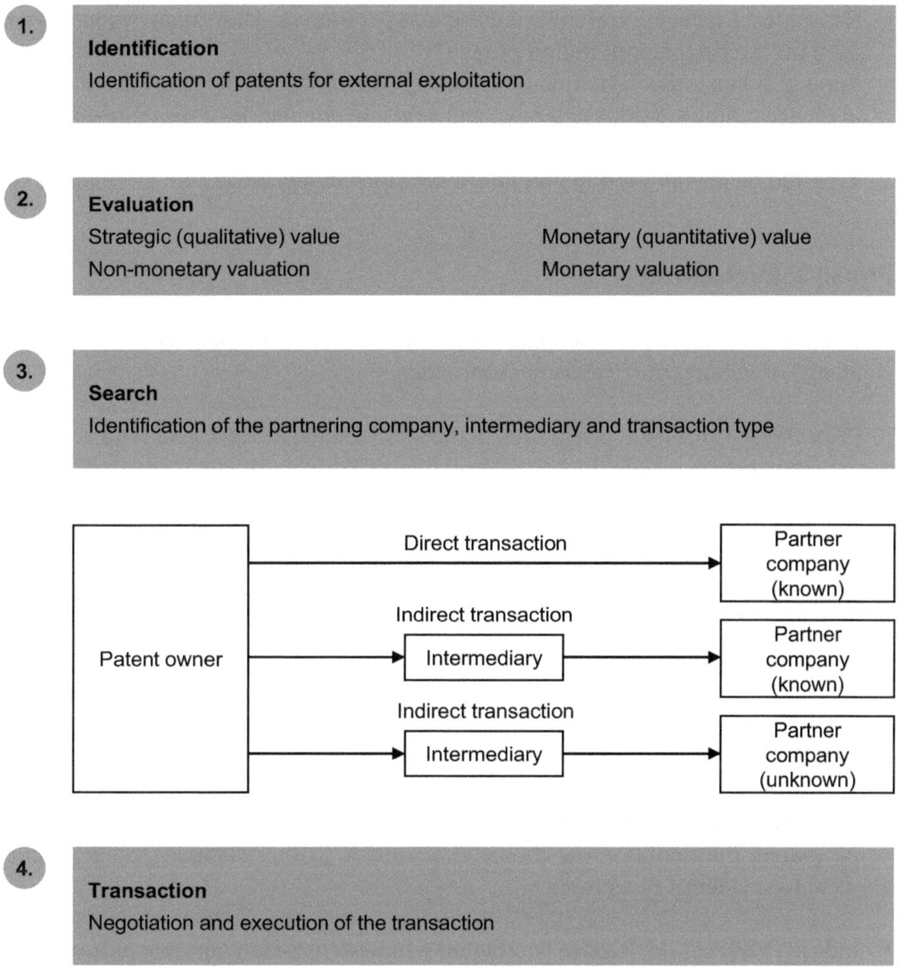

Fig. 4.7 The four phases of successful patent exploitation (Ziegler et al., 2011)

Phase 1: Identification

The challenge of this phase is to identify possible patents from the portfolio that are to be exploited on the basis of the company's internal exploitation motives, whether they are monetary or strategic.

The following decisions have to be made:

- Keep or Sell: Which technologies, products, or business models have the potential to be out-licensed? What should be kept, and what should be sold? What kind of patents should be sold (core patents and non-core patents)?
- Motives: What goals does the company pursue with patent exploitation? Are they more strategic or more monetary in nature?

- Resources: Licensing activities require many resources. How many resources are used for the patent exploitation project?
- Timing: When is the right time for licensing (depending on the development phase of the technology, market situation, and strategic orientation of the company)?
- Responsibility: Who is responsible for organizing and coordinating external exploitation and all current and future activities in this area?

Phase 2: Evaluation

Once the patents to be exploited have been identified, the company is faced with the challenge of valuing the patents appropriately:

- Price: What is the right price? Due to the lack of standardized, generally accepted valuation methods (qualitative, quantitative, or both?), pricing, when transferring patents, remains a major challenge.
- Valuation method: Should a qualitative or a quantitative method be used? (see Chap. 3).
- Risks: What risks are taken in relation to the company's core business?
- Exclusion factors: What factors speak against external exploitation (loss of market share, unprofitable cost–benefit estimates)?

Phase 3: Search

In the third phase, it is necessary to consider whether a direct or indirect transfer is being sought. Furthermore, the choice of a suitable partner company or intermediary is at the center of this phase:

- Industry: Should the license be granted within or outside your own industry?
- Licensing partners: Who is the right licensing partner? How is this partner to be found and then convinced?
- Competition: Is the company willing to sell to a direct competitor?
- Utilization channel: Will the patent be licensed out directly to a third party, or should the company resort to the support of patent intermediaries (e.g., patent brokers and patent auctions)?
- Resources: Does the company have the resources and expertise to find a suitable partner company itself and to carry out the transaction? Is an intermediary necessary?
- Intermediary: Who is a suitable intermediary to support the patent exploitation?
- Responsibility: What tasks should the intermediary perform, and what tasks are performed internally?

Phase 4: Transaction

The fourth and final phase will focus on negotiations on the terms and conditions of the patent transaction and its execution:

- Make or Buy: What should be self-generated, and what should be in-licensed?
- Exclusivity: Should exclusive or nonexclusive licenses be granted?
- Scope and content of the transaction: Should the patent be out-licensed with or without knowledge transfer? What services are associated with the license, from pure patent exploitation to full know-how transfer and process support?
- Regional delimitation: For which region is the license valid, for example, only in Germany or worldwide?
- Willingness to compromise: Which demands can be downplayed in negotiations, and which ideas are central?
- Consideration: What does the company expect in return (a lump sum, licenses, and know-how)?

10 Factors of Success for Commercializing Patents

- *Corporate strategy:* The adaptation of the exploitation strategy to the corporate and R&D strategy is central to successful exploitation. Inconsistencies can lead to confusion and inefficiency.
- *Industry:* The decision as to whether patent exploitation should be pursued within the industry itself, or outside of it, must be reflected in the exploitation strategy.
- *Market know-how:* For a successful patent exploitation it is essential to know the characteristics and market structures of the target industry in order to identify a possible demand for the patent.
- *Target definition:* Only with a clear target definition of the patent exploitation strategy can the right patents for the exploitation process be identified and selected.
- *Commercialization channel:* The path of commercialization must be chosen with regard to the external resources and competencies required, for example, direct or indirect transfer with the help of an intermediary.
- *Partner companies:* The choice of companies to which the patent rights are to be transferred must be made carefully in relation to the objectives of patent exploitation. The competence of the partner company is particularly important for projects with know-how transfer.
- *Evaluation model:* There is no perfect method for patent evaluation. The choice of valuation and evaluation methods always depends on the occasion and the objective and must be chosen accordingly.
- *Organizational structure:* A successful exploitation strategy requires appropriate organizational structures, such as organizational units specialized in patents and with clear resource allocation.
- *Management:* A successful exploitation strategy requires the strong and active support of the management.
- *Organizational culture:* External patent exploitation is an exception for many companies. In order to enable successful exploitation in the long term, incentives must be created within a company not only for patent generation but also for external exploitation.

References

Bader, M. A., Gassmann, O., Jha, P., Liegler, F., Maicher, L., Posselt, T., Preissler, S., Rüther, F., Tonisson, L., & Wabra, S. (2012a). Creating an organised IP rights market in Europe. *Intellectual Asset Management Magazine, 26*, 33–38.

Bader, M. A., Gassmann, O., Jha, P., Liegler, F., Maicher, L., Posselt, T., Preissler, S., Rüther, F., & Wabra, S. (2012b). *Creating a financial market for IPR*. European Commission.

Bader, M. A., & Liegler, F. (2013). Ein europäischer (Finanz-)Markt für Geistiges Eigentum? *Mitteilungen der deutschen Patentanwälte, 104*(1), 25–26.

Bader, M. A., & Süzeroglu-Melchiors, S. (2023). *Intellectual property management for start-ups – Value-enhancing approaches and practices for leveraging the potential*. Springer Nature.

Bessen, J., & Meurer, M. J. (2013). Direct costs from NPE disputes. *The Cornell Law Review, 99*, 387.

Bessler, W., Bittelmeyer, C., & Lipfert, S. (2003). Zur Bedeutung von wissensbasierten immateriellen Vermögensgegenständen für die Bewertung und Finanzierung von kleinen und mittleren Unternehmen. In J.-A. Meyer (Ed.), *Unternehmensbewertung und Basel II in kleinen und mittleren Unternehmen* (pp. 309–334). Eul.

Ewing, T., & Feldman, R. (2012). The giants among us. *Stanford Technology Law Review, 1*, 1–61.

Gambardella, A., Giuri, P., & Luzzi, A. (2007). The market for patents. *Europe Research Policy, 39*, 1163–1183.

Gassmann, O., & Bader, M. A. (2024). *Patentmanagement: Innovationen erfolgreich nutzen und schützen* (5th ed.). Springer Gabler.

Gassmann, O., Krech, C.-A., Bader, M. A., & Reepmeyer, G. (2016). Out-licensing in pharmaceutical research and development. In A. Schuhmacher, M. Hinder, & O. Gassmann (Eds.), *Value creation in the pharmaceutical industry – The critical path to innovation* (pp. 363–380). Wiley-VCH.

Gassmann, O., Schuhmacher, A., Reepmeyer, G., & von Zedtwitz, M. (2018). *Leading pharmaceutical innovation – How to win the life science race* (3rd ed.). Springer.

Gassmann, O., Ziegler, N., Bader, M. A., & Nowak, R. (2010). *IP management in practice*. University of St. Gallen (ITEM-HSG).

Grindley, P. C., & Teece, D. J. (1997). Managing intellectual capital: Licensing and cross-licensing in semiconductors and electronics. *California Management Review, 39*(2), 8–41.

Hall, B. H., von Graevenitz, G., & Helmers, C. (2021). Technology entry in the presence of patent thickets. *Oxford Economic Papers, 73*(2), 903–926.

Heller, M. A., & Eisenberg, R. S. (1998). Can patents deter innovation? The anticommons in biomedical research. *Science, 280*(5364), 698–701.

Hess-Blumer, A. (2009). *Patent trolls – Eine analyse nach Schweizer Recht* (pp. 851–865). *sic!*.

Hyundai. (2018). *Hyundai motor group and Audi partner in fuel cell technology*. Retrieved June 11, 2025, from https://www.hyundainews.com/en-us/releases/2557

IP Watchdogs. (2013). *Why bash individual inventor owned or controlled companies?* http://www.ipwatchdog.com/2013/06/30/why-bash-individual-inventor-owned-or-controlled-companies/id=42613/

IPXI. (2015). *Corporate announcement*. Intellectual Property Exchange International. https://www.ipxi.com/corporate-announcement.html

Kamiyama, S., Sheehan, J., & Martinez, C. (2006). Valuation and exploitation of intellectual property. *OECD science, technology and industry working papers*, no. 5. OECD.

Krech, C.-A., Rüther, F., & Gassmann, O. (2015). Profiting from invention: Business models of patent aggregating companies. *International Journal of Innovation Management, 19*(3), 1–26.

Lerner, J., Strojwas, M., & Tirole, J. (2007). The design of patent pools: The determinants of licensing rules. *The RAND Journal of Economics, 38*(3), 610–625.

Lloyd, R. (2018). Uber's patent transactions head explains how the company built its portfolio through savvy deal-making. *Intellectual Asset Management (IAM)*.

Marcum LLP. (2024). 2024 *Marcum patent litigation study*. Retrieved July 29, 2025, from https://ipwatchdog.com/wp-content/uploads/2024/12/2024-Marcum-Patent-Litigation-Study.pdf

Microsoft. (2004). *Siemens and Microsoft to cross-license patent holdings*. Retrieved June 11, 2025, from https://news.microsoft.com/source/2004/05/03/siemens-and-microsoft-to-cross-license-patent-holdings/

OECD. (2019). *Licensing of IP rights and competition law*. OECD.

Parr, R. L., & Sullivan, P. H. (1996). *Technology licensing. Corporate strategies for maximizing value*. Wiley.

PricewaterhouseCoopers. (2018). *2018 patent litigation study*. https://www.pwc.com/us/en/forensic-services/publications/assets/2018-pwc-patent-litigation-study.pdf

Reuters. (2014). *RPX buys Apple-backed Rockstar patents for $900 million*. http://www.reuters.com/article/2014/12/23/us-rpx-rockstar-ip-idUSKBN0K11AI20141223

Reuters. (2018). *Alexandria Sage, Dan Levine, Heather Somerville*.

TechInsights. (2018). *What does Uber's patent landscape look like?* https://www.techinsights.com/blog/what-does-ubers-patent-landscape-look

Treija. (2016). *Uber, what? Taxify is the most popular taxi startup in the Baltics*. EU Start-Ups.

UKIPO. (2013). *A study of patent thickets*. The Intellectual Property Office.

Ziegler, N., Bader, M. A., & Rüther, F. (2011). *Handbook: External patent exploitation: Motives, forms, the role of intermediaries, and a guideline*. University of St. Gallen (ITEM-HSG).

Organizing Patent Management 5

5.1 Corporate Governance vs. Service Department

As internal service providers, patent departments operate in constant tension between strategic control and governance on the one hand and providing services on the other (based on Loebbert, 2000). Internal customer relationships are maintained at three levels (see Fig. 5.1):

- *Executive and strategic level:* Management's mandate concerning the patent department must be clear and unambiguous. The widespread requirement of only regarding the number of patents is far from sufficient. Clear statements on the strategic thrust are important (see Chap. 2).
- *Operative level:* The provision of services for the internal client must be balanced (give and take, duties and rights).
- *Project level:* The moderation and alignment role of the patent department between the strategic client and the internal business line and staff department clients must be balanced.

The tasks of a patent department therefore include (but are not limited to):

- Clarification of inventions;
- Productive promotion of inventions;
- Litigating patents and other intellectual property rights plus monitoring of external law firms;
- Advice, support, searches, due diligence (methodology, analysis, support, and patent strategy);
- Inventor remuneration for employees and incentive systems;
- Standardization issues;
- Patent portfolio management (database and information management);

M. A. Bader et al., *Patent Management*, Management for Professionals,
https://doi.org/10.1007/978-3-032-12030-4_5

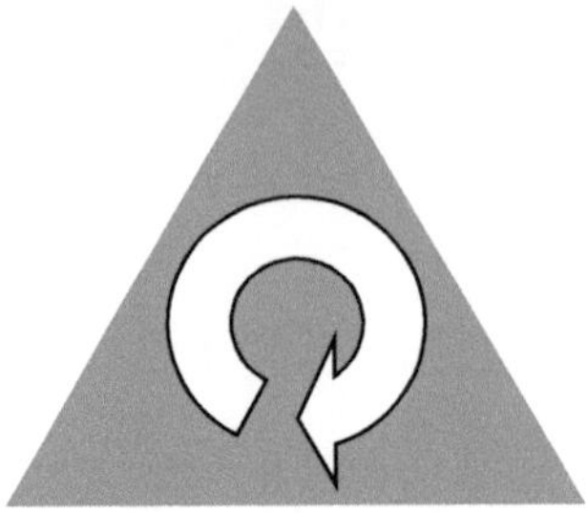

Fig. 5.1 Levels of the customer relationship of an internal patent department (authors' own figure)

- Administration of patent processes (deadlines and fees);
- Suggestions for improvement; and
- Knowledge management (idea management, state-of-the-art overview, invention disclosures, own patents, and patents of competitors).

The services provided by central patent departments often come under continual criticism in a lot of companies because the service aspect is forgotten in many companies. Instead, some patent departments act as censors and inhibitors rather than as catalysts of innovation. Those responsible often find it difficult to take timely measures based on the benefits and costs of providing services and having to balance them between the different groups of interest. It is important to keep and see Research and Development (R&D) and business units as customers. Three levels can be distinguished:

- *Executive and strategic level:* Mission statement from the executives should be clear and definite;
- *Operative level:* Services for internal clients must be adequate and valuable; and
- *Project level:* Balance between the strategic principal and the service clients (see Fig. 5.1).

Factors for Successfully Managing a Patent Department

The management of a patent department is highly dependent on the interaction within the entire company. It requires:

- Full backing and support from top management, line management, and project managers;
- Internal networking: Availability of internal specialists as well as decentralized, supporting coordinators that are, for example, embedded in the R&D department;

(continued)

(continued)

- Cooperation between the Intellectual Property, R&D, and Marketing/Sales departments;
- Regular patent awareness training and further education for R&D, management, and marketing/sales as well as in the patent department;
- Clear evaluation and selection system for inventions and patent portfolio with corresponding processes, taking into account cost/benefit aspects;
- Defense against warnings and patent infringement proceedings through the rapid availability of a centrally coordinated core team, which can also draw decentrally on specialists and decision-makers;
- Licensing and enforcement of intellectual property rights, taking into account the availability of suitable intellectual property rights, financial resources, and in-house capabilities;
- Promoting an appropriate invention culture, including an adequate incentive system;
- Controlling both material and immaterial incentives for all parties involved, for example, for inventors or licensing experts; and
- Determination of resources concerning headcounts and financial framework.

5.2 Governing Outsourcing and Compliance

Over the past decades, the requirements placed on corporate patent organization and management have increased markedly—both for internal strategic advisory work and for externally sourced services, in particular patent-attorney legal services. What follows are implications for internal patent management and an overview of the challenges and conflicts that must be managed.[1]

The *New Institutional Economics (NIE)*—shaped decisively by Coase's 1937 article on the nature of the firm—offers deep insights into the coordination of economic activities within institutions such as firms and markets (Coase, 1937). Coase argued that internal coordination can, under certain circumstances, be more efficient than market-based transactions because it lowers transaction costs (e.g., for information search). Building on this idea, NIE evolved in the 1960s around three foundational assumptions: methodological individualism, stable individual preferences, and bounded rationality (Thommen et al., 2023).

- *Methodological individualism:* Institutions are aggregates of individual actions and decisions rather than monolithic actors;
- *Stable individual preferences:* Individuals seek to maximize their own utility; and

[1] A selected portion of this section was previously published in the chapter Bader, M. A., & Mohr, C. A. (2025). Patentanwalt und Patentmanager – zwei Rollen im Wandel der Zeit. In U. Fitzner (Ed.), *Festschrift zum 125-jährigen Bestehen des Patentanwaltsberufs.* Hürth: Wolters Kluwer, 131–152. Used with permission.

- *Bounded rationality:* Individuals act rationally within limits of information-processing capacity; fully rational behavior is excluded.

Three complementary NIE lenses are particularly relevant for patent management design: property rights, the transaction-cost approach, and principal–agent theory (Thommen et al., 2023).

1. *Property-rights theory:* The value of an asset is codetermined by the bundle of rights attached to it. Clear allocation and enforcement of rights create incentives for stewardship and efficient use—central to allocating, managing, and monetizing patents.
2. *Transaction-cost approach:* Institutions are compared by the costs for initiating, negotiating, and enforcing contracts (e.g., information search, bargaining, contracting, monitoring, and adaptation). These costs can be monetary or non-monetary and are pervasive in patent prosecution, portfolio curation, and enforcement.
3. *Principal–agent theory:* It addresses relationships where a principal delegates to an agent under information asymmetries and divergent risk preferences—conditions that characterize many patent tasks outsourced to external advisers.

In practice, these perspectives help decide which patent-management tasks should be internalized (governed) versus outsourced (market) and how to structure contracts and controls when external work is unavoidable. This is especially pertinent for allocating roles between *patent attorneys of external firms* and *in-house patent management* (see Fig. 5.2).

Outsourcing Through the Lens of Principal–Agent Theory

Readers will readily accept that companies routinely seek legal advice—either from in-house counsel (e.g., corporate or in-house patent attorneys) or from patent

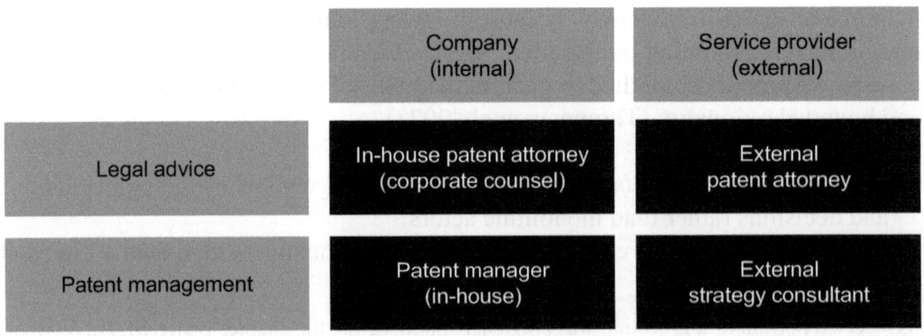

Fig. 5.2 Principal–agent dilemma in patent management—and the tension between external legal advisory services and internal patent management (Bader & Mohr, 2025)

attorneys from external law firms or external service providers. Often, internal and external experts work closely together or cross-check each other's assessments.

While the "classic" patent work (drafting, prosecution, and litigation) is frequently anchored with employed specialists because they are embedded in corporate structures and have easier access to strategy-relevant information, companies increasingly purchase external services across a broad spectrum—from engineering support to complex strategy consulting. Where no internal patent manager exists (especially in SMEs), external patent attorneys often have to assume parts of that role. The aim here is not to judge the fundamental suitability of freelance patent attorneys for such a complex role, but to use *principal–agent theory* to analyze and explain the dynamics between companies and their external patent-attorney firms.

The theory highlights the *divergent objectives* and *information asymmetries* between the internal patent management (*principal*) and external patent attorneys (*agents*). Hence, careful steering and monitoring of external firms are required, as they may rationally pursue business interests not always aligned with the firm's strategic goals. External patent attorneys operate within professional rules of conduct.[2] For example, some codes state that the *independence of the patent attorney is jeopardized whenever personal economic considerations drive the handling of a mandate*. Whether such rules are sufficient—both to protect companies and to protect the profession itself—remains a compliance question to be addressed by corporate governance.

A *robust internal patent management capability* is therefore essential to ensure that external activities align with corporate objectives and are efficiently governed. A strong, independent in-house team can effectively control and coordinate external advisers, reduce the risk of conflicts of interest, and help the company reach its innovation goals without undue dependency on external influences. Building competence and strengthening the internal processes enable the in-house function to act as the principal—defining scope and quality for agents' services. This supports strategic alignment, protection of corporate value, and cost efficiency across IP activities. What, then, are the consequences for the integrity of external patent attorneys as officers of their legal system if such internal capabilities are missing or underdesigned—especially in SMEs?

Walking the Tightrope Between Compliance and the Principal–Agent Dilemma

The role of external patent attorneys is characterized by the need to balance *strict compliance obligations* with the *commercial interests* of their firms. Patent attorneys are subject to stringent professional and ethical rules (e.g., independence, confidentiality, and avoidance of conflicts of interest) set forth in their applicable

[2] Professional codes of conduct (e.g., national patent-attorney regulations) are jurisdiction-specific; where examples are cited in the text, they serve as illustrative references for compliance design rather than jurisdiction-binding guidance.

patent-attorney acts and codes of conduct. Yet, as independent businesses, they also face commercial pressures. This duality creates potential areas of conflict:

- *Maximization of own remuneration:* Business models may incentivize the expansion of billable services, potentially clashing with the client's interest in cost-efficient advice and the attorney's duty to provide such advice;
- *Client-base expansion:* To grow market position, firms seek new clients, increasing the risk of accepting mandates that could create *conflicts of interest*; and
- *Economic pressure:* The need for competitive profitability can, at times, conflict with the objective, impartial advice companies expect.

Navigating the Principal–Agent Dilemma in Patent Management

Managing this dilemma requires a balance that upholds legal–ethical standards and secures the firm's economic viability. Companies that engage external patent attorneys or legal advice must recognize this dual nature and implement *oversight and control mechanisms* to ensure that their interests are represented effectively and efficiently.

In the domain of *classical legal expertise*—particularly in large companies with in-house patent managers—both sides can control the relationship relatively well for tasks such as drafting applications, handling procedures before patent and trademark offices, and enforcing patents in court. Reference checks and market comparisons enable companies to make relatively transparent choices; external attorneys and service providers can contribute by offering transparent fee structures.

By contrast, the internal patent-management domain is more complex. Here, *cost-relevant corporate decisions* (and commercially relevant decisions for the firm of the agent) are made—for example:

- Which inventions should be filed at all?
- How many applications, in which countries, with which foreign associates?
- Which procedures should be continued, how long, or abandoned?
- Which patents should be enforced, where, and how?

Against this backdrop, a structural separation between *strategy-related decision-making* (principal) and *operational execution* (agent) appears not only sensible but often necessary (*"do not set the fox to guard the henhouse"*). This requires sufficient, independent in-house competence to cover the broad task spectrum of patent management, make sound strategic decisions, and efficiently steer external firms.

Integrating Expertise and Strategic Corporate Leadership

Therefore, in today's IP landscape—where challenges and dynamics keep intensifying—a *clear division of tasks* between in-house patent management and external patent attorneys for all strategy-shaping decisions is essential for effective and efficient corporate leadership. External attorneys contribute deep legal expertise in assessing patentability and in representation before authorities and courts. Their challenge is to consistently champion the client's interests while managing the economic goals of their own practice; in reality, this ideal cannot always be followed stringently, especially when advising SMEs that often lack experienced patent managers—or any at all—thus imposing heightened moral and ethical responsibility on external counsel.

Full integration of patent management into the company offers considerable advantages: direct embedding in strategic and operational processes, immediate focus on corporate goals, and tight steering of patent activities to support those goals. This reduces principal–agent frictions because the in-house patent manager's objectives largely coincide with those of the company. It also optimizes oversight of freelance attorneys to ensure that their services align with corporate strategy and are executed efficiently and cost-consciously. The decisive prerequisite is that the in-house function possesses the competence to make strategic decisions and effectively govern external providers.

Nothing argues against involving freelance patent attorneys in operational patent or innovation-management tasks, and in many cases, this is desirable. Yet, from a principal–agent perspective, activities that directly or indirectly lead to paid assignments for the external attorney should be treated as problematic if the same person or firm also influences the decisions that create those assignments. Unproblematic examples include support for idea generation, development of design-around solutions, and contributions to (patent-law) evaluation of ideas. However, influencing the patent budget—such as determining the number of filings stemming from ideation—should be avoided by those agents who stand to benefit commercially. Decisions in patent management should be structured to minimize the principal–agent dilemma so that the principal's interests are represented effectively and without conflicts by the agent.

Both external counsel and in-house patent management must remain conscious of the dilemma and strive to reduce risks and ethical conflicts. A clear separation between *in-house decision-making* and *external execution* helps prevent conflicts of interest and is indispensable for a trust-based, efficient collaboration. To support this, companies should implement mechanisms that foster transparent and auditable decision-making, including:

- Clear collaboration guidelines for external patent-attorney engagement;
- Controls enabling independent review of external attorneys' work; and
- Incentive systems aligning the goals of external attorneys with those of the company (e.g., outcome-focused fee models where appropriate and compliant).

These measures are foundational to ensure that both parties can fulfill their roles without compromising ethical standards. The moral and legal obligations of external patent attorneys are central: They are expected to act with the highest integrity and to put clients' interests ahead of their own commercial interests. These obligations are not only matters of law and professional regulation; they are a core aspect of professional identity that goes beyond mere compliance. By adhering strictly to these principles, external patent attorneys strengthen trust with corporate clients, enabling long-term, successful partnerships and helping maintain a fair and effective patent-management system that serves all stakeholders and meets the profession's standards.

From an organizational perspective, separating *(internal) patent-management decision-making* from *(external) legal execution* is the safest and clearest measure for mastering the principal–agent dilemma—though it requires commensurate internal resources and competencies. Where full separation is not possible or expedient, both principal and agent must organize decisions to minimize the resulting risks. In nearly all jurisdictions, external patent-attorney codes of conduct already impose a high duty to cooperate in that effort, but it remains the responsibility of the company, as the principal, to govern, to manage, and to control their agents.

Compliance Design Principles for Patent Departments

The management of a patent department is highly dependent on the interaction within the entire company. It requires:

- *Mandate clarity:* Separate strategy decisions (principal) from execution (agent); specify the boundary in engagement letters and SOPs.
- *Conflict of interest (COI) safeguards:* Require COI checks, client matter screening, and, where needed, ethical walls at external firms.
- *Transparent economics:* Use clear fee schedules, alternative fee arrangements where appropriate, and matter budgets owned by the principal.
- *Performance and quality controls:* Define service levels (timeliness, quality criteria for drafts, and country filing rationales) and conduct periodic audits.
- *Documentation and audit trail:* Maintain invention to decision documentation (e.g., why filed or abandoned) to evidence objective, strategy aligned choices.
- *Capability building:* Invest in in-house skills (portfolio analytics, prosecution strategy, valuation, and enforcement economics) to reduce information asymmetry.

5.3 Costs and Benefits of a Patent Department

The pressure in companies to optimize costs and benefits has led to greater attention being paid to intellectual property issues while at the same time improving processes. Our studies show that 75% of companies pursue legal protection strategies and have a well-formulated patent strategy that is aligned with the company's strategy, implemented across the organization, and regularly reviewed and updated. R&D departments, in particular, are actively involved in the strategy process.

Those studies also show that the main thrust of patent strategies is becoming increasingly directed not only toward pure defense and the protection of intellectual property but also toward the generation of license revenues through external exploitation of industrial property. In general, patents are already being marketed externally by every second company. Here, however, a differentiated approach is necessary since, as a rule, the core competencies and comparative competitive advantages of companies are affected.

The direct costs of an existing patent department are relatively easy to determine. In addition to personnel costs, infrastructure costs and costs of external services such as search costs, office costs, and fees must also be taken into account. However, it is relatively difficult to always see the costs of the entire patent management process, taking into account all internal and external stakeholders.

It has therefore proved advantageous in numerous companies to introduce cost transparency on the basis of individual activities or process steps. These must be accounted for internally according to the polluter-pays principle. The overall performance is divided into performance groups. This results in a regulatory between the expected benefit, the effort, and the associated costs of service provision.

Within the framework of the settlement of individual services, various settlement models exist:

- Allocation;
- Hourly billing; and
- Flat-rate billing on a case-by-case basis.

In allocation accounting, the costs incurred are allocated to the various stakeholder groups, e.g., business units. Cost centers are often used for allocation. The criteria for the distribution key can be the sales of the enterprise areas, their R&D budget, or the number of R&D employees. The advantage of this type of allocation is that it is very simple. In practice, the low influenceability and lack of transparency of the allocation keys are often seen as a disadvantage.

Hourly billing, analogous to external service providers, is characterized by high transparency and accuracy. The internal effort, however, is usually much higher and involves the difficulty of allocating hours that cannot be charged directly.

The flat-rate billing per case represents a compromise, since sufficient accuracy can be achieved with a justifiable effort. Particularly suitable work processes for flat-rate invoicing are the preparation of notifications, notices, and expert opinions, administrative portfolio maintenance and information. Other service processes, such as infringement matters or innovation consulting, are difficult to compute as a flat rate due to the very case-specific expense and are therefore usually charged on a time and material basis.

The general disadvantage of settlement models consists of the dominance of particular and business interests in the sense of "who pays, creates." Even more problematic than the costs *per* se is the benefit of a patent department, which is therefore always under increased scrutiny. In other words: What would be the opportunity costs if no patent department existed? The directly monetary measurable benefit through license revenues usually represents the smallest part. Much more important is the trouble it causes to prove that competitors were able to circumvent a good patent with difficulty and that therefore no imitator is active as a competitor (temporary monopoly profits). The extent to which competitors are effectively blocked by their own patents can only be determined in exceptional cases (e.g., *Gore-Tex* patent). In practice, however, these blockade effects cannot really be assessed in monetary terms.

Performance Evaluation

The consumer goods manufacturer *Henkel* uses the number of oppositions against its own patents as the indicator for assessing the quality of the patent filing activity of the patent department. This seems to be a simple and effective indicator for the purpose.

Complex Patent Department Reshuffle: Infineon Technologies

The semiconductor company *Infineon Technologies* was a spin-off from its mother entity *Siemens* in April 1999. *Infineon* was already one of the top ten semiconductor companies worldwide at the time and had a patent portfolio of over 20,000 patents and patent applications at the time of the spin-off. This case is particularly instructive since the intellectual property (IP)-related arrangements were central to the success of the new company, and supporting IP organization was very complex.

Infineon's initial philosophy was to become independent of the former parent company as quickly as possible. As numerous services had previously been provided centrally by *Siemens* but had not been spun off, it was important to make greater use of externally available sources, especially in the service sector. This particularly affected the patent and trademark departments. This initial situation gave rise to different perspectives:

- *Infineon's* consideration: How can *Siemens'* previous semiconductor patent department be committed to support *Infineon's* patent and trademark department for as long as possible?
- *Siemens*' consideration: What should happen to the former semiconductor-specific patent department? → Internal absorption and independence as an external law firm.

In setting up an intellectual property service, short- and long-term goals had to be balanced out. In the short term, it was necessary to completely transfer the previous intellectual property support from *Siemens* to *Infineon* until the planned Initial Public Offering (IPO), only 1 year later in April 2000. In the long term, the company wanted to build up its own competitive intellectual property support with a sophisticated range of services.

However, the conditions were very risky for the establishment of an internal patent department. A very large number of inventions and patent applications had to be processed. More than 1000 patent applications were filed annually in 1998/1999. In addition, there was a very high active file inventory with more than 10,000 patent dossiers. A large number of infringements and other legal disputes as well as a generally high need for legal advice, such as for product clearings and redesign, placed high demands on the department's advisory capacity and quality. In contrast, only a small number of freely available IP professionals were available on the labor market for the high-tech area of semiconductor technology. In addition, there was generally strong demand for freelance IP professionals.

The starting position described above suggested outsourcing the provision of services in the patent application process. In addition, it was obvious that the service package had to be divided among several external patent law firms.

A comprehensive set of measures was outlined by *Infineon* and *Siemens* to enable the independence of the intellectual property activities at *Infineon*. Approximately one-third of the specialist staff of *Siemens'* semiconductor patent department was successfully hived off as an independent law firm. In this context, *Infineon* temporarily assured the firm of minimum reference values. In addition, the *Siemens* patent department, which had previously been responsible for the semiconductor sector, already had relationships with an external network of law firms. Peak workloads have already been outsourced as the so-called "colleague work," but without the assignment of mandates. These activities resulted in relationships with about 30 law firms in Germany, which should now be increasingly accessed. A transitional arrangement between *Siemens* and *Infineon* got *Infineon* the temporary support of a handling team of the *Siemens* patent department as well as the continuity of administrative handling. At the same time, *Infineon* began setting up its own intellectual property department. The prerequisite for the outsourcing of intellectual property processes, however, was the establishment of *Infineon*-specific IT infrastructure in order to create a so-called "law firm capability" (see Fig. 5.3).

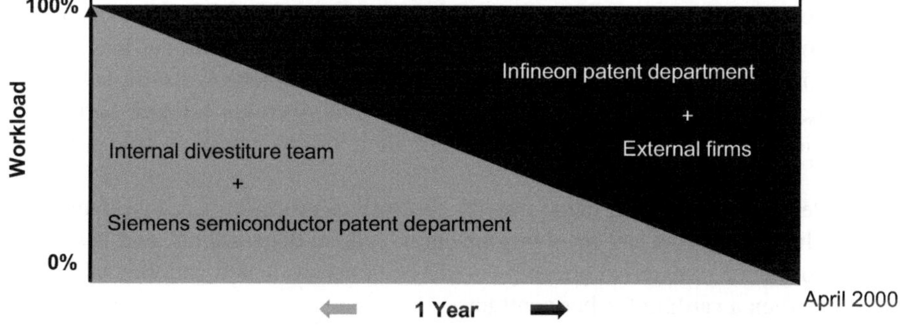

Fig. 5.3 Transition to new patent department and external providers (authors' own figure)

Managing Outsourcing

The goal at *Infineon* was to put in charge as few law firms as possible in order to maintain the greatest degree of controllability possible. An important selection criterion was that the law firms had sufficiently technically qualified employees and that they had the opportunity to expand this knowledge. The technically relevant areas mainly concerned semiconductor technology and communications technology, along with some security know-how. Another important factor was the general willingness of the law firms to act, for example, to achieve certain growth by hiring additional employees.

Infineon avoided relying on a single firm. Therefore, at least a second, sufficiently qualified and suitable law firm was mandated in relevant subject areas. This was intended to simplify performance and price comparisons at a later date and to make capacity shifts practicable.

A particularly decisive factor in the selection was, however, the extent to which a law firm was able to handle not only new applications but also ongoing proceedings. On average, the quantity ratio was about 1:4: For each new application, four ongoing application procedures had to be taken over. In this respect, of course, those law firms that had previously provided "colleague work" as an extended workbench for the *Siemens* semiconductor patent department were generally at an advantage. *Infineon* chose to standardize as much as possible during the selection process:

1. *Infineon* created standard interfaces linking to law firms, for example, by establishing:

- Lawyer ↔ Infineon patent department channels.
- Law firm ↔ inventor channels.

2. Decision processes were standardized.
3. Technical application fields and channels for office capacity requirements were identified.
4. *Infineon's* ability to work with law firms was an important prerequisite for enabling outsourcing, for example, the establishment of a specific IT infrastructure for the patent and trademark administration.

Managing Quality

Strong, pragmatic, and consistent quality controlling was established to evaluate the quality of external patent services. *Infineon's* purchasing department was significantly involved in this process. When negotiating conditions with the law firms, price and performance, including time requirements, were an integral part of the negotiations. Framework agreements were then drawn up with law firms on this basis.

By developing a standardized quality controlling process covering quantitative and qualitative aspects and involving inventors, patent departments, and law firms, the performance of external attorneys could be better evaluated and thus taken into account when awarding further contracts.

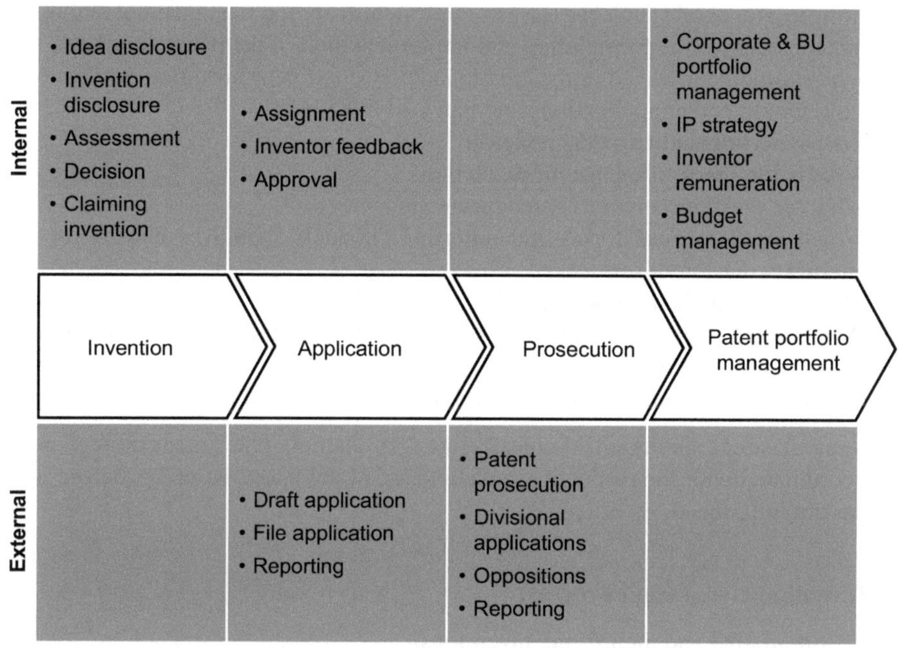

Fig. 5.4 Internal and external processes at *Infineon Technologies* (authors' own figure)

Managing Processes

Infineon has largely outsourced the operational patent application process (see Fig. 5.4). While the *internal* focus is on strategy, coordination, and decision-making processes, the *external* focus is on ensuring that patent applications are handled quickly and in line with requirements, which has led to a minimal backlog of patent applications in progress.

5.4 Core Processes of Patent Management

Determining the correct "dosage" of freedom to operate, competitive differentiation, and license revenues that a company wants to achieve through the use of patents is also referred to as a patent strategy. If the company is divided into different business areas, a two-pronged strategy development is recommended, which is divided into company and business area levels. At the corporate level, the general patent strategy tailored to the enterprise is defined, specifying, for example, how offensively or defensively the enterprise wants to behave. At the business unit level, it is primarily the application strategy that has to be formulated, which includes the main areas of invention, selection criteria, and country portfolios.

The comparison of top-down and bottom-up strategy elements is an iterative process. The best strategy is good-for-nothing if it is not consistently implemented. This requires suitable structures and processes within the company. The following questions arise in particular:

- How do you obtain the necessary commitment from top management and other stakeholders for the formulation and implementation of the patent strategy?
- Who should be involved in the creation and evaluation of invention disclosures? How should patent applications and patents be pursued?
- How are cost/benefit aspects reviewed?
- What is the scope of the patent protection?
- What are the alternatives to patent protection?
- Which organizational forms and reporting channels should be chosen for the internal provision of services?
- What are the typical implementation measures?
- How can external service providers be involved, and how can the quality provided be monitored?
- Which culturally influencing factors should be considered?

Regardless of the internal complexity, the formulation of the patent strategy must be coordinated with the respective stakeholders, at the latest, however, before processes are introduced.

Invention Generation Process:

1. Stimulating and identifying inventions.
2. Evaluating and selecting inventions.

Procedures before Patent Offices:

3. First filings.
4. Divisional applications and applications abroad.
5. Maintaining patents and other protection rights.

Strategy rounds, often referred to as *Strategic Patent Committees*, are suitable for implementing the strategizing process in large companies. These are conducted regularly, for example, annually, and can be prepared by the patent department. However, their general implementation requires the explicit support of the management.

An essential component of patent management is the conduct of proceedings in the patent application procedure before the patent offices (*patent prosecution*). Typically, this is divided firstly into the process of generating inventions and secondly into the conduct of proceedings before the patent offices:

Invention Generation Process

1. *Stimulating and Identifying Inventions:* This first step begins with the generation and search for suitable ideas. This includes, for example, idea generation, associated discussions with inventors and project managers as well as reviews of project milestones. In addition to the rather passive recording of patent ideas during project reviews, the patent attorney also plays an active role: They moderate and stimulate ideas for possible patent applications in order to find not only concrete

product concepts but also far-reaching innovation ideas. Furthermore, the patent attorney helps to abstract from existing product concepts and to break out of familiar thinking structures. A new combination of knowledge and experience as well as a moderated change of perspective stimulates new patent ideas. The following steps have to be clearly subdivided:

- Problem clarification: System delimitation and problem definition of the area to be patented;
- Idea generation: Creativity and divergent thinking dominate; helpful here are creativity techniques, for example, the morphological box, the TRIZ, 6-3-5 method, or ordinary brainstorming. It is important to stimulate ideas in this phase, but not to evaluate them yet;
- Idea selection: Preliminary selection of ideas that should at least be followed up. The focus here is on structuring, evaluating, and condensing the ideas into the most promising solution approaches; and
- Implementation: Creation of invention disclosures.

2. *Evaluating and Selecting Inventions:* An assessment is preferably made in a team in which the areas of patent function, R&D, innovation management, operations, and marketing are represented. It is an advantage if regular meetings take place. In addition to the composition of the evaluation team, it is also important that the evaluation is not carried out by individuals but by the entire team. In addition, a written individual evaluation can also be carried out according to precisely defined criteria specified by the patent department (see Chap. 3).

Procedures Before Patent Offices

3. *First Filings:* This step includes searches and filing with a patent office. Approvals should be country-specific. General prior art publications can be made by publication in journals, showcases, the Internet, or other media.

In general, before filing the first application, it should be looked into whether the attainable benefit of a later patent is at all in a reasonable proportion to the costs (see Sect. 5.2.4). In addition, if there is a problem that potential infringement will be difficult or impossible to prove later, consideration should be given to keeping the invention secret instead of filing a patent application. This is often the case, for example, with production processes, since these take place in production facilities that are inaccessible to outsiders and are also very company-specific.

If, however, there is a danger that third parties could obtain interfering patents in the same area, then, in order to avoid this, self-induced state of the art can be created by publishing generic improvements by means of the so-called prior art publications (see Sect. 2.5). The general process of the European patent procedure and that of the grant procedure at the European Patent Office (EPO) are displayed in Figs. 5.6 and 5.7 (see also WIPO, 2017).

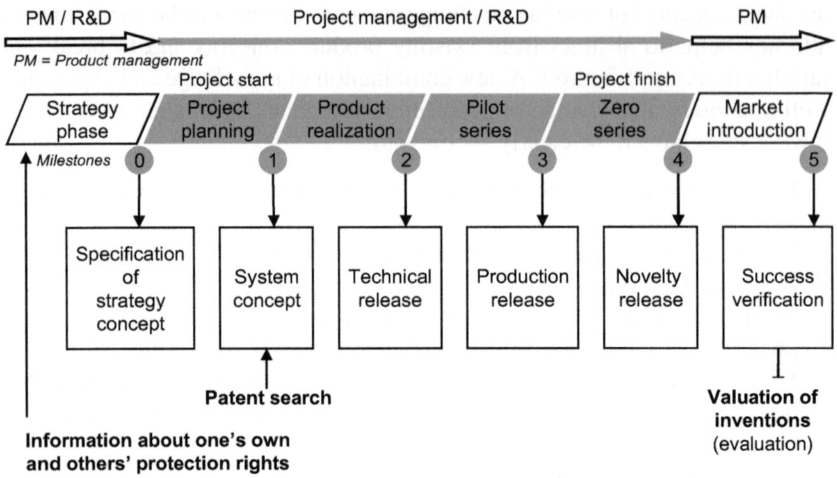

Fig. 5.5 Inclusion of the different patent processes at *Festo* (authors' own figure)

Example—Festo Sets Clearly Defined Milestones

The German multinational industrial control and automation company *Festo* has set clearly defined milestones in the development process (see Fig. 5.5). Based on this, Festo conducts patent searches, analyzes patent information, evaluates inventions, and carries out a portfolio evaluation to control the patent application process. ◀

4. *Divisional Applications and Applications Abroad:* After one has already filed a first application, e.g., a national one, one can file a second application, e.g., to gain a more international patent protection, and maintain the original filing date. The filing date of that original application then becomes the priority date of the second application. The priority date applies only to elements the two applications have in common. When placing second applications, it is then ideally investigated whether the assessment criteria on which the initial application is based are still current. This phase also involves the cost-intensive selection of countries in which further industrial property rights are to be obtained. Particularly suitable criteria are the sales market countries and the countries in which the competitors' production facilities are located.

Example—Identification of Invention Disclosures at Henkel

For the German chemical and consumer goods company *Henkel*, a multinational active both in the consumer and industrial sector, an important prerequisite for the identification of invention disclosures is a good understanding of the state of the art and the competition. Henkel uses the services offered by *Derwent* and *MicroPatent* to monitor the competition. Approximately 5000 patent specifications are processed manually each year. The focus is on the activities of the competitors.

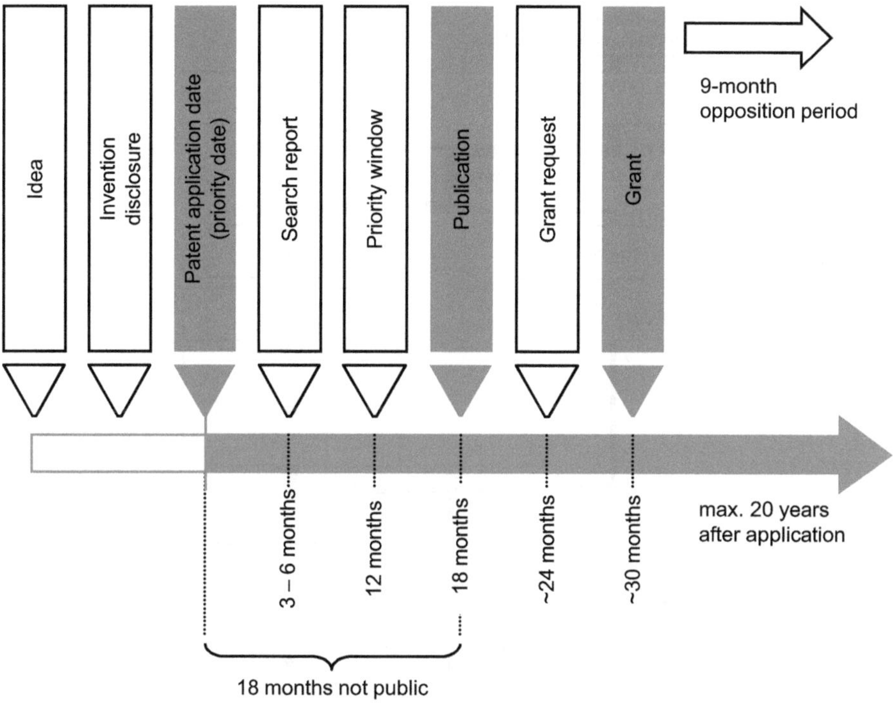

Fig. 5.6 Process of the European patent application procedure (authors' own figure)

In addition, keyword searches are used to monitor the fields of technology. The responsible technology specialists are responsible for monitoring and evaluating the patent documents. As a rule, these are the heads of the R&D groups. For example, the head of development for detergent tablets is responsible for the "Tablets" search field. Although the group leaders bear responsibility in the first instance, they can fall back on the input of other designated technology experts in their team. The R&D manager receives regular and direct reports on the patent situation from the heads of the R&D groups. At Henkel, great attention is paid to the regular and intensive work of the R&D specialists with patent documents and information. After reviewing the documents, the second step is to derive appropriate action measures based on the new understanding. ◀

5. *Maintaining Patents and Other Protection Rights:* A separate process step must be dedicated to the maintenance of intellectual property rights, during which the assessment criteria are reexamined before the official fees are paid. The maturity of the costs in the individual countries plays an important role here. While annual fees are charged in European countries, in the USA, they are due only every 4 years after they have been granted. As a rule, property rights are not explicitly dropped, but simply no fees are paid and thus expire. In particular, this has the advantage that in the event of a wrong decision, the property right can possibly be reactivated.

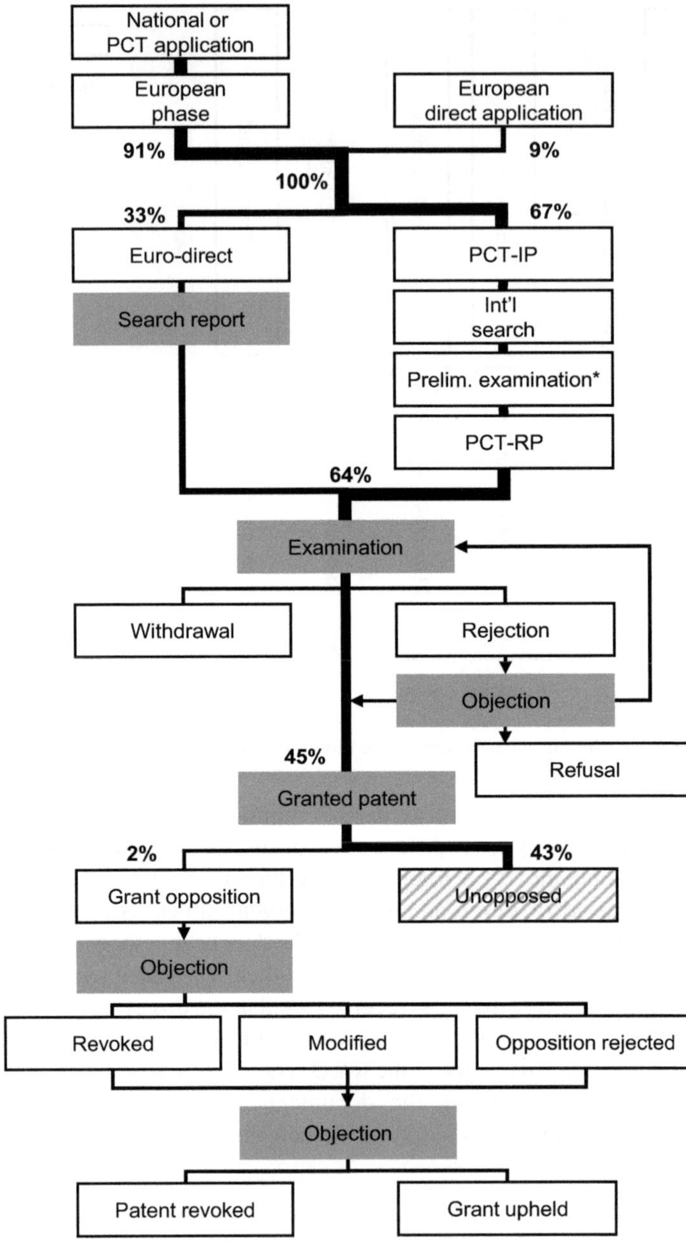

Fig. 5.7 Grant and opposition procedure at the European Patent Office (EPO)

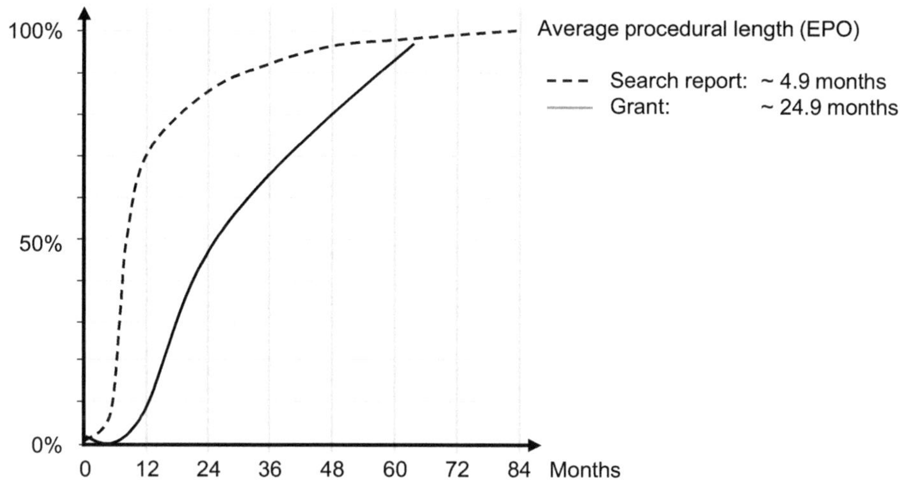

Fig. 5.8 Average procedural length at the European Patent Office (EPO)

The generation of patents is usually based on individual decisions made by individuals in Small and Medium Enterprises (SMEs) and by teams of experts in larger companies. Such teams, also known as *patent liaisons* or *operational patent committees*, are composed of several experts with market, technology, and patent expertise. These teams often meet once a month or quarter to assess new invention disclosures, initial and subsequent applications, and patent maintenance. This process may take several years before the patent is granted. Patent offices worldwide have been trying to cope with the backlog and recently have been bringing down the time previously needed for this. Patent applications before the European Patent Office, for example, are granted only after 2–3 years, and patents are held for an average of 12 years (see Figs. 5.8 and 5.9). For the search report, it is almost 4.9 months; for the grant, it has been about 30 months; as of 2024 the granting time has come down to 24.9 months; 95% of the applications are done within 63.3 months (EPO, 2024). The USA offers a fast-track program, which aims to grant after 1 year. Japan has drastically reduced its pendency, with time to first action down from ca. 26 months in 2011 to around 10 months now and by getting a final decision made at around month 20 (WIPO, 2017).

5.5 Generative Artificial Intelligence in Patent Management

Generative Artificial Intelligence (GenAI) represents a paradigm shift in IP management, as it transforms AI from a passive analytical tool into an active partner in the creation and strategic handling of innovation. While traditional IP management relies on labor-intensive processes (Ashrafi et al., 2024), GenAI, powered by Large

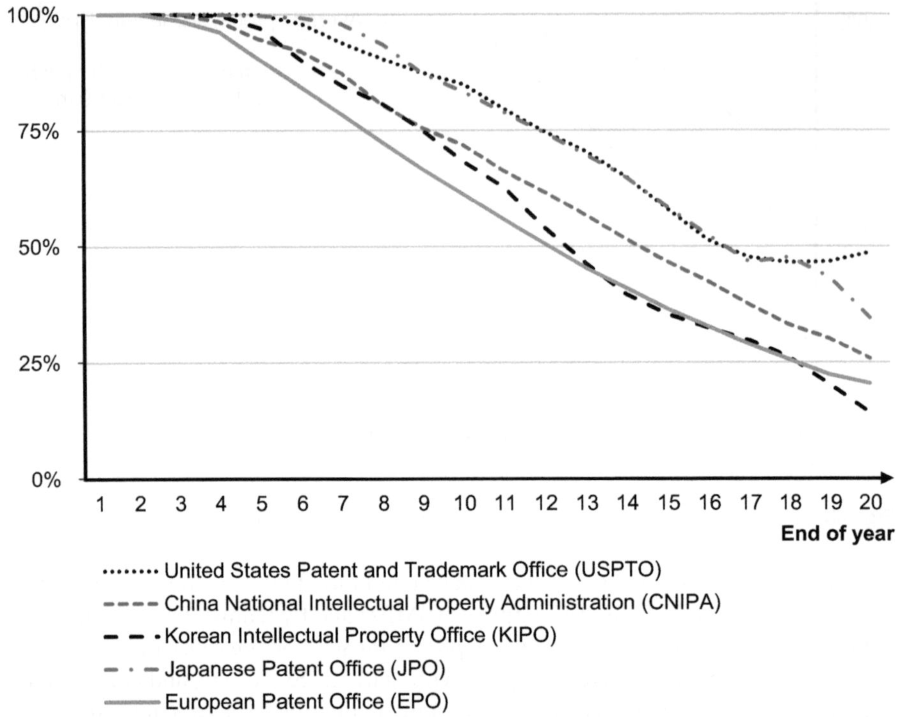

Fig. 5.9 Average patent lifetimes (Five IP Offices, 2024)

Language Models (LLMs), automates and enhances cognitive tasks (Engberg et al., 2025; Obschonka et al., 2024) such as synthesizing technical data, drafting legal arguments, and identifying patterns in prior art. This section analyzes this transformation by defining the unique capabilities of GenAI, applying them to different stages of the patent life cycle, and confronting the strategic, legal, and ethical implications for the IP profession.[3]

The Generative AI Paradigm

The impact of Generative AI goes beyond the predictive capabilities of legacy AI, providing cognitive capabilities previously supplied solely by human expertise. Whereas previous AI systems analyzed existing data to make classifications or predictions, GenAI's can create and perform cognitive tasks that incorporate context (Chang et al., 2024). This is enabled by technologies like LLMs, which are trained on vast datasets to understand and generate novel, contextually coherent human-like text. Other architectures, such as Generative Adversarial Networks (GANs) and

[3] This section has been authored by Ashkan Fredström, University of St. Gallen, Switzerland.

Diffusion Models, extend this creative capacity to other data types like images, allowing GenAI to produce a wide range of new content.

This technological leap provides a suite of capabilities directly applicable to patent management. Advanced Natural Language Understanding and Generation (NLU/NLG) allows GenAI to parse complex patent claims and technical descriptions and, conversely, to draft detailed invention descriptions or persuasive legal arguments. Text Summarization and Synthesis enables the distillation of critical information from voluminous prior art documents or prosecution histories, accelerating analysis. Multimodal Content Generation facilitates the translation between data types, such as creating a block diagram from a textual description of a process. Besides content creation, GenAI can be applied to Data Analysis, identifying conceptual clusters in a patent portfolio or anomalies in an examiner's rejection patterns. For software inventions, its capacity for Code Generation and Analysis can help demonstrate enablement or find evidence of use in a competitor's product.

To appreciate this shift, it is necessary to consider the legacy tools used in patent management. The field progressed from early statistical analysis of patent databases and rigid Boolean search methodologies, which required significant user expertise to construct precise keyword queries (Garcia et al., 2025). This was followed by first-generation semantic search tools, which used early AI to understand synonyms but often lacked deep contextual understanding. Concurrently, predictive AI models were developed for automated patent classification, increasing administrative efficiency but remaining an analytical, not a creative, function. This represents a changing relationship between the professional and the machine: from an operator of passive databases, to a guide for early analytical AI, and now to a collaborator with a generative partner. The dynamic elevates the role of the IP professional to that of a strategist, prompter, and most critically, a validator of the AI's output.

Generative AI Across the Patent Life Cycle

The capabilities of GenAI have direct applications at various stages of the patent management life cycle, which drive efficiency and enable more strategic decision-making. An example of generative AI capabilities across the patent life cycle is given in Fig. 5.10. An overview of examples of new and existing tools applying GenAI in IP management is given in Table 5.1.

Invention Capture and Disclosure

The initial capture of an invention is often challenging, as inventors may struggle to articulate its novelty. GenAI can power interactive disclosure forms that engage inventors in a dialog, asking targeted questions to elicit missing technical details or clarify ambiguities. Such systems can analyze free-form text, generate standardized summaries, and even perform a preliminary, real-time similarity check against public databases. This provides immediate feedback, allowing inventors to refine their concepts, and ensures that the initial disclosure is robust, lowering the barrier to high-quality submissions and reducing subsequent rework for patent attorneys.

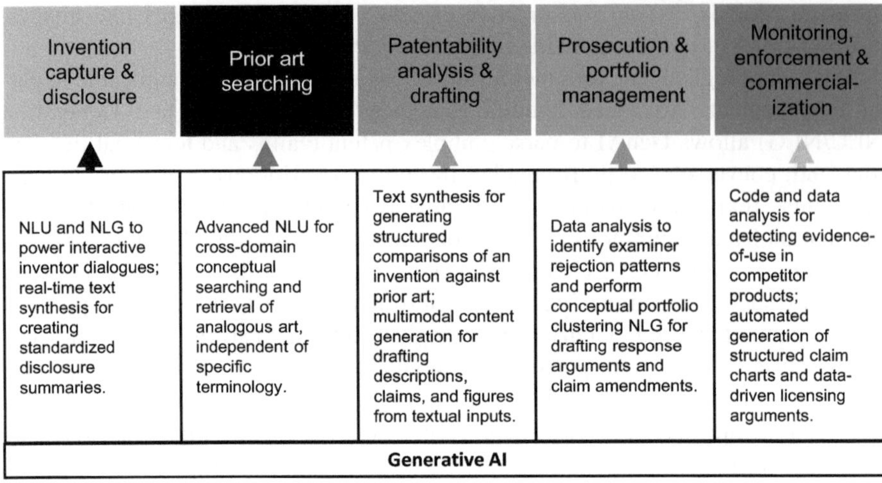

Fig. 5.10 Example of generative AI capabilities across the patent life cycle

Table 5.1 Examples of new and existing tools applying GenAI in IP management

Tool name	Primary IP category	Key features	Target user and use case
IP Copilot	Invention capture and disclosure	AI idea harvesting from messages and documents; smart disclosure assessments (scoring merit, prior art, and detectability); automated workflows and docketing; instant prior-art search	Inventors, R&D teams, and IP counsel in companies of all sizes, from startups to large corporations
Patlytics	Prior art searching; portfolio management; monitoring and enforcement	AI-powered prior art search; advanced portfolio classification; infringement detection; automated claim chart generation; and patent-to-product mapping	Law firms (Am Law 100), corporate IP departments (Fortune 500), and enterprise innovators
DeepIP	Patent drafting; prosecution; patentability analysis	Integrated as a Word add-in; patent preparation (summarize, define); drafting assistance (claims and descriptions); office action response drafting; and multi-format input including audio	Patent professionals seeking an AI assistant to augment their existing workflows in Microsoft Word

(continued)

Table 5.1 (continued)

Tool name	Primary IP category	Key features	Target user and use case
IPRally	Prior art searching; monitoring and enforcement	Graph-based AI search for visual and transparent results; conversational patent review ("Ask AI"); continuous monitoring for new filings; FTO analysis; and portfolio classification	Patent searchers, managers, and attorneys focused on in-depth search, analysis, and monitoring
Solve Intelligence	Invention capture; patent drafting; prosecution	Full application drafting (claims, figures, and chemical structures); office action response drafting with multi-source citations; and customization for drafting style and jurisdiction	Attorneys and firms with complex portfolios seeking an end-to-end, highly customizable solution
Questel	Patent drafting; prosecution	Hybrid AI models combining AI with attorney knowledge; NLP for optimizing claims; diagram generation; and prosecution toolkit with case law and guidelines	Patent applicants and attorneys looking for a comprehensive, all-in-one drafting solution
PQAI	Prior art searching	User-friendly AI-powered search tool for patents and scholarly articles; provides sample queries to demonstrate functionality; and no tracking or logging of search queries	Professionals or non-specialists needing a straightforward, privacy-focused tool for preliminary searches
SenseIP	Monitoring and enforcement; FTO analysis	AI-driven FTO analysis that flags and rates existing risks; continuous, daily monitoring with instant notifications; and cost-effective subscription model	Individual inventors, startups, and corporate IP departments needing affordable, continuous FTO analysis
ClaimMaster	Patent drafting and review	Focuses on application review and automating simple, tedious tasks; boilerplate incorporation; and checks for antecedent basis issues and ensures internal consistency	Patent practitioners focused on reviewing and finalizing patent applications
Edge	Invention capture and drafting	Specializes in invention disclosure creation and patent drafting; browser-based workspace with guided forms; and user-specific customization	Patent professionals who want more control and visibility over how AI generates each part of the application

Prior Art Searching

Prior art searching is transformed by the shift to conversational, semantic search. Instead of constructing complex Boolean queries, a user can provide a GenAI-powered engine with a full invention disclosure. The AI uses its deep conceptual understanding to find similar documents, regardless of the specific terminology used or the technical domain. This mitigates the primary weakness of keyword searching—the risk of missing analogous art described with different vocabulary—and can uncover connections across disparate fields, such as a mechanism in an industrial patent that is conceptually similar to one in a medical device. This democratizes the search process, enabling non-specialists to conduct effective preliminary searches (Moeller & Moehrle, 2015).

Patentability Analysis and Drafting

Following a search, GenAI can accelerate the analysis by taking multiple prior art documents and the invention disclosure as input. It can summarize each reference and generate a structured comparison, mapping the features of the invention against the prior art disclosures. From this analysis, the AI can produce a complete first draft of a patentability opinion, including summaries of cited art and preliminary arguments for novelty and non-obviousness. This drastically reduces the manual labor involved. However, the output requires rigorous human verification to mitigate the risk of AI "hallucinations" or the generation of plausible but factually incorrect information. Similarly, in application drafting, AI serves as a "copilot." Given attorney-drafted claims, AI tools can generate a consistent first draft of the detailed description, background, and summary. They excel at ensuring internal consistency, such as verifying that all claim elements are described in the specification and that reference numerals are correct. This reduces drafting time and the risk of costly errors, allowing attorneys to concentrate on crafting the strategically critical claims (Tseng et al., 2007).

Prosecution and Portfolio Management

During patent prosecution, GenAI tools can analyze an office action, identify the examiner's specific grounds for rejection, and summarize the cited prior art. Based on this, the AI can suggest counterarguments and claim amendments designed to overcome the rejection, serving as a brainstorming partner for the attorney. This accelerates the preparation of responses and allows the professional to focus on crafting the most persuasive legal and technical arguments (Chu et al., 2024). For portfolio management, GenAI enhances analysis by moving beyond keyword or classification-based clustering. It can perform context-aware classification, grouping patents into custom, conceptually coherent taxonomies based on the technology they describe. The integration of patent data with external sources like market reports makes it possible for the GenAI to assist in valuation and provide predictive analytics, enabling more strategic decisions about which patents to maintain, license, or abandon.

Monitoring, Enforcement and Commercialization

To leverage a patent, GenAI powers intelligent monitoring services that provide more relevant alerts on new patent filings by understanding their conceptual substance. This same understanding improves Freedom-to-Operate (FTO) analysis by identifying potentially blocking patents even if they use different language. For enforcement and licensing, GenAI can scan product websites and technical manuals to identify potential infringement and automate the initial creation of evidence-of-use or claim charts. This systematically compares a patent's claims against a product's features, providing a data-driven foundation for licensing negotiations or litigation and significantly increasing the potential for monetization. The application of GenAI across these stages creates a "digital thread," allowing data and context to flow seamlessly from invention disclosure to commercialization, fostering a more holistic and strategic approach to IP management (Mangubat et al., 2025).

Strategic and Ethical Frontiers

The integration of GenAI forces a confrontation with foundational legal principles, introduces significant operational risks, and reshapes the role of the IP professional. The core challenge is one of professional responsibility, as the tenets of confidentiality, accuracy, and human accountability are tested by the nature of current AI models.

The Human–AI Inventorship Dilemma

The most profound legal challenge concerns the personhood of the inventor. Patent law globally is founded on the principle that an inventor must be a natural person. This was affirmed in the USA in *Thaler v. Vidal*, where the U.S. Court of Appeals for the Federal Circuit ruled that the Patent Act interpreted an "inventor" to be a natural person. Similar rulings from the European Patent Office (EPO), the United Kingdom, and Australia have established a strong international consensus against non-human inventors (Chimuka, 2019; see Chap. 7).

In response, patent offices have issued guidance clarifying the boundary between permissible AI assistance and impermissible AI generation (Yakubovich & Wu, 2025). The USPTO's 2024 Inventorship Guidance established a "significant human contribution" test. Applying factors from *Pannu v. Iolab Corp.*, (Aboy et al., 2025), the guidance states that a human must contribute significantly to the conception of the invention; merely presenting a problem to an AI is insufficient. The EPO treats AI-related inventions as "computer-implemented inventions," which are patentable only if they provide a "technical effect." This guidance provides a temporary framework but leaves critical questions unanswered. In sum, AI models are challenging the traditional concept of inventorship, as they become more autonomous, and as the line between a human "significantly contributing" and merely directing a more capable AI blurs.

Confidentiality, Hallucinations and Bias

The use of GenAI introduces severe practical risks. The duty of confidentiality is paramount, as any non-confidential disclosure of an invention before filing can forfeit patent rights. Using public-facing GenAI tools whose terms permit user inputs for model training could be deemed a public disclosure, creating an unacceptable risk. Mitigation requires using AI platforms with contractual guarantees of data security, such as zero-data-retention policies, or deploying private, on-premise models.

A second major risk is accuracy. LLMs are probabilistic systems that can "hallucinate"—generating fluent, confident, and entirely false information, such as inventing non-existent legal cases or fabricating technical data. Relying on such output without rigorous verification constitutes a breach of the professional duties of competence and candor to the patent office (Warraich et al., 2025). This underscores the non-negotiable necessity of maintaining a "human-in-the-loop" to fact-check and assume responsibility for all work product. Finally, the risk of bias exists, as models trained on historical data may learn and amplify existing biases related to gender, geography, or technology, an ethical concern the profession must actively address.

The Evolving Role of the IP Professional

GenAI will not render patent professionals obsolete but will fundamentally reshape their work. The value proposition is shifting from the performance of routine tasks to the exercise of high-level strategic judgment. As AI automates initial searches and the drafting of boilerplate text, the professional's value will increasingly lie in providing strategic advice, developing sophisticated litigation strategies, and exercising nuanced legal judgment.

To thrive, professionals must cultivate new skills. These include strategic advisory, leveraging AI-driven analytics to offer deeper insights; AI tool mastery, including the art of "prompt engineering" to elicit optimal outputs; and critical validation, serving as the final arbiter of quality and integrity for all AI-assisted work. This technological shift also challenges the traditional billable hour model. The efficiencies gained from AI create a disincentive for hourly billing, likely accelerating the move toward alternative fee arrangements like fixed fees or value-based pricing that reward outcomes over time spent.

Takeaways GenAI in Patent Management

The integration of Generative AI into patent management introduces fundamental changes to professional roles, operational risks, and strategic decision-making.

- GenAI transforms the IP professional's role from a performer of routine tasks to a strategic validator and director of AI-powered tools, which demands new skills in prompt engineering and critical oversight.

(continued)

(continued)

- The technology offers tangible efficiencies across the entire patent life cycle, from automating invention disclosures and enhancing prior art searches to drafting initial applications and identifying infringement.
- A critical legal friction point remains, as global patent law requires a "natural person" as an inventor, a standard that current guidance addresses by mandating a "significant human contribution" to the invention's conception.
- The use of GenAI carries non-negotiable risks of confidentiality breaches, factual "hallucinations," and algorithmic bias, which make rigorous human-in-the-loop verification an absolute professional necessity.

5.6 Blockchain and DLTs in Patent Management

Society often needs a canonical record of ownership, legal, and administrative transactions. In the past, this function has typically been assumed by a trusted party, such as a (central) bank or governmental land registry. In that system, each change in status or ownership is recorded and executed by the trusted party, who maintains all those canonical records. The advantage of this system is that it is not technically complex—land registries still keep simple paper records in some parts of the world. There is no external validation required and transactions can happen very quickly as soon as the registry or trusted party makes a change in the ledger. This trusted party system has been the only real practical one until recent technological developments.

Cheap computational power and software have made distributed ledgers feasible. *Distributed Ledger Technologies (DLTs)* are typically databases where multiple participants have access to the records in their respective locations. They distinguish themselves from centralized ledgers in that each participant has a copy of the records or a unique hash of the records. All participants can typically view all the records and observe all of the changes made to the registry. Those same agents also act as guarantors of the registry integrity through cryptographic or chain of custody algorithms. Currently, there are many technologies vying for a place in our collective distributed ledger future. The "blockchain" is just one subtype of a distributed ledger system. Figure 5.11 presents a synopsis of some of the key features of new DLTs.

DLT is not explained in detail here, but its implications for IP, which are many, are explored. In the field of IP, WIPO has recognized the huge potential of this technology and hosted a 2-day conference in 2019 to scan the horizon and explore the meaning of the technology for intellectual property. DLT has already made inroads in the music industry where projects like *Audius* or *Ujo Music* track usage and payments using distributed leger technologies; the latter runs on the Ethereum network and integrating crypto micropayments. While the issues and industries are different, it stands to reason that DLT could be used to manage patents, trademarks, and designs.

	Blockchain	Directed Acyclical Graph (DAG)	Hashgraph	Holograph
Mining	Consensus token creation	Proof of work to send data	Consensus through virtual voting	Variable distributed hash table
Speed/capacity	Limited throughput and volume	Theoretically speed of light	Limited to bandwidth	Limited to computation on subchains
Data	Chained in blocks confirmed by miners	"TANGLE" with sharing with hashed integrity	Shared graph structure	Agents' hold their own hash chain
Validation	Chain with blocks confirmed by miners	Previous transaction validates next	Gossip about data network	"DNA", gossip, private key
Example	bitcoin	IOTA	Hedera Hashgraph	HOLOCHAIN

Fig. 5.11 Examples of distributed ledger technologies (authors' own figure)

In this section, there is a look first at DLT as the object of IP, then at how it might be used to secure innovation, and lastly, at how it might be used to fundamentally alter the fabric of global patent administration and marketplace.

Blockchain as the Object of IP

The most obvious intersection of blockchain and intellectual property is the patenting of blockchain and DLT itself. Starting in 2013, blockchain and distributed ledger patents started to appear in the patent record; there are currently about 2500 of these patent families published already, of which about 500 have been granted thus far. Many of the usual suspects, *Goldman Sachs*, *Qualcomm*, and *Intel*, are among the assignees of these patents. In the face of this growth in patenting and the novelty of the technology, there have been a number of mediocre legal articles written on the patentability and legal implications of the blockchain.

But, at its core, the blockchain and DLT are really software with a source code base like any other program; it defines a protocol. As such, it is software and is protected by copyright. There is no mystery about the patentability of such a technology: The same rules that apply to software and business methods apply to these patents, which are discussed below (see Sect. 7.4).

The practical bottom line with blockchain patents has been that patenting the technology is often at fundamental odds with free use of the technology (Yanisky-Ravid & Kim, 2019). Since the economic and social values of a network are proportional to the number of nodes connected to it, DLT in most cases benefits from more devices and agents using the network and system. Before any commercial players will use a system, they often need assurance that they will not be subject to licensing fees or lawsuits. Hence, free use is often required to achieve the network effects that enable widespread use, which DLT often aims to achieve. For this and ideological reasons, most of the major DLT projects are open-source projects or controlled by public foundations. Propriety blockchain systems, offered by *IBM* or *Amazon*, resemble much more traditional software as a service business model—even if they rely on blockchain or DLT.

Using Blockchain to Secure Innovation

Perhaps more exciting than blockchain as the object of IP is the fact that it can be used as a guarantor or compliment to IP. According to the European Observatory on Infringements of Intellectual Property Rights (EUIPO, 2018), losses to counterfeiting are at least on the order of US$30 billion annually. Hence, one idea, elucidated in Clark and Burstall (2018), is the use of blockchain technology to prevent counterfeiting drugs in the pharmaceutical industry; their argument is that packaging and coding can be immutably etched into the blockchain. At each stage in the supply chain, certified actors can register events in the blockchain—for example, when the pharmaceutical compound leaves the production facility to be packaged, the packager can certify the chain of custody and record her own reception into her packaging facility. Similarly, when the drug leaves the packaging facility and goes to the shipper another entry in the blockchain could be made. Analogously, when the package is indeed received from the other recipient, the shipper records her own entry, and thus the supply chain continues via distributors and pharmacies. This record for chain of custody would go all the way to the consumer, who could in theory read all the events in the blockchain. Since all the events are recorded, counterfeit drugs introduced into the supply chains by unscrupulous distributors, and thereby not part of such a system, would be left out in the cold. Aside from the revenue losses, expiration and batch information may allow public health officials to take action and prevent bad drugs from entering the supply.

As of February 2019, Europe has addressed this issue with a unique identifier (a two-dimension barcode) and anti-tampering device requirements for authorized drugs. Naturally, this territorial solution is not necessarily the first-best technological or global regulatory design, but blockchain was only in its infancy when the original 2011 directives came out. Currently, the blockchain is unlikely to make many inroads to protect pharmaceuticals due to the heavily regulated nature of the industry. Moreover, the amount of money at stake has meant that pharma spends about US$100–165 million per year lobbying both the U.S. Congress and the EU to press governments and international organizations to expend public resources to enforce its private intellectual property, which seems like a bargain when perhaps up to US$100 billion annually in global counterfeit medication is at stake. Estimates vary, but various transparency watchdog groups, like reports that the U.S. Congress receives anywhere from 100 to 200 million a year depending on the election cycle and legislative docket. Amounts spent lobbying the EU for action are on a similar order of magnitude. According to the EU transparency register, *Bayer*, a major pharmaceutical manufacturer, has spent ~6.2 million euros lobbying in Brussels (LobbyFacts, 2025). According to *OpenSecrets*, the spend hit a whopping US$272 million a year where "Lobbying efforts focus on the patent system, research funding and Medicare" (opensecrets.org).

Despite the predominance of traditional protection mechanisms (border enforcement, police action and interdiction, and lawsuits) in pharma, blockchain still could play a vital, engaging, and interesting role for certain innovative products. For example, a luxury brand with an innovative product or design might use the blockchain in the same manner to protect the authenticity of a product and the embedded design patent, while, say, showing the chain of fine materials or artisanal manufacturers used to produce it. More mundane but essential products, like patented spare parts, could be tracked and validated analogously, along with their service history; this might guarantee the quality and service while protecting the intellectual property at the same time. Thus, in sum, distributed ledger technologies hold out both the promise of intellectual property protection and the potential of creating customer value. A hallmark of great IP management appropriates value to the innovator while creating an added-value proposition for the customer. Our faith in this strategy stems not just from it being good business practice, but from its ability to create a decentralized and vested interest in the end user to help enforce the IP and lessen demand for infringing products, as was seen with *Bayer's* seed technology.

Beyond patents and physical goods, there are some postulated uses of blockchain for copyright, which are in a similar vein as patent protection. The *Society of Music Authors, Composers, and Publishers (Sacem)* and *IBM* have been working together to track and capture creators' rights using DLT and the hyper ledger (Sacem, 2019). DLT lends itself well to micro-rights and micro-residual payments, and the platform holds out the possibility to gather additional intelligence on users.

Beyond these more immediate uses, the blockchain is also being hypothesized as a way of tracking micropayments to photographers or graphical artists. Perhaps even more radical is using the technology of recording who had an innovative idea to determine prior art or ownership in collaborative pools across organizational boundaries. While the threshold to obtain a patent is quite high, by lowering the barriers to an IP system, it may be possible to better record and trace inventorship using DLT and blockchain.

Blockchain as the Solution to IP

This brings us to our final and perhaps most salient and realistic use of DLT for IP, which is the embryonic effort to deploy the technology as a way of publishing and recording administrative procedures. The following is a decision flow chart published by the *US National Institute of Standards and Technology's (NIST)* white paper for the use of Blockchain Technology Overview (Yaga et al., 2018), an oft-cited good technical reference on this new technology.

In the following, the *NIST* template is used to structure and to understand the patent office's decision to explore the use of blockchain—and to provide a decent managerial checklist (see Fig. 5.12):

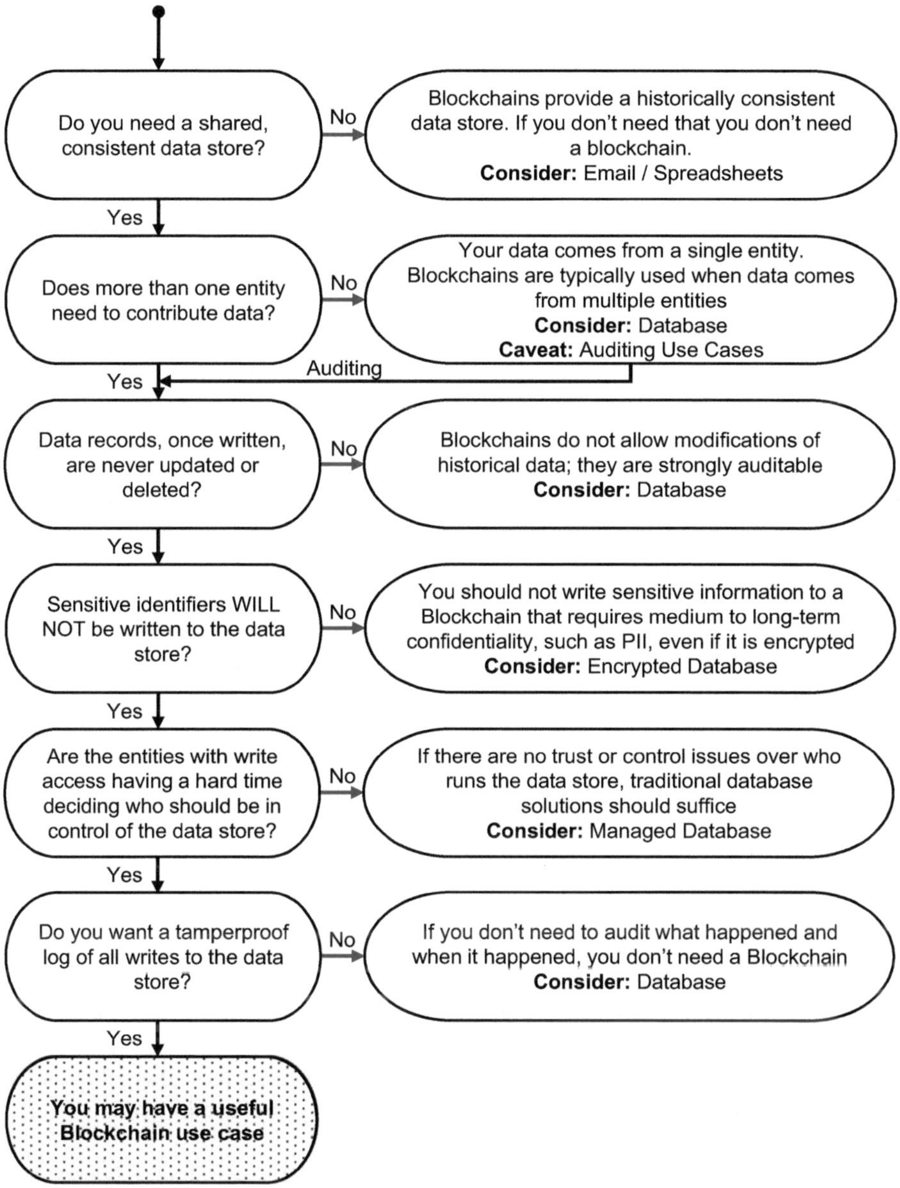

Fig. 5.12 Flowchart for deciding whether the use of blockchain is appropriate (Yaga et al., 2018)

1. Are sharing and consistency necessary? There is a need for a consistent and shared data store. Intellectual property (IP) records have to be consistent to understand ownership, and all economic agents in the system need to have easy access to that datastore in order to make informed decisions.
2. Are there multiple authors? Whether more than one entity needs to contribute is a bit questionable. In terms of patents, courts occasionally issue invalidity rul-

ings—these are then passed to the patent office that registers the events. Banks will occasionally put liens on patents, which again would require an office to show that the property is collateral.

3. Is record modification required? Patents and their registry events are never deleted. In this sense, the blockchain is very appropriate. While we have seen that schlepping the entire transaction history has prevented blockchain from becoming a truly viable solution for payment systems, this indelible history is very appropriate for legal events and entitlement, which are integral to how the patent system operates.
4. Does it involve sensitive information? With the exception of some classified military technologies, most, if not all, of the patent record is and/or should be publicly available. In this sense, there are few, if any, sensitive identifiers in the patent record.
5. Are there control issues? In general, IP and patent offices around the globe are trustworthy institutions. They tend to be outside of the main political fray and are staffed with highly specialized technical and legal personnel. There is not necessarily a trust or control issue in this sense, and this is perhaps one reason why IP offices have not had to cede control over their own data.
6. Is auditing required? There is not a massive need to audit IP registry data. Some IP offices have been keeping records longer than even land registries. There has been no great concern about the integrity of the registry entries, thus obviating one of the major benefits of blockchain technology.

Those last two dubious reasons notwithstanding, after making this type of assessment, the WIPO and some offices, notably Russia and the Australian patent office, *IPAustralia*, are pushing ahead with DLT. The Russians are making good use of their famed cyber skills and have already set up the *IPchain*, a consortium of Russian governmental agencies, that maintains a prototype system. *Rospatent* has been experimenting with a patent record that is mirrored in the blockchain. The idea is that applications would be recorded, along with grant and examination data, which would then subsequently enable commerce to take place on the backend of the process. The country has had a blockchain gazette service for patents since October of 2019 and a prototype for IP management of trademarks since November of 2018. The Russian *IPchain* is built on the hyper ledger.[4] Russia has moved quickly on the legal front with the Russian IP court also supporting the administration's foray into DLT.

While Russia has moved ahead on the technical side, IPAustralia has been working, as coleader of the *CWS Blockchain Task Force*, to map the needs of WIPO members. IPAustralia is also working to develop a common vernacular to discuss the issue and is spearheading the effort to achieve a standard around which the Russians can build the technological platform.

[4] https://www.hyperledger.org. This effort is part of a broader Russian initiative to advance blockchain technologies, spearheaded by the *IPchain Association* (https://ipchain.global/association/). This system can be accessed using the blockchain node at peer-1.ipchain.ipchain.ru (specialized software required).

There is absolutely no reason that such a comprehensive solution need be privately run. In theory, there could be some enabling legislation that would allow the patent system to be moved to the "chain" without a supervisionary patent office, but whether that could get off the ground without serious coordination and backing is dubious.

Since the Russian initiative began, the EUIPO has linked its *TMView* (trademark search) and *DesignView* (design search) platforms using blockchain technology in 2021. Since 2023, the EUIPO has had a new initiative, *EBSI-ELSA*, which integrates information from IP-rights holders, customs, and IP offices on chain using blockchain technology with the ultimate goal of combating counterfeit products in the supply chain (European Commission, 2025). As of 2025, this program has not been implemented at scale.

Example—IPWe: AI and Blockchain Help Discover and Transact IP

Aside from these public initiatives, one privately run technology based on DLT comes from *IPwe* (see Fig. 5.13). Their platform is based on *IBM's* Hyperledger blockchain technology (Alpana Ventures, 2021). They aim to drastically lower the cost of patent transactions. One of the main differences between patents and

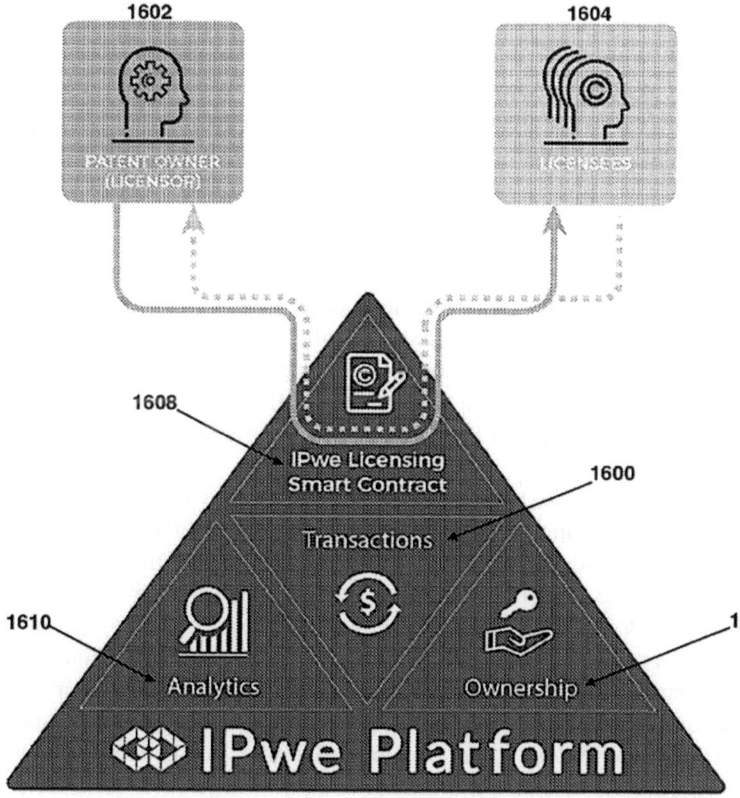

Fig. 5.13 IPwe: System and method for a decentralized innovation platform driven by proprietary artificial intelligence and blockchain technologies (US 2023/230185 A1)

other assets is that the price and contractual terms of intellectual property sales and licenses change depending on the buyer and licensee, as there are often balance-of-power considerations (IBM, 2021).

IPwe's technology not only facilitates transactions but also offers the possibility of providing a collective legal shield. Patent owners on the platform can instantaneously summon a massive patent portfolio to deter legal aggressors. This would certainly alter the balance of power in the patent space, especially if any agent in the system, through the use of AI and smart contracts, could dynamically summon a massive IP shield in response to litigation, possibly deterring patent trolls.

Since ownership is tracked, inventors can also pledge patents quickly and legally through special-purpose vehicles traced by the chain. This would also possibly solve another one of the liquidity issues of patents in that, as an inventor, there is a lengthy search process to find investors and/or lenders to finance inventions, and once found, there are still complicated legal arrangements to fix mutually agreeable terms. The cost of all this prohibits transacting in all but the most valuable inventions. With IPwe's technology, each license could be securely recorded, and payments automated via smart contracts. This would enable complete and efficient controlling and due diligence of such assets by, say, tax authorities.

Making patents more liquid, administratively tractable, and transparent is undoubtedly in the economic interest of the public. Whether this is in the economic interest of the major actors in the patent space, who also essentially dictate the political economy of patent policy, remains to be seen. ◀

Takeaways Blockchain and DLTs

- *Challenging the Status Quo:* Blockchain is a type of Distributed Ledger Technology (DLT) that functions as a decentralized, shared database. It challenges the need for traditional, centralized trusted parties (like banks or registries) by creating an immutable record of transactions.
- *A Dual Role in IP:* DLT has a dual role in the IP world. It can be the object of IP itself (e.g., patented blockchain methods), and it can be a tool for securing other IP rights.
- *The Patenting Paradox:* While blockchain technology can be patented like other software, doing so often conflicts with the open-source ethos that helps build the widespread network effects necessary for the technology to be valuable. The underlying code is also protectable by copyright.
- *A Tool for Protection:* DLT can be used to create a secure, immutable record of a product's chain of custody, helping to combat the counterfeiting of pharmaceuticals, luxury goods, or patented parts. It also offers a way to manage digital copyrights and automate micropayments to creators.
- *Transforming IP Administration:* Global IP bodies and national offices are exploring DLT to create a more transparent and efficient system for publishing and recording administrative IP procedures.

(continued)

(continued)

- *Digital Rights Management:* Blockchain can create fast immutable records of ownership, with fast decentralized verification of rights. Smart contracts can automate payments or permit complex revenue sharing arrangements at the transaction level.
- *The Future Marketplace:* Private platforms are already leveraging DLT and AI to create new marketplaces for IP. The goal is to make patents more liquid, lower transaction costs, and provide tools to deter patent trolls, ultimately making IP assets easier to finance and trade.

References

Aboy, M., Liddell, K., & Lath, A. (2025). Inventorship in the age of AI: Examining the USPTO guidance on AI-assisted inventions. *Journal of Intellectual Property Law and Practice, 20*(7), 495–502. https://doi.org/10.1093/jiplp/jpaf019

Alpana Ventures. (2021). *IBM and IPwe team up to disrupt the patent ecosystem with blockchain and AI.* Alpana Ventures. Accessed July 16, 2025, from https://alpana-ventures.ch/ibm-ans-ipwe-team-up-to-disrupt-the-patent-ecosystem-with-blockchain-and-ai/

Ashrafi, A., Constantinides, P., Mehandjiev, N., & Thatcher, J. B. (2024). Mobilising new frontiers in digital transformation research: A problematization review. *Information Systems Journal, 35*(1), 97–139. https://doi.org/10.1111/isj.12531

Bader, M. A., & Mohr, C. A. (2025). Patentanwalt und Patentmanager – zwei Rollen im Wandel der Zeit. In U. Fitzner (Ed.), *Festschrift zum 125-jährigen Bestehen des Patentanwaltsberufs* (pp. 131–152).

Chang, Y., Wang, X., Wang, J., Wu, Y., Yang, L., Zhu, K., Chen, H., Yi, X., Wang, C., Wang, Y., Ye, W., Zhang, Y., Chang, Y., Yu, P. S., Yang, Q., & Xie, X. (2024). A survey on evaluation of large language models. *Acm Transactions on Intelligent Systems and Technology, 15*(3), 39. https://doi.org/10.1145/3641289

Chimuka, G. (2019). Impact of artificial intelligence on patent law. Towards a new analytical framework—[the multi-level model]. *World Patent Information, 59*, 101926. https://doi.org/10.1016/j.wpi.2019.101926

Chu, J., Lo, H., Hsiang, J., & Cho, C. (2024). From Paris to le-Paris: Toward patent response automation with recommender systems and collaborative large language models. *Artificial Intelligence and Law.* https://doi.org/10.1007/s10506-024-09409-7

Clark, B., & Burstall, R. (2018). Blockchain, IP and the pharma industry—How distributed ledger technologies can help secure the pharma supply chain. *Journal of Intellectual Property Law and Practice, 13*(7), 531–533.

Coase, R. H. (1937). The nature of the firm. *Economica, 4*(16), 386–405.

Engberg, E., Koch, M., Lodefalk, M., & Schroeder, S. (2025). Artificial intelligence, tasks, skills, and wages: Worker-level evidence from Germany. *Research Policy, 54*(8), 105285. https://doi.org/10.1016/j.respol.2025.105285

EPO. (2024). *Services and activities – Quality – Statistics – Examination.* Retrieved July 30, 2025, from https://www.epo.org/en/about-us/services-and-activities/quality/statistics/examination

EUIPO. (2018). *2017 situation report on counterfeiting and piracy in the European Union.* European observatory on infringements of intellectual property rights. Accessed July 7, 2025, from https://euipo.europa.eu/ohimportal/en/web/observatory/observatory-publications

European Commission. (2025). *The European Union Intellectual Property Office (EUIPO) and European Blockchain Services Infrastructure (EBSI) have joined forces to undertake the EBSI-ELSA project*. European Commission. Retrieved August 20, 2025, from https://ec.europa.eu/digital-building-blocks/sites/display/EBSI/EBSI-ELSA+EUIPO

Five IP Offices. (2024). *IP5 statistics reports 2023 edition*. Edited by Korean Intellectual Property Office, Nov 2024. Retrieved July 30, 2025, from https://link.epo.org/ip5_2023_Stats_Final_pdf

Garcia, M. B., Rosak-Szyrocka, J., & Bozkurt, A. (Eds.). (2025). *Pitfalls of AI integration in education: skill obsolescence, misuse, and bias: Skill obsolescence, misuse, and bias*. IGI Global. https://doi.org/10.4018/979-8-3373-0122-8

IBM. (2021). *IPwe creates world's first blockchain-powered patent platform*. IBM Corporation. Retrieved July 16, 2025, from https://www.ibm.com/case-studies/ipwe

LobbyFacts. (2025). *LobbyControl*. Corporate Europe Observatory & LobbyControl. Retrieved August 8, 2025, from https://lobbyfacts.eu/datacard/lobbycontrol?rid=6314918394-16

Loebbert, M. (2000). Interne Dienstleister: Was sie alles können müssen. *Harvard Business Manager, 3*, 49–57.

Mangubat, J. C., Mangubat, M. R., Uy, T. B. L., Acut, D. P., & Garcia, M. B. (2025). Safeguarding educational innovations amid AI disruptions: A reassessment of patenting for sustained intellectual property prote. *Pitfalls of AI Integration in Education Skill Obsolescence Misuse And Bias, 297–318*. https://doi.org/10.4018/979-8-3373-0122-8.ch013

Moeller, A., & Moehrle, M. G. (2015). Completing keyword patent search with semantic patent search: Introducing a semiautomatic iterative method for patent near search based on semantic similarities. *Scientometrics, 102*(1), 77–96. https://doi.org/10.1007/s11192-014-1446-9

Obschonka, M., Grégoire, D. A., Nikolaev, B., Ooms, F., Lévesque, M., Pollack, J. M., & Behrend, T. S. (2024). Artificial intelligence and entrepreneurship: A call for research to prospect and establish the scholarly ai frontiers. *Entrepreneurship Theory And Practice, 49*(3), 620–641. https://doi.org/10.1177/10422587241304676

Sacem. (2019). *Ascap, Sacem, and PRS for music initiate blockchain project to improve data accuracy for rightsholders*, press release dated 2019-03-12.

Thommen, J.-P., Achleitner, A.-K., Gilbert, D. U., Hachmeister, D., & Kaiser, G. (2023). *Allgemeine Betriebswirtschaftslehre* (10th ed.). Springer Gabler.

Tseng, Y., Lin, C., & Lin, Y. (2007). Text mining techniques for patent analysis. *Information Processing And Management, 43*(5), 1216–1247. https://doi.org/10.1016/j.ipm.2006.11.011

Warraich, M. K. S., Usman, H., Zakir, S., & Mehboob, M. (2025). Ethical governance of artificial intelligence Hallucinations in legal practice. *Social Sciences Spectrum, 4*(2), 603–615. https://doi.org/10.71085/sss.04.02.297

WIPO. (2017). *Patent office operations: Application processing times, examination capacity and examination outcomes*. World Intellectual Property Indicators 2017. WIPO. Retrieved July 1, 2025, from https://www.wipo.int/edocs/pubdocs/en/wipo_pub_941_2017-chapter1.pdf

Yaga, D., Mell, P., Roby, N., & Scarfoneet, K. (2018). *Blockchain technology overview*. National Institute of Standards and Technology, U.S. Department of Commerce. https://doi.org/10.6028/NIST.IR.8202

Yakubovich, V., & Wu, S. (2025). Orgtech: Evidence of organizational innovations in patent data. *Research Policy, 54*(5), 105209. https://doi.org/10.1016/j.respol.2025.105209

Patent Management by Industry

6

The effect of patents is strongly sector-dependent. Some industry-specific aspects of patent management are presented and discussed below.

We here give an overview of the following industry sectors, highlighting case study examples on specific aspects of patent management:

1. Pharma
2. Chemistry
3. Crop Science
4. Life Sciences
5. Consumer Goods
6. Retail
7. Machinery
8. Electronics and Electrical Equipment
9. Automotive and Connectivity
10. Information and Communication Technology
11. Financial Services and Fintech
12. Transport and Logistics

6.1 Pharma

In the pharmaceutical and chemical industries as well as in the biotechnology sector, patents grant an effective monopoly on the active ingredients and products to be protected (Gassmann et al., 2016, 2018). In the pharmaceutical industry, in particular, products are essentially entirely dependent on patent protection. Revenues from the so-called blockbuster products with sales of more than US$1 billion each and an average annual sales growth of more than 20% can usually only be achieved with patent protection. The entire generics market is based on bioequivalent products for

M. A. Bader et al., *Patent Management*, Management for Professionals,
https://doi.org/10.1007/978-3-032-12030-4_6

which patent protection has expired. In extreme cases, generic products can cause sales losses of more than 50% in the first few months after patent protection expires. Pharmaceutical companies are vulnerable to sales losses when blockbuster drugs come off patent. For example, major companies like *Pfizer* (Lipitor), *AbbVie* (Humira), *GlaxoSmithKline* (Advair), *Johnson and Johnson* (Remicade), *AstraZeneca Bristol-Myers Squibb* (>40%), *Eli Lilly* (>40%), *Schering-Plough* (>50%), *Amgen* (>60%), *TAP* (>90%), or *Novo Nordisk* (>50%) have faced this challenge.

It is therefore a major challenge in the pharmaceutical industry to protect sales of successful products from rapid price erosion, to replace them with replacement products, and to operate proactively in patent management (see Fig. 6.1). Due to the time it takes to approve a drug, pharmaceutical patents enjoy special extensions, and companies derive value through:

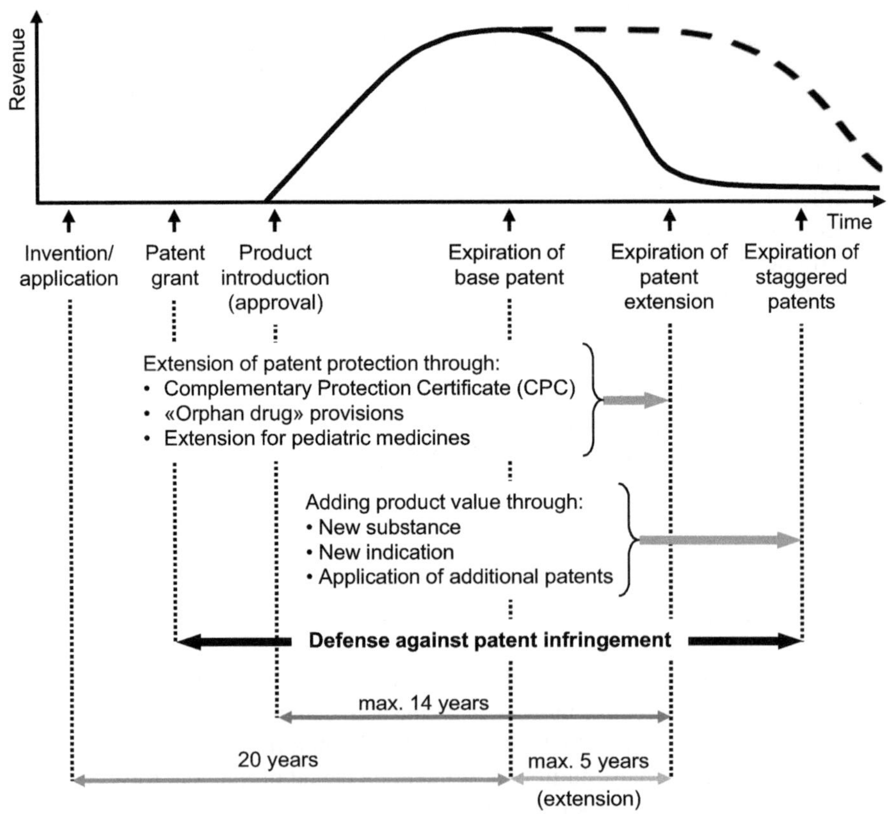

Fig. 6.1 Patent protection extension strategy in pharma (Gassmann & Bader, 2024)

- Supplementary protection certificates for drugs for a maximum of 5 years;
- So-called orphan drug provisions for niche drugs with an additional protection of 7 years in the USA, and a maximum of 10 years in the EU;
- Extension of protection for pediatric medicines for 6 months in the USA and Europe;
- Continuous increase in product value through new active ingredients and new indications;
- Aggressive defense of intellectual property rights against patent infringers;
- Securing sales after expiration of patent protection by changing the drug status to an OTC drug or introducing a generic brand; and
- Reduction of dependence on key products through investments in the life cycle and portfolio management, licensing to third parties, and mergers and acquisitions.

Example—Bristol-Myers Squibb vs. Gilead Sciences

Pharma is an industry where patents add a large amount of value. Society is willing to pay huge amounts in the effort to save and maintain life, and pharma meets that basic demand. In a recent court case, a Los Angelean jury found that *Gilead's Yescarta* (axicabtagene ciloleucel) cancer treatment had violated *Bristol-Myer's* licensed patent. Bristol-Myers was awarded US$752 million in damages plus a 27.6% royalty on all future sales of Gilead's Yescarta. The technology licensed from the *Kettering Cancer Center* in New York is both novel and powerful since it reprograms the patients' immunological T cells to attack the cancer. Gilead asserted that "Given that *Kite* independently developed Yescarta and took all the risk in its discovery and development, we do not believe *Sloan Kettering* and *Juno* are entitled to any level of damages" (Wolfe, 2019). ◀

Takeaways Pharma

- The productivity paradox in pharma is becoming more pronounced (Gassmann et al., 2018): Only one out of 10,000 substances tested preclinically becomes a marketed product.
- The overall R&D pipeline output is low at the average.
- Lower risk tolerance of both regulators and society contributes negatively to new molecular entities.
- The pressure to commercialize the R&D investment increases as clinical studies become larger and more complex and drug discovery technologies more expensive.
- Time that is available to monetize patents gets shortened, since the innovation process slows down.
- Time delays are caused by licensing, co-development, and joint venture negotiations. These processes must be accelerated.
- The imperative for blockbusters (1-billion-dollar drugs) increases the importance of single patents.

(continued)

(continued)

- New technologies such as artificial intelligence are starting to play a strategic role in the pharma industry.
- New entrants in the healthcare sector are often data-based companies, e.g., wearables from consumer electronics.
- Regulators play a crucial role in the value of innovation and patents: new product registration, R&D experiment regulations, price regulations, health care financing laws, but also patent protection policies in developing countries.

6.2 Chemistry

In the chemical industry, the rule is, "Whoever has the formula has the power." With regard to the handling of patents, licensing, and market structures in the chemical industry, patents are used in conjunction with other instruments, such as secrecy. This applies in particular to process innovations. Depending on the underlying field of knowledge, attempts are made to cover entire fields of technology with patent clusters. License agreements are often part of technology packages. In general, companies in the chemical industry are increasingly willing to license their products and technologies.

An important driver for technology exploitation is the commercial usability by third parties. Technologies, products, or even business models are licensed as the degree of maturity increases and the business risk decreases. A typical challenge, however, is the valuation of IP and know-how, which can lead to the licensor demanding an excessive license fee. As a result, the licensee's market success is jeopardized due to high market prices and too low contribution margins. There is thus a risk of losing potential profits for both the licensee and the licensor. In order to maximize profits, the licensor and licensee may therefore at least strive to optimize the contribution margin jointly. While for mature products a realistic net present value risk assessment distribution for licensor and licensee is often 60%–40%, for immature or untested products, a risk value of 30% is more appropriate for the licensee.

Example—Covestro

Covestro was formed in September 2015 from *Bayer MaterialScience*. Bayer announced its intention to divest Covestro and float the polymer division on the stock exchange in early 2016 to focus exclusively on the life science businesses. In the 2019 fiscal year, Covestro had sales of 12.4 billion euros and employed about 17,200 people at about 30 sites worldwide. Its main competitors are: *Dow Chemical*, *GE Plastics/Sabic*, *BASF*, *Huntsman,* and *Wanhua*.

Covestro had a portfolio of about 2500 patent families with about 12,900 patent family members (2019). In 2019, about 290 new patent applications were filed. The initial applications are usually at first made in Germany, the USA, or

China and are filed for disclosure and protection purposes. Subsequent applications are made abroad after careful consideration. Opposition is used where appropriate.

Covestro has set itself the goal of exploiting its own technologies. The company's earnings are to be further increased through intangible assets. As a prerequisite for this, valuable technologies are protected by legal rights. To achieve this and enable optimum exploitation, intangible assets, i.e., patents and know-how, are managed in a similar way to property, plant, and equipment:

- Targeted development of intellectual assets within the framework of risk-assessed R&D projects;
- Professional patent portfolio management;
- Prevention of misuse by third parties; and
- Consistent enforcement of own prohibition rights.

A patent committee has been set up for each field of technology, comprising: IP Department, R&D, marketing, and process and technology. Regular meetings of the patent committee form the basis for coordinated decisions concerning intellectual property. For IP asset management, Covestro involves the IP Department, R&D, process, and technology as well as marketing.

R&D projects are evaluated at Covestro on a regular basis. As part of the innovation and R&D process, intellectual-property-related aspects are taken into account at every milestone based on a stage-gate philosophy: from idea generation to product release. Technology is handled as an important asset class at Covestro. Technology exploitation can thus begin well before a product is even marketed. Covestro has even a special division for asset exploitation such as in—and out-licensing. Covestro mainly uses direct marketing to exploit its technologies. Though the direct sale of know-how and IP is not part of Covestro's core business, its importance is increasing significantly. Very valuable are technology partnerships, which often result in mutual technology licensing. In addition, with a specialized litigation function, Covestro takes consistent action against patent infringers, where considerable difficulties exist with piracy from the Asia-Pacific region. ◀

Takeaways Covestro

- IP department reflecting business units in substructures with group-wide governance.
- Interdisciplinary patent committees with decision-makers for each technology area.
- IP processes attuned to the R&D processes.
- Use of R&D cooperation and technology partnerships to generate and exploit IP.

6.3 Crop Science

Plant varieties produced by traditional methods are not patentable. In the case of a patent for corn with an increased oil content, the patent was revoked on the basis of this rule. The patent filed by *DuPont* with the European Patent Office in 1995 covered corn grains with an increased oil content, the oil obtained from these corn grains, and the use of the oil in foodstuffs. The maize was obtained from a cross between two different maize varieties, one of which had been chemically modified (mutated). *Greenpeace*, the Episcopal relief organization *Misereor,* and the government of Mexico have challenged the patent. The patent was rejected, among other things, because the maize was considered bred and therefore not patentable. If the company had achieved the same result with a genetic engineering process, the patent would probably have been granted.

In Europe, patent number EP 546 090 covers a genetically engineered type of soy: The US company *Monsanto* is the owner of a transgenic soy variety that is resistant to the herbicide *Roundup*, which is also approved in Switzerland in food and animal feed. With this patent, Monsanto not only has exclusive rights to use for all genetically modified soy varieties that are resistant to herbicide Roundup but also to all genetically modified plants containing artificially induced "Roundup-Ready" resistance, such as wheat, rice, soy, cotton, sugar beet, rapeseed, flax, sunflower, potato, tobacco, tomato, alfalfa, poplar, pineapple, apple, and grape. The patent also extends to all subsequent plant generations. In the USA and Canada, farmers who reuse patented seeds from their last crop for sowing are prosecuted by Monsanto.

After the So-Called Broccoli/Tomato Rulings on Breeding Methods for Plants[1]
Practice before the European Patent Office (EPO): Processes of production of plants or animals that contain one or more steps of sexually crossing whole genomes are excluded from patentability. But, genetic engineering methods for introducing new traits into plants or animals are not excluded from patentability.

[1] EPO (2019) on the patentability of (essentially) biological processes:

EP 1 069 819 (G 2/07, "Broccoli"): Method for production of *Brassica o.*, comprising steps of crossing and selection, wherein molecular markers are used to identify desired hybrids, and claims to plants per se;

EP 1 211 926 (G 1/08, "Wrinkled tomato"): Method for breeding tomato plants that produce tomatoes with reduced fruit water content, comprising crossing and selection steps, followed by allowing fruit to remain on the vine until it is partially dried... and claims to plants per se.

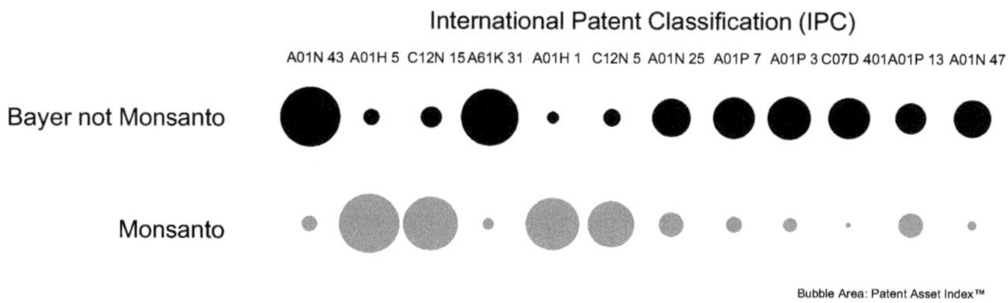

Fig. 6.2 Technology matrix *Bayer–Monsanto* (based on IPI/PatentSight, 2020)

Example—Monsanto Canada

Bayer acquired *Monsanto* in 2016 to complement its crop science technologies and business. As a patent portfolio analysis confirms, Bayer is strong in pharma and "classic" agrochemistry, while Monsanto is strong in genetic plant engineering (see Fig. 6.2).

Technology Protection Monsanto Canada ULC, now also part of Bayer AG, created its IP protection program in 1997 to help maintain a level playing field for Canadian farmers and ensure that farmers who have not paid for its patented technologies are not benefiting unfairly.

Why Does Bayer Enforce its Patents? If someone other than the patent holder tries to make, use, or sell the patented invention without the permission of the patent holder, they may be guilty of patent infringement. Monsanto Canada ULC profits from its developments in crop sciences. If farmers plant and harvest Bayer's patented trait technologies without a *Technology Stewardship Agreement*, they would be infringing Bayer's patent rights. The Technology Stewardship Agreement gives farmers permission to use Bayer's patented trait technologies. By signing this agreement, the farmer has a license to use their patented technologies subject to certain terms and conditions. There is nothing unusual about including terms and conditions in the agreement. It is a limited use license; it does not allow farmers to distribute, transfer, or sell patented technologies; and it only allows them to plant the seeds on their own farm for a single season.

Monsanto invests in the enforcement of its patent rights for three key reasons:

- No business can survive without being paid for its product.
- Monsanto currently invests millions of dollars per day to develop and bring new products to the market. If only some growers are paying the required technology fees, our ability to invest in research and development to create new products thereby decreases.
- Monsanto enforces its IP and agreements against violators as a matter of equity to those farmers who honor the agreement and respect Canadian IP law.

Seeds with the technology cannot be saved. The vast majority of farmers honor the agreement. They are prepared to purchase new patented seeds for each growing season, mainly because they are getting the benefits they want and need on their farm.

Monsanto also maintains an anti-piracy program. In 1997, Monsanto started enforcing its patent rights in Canada. This action was taken after 2 years of educating growers across Canada. During this time, the rules and obligations associated with growing Monsanto's patented seed technology on their farms were explained. It offers a technical support line, which looks into possible illicit use of Bayer's technology. When Bayer discovers issues of patent infringement, it does not immediately rush to file suit; it tries to settle matters amicably and outside the courtroom. ◀

Takeaways Crop Science

- Plant varieties produced by traditional methods are not patentable.
- Plants obtained from an "essentially biological process" are not patentable (EPO G3/19, 2020).
- Natural contractual incentives of licensees to enforce IP.
- Easy process to flag infringement with helpline.
- Industry is highly influenced by data analytics and new platforms in agriculture; technologies around data analytics will play a more important role.

6.4 Life Sciences

Patenting in life sciences has a long history: In 1873, *Louis Pasteur* was granted a patent for purified yeast. In 1953, the DNA's structure was discovered, which led to the commercial use of genetic engineering since the 1980s. Drugs such as human insulin for the treatment of diabetes, erythropoietin for the treatment of anemia, and monoclonal antibodies for cancer therapy are based on biotechnological manufacturing processes. In agriculture, biotechnology is used to modify plants to make them more resistant to diseases, herbicides, and difficult environmental conditions or to increase yields (see also EPO, 2019).

Example—Prionics

Prionics is a high-tech and innovative life science SME, which is now part of *Thermo Fisher Scientific*. The company was founded in 1997 as a spin-off of the University of Zurich and is based in Schlieren, Switzerland. The life science company manufactures products in the field of farm animal diagnostics, diagnostic solutions for prion diseases, and animal identification solutions. Prionics manufactures approximately 300 products. The majority of these are government-mandated and subsidized test systems for farm animals.

Prionics' first and best-known product is the test for bovine spongiform encephalopathy (BSE), which was launched in 1999. Today, Prionics is the world's number two in farm animal diagnostics, offering diagnostic solutions for the ten major farm animal diseases. Prionics' strategy is to expand along the food value chain with the continuous development of new diagnostic systems.

Defending One's Intellectual Property as a Small Life Science Company[2] Prionics gained a world market share of 40%–50% in the last 10 years with their antibody-based BSE tests. They could have prospered from this alone. Nevertheless, the company with Markus Moser as CEO has launched ten more diagnostic products for cattle, sheep, goats, and pigs.

At present, the Prionics' portfolio includes 29 international patents, and three or four more are added each year. They come either from their own 20-man strong research department or are licenses acquired from the academic world. "Basically, each of our innovation projects aims at a formal IP right," says Moser. Therefore, the Zurich-based company has built up a highly complex process that ranges from the combined patent and literature search (technology search) at the IPI as well as a bi-monthly monitoring of all projects and products to the creation of an internal database with selected third-party patents.

However, this is not enough for the life science markets because, as has been the case in the pharmaceutical industry for a long time, a kind of balance of terror prevails in these markets. The market operators build up entire protective barriers around their products and fight on all relevant technological fronts for every inch of the market.

"Even we can be very aggressive when it's about our IP," says Moser honestly. For example, Prionics also defends its IP abroad by protecting products with a patent in every country in which a competitor could earn money with an imitation product. "It is not just a question of money, but also a matter of principle," explains Moser. Prionics is serious about things when it comes to a court case. In Germany, for example, a lawsuit is currently pending because somebody tried to free ride on the back of the company.

There are years when Prionics is forced to spend over a million francs on its IP protection. For a company with approximately 100 employees, this is a lot of money. But Markus Moser is certain: "If we did not do so, we would soon be out of the market." ◀

Takeaways Life Sciences[3]

- Performing patent searches at the beginning of each invention is the best protection against later surprises (e.g., see Fig. 6.3).
- In the case of a blockade by a competitor's patent, it is initially sensible to work on workarounds.
- A best practice model is to focus on one "key" patent that is going to be the core patent of the company.

(continued)

[2] Extract from IPI (2019).

[3] Bader and Gassmann (2022a).

(continued)

- However, effective protection is often not provided by individual patents. Innovative SMEs should, therefore, set up a systematic patent cluster to secure competitive advantages.
- While broad patents have a stronger impact, they are also more vulnerable. The application of broad patents should, therefore, be considered especially at the beginning of a technology cycle.
- In addition to basic patents, various more specific design and application alternatives can be patented.
- In the event of a dispute, the own negotiation basis can be improved if an improvement solution is submitted based on a systematic analysis and evaluation of competing products, as this makes further development difficult for the competitor.
- In-licensing or patent license exchange enables the use of inventions and technologies patented by other parties.
- For patent invalidation actions, such as opposition or nullity proceedings, it is advisable to engage a patent attorney, as general technical–legal knowledge is not sufficiently available internally.
- Consistent and rigorous action against patent infringers has a deterrent effect and increases the imitation hurdles.
- Another option is to trade patent rights: Patents are regarded as real products that are traded as assets on a marketplace, including options such as barter, sale, or licensing.
- With regard to a later partnership with, or an exit scenario to, larger corporations, consider the early implications for establishing a business case-relevant patent portfolio, including a sufficient patent country coverage.

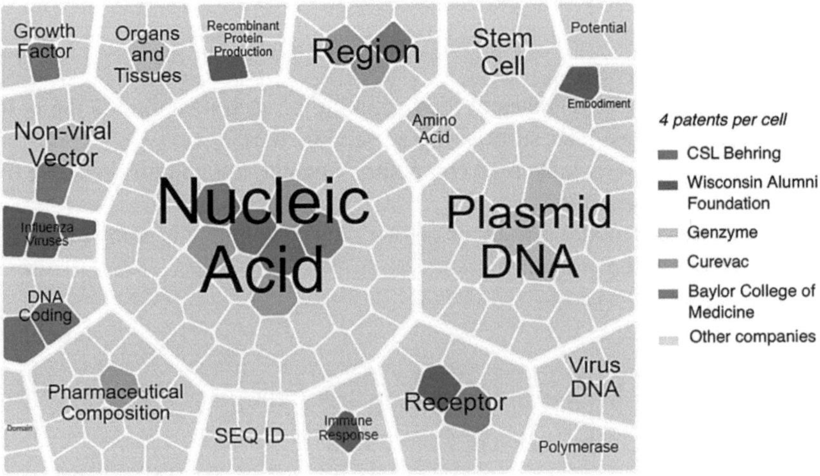

Fig. 6.3 Visualization of life sciences patenting (Picanço-Castro et al., 2020)

6.5 Consumer Goods

The consumer goods industry comprises sectors such as the food, beverage, cosmetics, and chemical industries as well as the textile, sporting goods, and consumer electronics industries. This industry therefore mainly produces goods that are intended for private use. Marketing and advertising therefore also play a central role in this industry in order to strengthen a brand. The annualized consumer goods market in Germany amounted to around 670 billion euros in 2024 (Singh, 2025). While *Henkel* was the strongest company in Germany with net sales of US$23.3 billion in 2024, *Nestlé* was the European leader in consumer goods with US$98.7 billion. This makes Nestlé one of the largest consumer goods manufacturers in the world, along with *Unilever*, *Anheuser-Busch InBev,* and *L'Oréal*, but also American companies such as *Procter & Gamble*, *Pepsi*, and *Coca-Cola.*

Example—Nespresso, the Game Changer

In the hotly contested consumer goods market, patents therefore also play an important role in protecting innovations and differentiating oneself from competitors. For example, *Nestlé* has filed over 2000 patents for its *Nespresso* machine since 1976 to protect its innovative capsules and brewing system (Brem et al., 2016; see Fig. 6.4). There has been a long fight over whether the earlier *Battelle* patent on a capsule apparatus from the year 1972 can be seen as the first step.

Today, there are over 85 competitors in the coffee capsules business in Europe alone. Since the early patents expired, Nestlé had to further develop and protect its business model. Through this extensive patent portfolio, Nestlé was able to secure its functional competitive advantages and strengthen the Nespresso brand through clever marketing activities. ◄

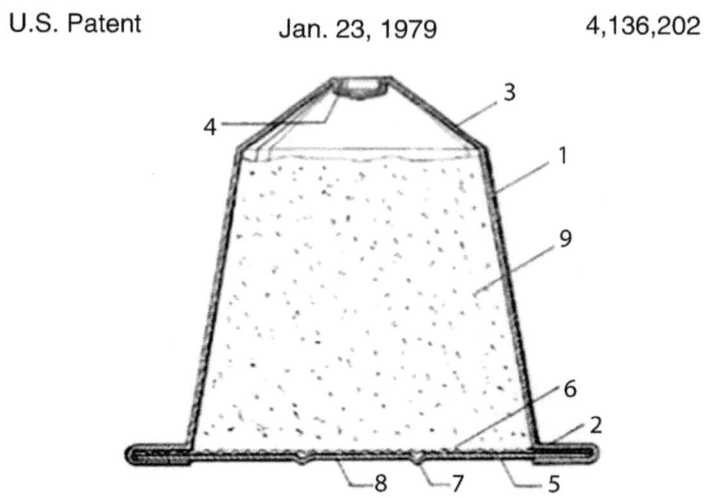

Fig. 6.4 US 4,136,202: Capsule for beverage preparation *(Nestlé)*

Example—Henkel's "Glocal" IP Strategy

Henkel sees brands as synonymous with trust and reliability. It is important for the company to have a clear understanding that customers act locally and that brands, therefore, have a local impact. The brand strategy employed by Henkel is caught between the need for *standardization* on the one hand and the need for *differentiation* on the other. The standardization of products and brands is advantageous for efficient and inexpensive production, low complexity, and a rapid introduction of new products. Differentiation is necessary in order to achieve the highest possible level of customer loyalty, to obtain flexible responses, and to be able to close regional markets. As a result, the brand strategy tries to do justice to both focal points. Henkel has come up with the made-up portmanteau word *glocal*, which is derived from combining the words "local" and "global."

Henkel's patent strategy distinguishes between core competence and non-core competence areas. In core competence areas, inventions are pursued as best as possible as patent applications in order to achieve the greatest possible differentiation from competitors. In these core areas, *Henkel* strives to provide exclusive protection for products, technologies, packaging, and ingredients. In non-core areas of competence, Henkel attempts to maintain the greatest possible freedom-of-action position: Often, inventions in these areas are not filed for patent, but are published in restricted publications to prevent them from being patented by competitors.

Henkel coordinates both the achievable protection through trademarks and the achievable protection through patents. While trademark protection is primarily suitable for protecting the customer interface, patents are mainly used to protect products and technologies. Since the protective effects of trademarks and patents have complementary effects in this sense, it is, therefore, necessary to coordinate the protective alternatives in such a way that an optimal overall effect is achieved on both the customer and the technology side. ◀

Takeaways Henkel

- Coordinated, complementary brand, and patent strategy.
- Determination of the permissible filing period depending on the potentially achievable scope of protection.
- Interdisciplinary teams to evaluate inventions in terms of market relevance and technical relevance.
- Four-stage decision-making and selection process, aligned to the patent application process.
- Supply exclusivity agreements in R&D cooperation as compensation for non-exclusivity in patent and trademark rights.

6.6 Retail

Over the past 10 years or so, the largest online and retail retailers have begun to build up their own patent portfolios. Progressive digitalization and technology applications in retail play a particularly important role here[4]:

- *Alibaba* has significantly increased its patent applications since 2013. In 2018, the Chinese technology and retail group registered 4622 patent families. Alibaba was founded in 1999 as a B2B e-commerce portal, originally to connect Chinese manufacturers with overseas buyers (see Fig. 6.5).
- *Amazon*, on the other hand, had its highest patent application date back in 2014, but overall has a largely granted, i.e., examined and enforceable, patent portfolio. The effects of the "Alice" decision after 2014 on the patenting of business methods in the USA (see Sect. 7.4 Software and Business Methods, and Sect. 7.5 Artificial Intelligence–based Business Models) can be clearly seen. Amazon was founded in 1994 as an online bookseller and has developed into the world's largest online retailer for books, clothing, electronics, and music, among other things, but also offers B2B solutions such as cloud storage solutions (see Fig. 6.6).
- *Walmart* has also started to follow suit. While parts of the older patent portfolio were given up again (also in this case, the "Alice" decision, see above), Walmart has recently made a strong comeback. Walmart is the world's largest and highest-selling retailer with a wide range of products, including food, clothing, furniture, household appliances, and electronics (see Fig. 6.7).

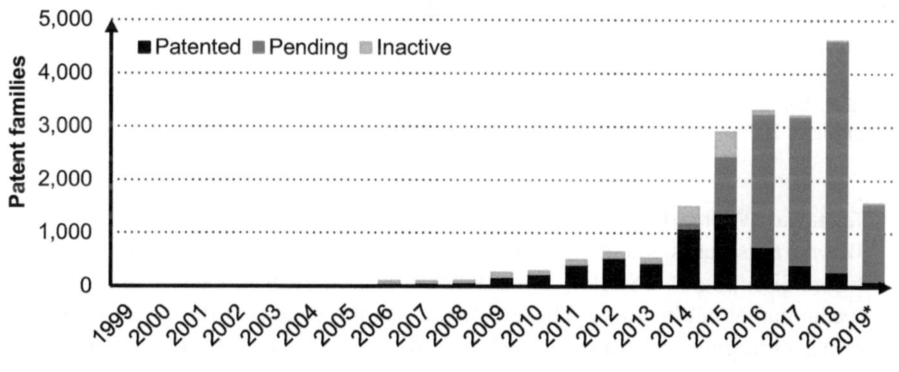

Fig. 6.5 *Alibaba's* number of patent families worldwide by filing year and legal status (LexisNexis PatentSight, 2020a)

[4]A selected portion of this section was previously published in the chapter Bader (2022). Innovationen im Handel nutzen und schützen. In M. Knoppe, S. Rock, & M. Wild (Eds.), *Der Zukunftsfähige Handel* (fourth ed.) Wiesbaden: Springer Gabler, 171–192. Used with permission.

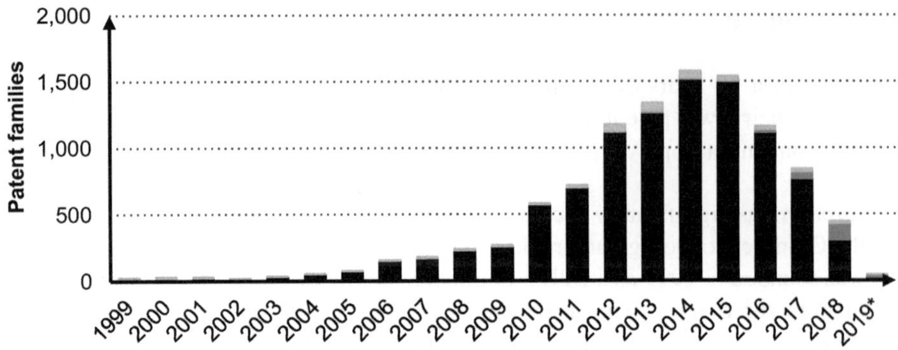

Fig. 6.6 *Amazon's* number of patent families worldwide by filing year and legal status (LexisNexis PatentSight, 2020b)

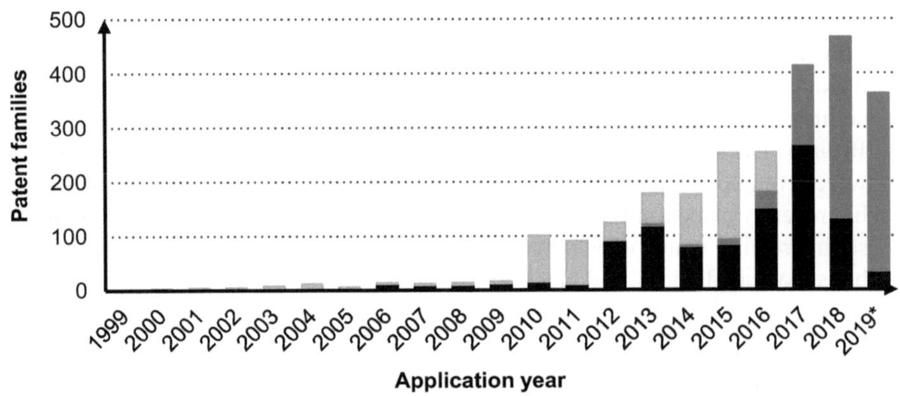

Fig. 6.7 *Walmart's* number of patent families worldwide by filing year and legal status (LexisNexis PatentSight, 2020c)

Takeaways Walmart: Patented Retail 2.0

Walmart also uses patents to protect its innovation projects: For example, the future direction of US retail giant Walmart can be gleaned from a number of recent patent publications. These indicate that the vision for the future is now to use emerging technologies to change the way customers shop. Walmart's latest patent filings also suggest that the company is trying to catch up with fierce rival *Amazon*, which is making inroads into every aspect of retail, including delivery and customer engagement (Internet of Business, 2021a, 2021b).

A recent example of a recent Walmart patent application is shown in Fig. 6.8. Other examples from Walmart's patent portfolio include:

(continued)

(continued)

- Customer wristband that logs customers into Walmart systems when they enter a store, tracks them as they move through the aisles, and logs them out when they leave the store: "Systems and methods for tracking wearable device users" (US 2018/082051 A1).
- Intelligent shopping cart program: "Systems and methods for autonomous item identification" (US 2018/082279 A1).
- Anti-theft system: "Autonomous vehicle content identification system" (US 2018/082249 A1).
- In-store drone assistance for price verification or to guide users to wanted products: "Systems, devices and methods for drone assistance" (US 2018/081375A1).
- Bee drones for autonomous pollination: "Systems and methods for pollination of crops by unmanned vehicles" (US 2018/065749 A1).

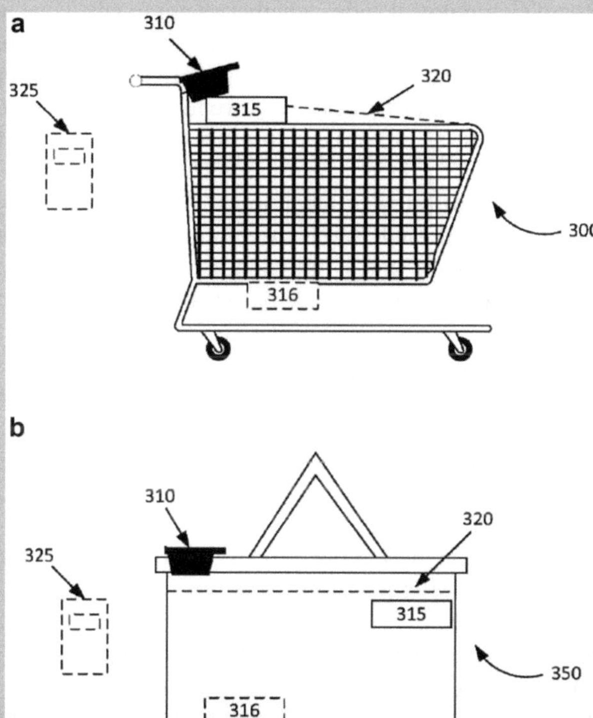

Fig. 6.8 Walmart US patent application: "Systems and methods for autonomous article identification" (US 2018/082279 A1)

6.7 Machinery

Example—Patent Management Processes at Schindler & Inventio

The Swiss manufacturer *Schindler* is a global leader in the market for elevators and escalators and today employs over 55,000 people, around 430 of whom work in central research and development. Its main sales markets are Europe, the USA, and Asia, with the Asian market showing high growth rates. The main competitors are *OTIS*, *ThyssenKrupp*, *Kone*, and *Mitsubishi*. There is a major price war going on in the industry. In addition to the development and production of elevator systems, maintenance and service as well as modernization are considered important areas of activity and sources of income. The vertical integration is still relatively high. Software development is playing an increasingly important role.

Schindler has a total patent portfolio of over 9000 active patents. About 80% of the patents come from the R&D department. About 80 new patent applications are made every year. In the event of a patent infringement of strategic importance, the Group Board Committee decides whether or not to take legal action.

Inventio is a separate company responsible for Schindler's global intellectual property business. The main features of the global intellectual property strategy are approved by the Board of Directors of Inventio. The head of central R&D is a member of the Inventio Board of Directors. This ensures that the R&D strategy is regularly aligned with the business strategy. The global implementation of the IP strategy is the responsibility of Inventio's management in coordination with product line management and R&D. Developmental cooperation exists with various technology partners and is initiated and implemented by R&D or the Board. Make-or-buy decisions are made by Inventio together with R&D and the market organization.

Schindler allows market changes and changes in internal goals to guide the strategy. Strategic building blocks that do not contribute to the desired success are redefined. The patent strategy is developed top-down, formulated in writing, and communicated internally. To implement the patent strategy, the patent portfolio must be aligned with Schindler's main activities. Core process steps for patent generation are shown in Fig. 6.9.

Schindler applies four basic core process steps for patent generation (see Fig. 6.9):

- *Trend Team:* Market analysis and technology scouting;
- *Exploitation:* Promotion and use of internal ideas;
- *Portfolio management:* Performing patent portfolio analyses, identifying opportunities and risks, monitoring competition, make-or-buy decisions; and
- *Invention Process:* Continuous invention disclosure process with classification.

In addition, patent analyses are used to generate new ideas. Patent analyses represent one of several sources of information on competitive activities. Schindler also uses patent analyses to expand its technological leadership and thus influence the industry technologically. The main general objective is to maintain the company's own freedom to operate.

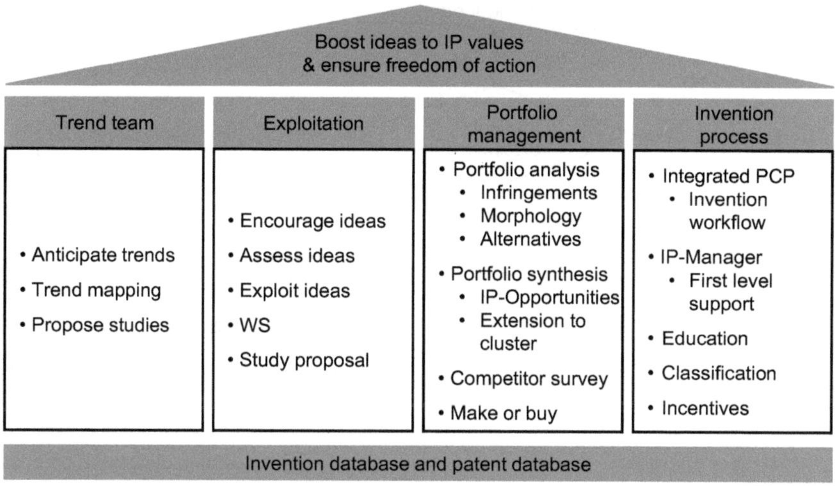

Fig. 6.9 Core process of patent generation at *Schindler* (authors' own figure)

Process The generation of invention disclosures is an important Research and Development (R&D) goal at Schindler and is therefore strongly weighted in the personal target agreements. The necessary decisions are made exclusively by Inventio, a separate company responsible for Schindler's global intellectual property business. The Schindler Invention Process consists of two subprocesses, starting with the idea evaluation and ending with the patentability evaluation (see Fig. 6.10):

- *Idea disclosure process:* Ideas are developed by the inventors and evaluated according to technical and economic criteria with the involvement of the supervisor.
- *Invention disclosure process:* Ideas are then examined for their suitability for patent application. An important criterion here is the ability to differentiate from the state of the art.

Initial registrations are initiated exclusively by Inventio. For subsequent applications, the relevance of the state of the art will be taken into account. Inventio obtains comments from Schindler product managers and selects the appropriate countries on this basis (see Fig. 6.11). The evaluation of such information and the investment decisions based on it requires many years of experience and foresighted thinking on the part of Inventio's management. As a rule, product managers are asked in writing every 2 years to maintain intellectual property rights. Ultimately, however, the decision is made by Inventio.

Portfolio Management Portfolio management is closely linked to product development and marketing. With regard to the influence on idea generation, certain focal points are maintained; for example, further developments mature into invention disclosures in joint R&D and Inventio workshops.

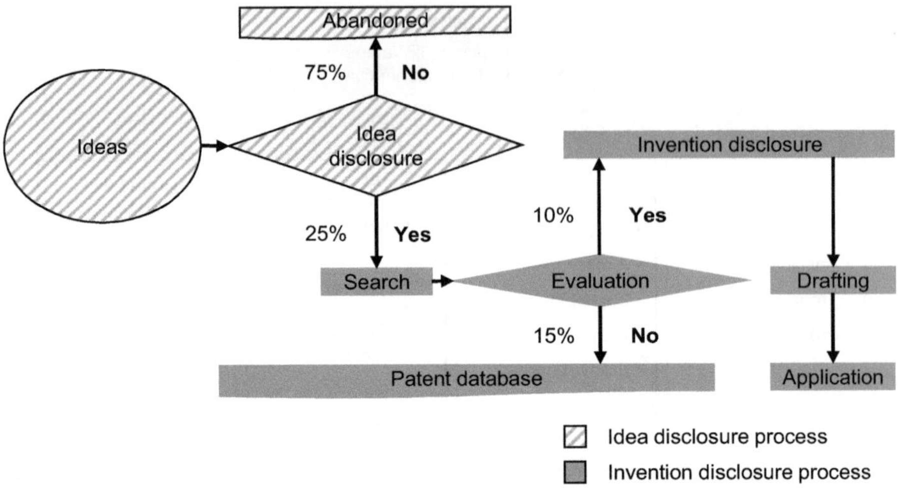

Fig. 6.10 Partial process of portfolio management at *Schindler* (authors' own figure)

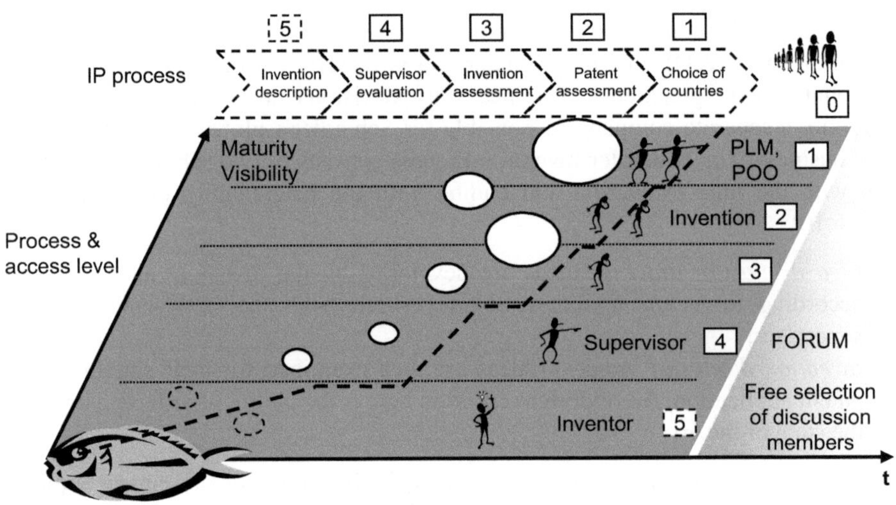

Fig. 6.11 IP process at *Schindler* (authors' own figure)

Portfolio information and the associated flow of information are provided by Inventio. Communication with Schindler takes place both traditionally via forms and postal delivery and electronically. As part of its intellectual property management, Schindler generally tries to prevent the launch of patent applications with a low probability of success, recognize possible infringements, and thus prevent possible legal actions.

Invention and Patent Database A virtual invention database provides valuable criteria for an efficient and pragmatic evaluation of ideas and inventions (see Fig. 6.12). A patent mapping function implemented in the invention database enables the active design of the Schindler Inventio patent portfolio.

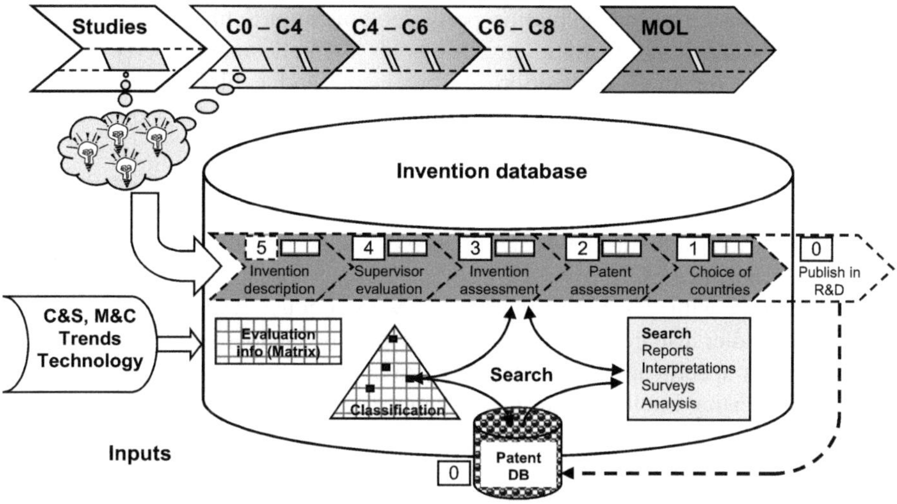

Fig. 6.12 Invention concept database at *Schindler* (authors' own figure)

Prerequisites for the successful implementation of the idea and invention disclosure process at Schindler are:

- Guaranteed privacy for the inventor to a certain extent;
- Simple involvement of colleagues, employees, and partners during studies and projects;
- Supervisor feedback, usually from project or R&D managers on ideas in order to create further added value;
- Extended information base for *Inventio*, R&D, and Product Line Managers;
- Greater availability of information within Schindler;
- Function sharing for all decision-makers;
- Coordination of the value chain process;
- Objective remuneration for inventions; and
- Management tool for patent mapping.

The invention database enables a simple documentation of ideas. Schindler first had to solve the problem that, on the one hand, the inventor's urge to communicate and, on the other hand, the confidentiality interests of the individual and the company had to be taken into account. Data transmission and communication between the parties involved take place within an encrypted intranet. Especially for the previously applicable requirements of US inventor law (first-to-invent principle), all documents receive an irrevocable time stamp that "freezes" the document and makes it unchangeable. In this way, inventions can be proved to have been made at a precise time. Different levels of access authorization have made it possible to regulate accessibility for user groups and thus the level of confidentiality. Through consistent introduction and communication, Schindler was able to achieve a high level of acceptance among users.

Organization The intellectual property department at Schindler has been outsourced to the subsidiary Inventio. Inventio holds all intellectual property rights and is responsible for their acquisition, enforcement, and exploitation worldwide. Inventio is internally described as customer-oriented, diverse, and cooperative and offers R&D support on important issues.

Cooperation and Licensing Schindler is open to granting licenses. In doing so, the company works mainly with suppliers. For key technologies that can be marketed worldwide, Schindler consistently strives for exclusivity in order to achieve competitive advantages.

Cooperation with development partners, who conduct R&D for Schindler, is typical. Schindler also cooperates with suppliers, who customize their components to Schindler's specifications, so that these components fit perfectly with existing systems. Licensing intellectual property rights in partnerships with suppliers tends to increase continuously. Cooperation with partners in research projects is rather rare. Within the framework of development projects, cooperation is also entered into where external know-how is required. The number of partnerships is large due to the number of technical areas that have to be covered: 15%–20% of the R&D budget is spent on cooperation.

In R&D partnerships, Schindler claims generated IP in full and handles the patent application process. In special cases, suppliers are granted a right of use outside the elevator and escalator sector. Schindler bears the patent costs for creation, application, and maintenance. Sublicenses are possible with component suppliers. ◄

Takeaways Schindler/Inventio

- Company remains the sole proprietor of IP.
- Clearly formulated patent strategy along with the core process.
- Two-tiered selection and decision process for filing a patent.
- Inclusion of patent experts in technological motoring and trend teams.
- Inventions database as an info platform for inventors.
- Generation of patent applications is an explicit part of R&D KPIs.
- Almost 20% of R&D budget flowing into R&D budget goes into partnerships.

6.8 Electronics and Electrical Equipment

Example—Patent Management at ABB

ABB is a globally active electrical engineering group with headquarters in Zurich. ABB was formed in 1988 from the merger of the Swedish *Allmänna Svenska Elektriska Aktiebolaget* (*ASEA*) and the Swiss *Brown Boveri & Cie* (*BBC*). ABB employs around 120,000 people, of whom about 6400 work in Switzerland. ABB's businesses are divided into five divisions: Power Products, Power Systems, Automation Products, Process Automation, and Robotics. The company has nine research centers with over 6000 researchers worldwide. In addition, the company has cooperation agreements with 70 different universities.

Patent Generation Strategy Technologies play a key role for ABB in that technologies are its source of value. ABB applies for about 700 new patents annually and holds 16,000 patents or patent applications worldwide. Expenditure on IP protection amounts to approximately CHF 36 million per year! ABB's patent management is strategically focused on generating patents that add value to the company and protect its products. ABB's company-wide patent strategy is linked to its business strategy and forms the basis for the specific patent strategies of the individual business units.

The aim of the patent strategy is to create patents that deliver added value. ABB distinguishes between a business and a strategic approach to creating value through patents. The business approach focuses on sustainably increasing and maximizing return on capital employed (ROCE). Intellectual property rights enable the maximum ROCE to be increased. In addition, patents can slow down the decline of ROCE after its maximum by reducing competitive pressure, i.e., it can achieve sustainability. The strategic approach puts the market and competition in the foreground. From this perspective, patents can reduce competitive pressure, secure market share, create new market access, and optimize pricing.

Patent Generation Processes To achieve the objectives of the patent strategy, ABB employs the following measures:

- *Gate model:* The development of new products follows a gate model in which questions and tasks relating to IP protection and the proactive avoidance of conflicts with third-party property rights are answered or processed at several gates. Without careful and complete processing and answering of these questions and tasks, it is not possible to move the development project forward.
- *Strategic patent workshops:* One-day events with an interdisciplinary group of participants to analyze the patent situation and further strategic orientation.
- *Cooperative approach:* Patent specialists are represented at all levels of the company and work closely with the internal patent attorneys.
- *Quality control*: Two-stage control concept prior to patent applications through review processes and peer reviews.
- *Patenting opinions:* Decision support for foreign applications.

ABB's goal is to create valuable patents. On the one hand, a valuable patent fulfills the claim of an optimal technical object. This means that it is an object that is in demand by the market and fits ABB's technology strategy. In addition, an optimal geographical scope of protection should be achieved. Depending on the area of application and market of the various technologies, priorities are set differently and a corresponding country strategy is developed. Thirdly, the optimal factual scope of protection must be ensured, i.e., when filing a patent application, the scope of protection must be examined and tailored to potential infringements.

Organizing Patent Generation ABB has developed an organizational structure that integrates patent management at all levels of the company. As the top level, the "Chief IP Counsel" is responsible for company-wide IP management. As the next level, each business unit has an assigned patent attorney. The third level is represented by local patent attorneys. For the future, ABB is considering establishing a fourth level with licensing specialists and the so-called patent enforcement specialists. The latter would have the task of actively searching for patent infringements by third parties. ABB has a total of nine IP departments worldwide with about 85 employees. ABB handles about 80% of its work volume through internal employees. External resources are only called upon in special cases.

Evaluating Patents ABB stresses the importance of regular reviews and feedback in the patent management process. The company, therefore, carries out a two-stage quality control process:

- *Check the invention:* Is the patent project aligned with the business strategy?
- *Check of the patent application:* Has an appropriate country strategy been selected? Are the claims formulated broadly enough?

ABB uses a four-field matrix to implement and monitor the patent strategy and patent portfolio (see Fig. 6.13). The axes reflect the strength of relative IP protection compared with the competition and the degree of differentiation of the product or market.

With weak patent protection and at the same time a low degree of differentiation, there is a risk of being blocked by competitors with stronger patents. Weak patent protection combined with a high degree of product differentiation makes it easy for

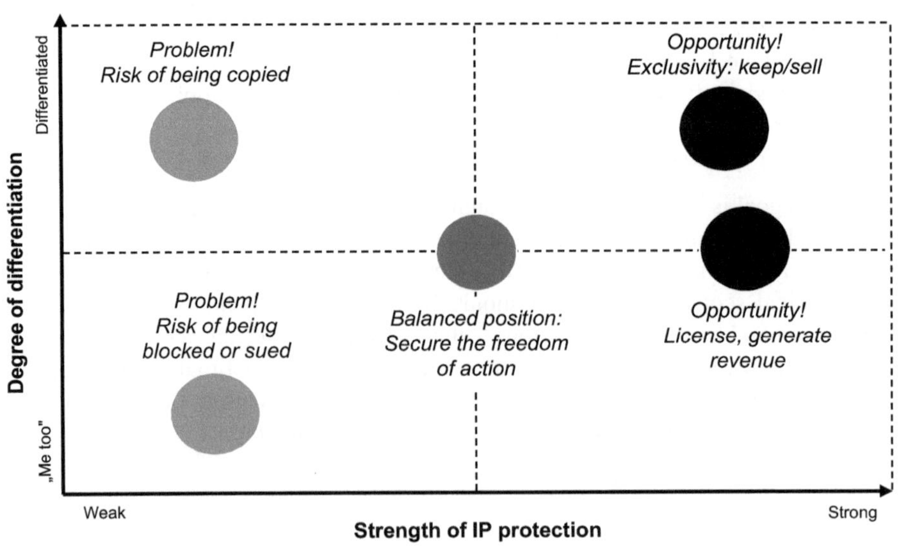

Fig. 6.13 *ABBs* patent evaluation matrix (Gassmann & Bader, 2024)

competitors to legally imitate an interesting product and thus increases the risk of being copied. Strong patent protection in a highly differentiated market means exclusivity for the patent holder. He has control over competitors and can determine the market. An opportunity for out-licensing arises from a strong patent on a medium-differentiated product. Here, an out-licensing strategy can generate additional revenues. With medium differentiation and medium patent strength, the product is in a balanced state and allows freedom to operate. Starting from the balanced position, the strength of the patent is the decisive factor. If the patent strength decreases, the product is quickly in one of the risk areas. Securing a valuable patent during the patent application process is therefore an important success factor.

ABB also uses this evaluation matrix as a tool for defining its patenting strategy. When defining the strategy of a product, it can be positioned in the matrix. The next steps are to consider which position is to be aimed for the product in the future and by which measures this can be achieved.

Below are two examples of ABB products and their assignment to the evaluation matrix.

Low-Voltage Products Low-voltage products such as switches or circuit breakers are mass products. There is a multitude of competitors and the margins are low. The differentiation is mainly based on price. Since there are hardly any technical possibilities for differentiating such a mass product, *ABB* has to assert itself through the strength of its intellectual property rights. As a supplement to a patent, design protection can increase the strength of protection. The aim is therefore to keep the position in the middle of the matrix stable (see Fig. 6.14).

High-Voltage Products ABB is the world market leader in the field of high-voltage products. Only a few competitors compete in this very sophisticated technological field. Market entry requires high investments and a high level of technological knowledge. ABB produces customized products and can generate high margins. In this example (see Fig. 6.15). ABB is in the top right quadrant of the evaluation matrix, with high differentiation and strong patent protection. This gives ABB an exclusivity advantage in the market.

Patent Commercialization ABB's primary goal in patent filing is to protect its own products. The external exploitation of patents is therefore not the primary focus. Nevertheless, ABB is in principle prepared to grant licenses if it is advantageous, for example, to broaden the market penetration of a product. Patents that are not central to securing ABB's own competitive advantage are reviewed for their external exploitation potential and released for commercialization on a case-by-case basis. ABB believes that in-licensing and out-licensing of technologies will play a more important role in the future and is therefore in the process of building up corresponding competencies. ◀

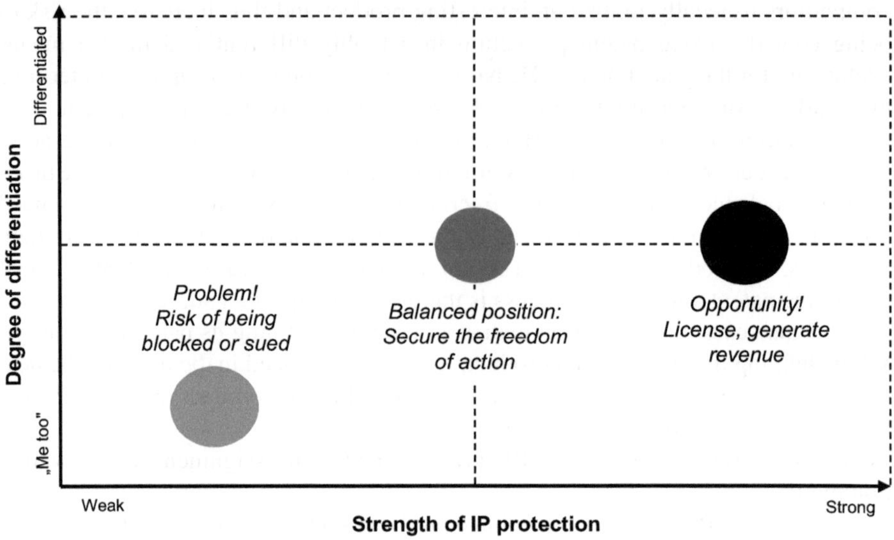

Fig. 6.14 Example from *ABB's* low-voltage products (Gassmann & Bader, 2024)

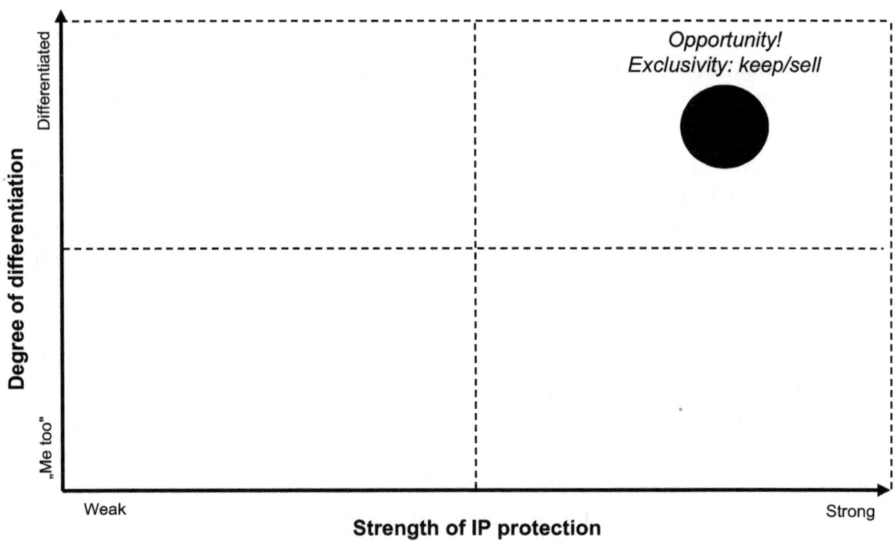

Fig. 6.15 Example from *ABB's* high-voltage products (Gassmann & Bader, 2024)

Takeaways ABB

- Patent strategy is embedded in the business strategy.
- Patents must generate added value.
- Patent management is a strategic instrument.
- Every business unit has a defined patent strategy.
- Organization uses a cooperative approach, where patent managers are represented at all levels.
- Evaluation matrix for implementing the patent strategy.
- Patents are reviewed for commercialization potential.

Example—Philips vs. Google

Beyond industrial electronics, *Google*, an advertiser, and *Philips*, a consumer electronics producer, fought in Germany over patent number EP 0 888 687, a User Interface for Television (see Fig. 6.16).

The legal dispute was the overuse of the technology in the area of mobile phones. Philips was in dispute with various manufacturers, and Google, the provider of *Android OS*, stepped in to defend their interests against Philips. The battle was fought in multiple jurisdictions simultaneously with the defendants *Wiko* and *Asus* being found to be infringing on Philips radio technology. Originally, the Circuit Court in Mannheim, Germany, had enjoined Asus not to sell any devices with Android 5.0 given that the interface may violate the Philips patent. The German Court of Justice ruled the European patent invalid for Germany. ◄

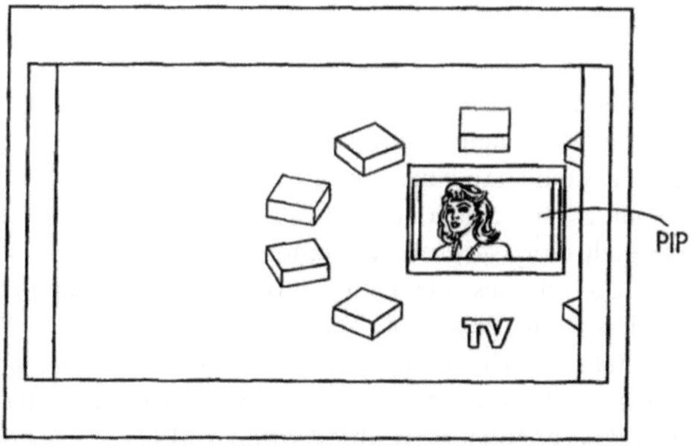

Fig. 6.16 *Philips* patent EP 0 888 687 B1: User Interface for Television

Takeaways Electronics

- Non-competing players in other industries can hold relevant technologies.
- A "small" patent can block an entirely unrelated and massive product line.
- Value of patents is getting increasingly monetarized by litigation.

6.9 Automotive and Connectivity

The global automotive industry suffered particularly badly from the consequences of the financial crisis and was confronted with the most difficult market conditions in history. Slumping sales figures and difficult credit conditions forced the industry to lay off workers and halt production. Since then, however, the automotive industry has been on the road to recovery and is experiencing its strongest growth phase in over 15 years. The automotive industry is also undergoing a strong concentration process: In 2001, the ten largest car manufacturers already produced almost 80% of the vehicles manufactured worldwide. The largest car manufacturers include *Volkswagen*, *Toyota Motor*, *Stellantis* (*PSA Peugeot Citroën* and *Fiat*), *Mercedes Benz*, *Ford Motor*, *General Motors*, *Honda Motor* and *Tesla Motors*, *Nissan Motors*, *Hyundai*, and *BYD* (Frost & Sullivan, 2025).

Due to greater involvement and commitment on the part of automotive suppliers, vehicle components are already being largely developed and manufactured by suppliers. More than 70% of the value added in development is generated by the suppliers, with the only exceptions being engines and transmissions (Wagner, 2015). The outsourcing of innovation activities to automotive suppliers has the consequence that these suppliers have to apply for industrial property rights more independently. According to the Head of Technology Management at *Daimler*, the major automotive suppliers are conducting research in the same areas as the Original Equipment Manufacturers (OEMs): "*Bosch* (a supplier) and Daimler (a carmaker) are tough competitors in automotive research." The main focus is on the battle for new knowledge and strategically strong patents. On the other hand, the purchasing departments of automobile manufacturers are exerting strong cost pressure on suppliers. In principle, attempts are being made to find several suppliers, the so-called second or third sources, for components. In practice, the respective suppliers can then only achieve exclusivity secured by patents on a temporary basis and at best get it for the luxury class vehicles. Only innovative and strong suppliers are able to maintain truly independent positions. The automotive suppliers *Bosch*, *Delphi*, *Mann + Hummel*, *Schäffler* (including *Continental* and *KAG Kugelfischer*), *Valeo*, and *ZF Friedrichshafen* have built up strong patent positions in the past and use them to strengthen their negotiating position with OEMs.

For example, the 6-speed transmission by *ZF Friedrichshafen* for *BMW* launched in 2002 had exclusivity for BMW only for a short period. This means that there is hardly enough time left for a sustained differentiation from automotive competitors. The leading OEMs, such as Daimler and BMW, therefore explicitly cooperate with technology-intensive non-suppliers (such as high-tech spin-offs from universities) in the early innovation phases in order to develop strategically important patents for the automotive sector. This is particularly relevant for system innovations. One example is the replacement of conventional steering systems by brake-and-steer-by-wire systems.

The development of various new drive forms, such as hybrid or electric drives, poses a challenge for automobile manufacturers. This effect is reinforced by political and social pressure to reduce CO_2 emissions and therefore improve the powertrain. Consequently, research activities for electric cars, for example, will be intensified. This is also reflected in a rapid increase in patent applications worldwide for electric cars in 2012, twice as many as for hybrid vehicles in the same period.

However, this development is also accompanied by a change in the automotive industry. More and more core technologies for electric cars are coming from other industries, and the automotive industry sees itself increasingly pushed onto the defensive. While over 80% of applications for hybrid technology still come from the classic automotive industry, this figure is just over 40% for electric drives (Grünecker, 2013). Such developments, as well as the research on autonomously driving cars, lead to a completely new market with participants pushing into the automotive sector. In some cases, these new market participants even own numerous patents in future-relevant areas such as infotainment systems (*Google, Apple,* and *Sony*) or battery technologies and hybrid/electric drives (*LG, Samsung*). An analysis of patent applications for automotive business processes also confirms this trend. Among the top 15 applicants in the field of automotive business processes in the period from 2001 to 2013, there was not a single automobile company. The patent landscape is dominated by companies from outside the industry like *IBM, American Express Travel*, and *Amadeus*, who offer scientific and technical services alongside travel services (Niemann, 2014).

Example—R&D Cooperation with Suppliers

The strength of automotive suppliers can hence be seen in the extent to which they are able to keep their own innovations exclusively in development cooperations with automobile manufacturers. This is currently only possible with the major suppliers. SME suppliers have less bargaining power: Automotive suppliers try to develop and patent inventions for fundamental innovations as independently as possible. Since, however, development work often only takes place in close cooperation with and on behalf of automobile manufacturers, the latter usually succeed in securing the development results as "contract developments" (see Fig. 6.17). Inventions and the resulting industrial property rights must then generally be transferred to the automobile manufacturer. The automotive supplier Z1 retains at most a simple right of use. The automobile manufacturer A1 can license the rights of use to further supplier Z2 in order to secure second and third suppliers for the development results achieved.

If the automotive supplier Z1 also wishes to supply A2 to another car manufacturer on the basis of its remaining usage rights, it is forced to pay licenses to A1. Frequently, it is also tied to an exclusivity period, usually 3–5 years, during which it may only deliver to the original car manufacturer A1. In return, it is guaranteed, for example, minimum purchase volumes.

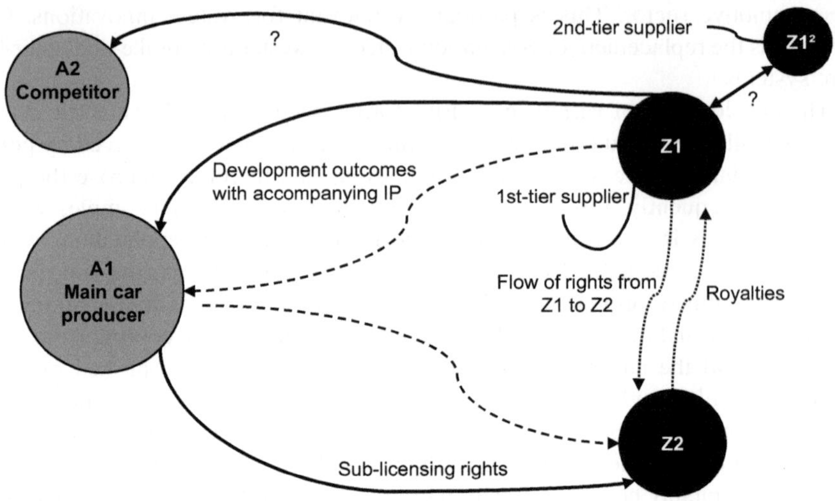

Fig. 6.17 Usage and licensing rights in the automotive sector (authors' own figure)

If, on the other hand, the automotive supplier Z1 has industrial property rights, which it alone can dispose of, the automotive manufacturer A1 generally demands a sub-licensable right of use, which can be passed on to the second and third supplier Z2. As compensation, the car manufacturer, A1, then pays quantity or turnover-dependent license fees to the owner of the industrial property right Z1, which are passed on to the second and third suppliers Z2 benefiting from the license through correspondingly reduced part costs. As a rule, the license fees are not of a magnitude to compensate for the development costs incurred.

It is possible, however, that automotive supplier Z1 will be forced to use intellectual property rights against license payments from third parties, for example from a second-tier subcontractor $Z1^2$, even without the "mediation" of the automotive manufacturer. These include in particular very large automotive suppliers such as *Bosch* or *Schaeffler*. The first-tier automotive supplier Z1 then has no choice but to try to pass on the license fees to the automobile manufacturer A1 in some way. In this scenario, however, the automobile manufacturer A1 has the risk that its second and third supplier Z2 may not be able to take licenses from the second-tier subcontractor $Z1^2$ or not at the same conditions. This may be the case, for example, because usage licenses are tied to the purchase of $Z1^2$'s subcontracted products. However, there are increasing efforts by second-tier subcontractors $Z1^2$ to enter directly into license negotiations with the automobile manufacturers A1. However, this has not yet been implemented in practice. ◀

Example—Tesla, the Pacemaker

Leapfrogging by Declaring Commons: One of the most interesting patent strategies of a very high profile and a large company is that of *Tesla.* Tesla renounced its IP in favor of any open innovation strategy. The following is an ungrammatically titled explanation from *Elon Musk* himself—it is not all that common for a CEO to directly discuss an IP strategy beyond a few platitudes.

"All Our Patent Are Belong to You":[5] Yesterday, there was a wall of Tesla patents in the lobby of our Palo Alto headquarters. That is no longer the case. They have been removed, in the spirit of the open-source movement, for the advancement of electric vehicle technology.

Tesla Motors was created to accelerate the advent of sustainable transport. If we clear a path to the creation of compelling electric vehicles, but then lay intellectual property landmines behind us to inhibit others, we are acting in a manner contrary to that goal. Tesla will not initiate patent lawsuits against anyone who, in good faith, wants to use our technology.

When I started out with my first company, *Zip2*, I thought patents were a good thing and worked hard to obtain them. And maybe they were good long ago, but too often these days, they serve merely to stifle progress, entrench the positions of giant corporations, and enrich those in the legal profession, rather than the actual inventors. After Zip2, when I realized that receiving a patent really just meant that you bought a lottery ticket to a lawsuit, I avoided them whenever possible.

At Tesla, however, we felt compelled to create patents out of concern that the big car companies would copy our technology and then use their massive manufacturing, sales, and marketing power to overwhelm *Tesla.* We could not have been more wrong. The unfortunate reality is the opposite: Electric car programs (or programs for any vehicle that does not burn hydrocarbons) at the major manufacturers are small to non-existent, constituting an average of far less than 1% of their total vehicle sales.

At best, the large automakers are producing electric cars with limited range in limited volume. Some produce no zero-emission cars at all.

Given that annual new vehicle production is approaching 100 million per year and the global fleet is approximately 2 billion cars, it is impossible for Tesla to build electric cars fast enough to address the carbon crisis. By the same token, it means the market is enormous. Our true competition is not the small trickle of non-Tesla electric cars being produced, but rather the enormous flood of gasoline cars pouring out of the world's factories every day.

We believe that Tesla, other companies making electric cars, and the world would all benefit from a common, rapidly evolving technology platform.

Technology leadership is not defined by patents, which history has repeatedly shown to be small protection indeed against a determined competitor, but rather by the ability of a company to attract and motivate the world's most talented

[5] Elon Musk, CEO June 12, 2014.

engineers. We believe that applying the open-source philosophy to our patents will strengthen rather than diminish Tesla's position in this regard.[6]

The Why: Beyond Elon's high-minded explanation lies actually some very savvy business acumen. By allowing others to use Tesla's technology, he helped roll-out the charging stations needed. Moreover, Musk's vision and attitude coincides with the Tesla brand. In short, the brand-value may be. It is also worth noting that Musk's phrase "initiate patent lawsuits against anyone who, in good faith, wants to use our technology" would not exactly convince legal experts at a major car company to allow cars to go into production. Most of Elon's value-added lies not in an ancient motor technology, but rather in the car's software, especially in the sophisticated AI and self-driving features—all of which is a trade secret and copyrighted.... ◀

Example—Avanci: Traditional Automotive Players Under Attack

Avanci is a patent pool in the ICT space (see also Sect. 6.10). *Volvo* along with 14 others, including major automotive brands, has signed patent licensing agreements with Avanci to get access to its patent pool. Cars increasingly rely on wireless connectivity.

The Avanci patent pool was conceived both to monetize patents and to eliminate a lot of the legal challenges in the space. Some of the Avanci members *(Nokia, Sharp,* and *Conversant)* have sued *Daimler* to coax the company to agree to its licensing terms. The case went into mediation, which eventually failed. *Continental Automotive Systems* argued that Avanci in acting for its members violated (Fair, Reasonable, and Non-Discriminatory) FRAND principles. Avanci would prefer to license to the end-user automotive company, but Daimler has resisted this since the royalty rates are then assessed not on the components, which suppliers like Continental make, but instead on the end product. To use a concrete case, consider that Continental needs a US$20 baseband chip—and Avanci demands a US$15 royalty per car. This royalty represents a 75% markup on the cost of that single component. By contrast, the entire connectivity module, which Continental sells, costs only US$75. Continental thus asserts that this is not reasonable or fair, considering that patent royalties conventionally have constituted only a 5%–15% markup, perhaps 2 dollars—so, whether the parties can close the gap remains to be seen (Juve, 2020; Pepe et al., 2019). European case law is still developing in the area of FRAND and Standard Essential Patents (SEPs) (cf. infra "Smartphone Patent Wars"). ◀

[6] https://www.tesla.com/about/legal#patent-pledge

Example—Chinas' Cars: Electronic Take-over of Automotive Industry

The automotive industry has started to shift toward China in the last years. *BYD*, one of China's largest electric carmakers, surpassed the mighty *Tesla* in 2024 in terms of units and revenues. The industrial nation has leveraged its advantage in the electronics industry supply chain and does not have the product burden of internal combustion engines. BYD's CN 118781682 A patent disclosure shows some step toward blending services using digital security in the automobile. Beyond electric cars and all the bells and whistles. Beyond car producers, we have seen smart device and consumer electronics makers like *Huawei* having 7300 patents related to self-driving, most of these being filed in the post-COVID era. *Apple*is now releasing CarPlay Ultra® to run the software side of *Aston Martin's* products. In short, the automobile industry is merging with the consumer electronics industry with China's makers leading the charge. Beyond the electronification of cars, their mobile connectivity opens up potentially different appropriation strategies like recurring licensing fees or subscriptions that likely differ from the past model where a supplier might have just added in development costs directly to the production cost of an electronic head unit. ◀

Takeaways Automotive and Connectivity

- Design and registered designs play an important role.
- Patents are exclusive rights, not license rights. This means that a patent prohibits third parties from imitating the protected invention, but does not automatically guarantee freedom to operate.
- Complex supply chains mean that cooperation between companies is very intensive, both vertically and horizontally.
- Value creation in the automotive industry increasingly comes from software, interconnectivity, and technology platforms and decreasingly from the hardware itself.
- Software, i.e., the code, is subject to copyright as such, but software and the algorithms used can generally be patented as computer-implemented inventions.
- Areas such as improved video services, real-time automation, monitoring and tracking, autonomous robots and vehicles, maintenance measurements, intelligent monitoring, and remote control are based on connectivity and have introduced a new culture of patent evaluation, licensing, and enforcement.
- Thinking in terms of business models is also becoming increasingly important in the automotive industry, while patents play an important role in enforcing and replicating the value of technologies (although this is still highly questioned by traditional players in the automotive industry).
- Value-oriented patent strategies, different licensing practices, and more aggressive enforcement of patents, for example, in the field of connectivity, are the new reality.
- Technology and platform leaders as well as patent exploitation pools often—at least for now—do not come from the same industry!

6.10 Information and Communication Technology

Since the 1980s, the *Information and Communication Technology* (*ICT*) sector has been a highly innovative and rapidly changing area. These technologies include computing and telecommunications and encompass new developments in emerging technologies, e.g., Artificial Intelligence (AI). More than a third of the patent applications received by the European Patent Office (EPO) concern ICT directly or indirectly (see Fig. 6.18). Given this importance, the EPO has even created a specialized ICT department, which brings together several of the EPO's examiners from various other technical sections like computers or semiconductors. This puts EPO examiners in the best position to assess the alleged novelty of inventions described in patent applications (EPO, 2018, 2025).[7]

In many areas of the electronics, semiconductor, and telecommunications industries, patents are interdependent. Almost no company in these sectors can still develop and sell products independently without being dependent on third-party patents. Accordingly, companies such as *IBM* or *Siemens* are increasingly forced to pursue an open licensing policy and conclude cross-licensing agreements on a broad scale.

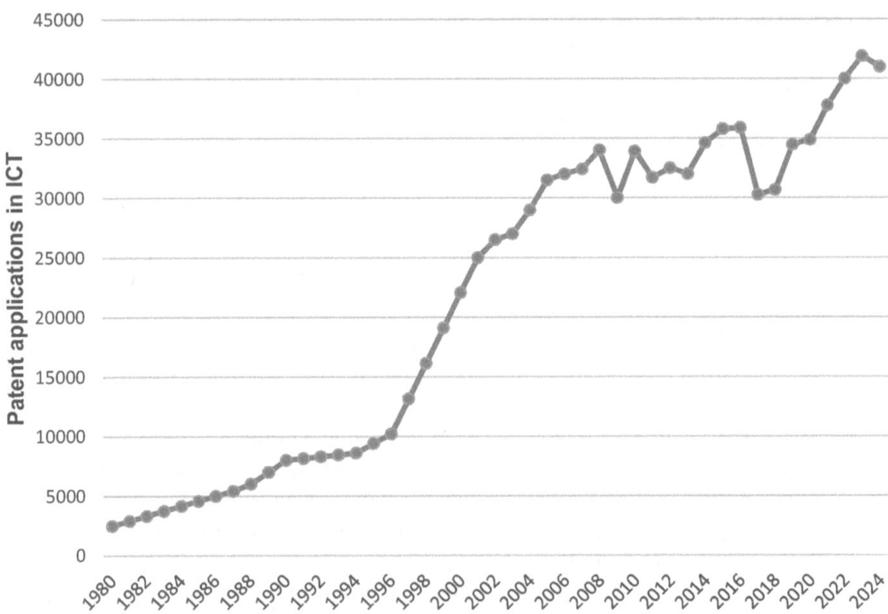

Fig. 6.18 Patent applications in ICT at the European Patent Office (based on EPO, 2017, 2025)

[7]A selected portion of this section was previously published in the chapter Bader and Gassmann (2022b). Patent Strategies in the Networked Economy. In O. Gassmann, & F. Ferrandina (Eds.), *Connected Business*. Cham: Springer Nature, 247–264. Used with permission.

Due to market requirements, there are often broad areas of technical overlap. On the other hand, there are usually numerous different technical solution variants that offer the same functionality but can still meet the needed requirements. Since users are demanding ever greater modularization of technical devices, international and cross-company technical standardization initiatives have become unavoidable. These are particularly pronounced in the field of mobile communications. In the standardization committees, however, the companies involved must generally be prepared to sacrifice their patent portfolios in favor of a common standard that is then made available to all participants.

Example—From GSM to UMTS Standard to 5G

In the late 1980s, when the *European Global System for Mobile communications (GSM)* standard was developed, the American company *Motorola* influenced the standardization process significantly using its own relevant patents, and it pursued a licensing policy that was unusually aggressive at the time (Granstrand, 1999). Thus, the GSM standard was kept away from countries in which *Motorola* pursued other interests. In addition, specific licensing conditions could be enforced, such as cross-licensing, which secured Motorola access to competitors' patent and technology portfolios and determined the structure of the GSM supplier market (Bekkers et al., 2002): Despite a small number of its own relevant patents, *Siemens* succeeded in joining the GSM standard at a later date. The French-German company *Alcatel* originally pursued a different technical solution, but this did not become the standard. Once the GSM standard had been defined, the company, therefore, had to build up a new patent portfolio.

The underlying patent portfolios also played an important role in the worldwide third-generation *Universal Mobile Telecommunications System* (*UMTS*) standard. There are significant technical dependencies on the *American Code Division Multiple Access* (*CDMA*) mobile communications standard. This was based on relevant patents of the American company *Qualcomm*, without which the UMTS standard could not be operated. The new race is now about who gets to be part of the new standard for the fifth-generation wireless technology for digital cellular networks "5G" (see Fig. 6.19). This standard was finalized in 2017 and became commercially available in the back-half of 2019. 5G is now already in its 19th version, which now incorporates non-terrestrial (space) networks.

Patent portfolios are increasingly getting used to keep previously uninvolved newcomers out of the market through raising high barriers to market entry. The initial major players who had patents for the 5G standard remain in place; the now-defunct Nokia patents are fewer, and ZTE has gain in relevancy (GreyB, 2020). The exact composition of the patents required for the technology evolves with the standards. Technical standards supported by patent portfolios and their licensing regulations force newcomers to disclose their own relevant intellectual property rights and make them available to standard participants. In return, a license to the standard is acquired. Such trade, however, comes up against its limits when standard-relevant patents exist but their owners themselves have no intention of marketing their own, standard-compliant products, but are instead primarily aimed at licensing revenues. ◀

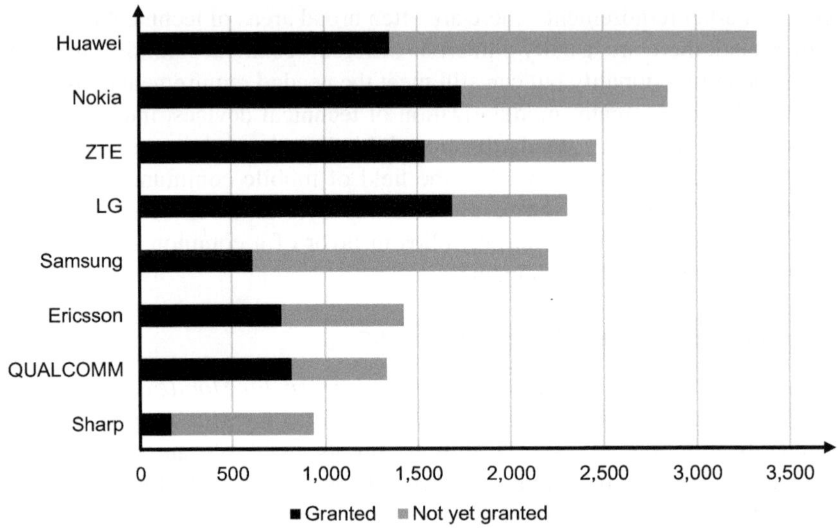

Fig. 6.19 The 5G patent owners' race: Companies that have filed the most 5G SEP patent families as of November 2019 (based on Buchholz/IPlytics, 2019). The exact pool of patents evolves with the standard

Example—The Smartphone Patent Wars

One of the more epic struggles in patenting took place around the so-called smartphone patent wars. As the smartphone was coming into its own, the various players in the industry realized the size and potential of the market. What ensued were dozens of lawsuits between *Apple*, *Sony Mobile*, *Google*, *HTC*, *Motorola*, *Microsoft*, *Nokia*, *Huawei*, *LG Electronics*, *Samsung*, and *ZTE*. This big battle entailed hundreds of thousands of patents ranging from the seemingly simple icon design, to sophisticated high-frequency modem chips, and it included everything in between. The iPhone was released mid-2007, marking a new era in connectivity—Nokia, a key player in the cell phone industry, kicked the war off by filing suit against Apple in late 2009, when the revolutionary device started to gain traction. The Nordic telecommunications equipment provider contended that Apple had not contributed to the patent pool surrounding the GSM, UTMS, and Wireless LAN standards and thus owed a royalty of 6–12 dollars per phone. Apple promptly countersued, alleging that Nokia stole some of its technology in 13 patents, the licensing terms of Nokia were not *FRAND (Fair, Reasonable, and Non-Discriminatory)*, and some of the patents in the standards were not enforceable (iam, 2015, 2016).

The enmity also brought other players, not even involved in consumer technology, like *Oracle*, to attack Google over the use of *Java* in *Android*. It underscores how patent infringement comes out of the woodwork when there is a lot of money at stake; Java had become widespread for the very reason that the language was considered an open technology after *Sun Microsystems* had become defunct, and perhaps, this is the main reason why it had become so popular.

The antagonism did not just involve the major big players of the industry, *EMG Technology*, a small Santa Monica company, alleged that Google had violated its patent (US 7,441,196 B2) for an "apparatus and method of manipulating a region on a wireless device screen for viewing, zooming and scrolling internet content." The method patent offers simplified navigation in a sister site. While numerous lawsuits were filed in Eastern Texas (a patent-friendly circuit court) over the technology—it never got invalidated, perhaps because the holder was willing to settle for a small sum. On its face, it is not clear that this patent would not be obvious for a skilled web developer in view of the state of the art in general. It is common for the core patent to never to be invalidated. For reasons of game theory, neither the owner nor the infringer typically has an incentive to invalidate it (Thompson, 2013). As an IP manager, it is often a good strategy to settle an invalidity suit rather than go to court because sharing a monopoly's profit is more than 1/2 of no monopoly profit. It is thus often very hard to know the extent of a company's IP strength by legal action.

In the ICT sector, *Standard Essential Patents* (*SEPs*) play a key role. SEPs are often subject to compulsory licensing terms under *FRAND* conditions (*Fair, Reasonable, and Non-Discriminatory*). The FRAND idea has had to be—and currently still is—interpreted by several courts as having to come up with an operationalizable concept. The main European FRAND case law comes from: *Unwired Planet* vs. *Huawei* vs. *Huawei* (UK High Court); *Huawei* vs. *ZTE* (European Court of Justice—ECJ); and *Sisvel* vs. *Haier* (German Higher Regional Court Dusseldorf).

The ECJ formalized the FRAND concept in its *Huawei* vs. *ZTE* case, wherein it outlined a general procedure to be taken when injunctive relief is sought under FRAND-committed SEPs (Pichler & Kastler, 2019):

- Before seeking an injunction, the SEP holder must give notice to the alleged infringer by designating the SEP in question and specifying how it has been infringed;
- The alleged infringer must express its willingness to take a license on FRAND terms.

The SEP holder must:

- Provide a written license offer on FRAND terms, specifying the royalty and how it should be calculated.

There is no universal formula for this, but the German courts have ruled that it should include a "claim chart" or a "proud list" to facilitate negotiates. The alleged infringer must:

- Respond to the SEP holder's offer in good faith by accepting the SEP holder's offer; or.
- Make a counteroffer on FRAND terms;
- Provide appropriate security; and
- Be able to render an account of its acts of use.[8]

Confidentiality and the obligation to conclude a *Non-Disclosure Agreement (NDA)*: In *Sisvel* vs. *Haier*, the court held that an SEP is required to produce comparable license agreements under an NDA. ◀

Example—Apple vs. Samsung

Apple sued *Samsung* in 2011; this case was launched in the broader context of the smartphone war (cf. supra). The lawsuit is a big conflict involving: Trademarks, patents, designs, trade dress,[9] technology standards, FRAND licensing, anti-trust law, and the patent doctrine of exhaustion.

While the lawsuit was centered on many software elements, trial documents show that these are very complex. The jury had to decide whether Samsung had violated rules surrounding "trade dress." It argued that *Samsung* copied its famously minimalistic packaging and design when marketing its devices in violation of its trade dress rights. The jury had to decide whether Apple's trade dress was famous and, by extension, protectable.

Apple also invoked its design rights, alleging that Samsung had copied its industrial designs filed for the iPhone. In the same suit, Samsung had alleged violation of several of its utility patents. The burden of proof in the case was whether it would be "proven by clear and convincing evidence that Apple's infringement was willful."

Apple had even claimed trademark violation under USC §1114 and general trademark law. This intellectual property right was used to cover its icons, design, user interface, and look and feel. On top of those types of rights, Apple had claimed various anti-trust violations by Samsung for certain Universal Mobile Telecommunications Service (UMTS) patents in violation of the US Sherman Anti-Trust Act of 1890. Furthermore, Apple claimed that Samsung had not offered its SEPs at a fair, reasonable, and non-discriminatory royalty (FRAND) rate.

Apple also invoked a more obscure defense against Samsung's claims. A doctrine of patent law is the concept of "exhaustion," which means that once the patented product has entered into commercial circulation—the patent right becomes exhausted. This reason for this doctrine is simple—it would be far too complex in an economy to manage a patent royalty right extending beyond the first sale. Apple alleged that Samsung had granted licenses to baseband chip suppliers, and that once they had done this, Samsung had "exhausted" its patent rights on the technology and could not then come after Apple for violation of these same patents, even if it incorporated Samsung's technology via these chips. ◀

[8] What it is, exactly, that constitutes security, is still a bit ambiguous. The court in *Sisvel* vs. *Haier* held that requiring secured royalties that are due in the future as being excessive and not FRAND-compliant. Again, the idea of good faith is the guiding principle.

[9] Trade dress deals with the visual presentation of the product, such as colors, shape, markings, fonts, a presentation that shows the consumer the source of the product (Sect. 1.3).

New Technology and Patent Exploitation Culture Through the ICT Sector

It can be assumed that in future, every sector into which information and communication technologies penetrate will be confronted with a different technology and patent exploitation culture. Some characteristics are:

- Value-based patent management, where the concrete value created by means of patents is in focus—compared to traditional cost-oriented patent management. *Google*, for example, bought *Motorola* primarily in order to acquire its patents and therefore be able to play in the field of connected business.
- New licensing models are imposed, compared to traditional fee per unit or fee per turnover as such approaches. One game-changing approach by the licensors is to take the value into account a license would have for the licensee in the future. Currently, the automotive industry is confronted with a new patent licensing culture being imposed by the telecom industry.
- Aggressive enforcement of patents, frequently processed by patent assertion companies, often also characterized as patent trolls. These firms file and/or buy patents, which they use for no other reason than suing manufacturing companies that might violate the patent. Various car manufacturers pay a two-digit amount of legal fees per year to defend themselves.

Many new product features and services are expected in the coming years as a result of 5G technology. For companies such as *Ericsson* (Ericsson, 2019), these will form the basis for licensing patents:

- Enhanced video services;
- Real-time automation;
- Monitoring and tracking;
- Connected vehicle;
- Autonomous robotics;
- Hazard detection and maintenance;
- Intelligent monitoring;
- Remote-controlled operations; and
- Augmented reality ("virtual reality").

The 5G patent licensing business is expected to become a multi-billion US$ royalty business again if compared to the so far patent licensing royalty incomes from 3G to 4G (see Fig. 6.20). In 2016, the top ten of the 3G/4G Standard Essential Patent (SEP) owners took 93% of the total licensing royalty income on mobile phones (Galetovic et al., 2018). The top earner is *Qualcomm* with US$7.7 billion, i.e., 54%. Ericsson revised its annual revenue forecast for 2023 upward to around US$1 billion after signing a multi-year global (cross-) license agreement with *Huawei*, covering key patents for standards relevant to both parties' products, including 3G, 4G, and 5G wireless technologies (Ericsson, 2023). In 2024, Qualcomm reported in its annual report US$5.572 billion from its technology licensing, which revealed a shifting balance of power.

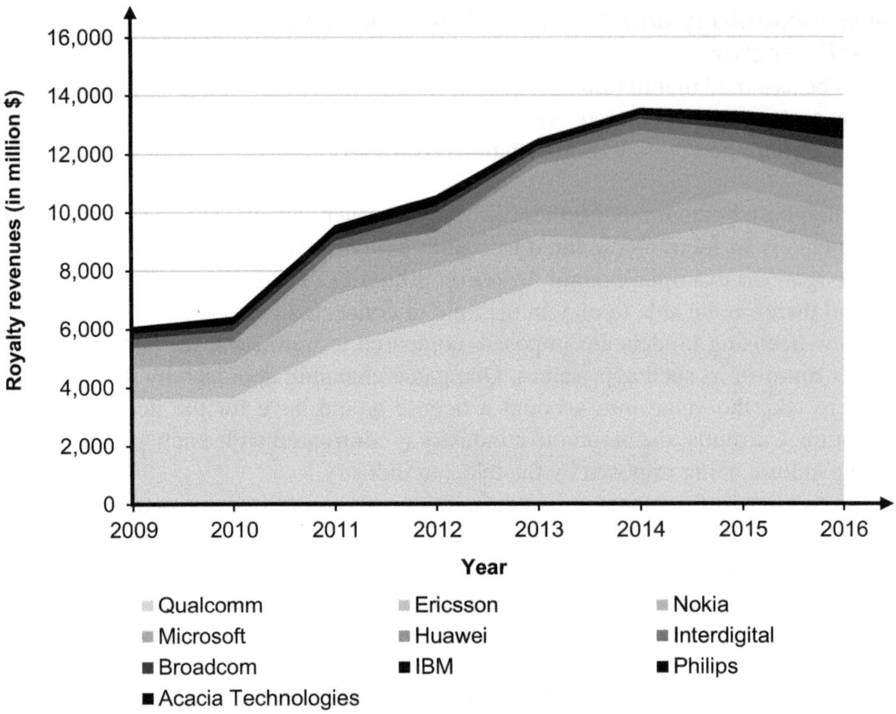

Fig. 6.20 Patent licensing royalty earnings of the top ten SEP holders in million US$ business based on 3G and 4G (not limited to), Galetovic et al. (2018) and Pohlmann et al. (2020)

Takeaways Information and Communications Technology

- Patents are extremely critical for patent pool negotiations.
- Patents and technologies directly determine capital expenditures as standards are formed.
- The ICT industry is characterized by several cross-licensing agreements on the one side and tough patent wars on the other.
- The acquisition of entire companies because of patents—as happened in the *Motorola* acquisition by *Google*—can be a strategic step to enter the connected world.
- ICT has a big influence on several industries, driven by the IoT (internet of things) economy.
- Several industries should pay close attention to the ICT sector and the patent behavior since there is a spillover as soon as connectivity enters the industry—and today, nearly every sector is driven by the strategic trend of connectivity.

6.11 Financial Services and Fintech

The financial services industry has been idle for a long time with respect to its own intellectual property activities compared to other lines of business, and only at a late stage did it begin to patent its developments (Glazier, 2003). This may seem unusual at first, since it is a highly developed industry in which software and system solutions, in which a lot is invested, play a central role. The emerging possibility of patenting business models could provide additional competitive advantages over competitors by preventing them from using the protected business model (Möhrle & Walter, 2009).[10] Also in the financial sector, a number of players had therefore begun to deal consistently with patents (Bader, 2007, 2008; Bader & Bischof, 2005; Bader & Cuypers, 2008).

The trigger for the incipient rethinking among financial service providers lay in particular legal disputes, which also met with a great response in the media due to their scope and novelty:

- *Data Treasury* vs. *JP Morgan Chase* et al.: The lawsuit pertains, inter alia, to the recording, data processing, and storage of cheques and credit card receipts;
- *LML Payments Systems* vs. *U.S. Bancorp* et al.: The lawsuit concerns, among other things, methods of converting paper cheques into electronic transactions;
- *NetMoneyIn* vs. *Bank One, Citibank, Wells Fargo*: The complaint relates, inter alia, to methods of accepting credit card payments over the Internet.

In the past decade, protection against lawsuits has also been the basic driving force behind the patent strategies, particularly in the finance and insurance sectors. The main thrust of which was to be able to prevent legal disputes with third parties by means of own patents. The banking sector's patenting has originally been driven in particular by institutions such as *Bank of America, Barclays, BNP Paribas, Capital One, Citibank, Credit Suisse, Deutsche Bank, Goldman Sachs, HSBC, JP Morgan Chase, Lehman Brothers,*[11] *Merrill Lynch, Royal Bank of Scotland, UBS,* and *Wells Fargo* (see Fig. 6.21). However, traditional tech companies, like *Alphabet, Amazon, Apple, IBM, Oracle,* and *Microsoft,* have started building up specific Fintech patent portfolios to protect their engagement in financial and payment services (see Fig. 6.22).

[10] Cf. Changes caused by *In re Bilski* decision. See the info-box *Patentability of Business Methods in the USA on Trial.*

[11] As part of the bankruptcy proceedings against *Lehman Brothers*, the patent portfolio went to *Barclays* in 2008: The industry breathed a sigh of relief that the portfolio didn't go to a PAE.

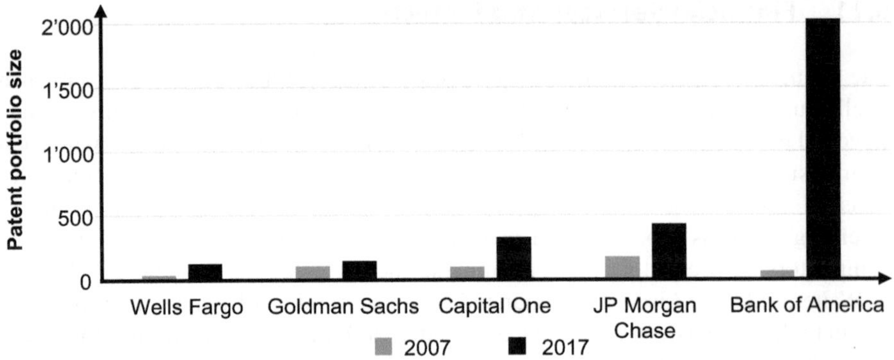

Fig. 6.21 Patent portfolio growth of largest US banks, 2007 versus 2017 (based on Bördin, 2019)

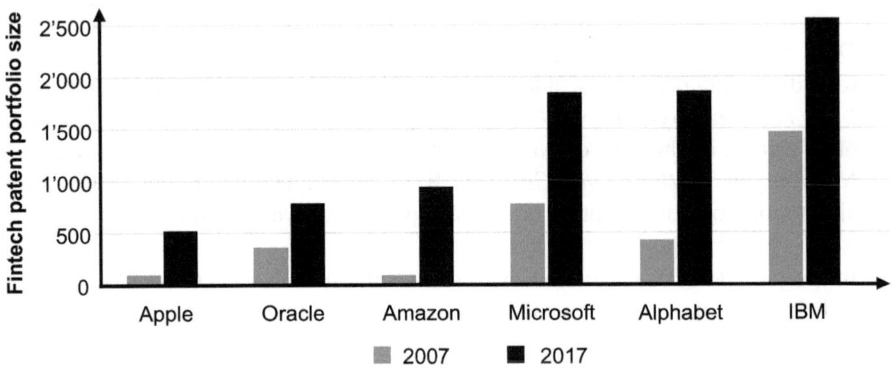

Fig. 6.22 Fintech patent portfolios of major tech companies (based on Bördin, 2019)

Example—Mastercard

Also, payment solution providers have significantly increased their patent filing activities. Hot spot patenting areas are especially blockchain, data security, and machine learning. The two market leaders, *Mastercard* and *Visa*, have increased their annual patent filings by six times since 2010, reaching a peak of about 650 filings in 2016 (Bördin, 2019; see Fig. 6.23). The total filings for both companies are now around 400. Visa filed roughly 444 patents in 2023; Mastercard filed about 371. Their portfolios have parted ways showing different strategic visions with Mastercard focusing on new areas like using AI or blockchain for payment processing, and Visa still filing highly technical patents, like in US patent application US 2025/0103708 A1, describing a way to save energy to make cryptographic defence more energy efficient.

Mastercard got a patent granted on a "Method and system for partitioned blockchains and enhanced privacy for permissioned blockchains" (US 10,097,344 B2, granted in 2018; see Fig. 6.24). The claimed concept allows multiple,

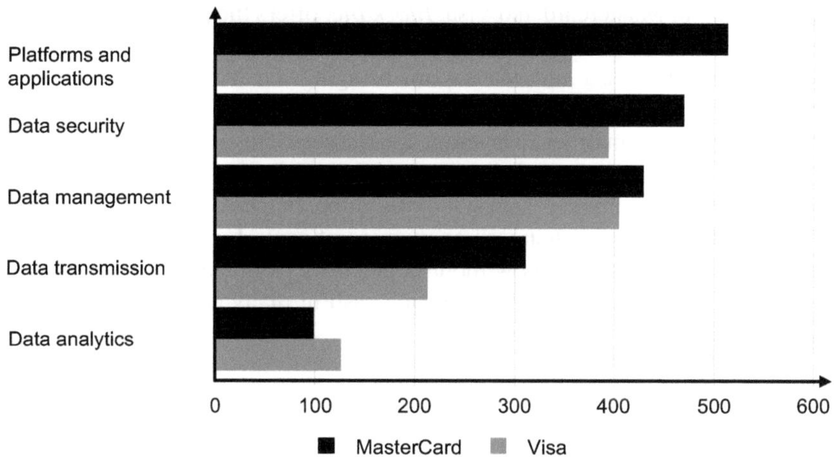

Fig. 6.23 *Mastercard* and *Visa's* technology distribution (based on Bördin, 2019)

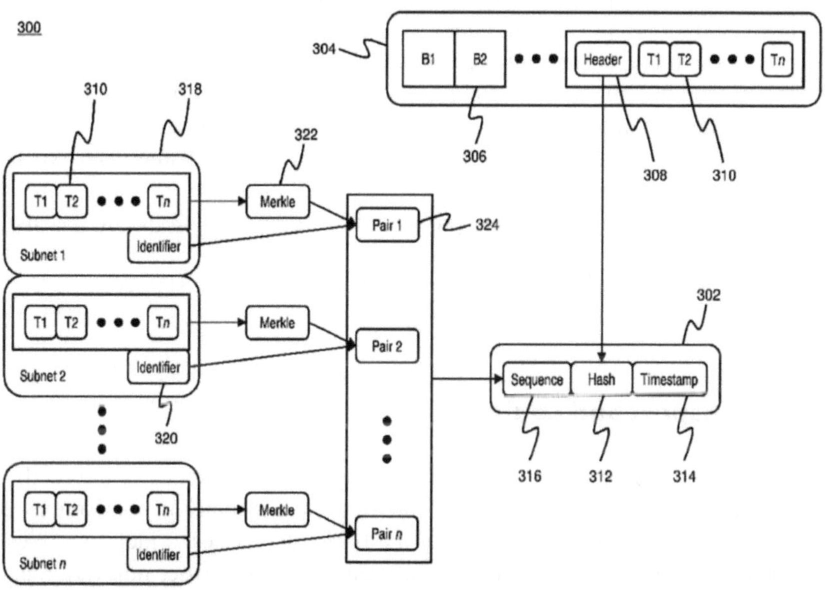

Fig. 6.24 *Mastercard* patent US 10,097,344 B2 on partitioned blockchains and enhanced privacy

different types of transactions to all be stored on a single blockchain. For instance, transactions for several different cryptocurrencies can all be stored in the single blockchain (see also Sect. 5.6).

Since COVID, a new contactless payment system has now come to dominate daily payments on basis of this recent payment technology. Since there are now over 4200 patents that reference the technology, and along with the traditional payment duo of Mastercard and Visa, *Block Inc.* offers the point of sales systems, *Capital One Services* furnishing credit and cars, and *Bank of America* offers clearing, with the Visa and Mastercard bringing the merchant networks. This type of patent pool for payments is more complementary, where the players need to find cooperation in order to leverage their assets. This is slightly different than in the telecom cases where *Samsung*, *Nokia*, and *Ericsson* had more substitute technologies in a more zero-sum standards game. In the case of *EMVCo*, the pool is more synergistic with network economies of scale for the players whom all have viable business models without contactless payments but have combined their technologies to completely displace cash in many economies like Iceland and Sweden. ◀

Takeaways Financial Services

- Finance is plagued by the same pitfalls of methods patents that the computer industry is, where the invention is often less definite than in other fields.
- The financial sector started quite late with patenting activities. Early starts have been done by US companies, namely the City Bank, which has been one of the most active banks, patenting at the European Patent Office.
- Innovation has not been a strong domain of the financial sector, but fintech companies are changing the rules and behavior of the industry.
- Customers are becoming more hybrid, loyalty is lower, and user experience plays an important role for customers.
- Blockchain technologies are part of the strategic outlook in the patent record.
- AI is starting to be deployed as a key aspect of payment services.

6.12 Transport and Logistics

The transport and logistics sector comprises companies that directly or indirectly dispatch or transport people and goods and "intelligently distribute" them. Companies in the sector are increasingly competing on the basis of services, which increases the importance of managing service innovation in general and logistics innovation in particular. The management of logistics innovations encompasses and refers to the planning, control, and monitoring of novel logistics products or processes in supply chains or within companies. Logistical production innovations crystallize through technologies such as "hardware" (e.g., new load carriers) and "software" (e.g., new advanced planning and scheduling systems) or a combination of the two (e.g., radio-frequency identification RFID use). Logistical process innovations, on the other hand, are primarily based on innovations in the area of process knowledge and the structure of the network of relationships. Logistics innovations also come from IT service providers as well as in industrial and commercial enterprises.

The logistics industry is therefore evolving from being seen as a cost center to a source of differentiation that promises sustainable competitive advantages. This trend is in line with the development of the industry into a knowledge or service society. Although numerous advances have been made in logistics in terms of increasing customer satisfaction, improving delivery services, or reducing costs, these achievements have little protection against imitation by competitors compared with other industries. Only a few companies in the logistics services sector systematically and comprehensively manage their intellectual property rights (Bader & Hofmann, 2006). Almost 15 years ago, there were no patent applications at all in the logistics services sector. In only 10 years, there has been a significant revival in patenting activities, with the major players playing a pioneering role. More than 180 new patent applications were published by *UPS* during this period, followed by *Deutsche Post DHL* with over 160, *United States Postal Service* with about 125, *FedEx* with about 20, and *La Poste* with about 10. Of these, most patents are filed not only nationally, but more than a third internationally. Nevertheless, it can be stated that logistics companies still make far too little use of the possibility of patenting business models and thus run the risk of losing innovative know-how and risking freedom-to-operate (Niemann et al., 2013). Since, Niemann's paper was published in 2013, the logistics services have upped their patent games a bit: UPS has filed about 250 patents, the *Deutsche Post* 180, *FedEx* about 50, and *La Poste* 6.

Example—MTel and United Parcel Service (UPS)

UPS was founded in 1907 as a courier service in the USA and is today the world's largest express and parcel delivery service. Over the years, UPS has expanded its service portfolio tremendously and today not only coordinates the movement of goods but also the information and financial flows that result from this. UPS has always placed great emphasis on innovation, standardizing customer service, and increasing reliability. UPS sees this as a sustainable way of differentiating itself from the competition. UPS applies three principles of innovation: First, business activities are continuously redefined, which UPS successfully implements with the strategic reorientation from "serving the small package delivery needs of our customers" to "enabling global commerce" and the entry into the service business; second, the importance of the long-term time horizon of innovation; and third, the important role of the corporate brand in communication during change are recognized.

Despite the fact that the UPS business model is enabled by a lot of logistics infrastructure, it has not been immune to patent lawsuits. It was sued by *Mobile Technology Technologies (MTel)* for infringement of U.S. Patent No. 5,786,748. The patent claims "to provide prompt notification of delivery of an express mailing to the addressee thereof, the page number of a person to be notified upon delivery of the express mailing is communicated to an express mail tracking network and to an operations center of a wireless paging service." The court applied the *Alice* Doctrine in its examination of the patent and found that the patent did not have the requisite inventive concept. *MTel* appealed to the court, arguing that the court had engaged in temporal bias. While the concept of notifying a sender of reception via telecommunications seems laughably trivial in 2016, it was not when the patent was filed in 1996. The court dismissed the appeal for reconsideration, holding that at its core the patent is simply an implementation of an abstract idea and that the patent's very subject was ineligible for patent protection under US law (*Mobile Telecommunications Technologies, LLC* vs. *United Parcel Service*, US District Court for the Northern District of Georgia, Atlanta Division, October 21, 2016). ◀

Example—Enlarging Logistics to Cloud Computing: Amazon

Although *Amazon* is commonly known as a major logistics player, it has substantial patent portfolios in logistics, drones, and aircraft technology.[12] As a recent analysis from Forbes points out (Columbus, 2019):

- Since 2010 Amazon has grown its patent portfolio from less than 1000 active patents in 2010 to nearly 10,000 in 2019, a tenfold increase in less than a decade;
- Amazon heavily cites *Microsoft*, *IBM*, and *Alphabet*;
- Amazon's patent portfolio is dominated by cloud computing, with the majority of the patents contributing to *Amazon Web Services (AWS)* current and future services roadmap;
- Amazon's ongoing developments in alternative delivery methods in Urban Logistics and Drones are mirrored by strong patents (see Fig. 6.25). ◀

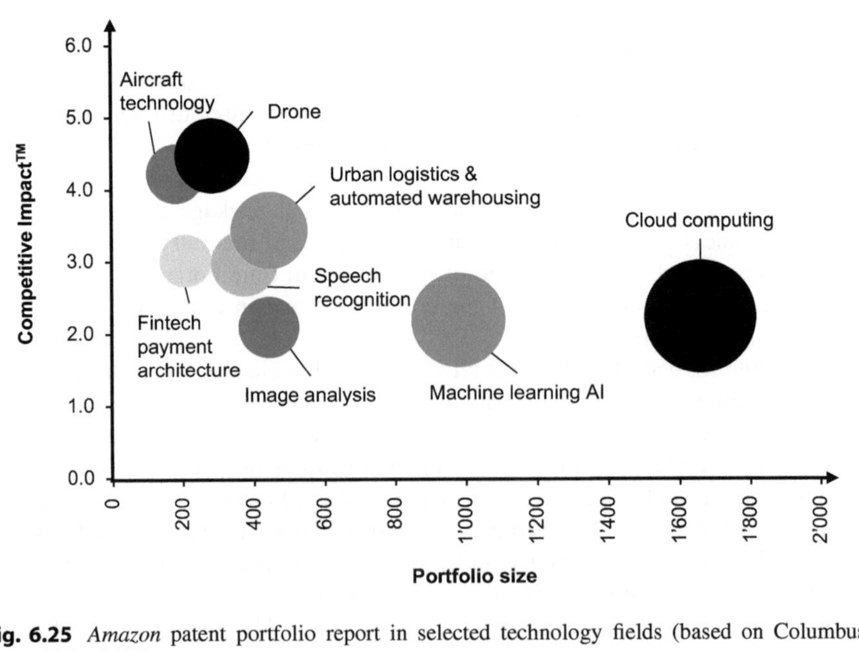

Fig. 6.25 *Amazon* patent portfolio report in selected technology fields (based on Columbus/PatentSight, 2019)

Takeaways Transport and Logistics

- The logistics sector is changing from a traditional low-tech sector to a data-based high-tech industry.
- Location-based services and traceability are becoming more important in the industry.
- The future of autonomous driving systems will revolutionize the logistics sector.
- Technologies as sensor systems, connectivity, 5G, and data analytics with neural networks drive the change of the industry.

References

Bader, M. A. (2007). Extending legal protection strategies to the service innovations area: Review and analysis. *World Patent Information, 29*, 122–135.

Bader, M. A. (2008). Managing intellectual property in the financial services industry sector: Learning from Swiss Re. *Technovation, 28*(4), 196–207.

Bader, M. A. (2022). Innovationen im Handel nutzen und schützen. In M. Knoppe, S. Rock, & M. Wild (Eds.), *Der Zukunftsfähige Handel* (4th ed., pp. 171–192). Springer Gabler.

Bader, M. A., & Bischof, D. (2005). Intellectual Property Management in der Finanzdienstleistungsbranche. In O. Gassmann & S. Albers (Eds.), *Handbuch Technologie- und Innovationsmanagement*. Gabler.

Bader, M. A., & Cuypers, F. (2008). Swiss Re: Global intellectual property management in the financial services industry. In R. Boutellier, O. Gassmann, & M. von Zedtwitz (Eds.), *Managing global innovation* (3rd ed.). Springer.

Bader, M. A., & Gassmann, O. (2022a). Patents in the biomedical sciences and industry—The case of the Swiss life science company Prionics. In M. Hinder, A. Schuhmacher, J. Goldhahn, & D. Hartl (Eds.), *Principles of biomedical sciences and industry*. Wiley-VCH.

Bader, M. A., & Gassmann, O. (2022b). Patent strategies in the networked economy. In O. Gassmann & F. Ferrandina (Eds.), *Connected business* (pp. 247–264). Cham.

Bader, M. A., & Hofmann, E. (2006). Intellectual Property Management in der Logistik. *Supply Chain Management, 6*(4), 7–13.

Bekkers, R., Duysters, G., & Verspagen, B. (2002). Intellectual property rights, strategic technology agreements and market structure: The case of GSM. *Research Policy, 31*(7), 1141–1161.

Bördin, J. (2019). Born from business need. *iam magazine*, autumn 2019. Retrieved July 1, 2025, from https://www.iam-media.com/patents/born-business-need

Brem, A., Maier, M., & Wimschneider, C. (2016). Competitive advantage through innovation: The case of Nespresso. *European Journal of Innovation Management, 19*(1), 133–148.

Buchholz, K. (2019). Who is leading the 5G patent race? Companies which have filed the most patents for 5G technology as of November 2019. *Statista*. Retrieved July 1, 2025, from https://www.statista.com/chart/20095/companies-with-most-5g-patent-families-and-patent-families-applications/

Columbus, L. (2019). *10 charts that will change your perspective of Amazon's patent growth*. Forbes. Retrieved July 1, 2025, from https://www.forbes.com/sites/louiscolumbus/2019/07/21/10-charts-that-will-change-your-perspective-of-amazons-patent-growth/

[12] As a side note, *Amazon* is now offering an *Amazon IP Accelerator* service, with pre-vetted legal professionals that can help companies to quickly accelerate IP and brand protection: https://brandservices.amazon.com/ipaccelerator

EPO. (2017). *Patents and the fourth industrial revolution. The inventions behind digital transformation*. Munich: European Patent Office. Retrieved July 1, 2025, from https://www.epo.org/en/news-events/in-focus/ict/fourth-industrial-revolution

EPO. (2018). *Information and communications technology patents at the EPO*. Munich: European Patent Office. Retrieved July 1, 2025, from https://www.epo.org/en/news-events/in-focus/ict/about-ict

EPO. (2019). *Patenting biotechnological inventions at the EPO*. Brussels: Dr. Harald Schmidt-Yodlee. European Patent Office.

EPO. (2025). *Statistics and trends centre*. Retrieved August 17, 2025, from https://www.epo.org/en/about-us/statistics/statistics-centre

Ericsson. (2019). *The internet of things: Challenges for IP and best practices (Dr. C. Tapia)*. Management Circle IP Service World: Munich, November 2019.

Ericsson. (2023). *Ericsson and Huawei renew global patent license agreement*. Retrieved June 26, 2025, from https://www.ericsson.com/en/press-releases/2023/8/ericsson-and-huawei-renew-global-patent-license-agreement

Frost & Sullivan. (2025). Global automotive outlook 2025. Retrieved January 9, 2026, from https://automotive.messefrankfurt.com/content/dam/messefrankfurt-redaktion/automotive/documents/exl/globalautomotive-outlook-july-2025.pdf

Galetovic, A., Haber, S., & Zaretzki, L. (2018). An estimate of the average cumulative royalty yield in the world mobile phone industry: Theory, measurement and results. *Telecommunications Policy, 42*(3), 263–276. https://doi.org/10.1016/j.telpol.2018.02.002

Gassmann, O., & Bader, M. A. (2024). *Patentmanagement: Innovationen erfolgreich nutzen und schützen* (5th ed.). Springer Gabler.

Gassmann, O., Krech, C.-A., Bader, M. A., & Reepmeyer, G. (2016). Out-licensing in pharmaceutical research and development. In A. Schuhmacher, M. Hinder, & O. Gassmann (Eds.), *Value creation in the pharmaceutical industry—The critical path to innovation* (pp. 363–380). Wiley-VCH.

Gassmann, O., Schuhmacher, A., Reepmeyer, G., & von Zedtwitz, M. (2018). *Leading pharmaceutical innovation—How to win the life science race* (3rd ed.). Springer.

Glazier, S. C. (2003). *E-patent strategies*. LBI Law & Business Institute.

Granstrand, O. (1999). *The economics and management of intellectual property. Towards intellectual capitalism*. Edward Elgar.

GreyB. (2020). *Who owns core 5G patents?—Essentiality check on 5G declared patents*. Retrieved August 17, 2025 from https://info.greyb.com/hubfs/5G%20Report%20-%201st%20Release.pdf

Grünecker. (2013). *E-Auto-Patentindex 2013*. Grünecker Patent—und Rechtsanwälte.

iam. (2015). *In search of the next patent war*. Retrieved July 1, 2025, from https://www.iam-media.com/litigation/search-next-patent-war

iam. (2016). *Innovation and survival: Lessons from the smartphone wars*. Retrieved July 1, 2025, from https://www.iam-media.com/innovation-and-survival-lessons-smartphone-wars

Internet of Business. (2021a). *New Walmart patents signal a push towards Retail 2.0*. Retrieved April 30, 2021, from https://internetofbusiness.com/walmart-patents-retail-2-0/

Internet of Business. (2021b). *Bee robotic: Walmart files patents on automating agriculture*. Retrieved April 30, 2021, from https://internetofbusiness.com/walmart-files-patent-autonomous-bees/

IPI. (2019). *Pulling no punches—How Prionics, a life science company in Zurich, defends its intellectual property*. Retrieved July 1, 2025, from https://www.ige.ch/en/intellectual-property/sme-portal/smes-report/detailseiten/prionics-ag.html

IPI/PatentSight. (2020). *Patent analytics as a support to business decisions*. IPI.

Juve. (2020). *Collision course set for Nokia and Daimler*. Retrieved July 1, 2025, from https://www.juve-patent.com/news-and-stories/cases/collision-course-set-for-nokia-and-daimler/ & *Hopes dwindle for peaceful settlement between Nokia and Daimler*. Retrieved July 1, 2025, from https://www.juve-patent.com/news-and-stories/cases/hopes-dwindle-for-peaceful-settlement-between-nokia-and-daimler/

LexisNexis PatentSight. (2020a). *Number of Alibaba patent families worldwide by filing year from 1999 to 2019, by legal status.* Statista. Retrieved July 9, 2025, from https://www.statista.com/statistics/1033899/number-of-alibaba-patents-by-filing-year-and-status-worldwide/

LexisNexis PatentSight. (2020b). *Number of Amazon patent families worldwide by filing year from 1999 to 2019, by legal status.* Statista. Retrieved July 9, 2025, from https://www.statista.com/statistics/1033929/number-of-amazon-patents-by-filing-year-and-status-worldwide/

LexisNexis PatentSight. (2020c). *Number of Walmart patent families worldwide by filing year from 1999 to 2019, by legal status.* Statista. Retrieved July 9, 2025, from https://www.statista.com/statistics/1034115/number-of-walmart-patents-by-filing-year-and-status-worldwide/

Möhrle, M. G., & Walter, L. (2009). *Patentierung von Geschäftsprozessen. Monitoring—Strategien—Schutz.* Springer.

Niemann, H. (2014). *Corporate Foresight mittels Geschäftsprozesspatenten: Entwicklungsstränge der Automobilindustrie.* Springer.

Niemann, H., Moehrle, M. G., & Walter, L. (2013). The development of business method patenting in the logistics industry—Insights from the case of intelligent sensor networks. *International Journal of Technology Management, 61*(2), 177–197.

Pepe, S., & Post, K. J., & Middleton, A. (2019). Continental Automotive v. Avanci: Wireless SEP licensing presents challenges for automotive industry. Ropes and Gray LPP on *Lexology*. Retrieved July 1, 2025, from https://www.lexology.com/library/detail.aspx?g=2e0a83b4-6e78-4faa-8311-9b6e4a0c945f

Picanço-Castro, V., Pereira, C., Covas, D. T., Porto, G., Athanassiadou, A., & Figueiredo, M. L. (2020). Emerging patent landscape for non-viral vectors used for gene therapy, *Nature: Biotechnology*, 38, 151–157. Graphic released to public by Purdue University. Retrieved July 1, 2025, from https://www.purdue.edu/newsroom/releases/2020/Q1/novel-techniques-for-mining-patented-gene-therapies-offer-promising-treatment-options-for-cancers,-other-diseases.html

Pichler, R. & Kastler, H. A. (2019). FRAND case law in Europe after Huawei vs. ZTE. *Morrison Foerster LLP on Lexology*. Retrieved July 1, 2025, from https://www.lexology.com/library/detail.aspx?g=f4c5633a-21ed-4aec-a1d2-23803d5d1806

Pohlmann, T., Blind, K., & Heß, P. (2020). *Studie zur Untersuchung und Analyse der Patentsituation bei der Standardisierung von 5G.* Study on behalf of the German Bundesministerium für Wirtschaft und Energie.

Singh, S. (2025). *Germany fast moving consumer goods market research report.* ID: MRFR/CR/42607-HCR. New York: Market Research Future, WantStats Reasearch and Media. Retrieved July 1, 2025, from https://www.marketresearchfuture.com/reports/germany-fast-moving-consumer-goods-market-44286#

Thompson. (2013). Costs of Swiss patent litigation. *Sic!* June, 2013.

Wagner, R. (2015). Wichtige Trends in der Automobilindustrie. In R. Wagner & G. Hab (Eds.), *Projektmanagement in der Automobilindustrie* (pp. 3–9). Springer Fachmedien.

Wolfe, J. (2019). *Bristol-Myers wins $752 million in US patent case against Gilead Reuters.*

7 Patent Management in New Technology Environments

The intellectual property system dates back several 100 years to when the first patent was issued in Florence, Italy, in 1421, for a barge hoist. This concept of privileged use of this slowly spread throughout Europe. But the patent system in its modern incarnation goes back to the industrial age of the nineteenth century and is increasingly at odds with the physicality of the originally designed system. Throughout all this time, technology has undoubtedly progressed, but inventions have become less physical and more ethereal as well.

Contemporary inventions are starting to exert pressure against the legal framework of the patent system conceived in an age of steel. Knowledge about which genes control which biological function is certainly a discovery on par with, if not more powerful than, any physical invention of the industrial age, but biotechnology raises deep bio-ethical questions and questions about where invention ends and discovery begins. Artificial intelligence is already pushing the legal boundaries of human agency in the creation of IP. The following is a selection of these technologies, which are likely to be both relevant commercially and where there are implications for intellectual property.

This chapter covers:

1. Biotechnology
2. Nanotechnology
3. Industry 4.0 and Internet of Things
4. Software and Business Methods
5. Artificial-Intelligence-based Business Models

M. A. Bader et al., *Patent Management*, Management for Professionals,
https://doi.org/10.1007/978-3-032-12030-4_7

7.1 Biotechnology

In recent decades, biotechnology has been one of the faster-growing fields as well as being among the top ten technical fields in terms of the number of patent applications filed with the European Patent Office (European Patent Index 2024, see EPO, 2025a); this is a volatile area. About half of these applications come from scientific institutes and universities. As this field of science covers a wide range of fields from microorganisms to agriculture and medical applications and covers publicly controversial techniques and products, such as genetically modified plants, animal cloning, or the use of human embryonic stem cells, patents are discussed more vividly here than in other technical fields.

Patenting biotechnological inventions raises a host of questions, not only legal or economic ones but also ones that are ethical and social in nature. Patenting is polarizing, although numerous studies have dealt with this controversial issue (Dutfield, 2003; OECD, 2003; Straus, 2003; Thumm, 2001, 2003): For some, patents are important for economic and scientific development, for others, they represent an inadmissible commercialization of life or a barrier to the free exchange of knowledge. In collaboration with the Swiss Federal Institute of Intellectual Property (IPI) and the Group for Science and Research (GWF), the Science et Cité Foundation has illustrated various points of view in this regard (EPO, 2024; Stiftung Science et Cité, 2004):

Examples of Patentable Biotechnological Inventions

Like all other technologies, inventions in biotechnology are in principle patentable under the law, and the same general patent examination rules and processes apply as for inventions from any other technical field.

- Genes and nucleic acid molecules (e.g., disease-related genes for diagnostics or for the antisense procedure and siRNA molecules for therapy).
- Proteins (e.g., insulin, erythropoietin for therapy and cell receptors for drug screening).
- Enzymes (e.g., proteases for washing powder and cellulose-degrading enzymes for the production of biofuels).
- Antibodies (e.g., for cancer treatment, pregnancy tests, or diagnostics).
- Viruses and virus sequences (e.g., hepatitis C virus and HIV for blood tests and for the development of vaccines and therapies).
- Cells (e.g., hematopoietic stem cells for the treatment of leukemia).
- Microorganisms (e.g., bacteria for bioremediation and yeast for food production).
- Plants (e.g., herbicide-resistant soybeans, "golden rice" with a high content of provitamin A, and drought-resistant plants and algae that extract CO_2 from the atmosphere).
- Animals (e.g., disease models for research purposes such as the genetically modified "cancer mouse," donor animals for xenotransplantation and milk-producing animals that excrete medicinal substances in their milk). ◀

Examples of Non-patentable Biotechnological Inventions

The European Patent Organisation's member states have agreed on a number of special rules that define what is patentable and what is not in the field of biotechnology. These rules are in line with the EU Biopatent Directive and concern, among other things, "living matter", especially inventions related to plants and animals. The law also gives guidance on inventions that cannot be patented for ethical reasons.

- DNA sequences without known function (e.g., expressed sequence tags (ESTs) as a result of automatic sequencing).
- Genetically modified animals that have to suffer without there being a significant medical benefit, e.g., a genetically modified animal that is only used for cosmetic tests.
- Plant varieties (already protected by the International Convention for the Protection of New Varieties of Plants, e.g., apples of the "Golden Delicious" variety).
- Animal breeds (e.g., Holstein cattle).
- Human embryos.
- Procedures that inevitably involve the use and destruction of human embryos.
- Human germ cells (sperm and ova).
- Human–animal chimeras. ◀

Research Despite Patents Possible

In biotechnology, the use of basic procedures, for example, for the isolation of genes, is essential for research. If such processes are not available or are only available at a high cost because of patents, research can suffer as a result. The polymerase chain reaction (PCR) is an elementary process in genetic engineering with which very small amounts of DNA can be amplified at will. Duplication solves the problem that genetic material is often only available in extremely small quantities and thus eludes direct detection or analysis.

The PCR method has been the subject of numerous patents. These patents have made the research possible, as the granting of licenses has allowed the technology to be used by others. The exponential increase in the number of scientific publications referencing PCR technology between 1987 and 1997, which appeared after the publication of the PCR patent, is evidence of this. In general, when licenses are granted, the costs of research projects may increase because license fees have to be paid. Especially in basic research, costs are an important factor.

Biotechnological Inventions and Patents

According to the European Patent Convention (EPC), "biotechnological inventions" are inventions that concern a product consisting of or containing biological material—such as DNA sequences, genes, or proteins—or a process by which biological material is produced, processed, or used (Rule 26(2) EPC).

"Biological material" means any material containing genetic information and capable of reproducing itself or being reproduced in a biological system (Rule 26(3) EPC). This includes living organisms and DNA.

"Biotech patents" are patents for biotechnological inventions and may also cover plant, animal, or human cells, tissues, organs, or genetically modified animals and plants, as well as genetically modified seeds.

Biotechnology Patents at the EPO

In the following, excerpts from the EPO on the legal requirements on *biotechnology patents* (EPO, 2024) are displayed:

As with all other technologies, inventions in biotechnology are generally considered patentable under the law, and the same general patent examination rules and processes apply to all inventions.

At the EPO, biotechnology represents about 4% of all patent applications filed; in 2024, 8479 of the total number of 199,264 European patent applications received concerned biotechnology.

In the vast majority of cases, patent applications in this field are uncontroversial. Public debate concerns a very small number of patent applications related specifically to animals and plants.

The EPO examines all patent applications diligently. Across all technologies, fewer than half of the applications filed become a patent. In biotechnology, the grant rate is significantly lower: Less than 30% of the patent applications filed become a European patent.

Respecting Traditional Knowledge

The EPO uses powerful tools and very comprehensive databases when performing a search to determine whether the invention claimed in a patent application is new or not.

To avoid undue privatization of traditional knowledge already in the public domain, the EPO also searches specialized databases, such as the Indian Traditional Knowledge Digital Library, which provides information related to Indian traditional medicine for patent offices. In 2009, the EPO signed an agreement with the Indian government granting EPO examiners online access to this database. The EPO also consults databases relating to other traditional knowledge, in particular databases describing Chinese and Korean traditional knowledge.

Ethics

The EPO grants patents in strict accordance with its legal basis, the European Patent Convention (EPC) and takes ethical considerations into account when granting patents. Inventions whose exploitation is deemed to be contrary to Article 53 EPC are not patentable. The law lists exceptions to patentability for ethical reasons; among them are human cloning, modification of the human genome, and commercial uses of human embryos.

For patents in biotechnology, the rules of the EU's Directive on the legal protection of biotechnological inventions ("Biopatent Directive") also apply. The Directive, for instance, clarifies that human genes, plants, and animals are patentable when all conditions for a patent are fulfilled. The Directive became part of the EPC in 1999.

The EPO voluntarily follows the rulings of the European Court of Justice on the correct interpretation of the Directive and has incorporated such rulings into its practical work in biotechnology.

The EPO engages with stakeholders of the patent system and the public in open and transparent discussions. It closely cooperates with the EU institutions and informs them on important developments in the field of biotechnology patents. It recently began a close cooperation with the Community Plant Variety Office (CPVO) on questions relating to patents on plants.

Animals and Human Genes

Patents for a human gene often form the basis for many life-saving drugs. The EPO does not grant patents for genes without a known activity or for unidentified gene fragments. For a patent to be granted for a human gene, its activity must have been described in the patent application and not be obvious.

Patents for human genes do not confer any rights to the human body. Applicants tend to withdraw their applications when they receive negative reports from the EPO on the patentability of their invention. The number of patent applications refused by the EPO, therefore, is generally quite low. However, there are many examples of rejected patent biotech applications.

In the area of human genes, numerous applications were refused because the function of the gene had not been convincingly demonstrated in the application. Examples include application EP 097930715 A and EP 01981441 A, both concerning human gene sequences said to be promising targets for the manufacture of medications. Application EP 96903521 A was refused on ethical grounds because it was based on the use of human embryonic stem cells that at the time of filing could only be isolated by destroying human embryos, which is not allowable under the EPC.

Like plants, animals are patentable according to the law. The patent applications filed with the EPO mostly concern transgenic (genetically modified) mice and rats used in medical research. However, the EPO takes ethical considerations into account: If the transgenic invention is found to make the animal suffer, it may only be patented if it brings a substantial medical benefit to humans (or animals).

As with plants, conventional breeding methods for animals are not patentable either. No patents for farm animals produced by such conventional breeding methods have been granted by the EPO.

Patenting of the First Mammal in the USA

In 1988, the US Patent Office granted the first patent on a mammal, the Harvard mouse.[1] This genetically modified mouse was not a great success in practice and in economic terms. But since the patent was granted, the effects of patenting living matter have been the subject of controversial debate worldwide. In fact, biological matter was considered patentable a few years earlier in the USA, Europe, and Japan. Until then, however, patents had only been granted for microorganisms or plants. It was only with the granting of a patent for an animal that the fundamental discussion on the patenting of biological material, especially in Europe, was launched. In Canada, the patent was revoked by the highest court because higher life forms could not be considered inventions.

Different Views in the USA, Europe, and Japan[2]

Before 1980, living matter other than plants was not patentable in the USA. With a decision of the US Supreme Court in 1980, this view was thrown overboard and patentability was basically extended to any man-made biological material ("anything under the sun that is made by man"). In the US Patent Act, there are no general reservations with regard to public order or morality, as is the case in Europe and Switzerland, and to some extent, also in Japan. In the USA, therapeutic, diagnostic, and surgical procedures on humans are also patentable, which are excluded from patenting in Europe, Switzerland, and Japan. The European Patent Convention (EPC) defines specific exceptions to biotechnological inventions that are not patentable, such as processes for cloning human beings or the use of human embryos for industrial or commercial purposes. Such specific exceptions are not listed either in the US Patent Act or in the Japanese Patent Act.

CRISPR-Cas9 Patent Dispute

CRISPR-associated protein 9 (Cas-9)[3] is an enzyme, which uses CRISPR genetic sequences to cleave DNA (Deoxyribonucleic acid) at specific points. The system comes from a prokaryotic bacteria immune response to nucleic attacks from viruses

---

[1] US 4,736,866 ("Harvard Mouse"/"Oncomouse").

[2] Stiftung Science et Cité (2004).

[3] CRISPR = Clustered regularly interspaced short palindromic repeats.

and plasmids. The immune-response mechanism gets the foreign agents to integrate the sequences into their own sequence, and then the Cas-9 enzyme cleaves the subsequent RNA (ribonucleic acid)—disrupting the virus or plasmid.

This obscure biological mechanism is now at the epicenter of the biggest advance in biotechnology since the advent of PCR DNA amplification because it allows scientists to tailor how and where the CRISPR sequences get inserted into another sequence and to then cleave it in a precise way.

The universities in *Berkeley* and *Vienna* filed a patent in 2012, which was where Jennifer Doudna and Emmanuelle Charpentier had worked to discover the application of the naturally occurring biological mechanism. US 2012/61652086 P "provides methods of modulating transcription of a target nucleic acid in a target cell, generally involving contacting the target nucleic acid with an enzymatically inactive Cas9 polypeptide and a DNA-targeting RNA. Kits and compositions for carrying out the methods are also provided. The present disclosure provides genetically modified cells that produce Cas9; and Cas9 transgenic non-human multicellular organisms."

A competing team, led by Feng Zhang, at *Massachusetts Institute of Technology* (*MIT*) filed a similar patent just a few months later. This triggered an interference procedure. The *Berkeley–Vienna* group showed how CRISPR could be used in an in vitro experimental system to alter DNA (Jinek et al., 2012); the *Cambridge group* (*MIT and Harvard*) showed in US patent No. 8'697'359 about 1 year later how it might be used in eukaryotic cells, of the type found in humans. In contrast, the *Berkeley–Vienna group* showed and based their findings on prokaryotic cells, the type found in bacteria—but the patent claims were left in vague as to which cell type was meant.

The *Berkeley–Vienna group* then triggered an interference at the US patent office claiming that their patent covered what the *Cambridge group* had claimed. America at the time, before the "America Invents Act," granted the patent to the first party to invent—and not necessarily the first to file. So, there is a period in which inventors can present evidence as to which party invented it.

Interference Proceeding

At the US Patent and Trademark Office (USPTO), an interference proceeding is conducted by a quasi-judicial panel of administrative patent judges to determine which applicant has a legal claim to the patent:

(a) Two or more pending patent applications; or
(b) At least one pending patent application and at least one patent issued within a year of the pending application's filing date.

Appeals are heard by the United States Court of Appeals for the Federal Circuit or the United States District Court for the District of Columbia.

The *Cambridge group* moved to have the interference quashed, arguing that a person of ordinary skill in the art would not have had a reasonable expectation of success in applying the CRISPR-Cas9 system in eukaryotes. For both patents to be upheld, the subject matter must be "patentably distinct." The USPTO panel has a two-way test. They apply this test by asking the questions, "Whether a person of ordinary skill in the art would have been motivated to modify or combine teachings in the prior art, and whether he would have had a reasonable expectation of success"; see *In re Stepan Co.* , 868 F.3d 1342, 1345–46 (Fed. Cir. 2017).

The expert testimony and the panel concluded that the eukaryotic and prokaryotic systems are so distinct that applications in one cell type cannot be directly applied to the other with any certainty. Ironically, one of the lead inventors in the *Berkeley–Vienna group*, Jennifer Doudna, experienced many "frustrations" while getting CRISPR-Cas9 to work in human cells. For these reasons, the United States Court of Appeals for the Federal Circuit held that the Cambridge CRISPR patent was not anticipated by the *Berkeley–Vienna group's* patent.

In this epic battle, the scientific community was in luck because both breakthroughs had been made in publicly funded laboratories. All the universities involved have since then licensed the technology, which has advanced genetic engineering and biotechnology. Had such an advance been discovered and patented by a private lab, a king's ransom could have been charged for the breakthrough, and the story of this amazing technology-propelling medicine and crop science could have been a lot different.

In the latest conflict of the CRISPR important story, one of the European patents (EP 2 771 468) was declared invalid. The reason is legally highly technical. Patents filed abroad depend on a so-called priority document, which is the first patent application for a given invention. EP 2 771 468 cites a US application, US 2012/61736527 P, as its priority document. The priority invention exists as an independent legal right, but the inventor. Article 87(1) of the European patent convention states:

Any person who has duly filed, in or for (a) any State party to the Paris Convention for the Protection of Industrial Property (PCIP) or (b) any Member of the World Trade Organization (WTO), an application for a patent, a utility model or a utility certificate, or his successor in title, shall enjoy, for the purpose of filing a European patent application in respect of the same invention, a right of priority during a period of 12 months from the date of filing of the first application.

The EP 2 771 468 cites 12(!) priority documents, but the earliest documents are the essential ones because the novelty of the invention was subsequently destroyed as several researches had made their publications shortly afterward. In these cases, the initial US 2012/61736527 P applicant had to legally transfer the right within that period to the subsequent EP 2 771 468 applicant. This was not done within the time window of that year, legally, which legally meant that EP 2 771 468 was void. In any many other cases, this legal technicality might have gone unnoticed—but here there was a lot at stake scientifically and commercially, and thus, the patent was challenged at the EPO by nine different opponents. Upon reviewing the case, the Opposition Board at the EPO ruled the patent invalid; the applicants lost their appeal in January 2020. The invention is now free to be used in Europe (see also IPStudies, 2019; Ledford, 2016; SCBT, 2024; ScienceMag, 2017; Sherkow, 2015, 2018).

Aside from being highly relevant to biotechnology, the presented case is an example of bad patent management—letting such a legal technicality slip through cost millions of dollars in revenue potential. It is also the exact type of arcane detail that might get lost if a company does not have good patent management in place. Moreover, as the value of a patent goes up, it will be subject to more and more legal scrutiny and challenge. This is why it is important for management to strategically weigh the risks and rewards of a given IP right.

Figure 7.1 offers a visual depiction of the frenzy of cross-licensing activity that has taken place round the CRISP technology.

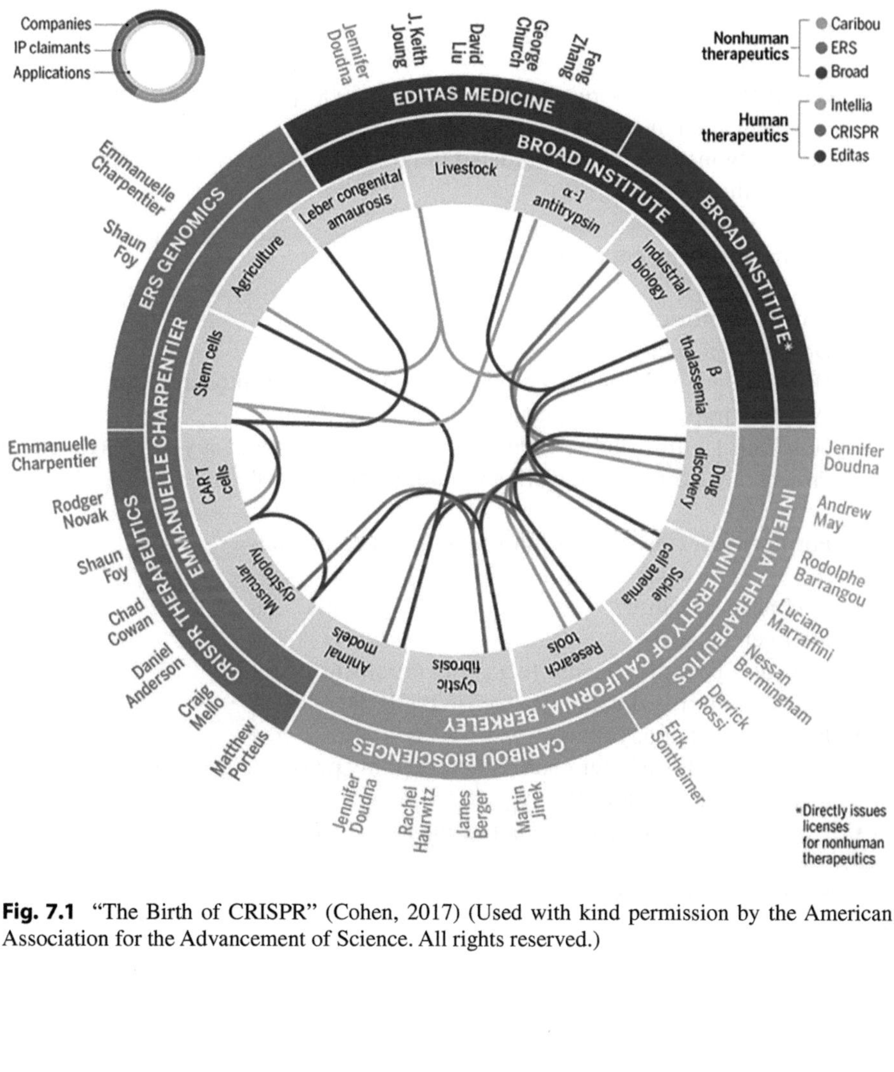

Fig. 7.1 "The Birth of CRISPR" (Cohen, 2017) (Used with kind permission by the American Association for the Advancement of Science.

Takeaways CRISPR-Cas9

CRISPR/Cas9 promises to be one of the most significant scientific and medical breakthroughs in modern history:

- Its precision and relative ease of use have already transformed how scientists study disease and the human genome.
- Use for therapeutic and diagnostic development, plant and animal breeding.
- The concept of using the CRISPR/Cas complex in animal and human cells is expressed in patent (applications) and disputed.

CRISPR IP battle falls mainly into two camps: *UC Berkeley* and the *Broad Institute at Harvard* and *MIT* (see Fig. 7.1).

- Both claimed IP rights to CRISPR technology shortly after its initial discovery in 2012.
- CRISPR technology results in more than 5000 patent families and 140 licensing agreements (IPStudies, 2019).
- EP family member was invalidated in 2020 during opposition on the legal technicality of entitlement.

For licensors (patent owners):

- Who is interested in my technology?
- Do I grant a license?
- How do I get paid for a license agreement (e.g., in cryptocurrency)?
- Will I be informed about changes in the IP landscape?
- How can I inform other parties and competitors about my other related projects to avoid double work and future IP problems?

For licensees (researchers, universities and companies):

- Do I need a license?
- Do I get a license?
- How do I pay for a license (e.g., with cryptocurrency)?
- Will I be informed about changes in the IP landscape?
- Is my project anonymized?
- How can I inform other researchers about my project to avoid double work and future IP problems?
- How can interested parties contact me to cooperate?

Source: BGW (2019).

7.2 Nanotechnology

Nanotechnology is the field of engineering of matter at the scale of less than 1 ten-millionth of a meter. It is a rapidly growing field and is regarded as one of the key technologies of the twenty-first century. In contrast to other domains, much of the research and development has been financed by state policy. In a Harvard law review done for the WIPO, Lisa Ouellete asserts that nanotechnology belongs to IP's "negative space," i.e., a domain where innovation takes place regardless of intellectual property rather than because of it (Ouellette, 2015). Many of the requisite technologies comprise basic research and physics. So, it is an interesting counterpoint to other domains where patents are the primary policy tool and incentive for innovation.

Given the fact that nanotechnology often relies on the discovery of something underlying it that is physical, some legal scholars have begun to question which parts of nanotechnology are actually patentable. Smalley (2014) writes, "The rules articulated in *Prometheus* and *Myriad* [US Supreme Court cases] may ultimately be applicable to nanotechnology. Compositions of matter that fall into the category of nanotechnology may already exist in nature or be a small-scale version of something that already exists in nature. For example, carbon nanotubes are naturally created in soot, but are the subject of thousands of patents. Further, the usefulness of nanotechnology inventions often comes from the unique properties of matter at the nanoscale, such as increased magnetism, conductivity, reactivity, or reflective ability. The 'product of nature' doctrine, as articulated in *Prometheus* and *Myriad*, may have substantial effects on the patenting of nanotechnology-related inventions because many such inventions involve discovering and harnessing the properties of material at the nanoscale or processes involving the use of nanoscale materials." As a concrete example, physicists Wang et al. (2008) have shown that the quantum tunneling effect can be used to drive an arrangement of carbon atoms to make a nanomotor. Their discovery begs the question of whether this is an invention, law of nature, or discovery, raising a fundamental question about patentability. Moreover, it raises other questions, namely whether a person sufficiently trained in the art would be able to create such a motor since presumably any quantum physicist would/should be able to predict the behavior of such an arrangement of atoms using the quantum and physical equations known to all—as they did using computer modeling. Such legal arguments might be used to attack many active patents in the nanotechnology space.

The role of state-sponsored R&D and legal patentability notwithstanding, numerous experts see nanotechnology as the major growth market after biotechnology. A volume of over US$75 billion is forecast for 2020. Against this background, it is not surprising that nanotechnology-related patent applications are growing at an above-average rate internationally. Korea leads with over 70%, followed by India, Poland, and China, which still show more than 40% growth (OECD, 2009). Among the top applicants are companies such as *IBM, Eastman Kodak, Micron, Hewlett-Packard, Xerox,* and *3M* but also *L'Oréal, BASF, Samsung* as well as the *Japan Science and Technology Agency* and *Matsushita* (Chen et al., 2008). In 2023, the European Patent Office (EPO) granted over 2700 nanotechnology patents, accounting for nearly 30% of the United States Patent and Trademark Office's (USPTO) total that year. The USA led with 801 patents, followed by Germany and France (Statnano, 2024). The search database of the European Patent Office has already classified more than 90,000 patent documents worldwide that can be attributed to nanotechnology.

Figure 7.2 shows the growth in nano-tech publications identified in the *Web of Science*, a former product of the Intellectual Property and Science business of *Thomson Reuters*. According to Zhu et al. (2021), in a more recent study using article relevancy rather than counts, China, USA, and South Korea still remain in the lead.

As with all new technologies, the patenting process often first had to develop and adapt (Huebner, 2008; Miller et al., 2005). One of the central questions regarding the patentability of nanotechnologies was whether already the miniaturization of a device known per se can be regarded as something new. As a rule, this is to be denied. If, however, a technical effect is reinforced by miniaturization, the practice

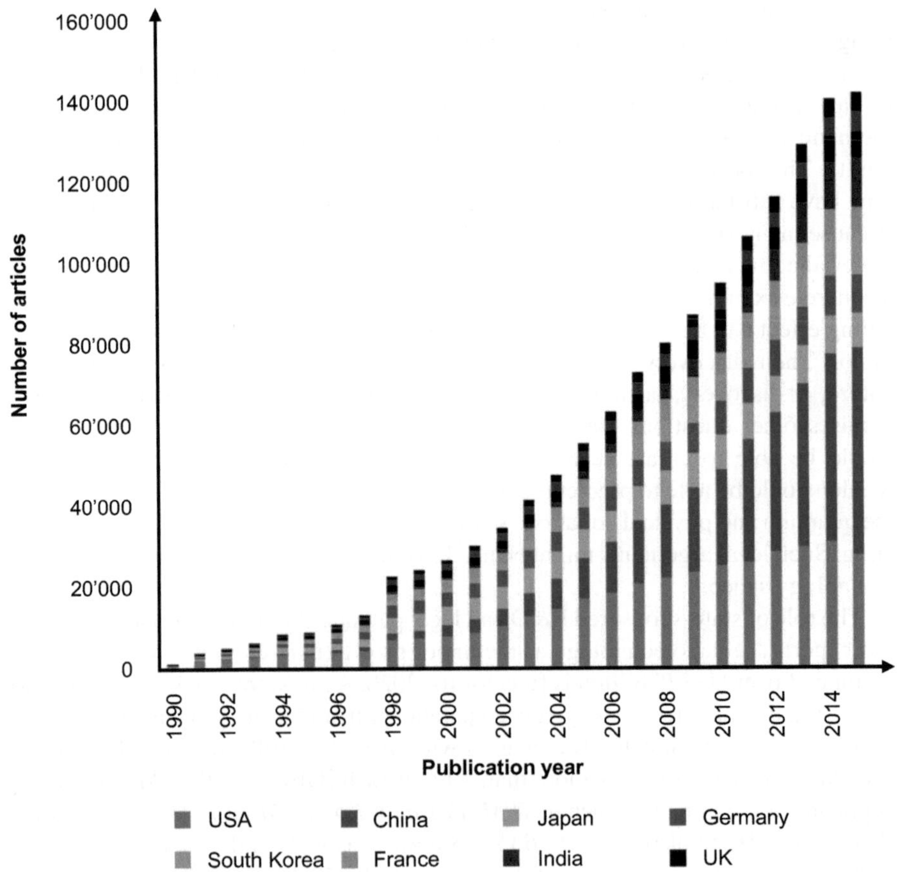

Fig. 7.2 Web of Science growth of nanotechnology publications (based on Youtie et al., 2016)

of the EPO assumes that the order of magnitude constituted an explicitly chosen path and that the novelty is thereby generally affirmed. If a sub-area of a larger area is selected, three criteria must be met to meet the novelty requirement (Kallinger et al., 2008):

- The defined scope/scale must be narrow in comparison to the known range.
- The defined scope must be sufficiently distant from scope/scale, which is known from examples known from the state of the art.
- A purely randomly selected subscale is not sufficient; rather, a new technical effect must occur that only occurs in the subscale.

It is also necessary for the inventive step to be substantiated that the specific or additional technical effect produced by the miniaturization is not obvious. Furthermore, it is important that the invention is sufficiently detailed and clearly described by the patent applicant in order to meet the requirements for patentability.

However, the practices might differ in different legislations, like the USA, where nano-patent applications are considered to get more likely granted than similar European applications (Costello-Caulkins, 2021).

Example—Patent Disputes Also in Nanotechnology

Despite the emerging case law in this field, there are already patent disputes. The US nanotech company *Nanosys*, which was only founded in 2001, filed a patent infringement suit against the British company *Nanoco* at the beginning of 2009, a kind of spin-off from the University of Manchester suit. Nanosys claims to have a portfolio of more than 500 patents and patent applications in the field of inorganic high-tech performance nanostructures, including five US patents that Nanosys had previously exclusively in-licensed from the *Massachusetts Institute of Technology* (*MIT*) (Nanosys, 2009). The in-licensed patents relate to luminescent quantum dot nanocrystals (based on a CdSe/ZnS core structure) that can be used in various areas, such as flat-panel displays. In mid-2009, Nanosys and Nanoco already compared themselves without compensation payments, but on the condition that Nanoco withdraws from the US market with heavy-metal-based quantum dot nanocrystals. Nanoco found patent disputes in the USA too costly as it was focusing on heavy-metal-free quantum dot nanocrystals. ◄

Practice of the European Patent Office (EPO)

In the following, excerpts from the EPO are displayed concerning the legal requirements on *nanotechnology patents* (EPO, 2013):

Basic Requirements for European Patent Applications

All European patent applications, including those relating to nanotechnology, have to meet the requirements of the European Patent Convention (EPC). To get your nanotechnology patent granted:

- The invention must be new (the principle of "novelty");
- It must involve an inventive step; and
- It must be susceptible to industrial application.

Furthermore, the invention must be adequately disclosed and the claims of the application must be clear, concise, and supported by the description.

When trying to determine whether or not your invention is new, it can be useful to look at catalogs and trade journals to see what is already on the market.

However, the single most important source of information for seeing what inventions already exist has to be the vast collection of published patent documents describing the relevant state of the art. A search of the patent literature using, e.g., *Espacenet* will help to give you an indication of whether or not the invention is new (see Sect. 9.5).

1. **Novelty and size.**

   For an invention to be regarded as patentable, it must be *new*, i.e., there must be no evidence that the same invention has ever been described before.

   With regard to nanotechnology, the question is whether making a known device smaller is in itself novel. Generally speaking, this is not the case. Patent applications directed toward the downscaling of an entity have to meet additional criteria if they are to comply with the requirement of novelty.

   A smaller version of a known device is considered new if it shows the same effect as the bigger one but to a greater extent, such that it is reasonable to assume that the size was selected on purpose.

   In general, if there is a technical effect that is enhanced in a selected subrange, the device is new and not just a part of the prior art.

Example—Novelty

In nanotechnology, inventions are often defined by a parametric range. For example, particle A has a diameter in the range of 20–30 nm. What if a particle B of the same material is known and has a diameter of less than 1 μm? At first sight, it seems that particle A is not new because the claimed range of 20–30 nm is already included in particle B's range of less than 1 μm. However, A will be considered as new provided that the selected subrange is—narrow compared with the known range—sufficiently far removed from any specific examples disclosed in the prior art and from the endpoints of the known range—not an arbitrary miniaturization of a known particle. ◀

2. **Inventive step.**

   To be patentable, an invention must also be the product of an inventive step.

   Novelty and inventive step are different criteria. Novelty basically exists if there is any difference between the invention and any prior art. The question—"Is there an inventive step?"—only gets raised if there is novelty. The answer to this question is positive if a person who is skilled in the technical field of the invention and familiar with the prior art would not—on his own—have arrived at the solution provided by the invention.

   When assessing whether or not a nanotechnology invention involves an inventive step, the key question is often whether the miniaturization of a known device is inventive. Is it just a random selection, or is there a new technical advantage to be had from making it smaller?

   If the inventor has simply taken the known prior art and made it smaller, without showing any particular technical advantage to making the invention this particular size, it is not inventive. In other words, there is no inventive step when the mere reduction of dimensions shows no additional or surprising effect and is arrived at arbitrarily.

   However, if the invention provides a new technical advantage that was not to be found in the prior art, and it was not an obvious thing for a skilled person with a thorough knowledge of the state of the art to arrive at, then the miniaturization could be considered inventive.

Example—Inventive Step

One of the features of an invention relating to a field-effect transistor was that it had an insulating layer with a thickness of 3–18 nm. When assessing whether this feature involved an inventive step, it was decided that the thickness range for the dielectric film merely followed a trend toward miniaturization in semiconductor devices. The applicant also failed to demonstrate any particular effects produced by the film having this specific thickness. The thickness in this case was deemed to be an arbitrary selection, and the patent was not granted. ◀

3. **Disclosure.**

   In many cases, nanotechnology is the product of highly sophisticated preparation methods and tools for manipulating materials in the nanometer or even molecular range. Some of these methods when applied to a highly specific problem go beyond the knowledge of the person of average skill in the field and even beyond that of experts.

   Sufficiency of disclosure, i.e., providing the skilled person with sufficient information as to how the invention is performed, is therefore a very important requirement for nanotechnology applications. The application as filed has to enable the skilled person to carry out the invention over the whole of the (broad) field claimed. To this end, the skilled person needs detailed information about the processes and tools used.

Example—Disclosure

It is not sufficient to say "nanoelectrodes with a diameter of 5 nm were deposited onto a substrate," since this cannot be done with commonly known methods. The precise conditions for carrying out the method have to be described. ◀

Takeaways Nanotechnology Patent Applications

- Clarity can be a problem in nanotechnology applications, particularly if relative terms or unusual terminology are used. It is important to use terminology that has a well-recognized meaning or to word the application more precisely.
- The application as a whole must disclose the invention in such a way that a person skilled in the art can carry it out.
- Making something smaller does not automatically make it new or inventive. Miniaturization-based inventions should always demonstrate an enhanced technical effect derived from the size.

7.3 Industry 4.0 and Internet of Things

The *Fourth Industrial Revolution* (*4IR*) or, in some regions known as *Industry 4.0* or *Industrial IoT* (*Internet of Things*), refers to inventions that can be assigned to three broad classes:

- *Core technologies* (hardware, software and connectivity) that make it possible to transform any object into a smart device connected via the internet.
- *Enabling technologies* (analytics, security, artificial intelligence, locating, power supply, 3D systems and user interfaces) that are used in combination with connected objects.
- *Application domains* (home, personal, enterprise, manufacturing, infrastructure and vehicles) where the potential of connected objects can be exploited.

Industrial IoT Innovation Is Taking off

The pace of global innovation in 4IR technologies has accelerated significantly over the past decade. From 2010 to 2018, international patent families (IPFs) in this field grew at an average annual rate of nearly 20%, compared to 12.8% between 2000 and 2009. Since 2010, the annual increase in IPFs for 4IR technologies has been almost five times higher than the growth observed across all technology fields (4.2%). As a result, smart connected objects represented more than 11% of all global patenting activity in 2018, with nearly 40,000 new IPFs filed that year alone (EPO, 2020a; see Fig. 7.3).

Connectivity has attracted the largest numbers of such patent applications so far, while the fastest-growing fields are data management, user interfaces, geo-positioning

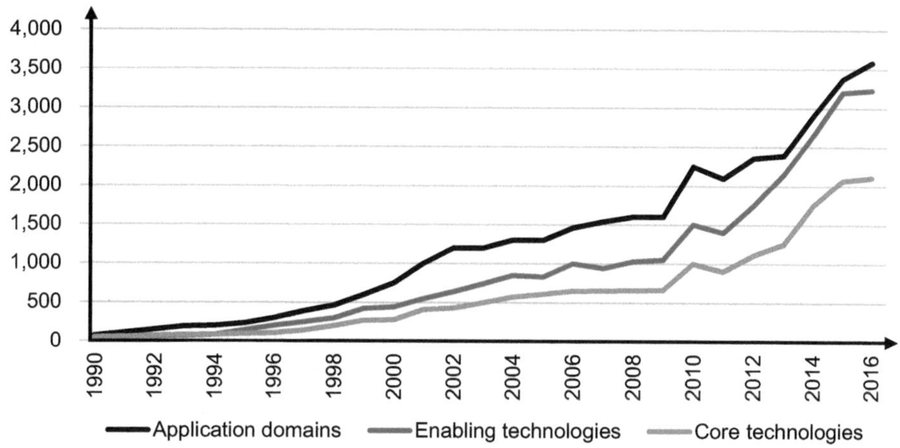

Fig. 7.3 4IR patent applications at the EPO by technology fields (based on EPO, 2020a)

and data protection. The core technologies underlying artificial intelligence (such as neural networks, deep learning and rule-based systems) show the strongest growth.

The rise in IoT inventions has been across all main subsectors. Application domains and core technologies capture a larger share of inventions, with the number of inventions relating to enabling technologies being significantly smaller. In recent years, the number of inventions involving core technologies has been increasing at a faster rate, almost catching up with the application domains.

In a 2024 follow-up study to the EPO 4IR patent study, Mertens and Scheufen (2024) found mixed evidence as to whether the EPO classification was useful at predicting forward citations. Instead, they found that it is the legal breadth behind these patents, which drives the relevancy of 4IR patents as measured by forward citations. Legal breadth in their study was defined as the number of words in the patent in the shortest independent claim of the patent document. Furthermore, I4R things technologies comprised AI, which encountered particularly strong growth as a subcategory in the last years, but I4R also comprised the general *computer technology* patents, which continued on a strong secular up trend (+56% applications per year in 2024 vs. 2016, EPO, 2025d).

Example—Dealing with the Anti-Commons

One of the academic debates that have been taking place for quite a long while is whether patents are actually harmful and in balance with certain technological areas where there are many players or where a technology requires dozens of different inventions to be viable. This economic situation is known as the *tragedy of the anti-commons* where too many owners of scarce resources mutually exclude other actors to the point that there is no longer any production taking place. There are a couple of sectors, like ICT or consumer electronics, where this is more likely to be the case because many players own a tiny slice of the technology needed to put a product together—a cell phone is a wondrous device, requiring many patents to make. In a study done for the WIPO, Reidenberg et al. (2015) identified some

314,000 *entities* with even more patents on everything from Liquid Crystal Displays (LCDs), software, on to modems. Any player trying to operate in this technological space is walking into an extensive legal minefield.

In the face of such obstacles, new entrants not only have to perfectly identify what is patented and what is not, a bewildering task in and of itself (cf. Freedom-to-Operate (FTO)), but they also have to negotiate with potentially dozens or even hundreds of entities. The transaction costs and asymmetries of information are so high that for some technologies and products, this is prohibitively expensive—and this is a "tragedy" since the product could be made but is not.

That is the pessimistic economic perspective, a more optimistic take is that where there is profit to be made, economic actors will organize to capture it. This *invisible hand* is precisely what will overcome the predicament. This is just what has happened for years in patent pools, where multiple inventors allow their innovations to be used by members of the pool—this legal cartel then can extract additional value from their inventions. These patent pools are sometimes very opaque, but a new entity, *Avanci*, has created a new type of open licensing platform in the space of wireless connectivity for the internet of things (cf. infra "Avanci—Traditional Automotive Players Under Attack"). "Avanci streamlines this process by offering a single license to patents owned by many companies, claiming fair, reasonable, and non-discriminatory (FRAND) terms" (see also Sect. 6.9). Just as theory predicts, *InterDigital*, a producer/patent troll entity, signed a patent agreement with Google in 2019 using this new platform (Google, 2019).

Though there is cause for optimism, the *internet of things* is still in its infancy, unlike the mobile space, so there is not much downside if the players toss their patents into a patent pool with a circumscribed objective. Moreover, we are much more likely to observe a patent pool rather than some forlorn inventor dead from exhaustion having tried to comprehend the legal implications of the patent record for her new invention. ◀

Top 4IR Applicants Active in Different Industries

The top 25 companies accounted for nearly 50% of all IPFs related to 4IR technologies between 2000 and 2018, highlighting a high level of concentration among key innovation leaders—many of them based in Asia (see Fig. 7.4). The top ten applicants alone were responsible for over a quarter of all 4IR IPFs during this period. Samsung remains at the top 10 in 2024 with Huawei taking the #2 spot (EPO, 2025d). Innovation in core technologies remains dominated by large firms in the *Information and Communication Technologies* (*ICT*) (see Sect. 6.10). In contrast, enabling technologies and application domains show a more diversified landscape, with leading applicants coming from a broader range of industries beyond ICT (EPO, 2020a).

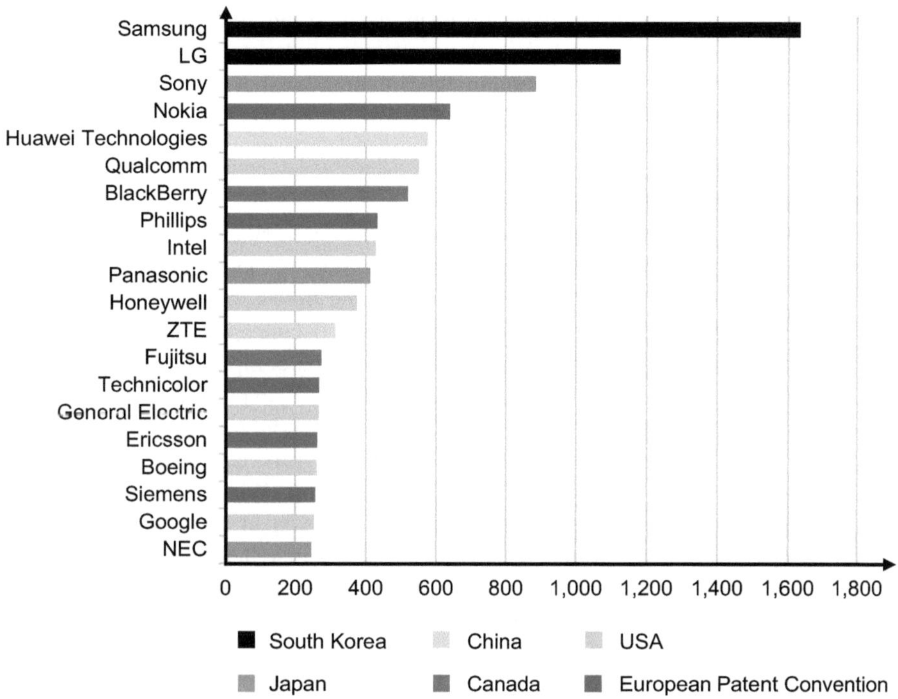

Fig. 7.4 Top 25 Industrial IoT patent applicants at the EPO 2011–2018 (based on EPO, 2020a, 2025d)

Europe, the USA, and Japan have been the main principle centers of innovation of Industrial IoT technologies since the mid-1990s. Large US, European, and Japanese companies from various sectors comprise the dominant applicants in the IoT enabling technologies. IoT innovation started later in China and Korea, which is dominated by a few ICT companies. *LG* and *Samsung* control 90% of the IoT applications in Korea; *Huawei* and *ZTE* control 70% of the 4IR patents in China.

In Europe, 4IR innovation tends to cluster in Munich and Paris. France and Germany are the dipoles of 4IR technological development. Germany has been the leader since the late 1990s, and it excels in the fields of manufacturing, vehicles, and infrastructure. The technological profiles of France, Benelux and Nordic countries are specialized more in AI, user interface, 3D processing, and security. *Philips*, *Nokia*, and *Ericsson* are key innovation players in those locations. Some forecast project that developments in the IoT will accelerate the advent of the fourth industrial revolution. If anything, the software and social organization to organize the underlying technology have been developing in these regions and organizations. Technology is outstripping the legal paradigm's ability to cope. For example, it has raised what legal and liability changes will be needed in order to allow for self-driving cars, which are arguably statistically safer than human drivers already, but where culpability and liability have not been clarified legally. Taken one step further, society has to consider legally when software and networked devices might allow each one to be its own economic agent using distributed ledger technology, such as the IOTA protocol from the *IOTA Foundation* (EPO, 2020a).

The Fourth Industrial Revolution[4]

The so-called *Fourth Industrial Revolution* (*4IR*)[5] describes a major technology trend that is being observed across a whole range of technical fields. This trend is primarily driven by the emergence of the *Internet of Things* (*IoT*) or *Industrial IoT* (which is close to the Industry 4.0 concept). It also encompasses a number of other technologies, such as cloud computing and artificial intelligence, technologies that make it possible to fully exploit the potential of smart connected objects in nearly all sectors of the economy.

The term "industrial revolution" reflects the pervasiveness and the disruptive potential of the latest technological developments. While previous industrial revolutions have led to the increasing automation of repetitive physical work, 4IR goes much further: it leads to the large-scale automation of whole groups of tasks, including repetitive intellectual tasks previously performed by human beings. 4IR can significantly enhance the efficiency and flexibility of production processes and augment the value of products and services (MGI, 2015). The transition toward "smart" factories operating autonomously has already been recognized as an important challenge by industry and policymakers in Europe[6] and beyond. Likewise, the deployment of connected objects in transport (autonomous vehicles), energy (smart grids), cities, healthcare, and agriculture profoundly changes the way these sectors are organized.

Like previous industrial revolutions, 4IR raises major economic and social issues (OECD, 2017). Increasing the automation of routine intellectual tasks changes the nature of human work and, hence, the balance of the labor market. It obliges companies to rethink their business models and to adapt to new forms of competition. Besides investing in the training of the 4IR workforce, policymakers face the challenge of supporting and regulating new digital infrastructures and of creating appropriate legal frameworks to safeguard competition, cybersecurity, and consumer rights in the digital age.

---

[4] Source: Definition extracted from EPO (2020a).

[5] Fourth Industrial Revolution is the term used by Klaus Schwab, Founder and Executive Chairman of the World Economic Forum, in his book on this subject (Schwab, 2017).

[6] See, e.g., "Industry 4.0" (Germany), "Nouvelle France Industrielle" (France), "Fabricca Intelligente" (Italy), "Industria Conectada 4.0" (Spain), "Made Different" (Belgium), "Prumysl 4.0" (Czech Republic), "Smart Industry" (Slovakia), "Production 2014" (Sweden), "MADE" (Denmark), "Produktion der Zukunft" (Austria), and "Smart Industry" (The Netherlands).

7.4 Software and Business Methods

"*Software eats the world*" was boldly proclaimed by the *Wall Street Journal* back in 2012. Software and algorithms are now finding their way into every industry. The so-called computer-implemented inventions have become omnipresent and can be found in almost all technical fields (Bader, 2022). Ninety percent of developments since the beginning of this century have been software-related (EPO, 2007). This is also reflected in patent applications. The inventive share is increasingly based on software-based developments.[7]

The development of software goes back to the 1960s (Boehm, 1976). In the past, software development was mainly focused on mainframe and minicomputer computing, whereas today, a distinction is already made between software development for personal, pervasive, and embedded computing. Whereas in the past, the legal protection of software was mainly covered by copyright in practice, numerous companies now also strive to protect software innovations by means of patents (see Table 7.1). It is interesting to note that the *SAP* software group did not start setting up its own patent department until 1998 and only held four software-related patents in May of 2001. The reason for establishing the patent department was the growing international competition in which patents played an increasingly important role.

The trigger for the "software patent boom" was a groundbreaking court decision, which in 1992 led to the so-called *Freeman–Walter–Abele* test, which enabled the patenting of algorithms applied in practice and thus of software in the USA. In 1998, this test was replaced by the so-called *State Street Bank* court decision in the USA, which was affirmed in 1999. Mathematical algorithms thus became patentable if the invention led to a concrete and tangible result. This heralded the start of the business method patents era in the USA. As a result, the number of patent applications and granted patents in the software sector skyrocketed internationally at the turn of the millennium (Hall & MacGarvie, 2010) to such an extent that there was increasing public criticism of patentability in this sector (Coriat & Orsi, 2002).

Table 7.1 Four types of protection for software (table compiled by authors)

Results of software development	Right
Documentation Screen appearance Code	Copyright/design patents/trade dress
Processes Algorithms	Patents
Branding	Trademarks

[7] A selected portion of this section was previously published in Gassmann and Bader (2024). *Patentmanagement: Innovationen erfolgreich nutzen und schützen* (fifth ed.). Berlin: Springer Gabler; and in the chapter Bader (2022). Innovationen im Handel nutzen und schützen. In M. Knoppe, S. Rock, & M. Wild (Eds.), *Der Zukunftsfähige Handel* (fourth ed.) Wiesbaden: Springer Gabler, 171–192. Used with permission.

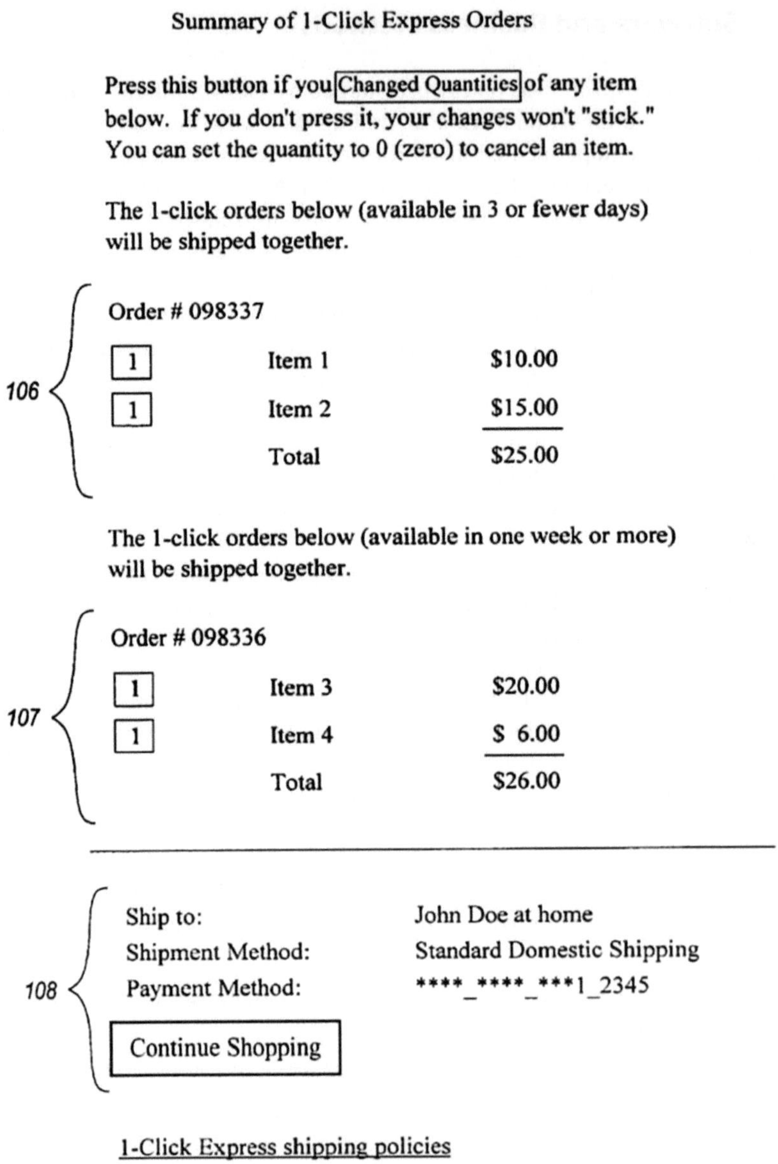

Fig. 7.5 Amazon's so-called "1-Click" US patent (US 5,960,411, Fig. 1C, Sept. 28, 1999)

One of the most (in)famous patents was *Amazon's* so-called *"1-Click"* patent, which concerns a technology that makes it possible to make online purchases with a single mouse click (see Fig. 7.5). Amazon's patent was granted in the USA in 1999. In 1999, Amazon filed a spectacular patent infringement suit against its competitor Barnesandnoble.com based on its "1-Click Patent," which initially forced the latter to introduce a 2-Click online shopping payment process. While the US patent was later confirmed with some limitations after a reexamination procedure by the

USPTO in March 2010, in Europe, however, the application from the same patent family was not granted by the European Patent Office. The procedural practice of the EPO in the field of computer-implemented inventions has largely consolidated after some confusion in the mid-1990s. The practice was again confirmed by the Enlarged Board of Appeal of the EPO in mid-2010.

The emerging patenting numbers gained considerable relevance in the software industry after the first patent infringement suits. Initially, mainly large companies were affected that generate large sales volumes and profits with a few product variants, such as *Apple*, *Google*, *Microsoft*, *SAP,* and *Oracle*. The Internet auction house *eBay* had to pay US$29.5 million in damages to *MercExchange* in 2003 after a patent infringement lawsuit, as MercExchange's patented proprietary auction technology also covered *eBay's* "buy now" feature. The damages were 30% of eBay's goodwill at the time. At the end of 2009, the Walldorf-based software group *SAP* was ordered to pay nearly US$140 million in damages to US competitor *Versata* following 2 years of patent infringement proceedings.

In addition to this, it is becoming increasingly clear that software, as a cross-sectional technology, has become a central factor in the convergence of technologies: The Taiwanese smartphone manufacturer *HTC* acquired a license from *Microsoft* after Microsoft accused the *Android* operating system, which now belongs to *Google*, of infringing several patents in areas of the user interface and the underlying system. The license agreement between Microsoft and HTC was concluded against the background that both companies' main competitor *Apple* had also sued HTC for infringing the *Linux*-based open-source operating system Android from Google out of 20 patents at the beginning of 2010. So even users of open-source software are not immune to patent infringement allegations. Microsoft in particular accused *Linux* that its operating system core infringes more than 230 of its patents and has already entered into license agreements with *Apple*, *Hewlett-Packard*, *Novell*, and *Amazon*. In the latter case, Microsoft also received licenses to Amazon patents in return, which gave the software group easier access to the tablet computer market. This includes e-bookstore solutions that Amazon, among others, has at its disposal.

The software technology sector is typified by the following challenges and risks (see also Fig. 7.6):

- Rapidly growing number of patents on software and business method applications requires a lot of monitoring effort.
- The quality and legal validity of numerous patents are questionable due to a lack of awareness of sufficient and relevant state of the art among applicants and patent offices.
- High risk of third parties getting involved in a costly and time-consuming patent infringement process, especially in the US market.
- The enforcement of own patents is associated with a high financial risk, especially in the USA.
- Heterogeneity regarding the general legal development in the various legislations regarding the patentability of software applications. Unlike more technical inventions, these patents are often subject to a wide variety of different national types of legislation.

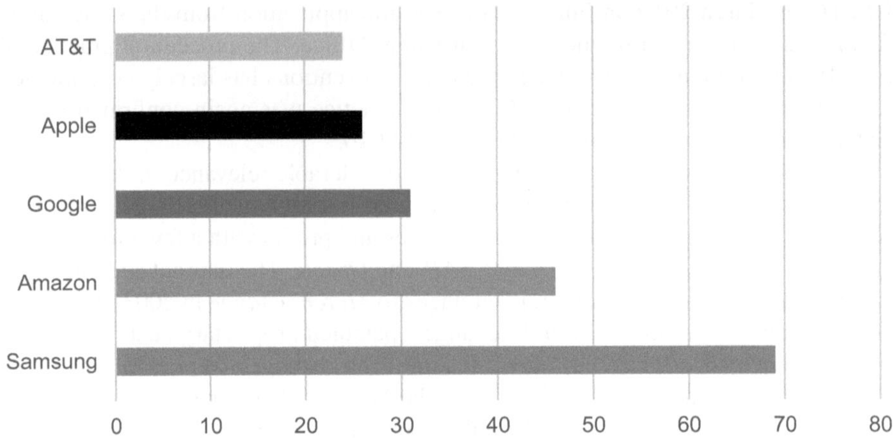

Fig. 7.6 The companies sued the most over patents: Number of US patent litigation cases against companies in the first half of 2024 (based on GreyB, 2025a)

Example—Microsoft

Like other large software technology companies, *Microsoft* started relatively late patenting its inventions. In 2004, Bill Gates announced that Microsoft was estimated to register twice as many software patents the following year than in the previous year. The announcement was made against the background that it became increasingly necessary for Microsoft to have its own patent portfolio: on the one hand, to negotiate cross-licenses and generate license income, and on the other hand, to transfer knowledge. At the venture capital conference in 2005, CEO Steve Ballmer once again underlined the great importance of patent management for Microsoft by announcing that the group often spends more money on the purchase or generation of patents than on the development of the actual technologies. At that time, Microsoft invested more than US$9 billion annually in research and development and, according to their own statements, held the largest and strongest patent portfolio in the software industry with nearly 60,000 patents in 2013.

One reason for the change in direction of the software company, which was previously inactive in the patent sector, is probably that Microsoft had faced around three dozen patent infringement lawsuits since 1998. The legal proceedings could often be ended in settlements, such as with *Time Warner* and their *Netscape* browser, and with mergers as with *AT&T*. Nevertheless, these were not necessarily cheap solutions, as can easily be seen when looking at the example given by *Sun Microsystems*. Microsoft had to pay the *Java House* a severance payment of US$1.95 billion. Small businesses also took action against Microsoft, such as *Inter Trust Technologies* in Santa Clara, California, which has patented approximately 30 patents with Microsoft regarding DRM (Digital Rights Management) technology. The settlement ended with a US$440 million payment to Inter Trust Technologies and a license to use the patent portfolio for Microsoft extending to end users of Windows operating systems. In a recent case, an American Court of Appeals upheld a ruling that allowed Microsoft, starting in 2010, to sell only a modified version of Microsoft Word 2007. The reason for this is the infringement of a patent by the small Canadian software company *i4i*. The patent relates to a method with which the architecture and content of documents can be processed independently of each another. Microsoft has been ordered to pay damages of US$290 million. Microsoft's patent strategy has changed fundamentally in recent years; the company is now more interested in getting to balanced patent license exchange contracts (Bader, 2006). Two companies license each other their respective technologies in exchange for corresponding back licenses from the contractual partner. *Microsoft* currently has such agreements with *Cisco Systems*, *Hewlett-Packard*, *IBM*, *SAP*, *Siemens*, *Sun Microsystems*, *Unisys*, and *Xerox*. Prior to this, Microsoft primarily employed an aggressive strategy (offensive patent enforcement).

In addition to the offensive strategy, Microsoft introduced an IP licensing program in 2003 with (technology) licensing programs and the *Microsoft IP Ventures Program*, which among other things was aimed at awarding ventures to technologies developed by Microsoft but not used by the company. Microsoft offers start-ups and small business owners a special license for these technologies. In return for its technology, Microsoft gets a share of the licensee's equity. If a new, internally developed technology has earnings potential of less than US$1 billion or does not fit into your own product portfolio in any other way, it is available to the IP Ventures program. According to David Kaefer, General Manager of Microsoft's Intellectual Property Licensing Team, the licensing terms are specifically agreed on a case-by-case basis. The licenses are granted nonexclusively. Microsoft, therefore, reserves the right to assign technology to different licensees.

Since its introduction, more than 600 license agreements have been made with the help of the IP license program, which is available to customers, partners, and competitors. Analysts rate Microsoft's licensing program as an intelligent move. The company has invested billions of dollars in research and development, which has led to a host of good ideas—probably more than Microsoft is able to turn into marketable products for itself. By making unused technologies available to the market, the shareholders' equity shares in return enable them to participate in their success without the need for further investments made in the licensed technologies themselves. In summary, Microsoft's patent strategy consists of four components:

- Building a larger patent portfolio as a starting point;
- Patent license exchange contracts for risk minimization and as technology access;
- Defense of one's own patent portfolio against patent infringers; and
- Awarding technology licenses to ventures in return for company shares for sustainable technology exploitation.

Microsoft has developed a sophisticated patent strategy over the past decade that goes beyond a purely offensive enforcement strategy. In addition to this, Microsoft attaches particular importance to human resource management, product development, and market launch, as well as organizational learning in the innovation process. Microsoft has also played a pioneering role in the latest developments in R&D, inside of global innovation networks. To meet this demand, Microsoft's Intellectual Property Team is led by *IBM* veteran Marshall Phelps, who was largely responsible for the licensing success of "Big Blue." ◀

The Practice of Computer-Implemented Inventions in Europe

The following excerpts from the EPO are displayed on *computer-implemented inventions (CII)* and so-called *software patents* (EPO, 2019):

The term "software" is considered to be ambiguous, because it may refer to a program listing written in a programming language to implement an algorithm, but also to binary code loaded in a computer-based apparatus, and it may also encompass the accompanying documentation. So, in place of this ambiguous term, the concept of a computer-implemented invention has been introduced.

A computer-implemented invention is one which involves the use of a computer, computer network, or other programmable apparatus, where one or more features are realized wholly or partly by means of a computer program.

Under the European Patent Convention (EPC), a computer program claimed "as such" is not a patentable invention (Article 52(2)(c) and (3) EPC). Patents are not granted merely for program listings. Program listings as such are protected by copyright. For a patent to be granted for a computer-implemented invention, a technical problem has to be solved in a novel and non-obvious manner (see Table 7.2).

The starting point for assessing the patentability of computer-implemented inventions is the fundamental provision that a patent should be granted for any invention, in any field of technology, provided that it is new, involves an inventive step, is susceptible of industrial application, and is not expressly excluded from patent protection (Article 52 EPC).

Table 7.2 Comparison of the term "invention" at EPO, JPO, and CNIPA (EPO & CNIPA, 2019; EPO & JPO, 2018)

European Patent Office (EPO)
Under Article 52(2) and (3) EPC, the following are not regarded as "inventions" if claimed as such: • Discoveries, scientific theories, and mathematical methods; • Esthetic creations; • Schemes, rules, and methods for performing mental acts, playing games, or doing business, and programs for computers; and • Presentations of information.

(continued)

Table 7.2 (continued)

Japan Patent Office (JPO)
The following are subject matters not corresponding to statutory "inventions" described in JPGL, Part III, Chap. 1, 2.1: • A law of nature as such; • Mere discoveries and not creations; • Those contrary to a law of nature; • Those in which a law of nature is not utilized, e.g., (i) Any laws other than a law of nature (e.g., economic laws), (ii) Arbitrary arrangements (e.g., a rule for playing a game as such), (iii) Mathematical formula, (iv) Mental activities of humans, or (v) Those utilizing only (i) to (iv) (e.g., methods for doing business as such); • Those not regarded as technical ideas, e.g., personal skill, mere presentation of information, or mere aesthetic creations; and • Those for which it is clearly impossible to solve the problem to be solved by any means presented in a claim.
China National Intellectual Property Administration (CNIPA)
Under Article 25.1 Chinese Patent Law, patent rights shall not be granted for any of the following: • Scientific discoveries; • Rules and methods for mental activities; • Methods for the diagnosis or treatment of diseases; • Animal or plant varieties; and • Substances obtained by means of nuclear transformation; and designs that are mainly used for marking the pattern, color, or the combination of the two of prints.

Patent Protection for Technical Creations While the EPC sets out the patentability requirements of novelty, inventive step, and industrial application in some detail (Articles 54, 56 and 57 EPC), it does not contain a legal definition of the term "invention." It has, however, been part of the European legal tradition since the early days of the patent system that patent protection should be reserved for technical creations. The subject matter for which protection is sought must, therefore, have a "technical character" or, to be more precise, involve a "technical teaching," i.e., instruction, addressed to a technically skilled person as to how to solve a particular technical problem using particular technical means. The problem solved by the invention must thus be technical, in contrast, for example, to a purely financial, commercial, or mathematical one. This must be satisfied in order for the invention not to be excluded from patentability (see Fig. 7.7).

Although the law does not define the term "invention," it does contain a list of subject matters or activities that are not to be regarded as "inventions." Among the particular examples mentioned in this list are "programs for computers." It should be emphasized that the subject matter or activities on the list are excluded only if the European patent application or patent relates to them "as such." Therefore, inventions having a technical character that are or may be implemented by a computer program are not excluded from patentability.

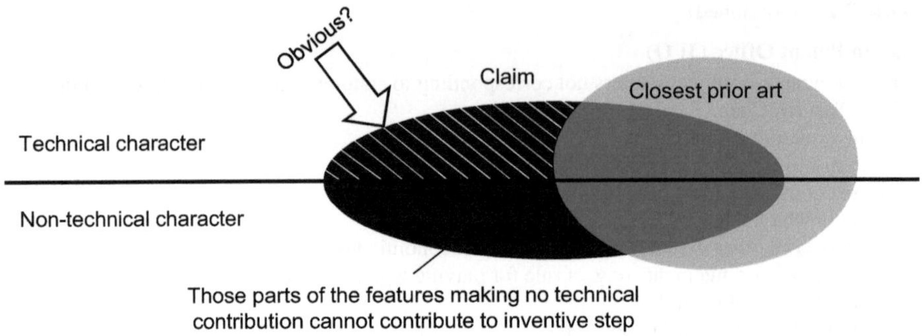

Fig. 7.7 How the inventive step for mixed inventions is assessed at the EPO (based on EPO & CNIPA, 2019)

The Case Law of the Boards of Appeal In the field of computer-implemented inventions, many decisions have developed the interpretation of the EPC provisions relating to the term "invention," providing guidance on what is patentable and what is not.

EPO case law says that controlling or carrying out a technical process is not excluded from patentability, irrespective of whether it is implemented by hardware or by software. Whether the process is carried out by means of special circuits or by means of a computer program has been found to depend on economic and technological factors; patentability should not be denied on the grounds that a computer program is involved.

A specific claim form for the protection of computer-implemented inventions is the "computer program/computer program product." It was introduced in order to provide better legal protection for computer programs distributed on a data carrier and not forming part of a computerized system. This claim form should not be confused with the term "computer program" as a list of instructions. Subject matter claimed under this form is not excluded from patentability if the computer program resulting from the implementation of the corresponding method is capable of bringing about, when running on a computer or loaded into a computer, a "further technical effect" going beyond the "normal" physical interactions between the computer program and the computer hardware on which it is run.

The normal physical effects of the execution of a program, e.g., electrical currents, are not in themselves sufficient to lend a computer program technical character, and a further technical effect is needed. The further technical effect may result, for example, from the control of an industrial process or the working of a piece of machinery, but also from the internal functioning of the computer itself (e.g., memory organization and program execution control) under the influence of the computer program.

For instance, a method of encoding audio information in a communication system may aim to reduce distortion induced by channel noise. Although the idea underlying such a method may be considered to reside in a mathematical method, the encoding method as a whole is not a mathematical method "as such" and, hence, is not excluded from patentability by Article 52(2)(a) and (3) EPC. Similarly, a method of encrypting/decrypting or signing electronic communications may be regarded as a technical method, even if it is essentially based on a mathematical method.

On the other hand, "schemes, rules and methods for (…) doing business" are not patentable; but a new method that solves a technical, rather than a purely administrative, problem may indeed be patentable.

Patents for Computer-Implemented Inventions Patents for CII may comprise claims to computers, computer networks, or other programmable apparatus, whereby at least one feature is realized by means of a computer program. If the invention concerns software that can be loaded into memory, transmitted over a network, or distributed on a data carrier, a claim to a "computer program" or "computer program product" may be present in addition to a computer-implemented method. However, in such inventions, although different claim structures are possible, the set of claims usually starts with a method claim, defining the steps performed by a computer, or other data processing means capable of running software, to achieve the desired technical effect (see Fig. 7.8).

A common type of CII patent relates to subject matter where all the method steps can be fully carried out by computer program instructions running on, e.g., a personal computer or the processors in a smartphone or printer. Other types of CII patents concern inventions where some method steps are performed outside a

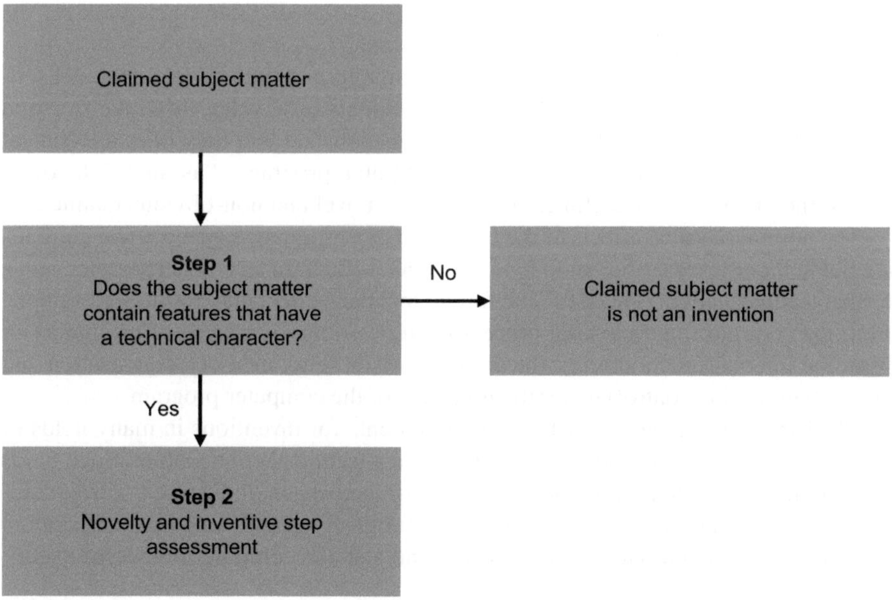

Fig. 7.8 The two-step approach for assessment of CII applications at the EPO (based on EPO & CNIPA, 2019)

computer, and require specific technical means, such as a sensor. For example, in a method for automatically braking in a self-driving vehicle, sensors measure the distance to the vehicle in front, and the signals received and produced by the sensors are used to control the braking process. Physical devices like sensors provide inputs and outputs for the invention, but the decisions as to how the devices operate are taken by a computer according to parameters and instructions, i.e., software. Any patent for such an invention would protect the combination of devices and computers carrying out the novel method.

Whereas mechanical inventions are represented with technical drawings in patents, for CII, the patent will often feature a flow diagram for the method, showing the decision steps in the process, and any interactions with devices and external inputs and outputs.

Regionally Different Treatment of Computer-Implemented Inventions[8]

Computer-implemented inventions (*CII*) are treated differently by patent offices in different regions of the world (see Table 7.2). In Europe, Article 52 of the European Patent Convention (EPC) excludes computer programs “as such” from patent protection. This exclusion does not mean that all inventions involving software are excluded from patenting; what it does mean is that tighter scrutiny of the technical character of these inventions is required.

Over the years, the case law of the EPO boards of appeal has clarified the implications of Article 52 EPC, establishing a stable and predictable framework for the patentability of computer-implemented inventions.

Like all other inventions, in order to be patentable, computer-implemented inventions must meet the fundamental legal requirements of novelty, inventive step and industrial application. In addition, it must be established that they have a technical character that distinguishes them from computer programs “as such.” In other words, they must solve a technical problem in a novel and non-obvious manner.

The normal physical effects of the execution of a program, e.g., electrical currents, are not in themselves sufficient to lend a computer program technical character, and a further technical effect is needed. The further technical effect may result, for example, from the control of an industrial process or the working of a piece of machinery or from the internal functioning of the computer itself (e.g., memory organization and program execution control) under the influence of the computer program.

The EPC thus enables the EPO to grant patents for inventions in many fields of technology in which computer programs make a technical contribution. Such fields include medical devices, the automotive sector, aerospace, industrial control, communication/media technology, including automated natural language translation, voice recognition, and video compression, and also the computer/processor itself.

[8] Source: Extract from EPO (2020a).

Example—Software Company und University Attack Web Economy

Due to patent infringement, *Microsoft* had to pay more than half a billion US dollars in August 2003. A US federal court awarded the software company *Eolas Technologies* in Chicago and the *University of California* damages of around US$520 million. Microsoft appealed, but then withdrew the lawsuit when the Federal Court of Appeals in Washington dismissed the claim to the lower court due to a procedural error but did not overturn the verdict. Microsoft then settled out of court with Eolas and paid an unknown amount to settle the dispute.

The court ruled that Microsoft had infringed a patent that Eolas' founder Michael Doyle University of California had co-developed at the University of California with his browser *Internet Explorer*. The patent concerns a technology that enables access to interactive programs embedded in Internet pages. Eolas was founded in 1994 to distribute the software; the University holds the corresponding patent. Eolas and the University have accused Microsoft of having integrated their development into their Internet browser Explorer. The patent has since been upheld several times by courts and the USPTO. The original patent was even extended in 2002 to cover newer applications. This extension of the patent protection now serves Eolas as a starting point from which to sue more illustrious names such as *Amazon*, *eBay*, or *Google* for patent infringement or non-payment of license fees. A total of 24 companies worldwide are affected by the mass action.

Critics wanted to exclude software and basic principles, such as Eolas', from patent protection in order not to hinder technological progress. Michael Doyle explained the matter to Spiegel: "We developed this technology more than 15 years ago and demonstrated it publicly, years before the market heard of web-enabled applications that remotely tap into powerful resources. To profit from the inventions of others without paying for them is deeply unfair. We only want what is rightfully ours" (Spiegel Online, 2009). ◀

Patentability of Business Methods in the USA

While the EPO and numerous national patent offices in Europe have maintained a more conservative, but more consistent, patent-granting practice with respect to computer-implemented inventions, the practice in the USA has been somewhat more dynamic with respect to software and business method patents:

The "Bilski" Decision 1997—The Rise In 1997, the two applicants Bernard L. Bilski and Rand A. Warsaw applied for patent protection in the USA for a business method relating to a method of hedging risks in commodities trading ("method of hedging risks in commodities trading"). After the patent application was rejected in two instances, first, the Board of Patent Appeals and Interferences (BPAI), and second, the United States Court of Appeals for the Federal Circuit (CAFC), the highest US court, the U.S. Supreme Court, dealt with the case on the patentability of process claims, which also include business methods and software in particular, from 2009 to 2010.

Until the "*Bilski*" decision, the question of patentability in the USA was based on the "*State Street Bank*" decision, in which implemented methods were patentable if they led to a "*useful, concrete and tangible*" result. As a result, a plethora of patents on pure business methods were granted in the USA. The CAFC now questioned not only these criteria in general but also the previously applicable *"Freeman-Walter-Abele" test*, which was applied to software patents to examine the patentability of mathematical principles and algorithms.

The so-called "*machine-or-transformation test*," introduced by the CAFC, was not confirmed by the U.S. Supreme Court as the sole test for examining patentability, but only as a "useful tool for investigation."

However, the legal validity of patents on business methods and software-based processes was now basically confirmed in the USA—Until the so-called "*Alice*" decision, which changed everything again more than 15 years later ....

The "Alice" Decision 2014—The Descent A few years later, the Supreme Court again dealt with the patentability of a business method in *Alice v. CLS Bank*. It declared a method of securing an intermediary settlement—a form of electronic escrow service—unpatentable. In invalidating the "Alice" patent, the court announced a two-step test based on the court's earlier decisions in *Mayo* vs. *Prometheus*, and *Funk Bros. Seed Co.* vs. *Kalo Inoculant Co.* This test first determines whether the claimed invention is directed to an abstract idea, a law of nature, a mathematical formula, or a similar abstraction. If so, the second step requires the court to determine whether the way in which the claimed invention implements the abstraction involves an inventive concept, as opposed to routine and convention. According to the "*Alice*" *test*, the claimed invention is only patentable if it contains an inventive concept.

The USPTO's working groups examining business methods reacted quickly to the Alice decision. Grants per month for financial-related patents dropped to 10% of their value prior to the "Alice" decision. The US Patent Trial and Appeal Board reacted in a similar way: Only about 20% of appealed rejections of US business method patents were reversed by the Board (see Fig. 7.9).

Takeaways Software and Business Methods

- Software eats the world—there is hardly an industry without "softwaretization."
- Software is *de jure* not patentable in Europe, it is their part of copyright law. But is de facto, in combination with a technical apparatus, one of the most patented areas.
- Software and methods portfolios are typically built around "mass" rather than quality.
- Software and methods patents are nuanced and complicated to monitor.
- Software and methods patents are not necessarily patentable everywhere.
- Generally, the "Alice" decisions changed the patentability and robustness of business method patents in the USA, including their enforceability.

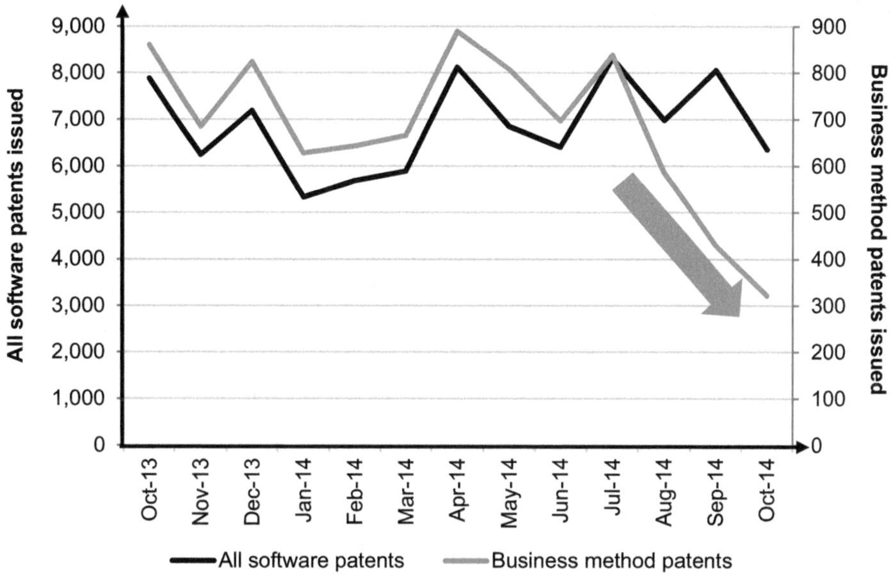

Fig. 7.9 Drop of business-method-related patents after the Alice decision compared to software (based on Stellbrink, 2016)

7.5 Artificial-Intelligence-Based Business Models

Formal and informal IP protection strategies also play a big role in Artificial Intelligence (AI)-based business models, taking into account the challenges given by an open innovation approach. Existing literature already distinguishes between formal and informal protection strategies and has tried to understand their influence on value capture for different business models. However, their application to the new field of AI is still a white spot. Therefore, this research aims at how formal and informal protection strategies can be applied in the field of AI-based business models, taking into account an open innovation environment that is relevant and current practice in AI-based innovation regimes. The managerial implications also cover how to balance open and proprietary innovation with a focus on entrepreneurship and start-up environments. Methodology: Qualitative research based on own empirical resources and analysis of empirical reports (see for this chapter also Bader & Stummeyer, 2019, 2024).[9]

Protecting that kind of intellectual property has become a relevant aspect depending on which business model is being operated and which elements of the value creation should be protected to gain high-value creation leverage. In a recent study based on an evaluation of different business model types, it could be emphasized that different business models need different optimization and complementation of formal and informal IP protection strategies (Bonakdar et al., 2017).

[9] A selected portion of this section was previously published in the chapter Bader and Stummeyer (2024). Innovation und geistiges Eigentum in KI-basierten Geschäftsmodellen. In L. Fend, & J. Hofmann (Eds.), *Digitalisierung in Industrie-, Handels—und Dienstleistungsunternehmen* (fourth ed.) Berlin: Springer Gabler, 293–323. Used with permission.

Challenge to Apply Formal IP Strategies to AI

Applying formal IP strategies to AI-based innovations faces a challenge when it comes to patenting AI-based inventions. The two main reasons are that, on the one hand, algorithms play a major role when designing AI concepts; as algorithms "as such" are seen as mathematical methods, they are per se excluded from patentability under the main patent legislation regimes. On the other hand, AI concepts are often directed at automating or conducting tasks and activities that are currently performed by the human mind—another reason for patent ineligibility; either for being just considered as a theoretical concept or due to lack of novelty.

However, many of the current AI-based inventions are based and implemented as software. As is the case in other fast-developing technical growth sectors. For example, more than 80% of the value added in the ICT sector is based on software and related services (OECD, 2017). So, patent legislation and practices relating to this have been built up during the past decades having to do with how to deal with software-based inventions:

In **Europe**, under the European Patent Convention, AI as a mathematical method per definition is excluded from patentability when claimed as such. However, if a method involves technical means (e.g., a computer) or a device, its subject matter may have a technical character when seen as a whole and for that reason is not excluded from patentability (the so-called computer-implemented inventions, CII: "The element in the technology which is new and inventive is actually a changed computerized algorithm or control mechanism which is responsible for bringing about an improved technical effect" (EPO, 2013, 2020b, 2024). When assessing patentability, the European Patent Office (EPO) applies the so-called two-hurdle approach for "mixed-type inventions" and checks whether "the AI method (steps) contributes to the technical character of the invention?" (EPO, 2023).

A central challenge for the patentability of AI-related inventions is the question of whether it is a technical or non-technical application or purpose (Best, 2022, see Fig. 7.10).

In this context, the EPO also recently updated their Guidelines for Examination with a specific section on "Artificial intelligence and machine learning," providing guidance on the assessment of whether an invention on AI and machine learning is based on the necessary "technical character" to be patentable and would feature examples relating to AI as well as detailed information on the technicality of CII based on decisions by the EPO's boards of appeal (EPO, 2025b).

In the **USA**, the patent eligibility so far presents a challenge, too, but due to a different legal philosophy. This is because, in the USA, abstract ideas are not considered patentable. Furthermore, the mere use of a computer to implement an abstract idea is not sufficient to gain patent eligibility (EPO, 2018, 2025b).

The most significant legal hurdle to obtaining a patent on an AI-related invention remains 35 U.S.C. §101, which limits patent-eligible subject matter to a "process, machine, manufacture, or composition of matter." However, judicial interpretations have narrowed this scope by excluding abstract ideas, laws of nature, and natural phenomena—the so-called "judicial exceptions."

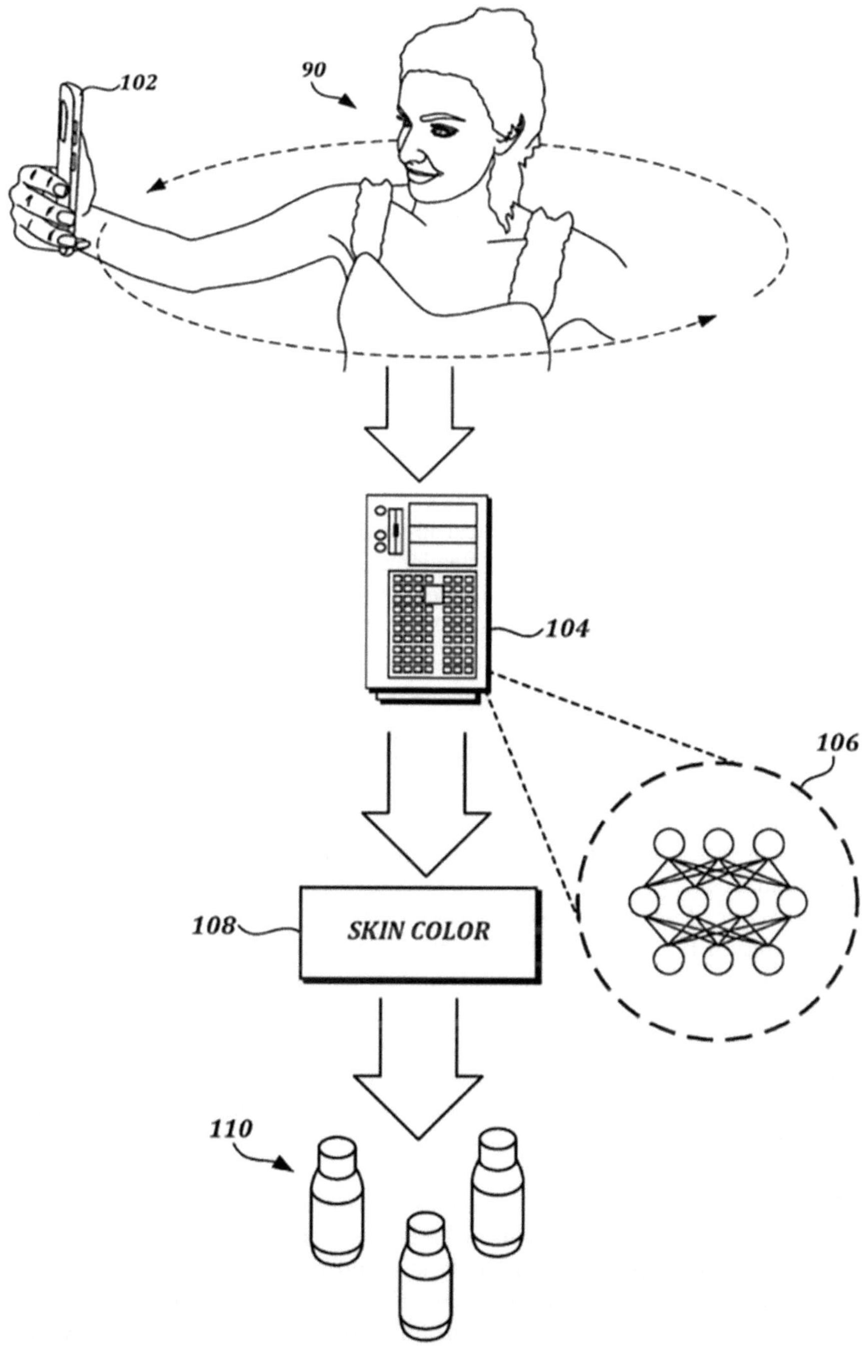

Fig. 7.10 L'Oréal (FR) & Christine Elfakhri (US): Techniques for identifying skin color in images having uncontrolled lighting conditions (EP 4 000 000 A1/ US 2022/0079325 A1)

The standard for determining subject matter eligibility became notably more stringent following two landmark U.S. Supreme Court decisions: *Mayo Collaborative Services* vs. *Prometheus Laboratories, Inc.* (2012) and *Alice Corp.* vs. *CLS Bank International* (2014). These cases established the now-fundamental two-step test—commonly referred to as the Mayo/Alice framework:

1. *Step One:* Determine whether the claims are directed to a patent-ineligible concept (e.g., an abstract idea, law of nature, or natural phenomenon).
2. *Step Two:* If so, evaluate whether the claim elements, individually or as an ordered combination, include an "inventive concept" sufficient to transform the nature of the claim into a patent-eligible application.

In *Alice*, the Court held that claims directed to "intermediated settlement" were abstract and lacked an inventive concept because they merely required a generic computer to perform conventional functions. This decision has had a profound impact on software and AI-related patents, with courts and the USPTO frequently rejecting claims that fail to demonstrate a practical application beyond the abstract idea itself.

Other jurisdictions have different standards on subject matter eligibility, as discussed in the USPTO's "Patent-Eligible Subject Matter: Report on Views and Recommendations from the Public" (USPTO, 2017):

- In **Japan**, a software invention is patentable if its information-processing aspects are required to be "specifically implemented by using hardware resources." Many view software inventions as being patent-eligible, as long as their claimed inventive steps are expressly tied to hardware.
- In **China**, according to the examination guidelines revised in April 2017, "the computer program-related invention" that has "technical characteristics will not be excluded from patentability." This revision is viewed by many as a broadening of the scope of patent-eligible subject matter.
- The **Korean** Intellectual Property Office's guidelines state that computer programs per se are not patent-eligible, but they also "indicate that if computer software is claimed in conjunction with hardware, then the combination, the operating method of the combination, and a computer-readable medium containing the software that implicates the combination is patent eligible." The Republic of Korea recently introduced an accelerated examination for patent applications pertaining to AI and other specified emerging technology fields.

Generally speaking, software inventions can be patented in these non-US offices if they are implemented with or sufficiently tied to hardware. Thus, some believe that the patent subject matter eligibility standard outside the USA might be less stringent than the Alice framework, although others believe that the recent developments indicate a convergence of the Alice framework, particularly with respect to its second prong, and the European practice.

In the USA, the *Mayo/Alice* framework[10] has been criticized for creating uncertainty and inconsistency, particularly in emerging fields like artificial intelligence and diagnostics (e.g., see Carroll et al., 2024). In response, the USPTO has issued evolving guidance to clarify when AI and machine learning inventions may be considered patent-eligible—especially when they are "integrated into a practical application" (USPTO, 2024).

DABUS: A Global Test Case About the Role of AI for Inventorship and Innovation
One of the most provocative frontiers in artificial intelligence is its potential to create intellectual property autonomously. While companies have already since earlier used AI techniques—such as genetic algorithms and machine learning—to optimize parameters and assist in innovation, there is now a shift taking place: AI systems are not just tools but are increasingly credited with generating novel, inventive outputs.

This shift raises profound legal and philosophical questions. If an AI system creates a new invention, who owns it? The developer of the AI? The owner? The user? Or no one at all? These questions are no longer hypothetical. A real-world test case emerged with *DABUS* (Device for the Autonomous Bootstrapping of Unified Sentience), an AI system developed by Dr. Stephen Thaler. DABUS was credited with inventing two products: A fractal beverage container and a neural flame-emitting flashlight for search-and-rescue missions (see Dabus patent application example in Sect. 9.2).

Dr. Thaler filed patent applications in over a dozen jurisdictions naming DABUS as the sole inventor. The applications were rejected in nearly all of them—including the United States, the European Patent Office, the United Kingdom, Germany, and most recently, Switzerland and Canada—on the grounds that only a natural person can be legally recognized as an inventor. The only exception was *South Africa*, which granted a patent without substantive examination.

The implications go far beyond DABUS. If AI systems can autonomously generate patentable inventions, they could be used to systematically mine the patent landscape, identify gaps, and flood the system with filings—potentially creating barriers to entry for competitors. This raises concerns about patent thickets, ownership ambiguity, and the risk of automated IP spamming.

Meanwhile, companies like *Novartis* and *DeepMind* already use AI to discover new drug compounds and protein structures, demonstrating that AI is not just a theoretical inventor but a practical one. As noted in the *Wall Street Journal* ("Can an AI System Be Given a Patent?", WSJ, 2019), the legal system is struggling to keep pace with these technological capabilities. ◄

[10] *Mayo Collaborative Servs.* vs. *Prometheus Labs., Inc.*, 566 U.S. 66 (2012); *Alice Corp. Pty. Ltd. vs. CLS Bank Int'l*, 573 U.S. 208 (2014).

As of 2025, legislative efforts such as the *Patent Eligibility Restoration Act* (*PERA*) have been introduced to redefine and broaden eligibility standards, aiming to reverse the restrictive effects of *Mayo* and *Alice* and restore clarity for innovators in AI, biotech, and quantum technologies (PERA, 2025).

Status Quo in Patenting AI-Related Innovations

As already indicated, AI-related innovations are often based on software and computer-implemented inventions, respectively. They might be directed to one or more specific AI application fields. Based on earlier and current legislation, various companies and research organizations have started filing patents also in the field of AI. The trend displayed in Fig. 7.11 (AI-related patent families and scientific publications by earliest publication year), nearly 340,000 patent families[11] have been filed and published since the 1960s. One can also see that AI has become a major field in science with a total of more than 1.5 million papers published up to mid-2018. That trend identified in the 2019 WIPO report has gone parabolic according to the 2025 WIPO

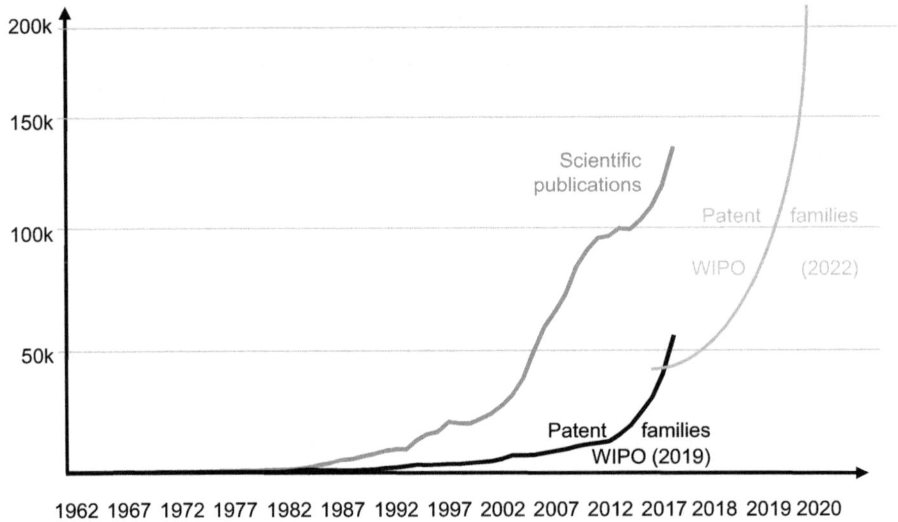

Fig. 7.11 AI patent families/scientific publications by the earliest publication year (based on WIPO, 2019, 2025)

[11] The terms "patent family," "patent application," "patent filing," or "invention" may be used interchangeably, referring to the representative patent family member and the corresponding invention. A patent family may include members for which patents have been granted, others not granted or still under patent examination. A patent family includes all those patents in different offices that relate to the same or similar technical content. The earliest application in the family has what is known as the priority number, and other applications in the family share one or more pieces of priority data for the purposes of novelty and inventive step. There are different definitions of patent families; for the displayed data and charts, patent families are used that are grouping together the same invention sharing the exact priority data seeking patent protection in different jurisdictions (WIPO, 2019, 2025).

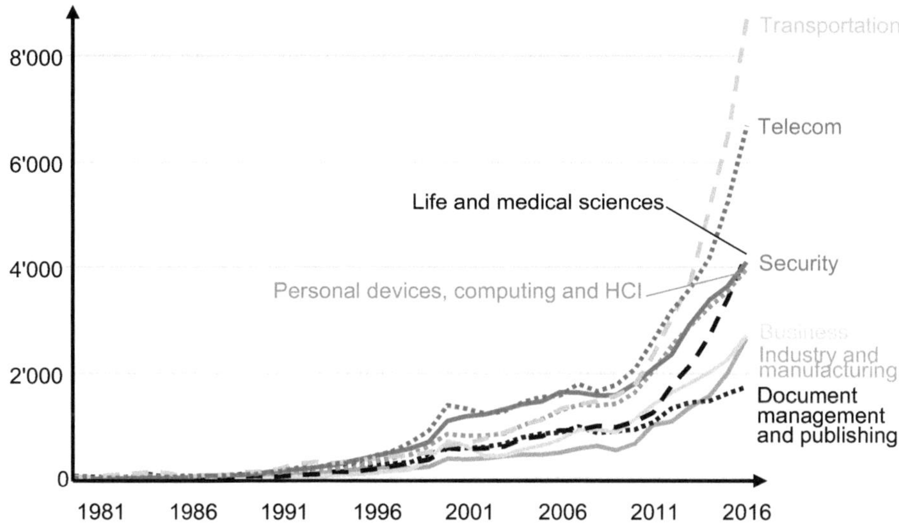

Fig. 7.12 Patent families for application field categories by earliest priority year (based on WIPO, 2019)

report, wherein it is documented (WIPO, 2025)! While the number of scientific publications increased significantly by the beginning of the 2000s (with an average annual growth rate almost doubling to 18% between 2002 and 2007), it took another 10 years for the patent publications to lift off (with an average annual growth rate of 28% between 2012 and 2017). A reasonable interpretation is that basic research primarily results first in scientific publications, while development efforts with regard to industrial applications take some time and result in patent publications.

Patent applications directed to specific application fields have been emerging since the mid-1990s (see Fig. 7.12).[12] The application fields for which patent protection is mainly sought are transportation and telecommunications. Please note that AI-related inventions are regularly directed to several application fields.

IP Protection Strategies for AI-Based Business Models

Current AI research and innovation are based on large monetary investments. Just the European Union alone wants to increase the overall investments (public and private sectors) within the EU region in AI to at least 20 billion euros per year beyond 2020 to make Europe a global leader in AI (European Commission, 2018, 2025).

[12] Note: A patent may refer to more than one category.

According to WIPO data, almost 3000 companies active in AI have received funding (almost half of all AI active companies), representing about US$46 billion in funding. Also, M&A has become a means of acquiring AI-based technologies, data access, and related patent portfolios. Almost 500 companies have been acquired, with more than half of them since 2016. This represents a great exit and co-funding environment for start-ups. Given the high investments in AI technologies and their applications, it is obvious that companies and investors are attempting to protect and monetarize their investments. While over 1.6 million publicly available scientific publications have emerged out of research, 340,000 AI-related inventions have been claimed for patent protection since artificial intelligence emerged in the 1050s. Enforcing patents has also made inroads into the field of AI, with thousands of AI-related patent families being mentioned in litigation cases (WIPO, 2019).

Also, in the field of AI IP protection, mechanisms are used and enforced to secure and to monetarize investments. Below, some of the applied key protection strategies for formal and informal AI-related IP are presented:

1. Protectability of AI-based inventions and innovations with *formal IP* means:

   (a) *AI algorithms → Patents:* There are typically three types of AI-related inventions (EPO, 2025b) that are eligible for patent protection (provided that the general legal requirements for patentability of software can be met, e.g., the two-hurdle approach to testing the technical character of the invention before the EPO in Europe or the passing of the *Alice Corporation* vs. *CLS Bank International* test in the US):

   - Core AI, including the challenge that algorithms as such, may not be patentable (e.g., if not implemented in an applied field and are then consequently considered as non-patent-eligible mathematical methods).
   - Trained models/machine learning, including the challenge to claim variations and ranges.
   - AI as a tool in an applied field, defined via technical effects.

   (b) *AI code → Copyright:*

   - AI software program code is generally considered as non-patent-eligible subject matter but is eligible for copyright protection.

2. Protectability of AI-based inventions and innovations with *informal IP* means:

   (a) *AI data → Trade secrets:*

   - Datasets (e.g., categorized training data for supervised learning may be classified and kept secret).
   - Data protection rules (e.g., the General Data Protection Regulation (GDPR) in the European Union, which may limit the exchange of or access to data).

In contrast to the above-mentioned IP protection strategies that aim to gain differentiation by gaining exclusivity, there is a second applied approach that is based on a standardization by access from and to the public domain. In the recent models of innovation management, both approaches have been practiced by innovation champions parallel to optimizing innovation speed and getting access to standards, while still monetarizing their own R&D investments (Bader, 2007; Gassmann & Bader, 2024).

However, when developing AI techniques there are two major challenges: (a) to develop the AI systems and algorithms from a technical point of view; and (b) to have access to qualified datasets (e.g., to optimize the AI algorithms or to train the AI systems). Access to datasets is already considered as a major competitive advantage between legal systems (e.g., China compared to the USA, but also for investors that invest in start-ups: which dataset is available? How much of the investment needs to first get burned for qualifying raw data? For public research organizations, it might be even more difficult to get data access due to limited financial budgets or data protection rules (e.g., in the field of life sciences).

Within the public domain, there might be open access to algorithms and software code (e.g., *TensorFlow* and *scikit-learn*, which are available on the collaborative developer platform *GitHub*) (Stone et al., 2016), but also to datasets (e.g., for training purposes) (Littman et al., 2021). Furthermore, public research organizations might dedicate their outcomes to the public domain. This can be for fundamental research (e.g. *MIT-IBM Watson AI Lab*, US$240 million funding in 2017, or due to a philanthropic approach (e.g. *MILA*, US$3.4 million funding from *Alphabet/Google* in 2016).

For entrepreneurial companies, it is, therefore, a comparative advantage when researching and/or innovating in the field of AI to practice both: Standardization in the open-source public domain (e.g., to speed up development or to centrally collect and enlarge datasets), and (!) differentiation by exclusivity applying formal and informal IP protection strategies to capture value (e.g., to leverage competitive advantages or to get access to VC investments).

Managerial Implications

AI has emerged not as a single technology mantra but rather as multiple sets of techniques, e.g., machine learning or deep learning based on multilayered neuronal networks being specifically used within certain application fields, e.g., for speech processing, computer vision, or robotics.

Although basic research is still ongoing and scientific publications have significantly increased since the 2000s, industry-sector-specific and cross-industry AI applications have become increasingly common since 2012, as patent application numbers clearly suggest. AI is increasingly being used and applied in business models, ranging from weak AI and narrow AI for limited tasks to strong AI in the (potentially near) future.

There has been various research and practical evidences that complementary formal and informal protection strategies are necessary for effective value capture in business model innovation. For AI-based business models, especially formal IP protection means [patents (e.g., for applied AI algorithms), copyrights (e.g., for AI code)] and informal IP protection [trade secrets (e.g., for AI datasets)] play a significant role. As the current systems primarily clarify how AI can be patented as being considered as software, applying AI algorithms, it is still up to legislation and professionals to tackle the remaining legal, practical, and ethical challenges, especially when it comes to patent protecting AI-based methods and systems.

From an innovator's point of view, the main challenge is how to balance public commons (e.g., getting access to specific datasets and/or specific AI algorithms), while the innovators' basic question is how and where to capture value/comparative differentiation (e.g., to monetarize the ownership/access to specific datasets). Figure 7.13 summarizes and integrates our findings from R&D cooperation and cooperation models and practices, as well as the above-outlined formal and informal complementary protection strategies.

Concerning entrepreneurship and start-ups, the accelerating progress of AI technologies has made it necessary to cope with a new and higher level of acceleration in business development, requiring a tremendous concentration of activities—attracting funding, attracting AI software engineers—at a rate not seen before, while still constructed around the comparatively and traditionally slow decision taking and reluctant adoption processes of large corporations (Šrámek, 2019). Especially when it comes to funding or direct investments, the critical questions of how to deal with public contribution and value capturing have become an important premise setting the pace for applying formal and informal protection strategies and balancing these.

To quote the Silicon-Valley-based private American venture capital firm, *Andreessen Horowitz* (Frank Chen, 2019): "When investing in start-ups, we think about where the pockets are that can make money in the shadow of the giants (i.e., *Amazon*, *Google*, *Microsoft*, and *Facebook*). These large companies are investing a lot in AI, so start-ups need to be thoughtful about what will differentiate them in a valley of giants. For instance, when we're looking at a company in the AI space, we look for start-ups that:

1. Have smart, ambitious teams ready to think outside the box;
2. Have access to a dataset that the giants don't (i.e., partnering with companies who may not want to give Google their business transaction data); and
3. Are not over-rotated on AI. In the computer industry, we've got dozens of billion-dollar companies and a lot of opportunities ahead. AI is not a panacea."

Potential AI-enabled systems are upcoming based on AI technologies that are already starting to affect urban life, with autonomous transportation as the currently most visible AI application (Grosz & Stone, 2018). The *Stanford One Hundred Year Study on Artificial Intelligence*, generally referred to as "AI100," is dedicated to assessing AI's influences on people, communities, and society and recently published their first forward-looking assessment on life in 2030: AI, in the long run, might challenge human cognitive jobs while enhancing the benefits of owning intellectual capital (Littman et al., 2021; Stone et al., 2016).

Proprietary innovation:

- Exclusive ownership
- Who pays owns case
- Owner can license, sell, sue, use, etc.
- No shared income

Bought Control Model:

- No loss of ownership, regardless of payment
- Full right to use, license, etc.
- No accounting problems
- Lower admin overhead

➔ Differentiation

Open innovation:

- Jointly own
- Who pays controls case
- All owners license to public for free

Free Public Commons Model:

- Ownership supports commons
- Full right to use, license, etc.
- No accounting problems
- For academic and commercial use

➔ Standardization

AI Specifics:

Means:

- Proprietary datasets, a/o
- Proprietary algorithm strategies, a/o
- Proprietary source code & libraries, a/o

Means:

- Access to common datasets & pooling of datasets to increase learning bias, a/o
- Publication of algorithm strategies , a/o
- Publication of source code & libraries, a/o

Effect:

+ Proprietary position, e.g. exclusive dataset, as basis to receive funding, investments, exit strategies
+ Application specific IP possible
+ Basis to financially leverage competitive advantage
- Potentially limited innovation progress
- Potentially unclear ethical standards

Effect:

+ Acceleration of innovation progress
+ Free flow of information
+ Open discussion
+ Foster publications
- Pressure to gain intrinsic R&D, public funding or philanthropic investments

Applied by (not limited to):

- Companies that want to tie specific innovation to their business model and keep exclusivity
- Start-Ups with need for external investment

Applied by (not limited to):

- Public institutions and research institutes, e.g. MILA Montréal
- Companies and institutions that need access to (also specific) datasets or want to accelerate their innovation progress

➔ Entrepreneurial AI pioneers use both models in parallel

Fig. 7.13 Balancing proprietary innovation and open innovation (Bader & Stummeyer, 2019, 2024)

Therefore, innovation in AI-based business models combined with value capturing based on formal and informal IP protection strategies retains its relevance. However, this approach is likely to be challenged by the public's appreciation of fairness and equitableness with regard to public goods and commons and the innovator's striving for appropriability.

Example—Anthropic's Patent Strategy: Building IP Leadership in Generative AI[13]

Anthropic, a recognized leader in large language models (LLMs) and AI safety, exemplifies how IP can be leveraged to protect innovation, shape market dynamics, and foster responsible technology deployment. For companies operating in generative AI, where innovation cycles are short and competition is fierce, a robust patent strategy is essential. Patents are a strategic instrument that define competitive advantage, influence industry standards, and secure long-term growth.

The Strategic Imperative of IP in Generative AI Generative AI is characterized by high research intensity, rapid technological shifts, and significant commercial potential. In this environment, patents serve multiple purposes:

- **Protection:** Safeguarding core innovations from competitors and non-practicing entities (NPEs).
- **Negotiation Power:** Providing leverage in partnerships, licensing, and cross-licensing agreements.
- **Market Signaling:** Demonstrating technological leadership and commitment to innovation.
- **Standard Setting:** Influencing the direction of industry norms and best practices.

For Anthropic, IP is not an afterthought—it is a foundational element of its business strategy, ensuring both freedom-to-operate (FTO) and the ability to shape the future of AI responsibly.

Proactive IP Defense in a Competitive Landscape The AI sector presents unique IP challenges. Rapid innovation creates overlapping claims, while the high value of AI applications attracts litigation risks. Anthropic addresses these challenges through:

- **Comprehensive Patent Coverage:** Securing patents across core technologies to deter infringement.
- **Portfolio Positioning:** Building a balanced portfolio that acts as both a defensive shield and an offensive tool in negotiations.
- **Litigation Preparedness:** Anticipating potential disputes with NPEs and competitors by maintaining strong legal and technical documentation.

[13] Based on GreyB (2025b).

This proactive approach reduces exposure to costly litigation and ensures operational continuity in critical technology areas.

Core Innovation Domains and IP Focus Anthropic's innovation strategy aligns closely with its mission to develop safe, high-performing AI systems. While exact filing numbers are confidential, the company's likely IP priorities include (innovation area—strategic patent focus):

- **Novel Model Architectures:** Patents on advanced neural network designs, transformer variants, and attention mechanisms that improve efficiency and scalability.
- **Advanced Training Techniques:** Patents covering reinforcement learning from human feedback (RLHF), self-supervised learning, and innovative data curation methods.
- **AI Safety and Alignment:** Patents for bias reduction, truthfulness verification, and misuse prevention—critical for ethical AI deployment.
- **Efficient Inference Systems:** Innovations enabling faster, resource-optimized model deployment for real-world applications.
- **Human–AI Interaction:** Patent protecting intuitive interfaces and control mechanisms that enhance user experience and trust.

This portfolio reflects a dual commitment: Pushing the boundaries of performance while embedding safety and ethical considerations into the technology.

Influencing the Broader AI Ecosystem Anthropic's patent strategy extends beyond internal benefits. Foundational patents can:

- **Shape Competitor Behavior:** Forcing rivals to adjust R&D priorities or seek licensing agreements.
- **Set Industry Benchmarks:** Establishing standards in areas like AI safety and alignment.
- **Foster Collaboration:** Enabling partnerships through licensing frameworks that encourage responsible innovation.

By defining what is considered novel and enforceable, Anthropic's patent portfolio influences the trajectory of AI development across the industry.

Patent Monetization and Licensing Opportunities Beyond protection, Anthropic's patents hold significant monetization potential. Licensing agreements can generate revenue streams while promoting interoperability and ethical standards. Strategic licensing also strengthens Anthropic's position in negotiations with major cloud providers, enterprise clients, and research partners.

IP as a Catalyst for Responsible AI Leadership Anthropic's case illustrates how a forward-looking patent strategy underpins both technological leadership and ethical responsibility in generative AI. By aligning patent filings with core innovation areas and safety principles, the company not only secures its competitive edge but also contributes to shaping a sustainable and trustworthy AI ecosystem. In an era where AI is transforming industries and societies, IP foresight will be a defining factor for market leaders. ◀

Scale AI's 20 Essential Business Principles for Patenting AI[14]

Todd Bailey of *Scale AI*, Canadian Artificial Intelligence Supercluster (an investment and innovation consortium of industry partners, research institutes, academia and government partners), suggests that these principles empower the application of business intuition and common sense to patents in context of AI business strategies:

1. Patents Are Business Tools.
2. Effective Patents Require Strategic Planning.
3. The Bar for Patenting Is Lower Than You Think.
4. Patenting Involves a Strategic Compromise.
5. Not All Patents Are the Same: The Role of the Claims.
6. No Patent Can Prevent Copying or Stop Competitors.
7. Most Patents Miss Their Potential Business Value.
8. Detectability: The Hallmark of Effective Patents.
9. The "Goldilocks" Time for Filing a Patent.
10. Patenting AI is Different Than Other Technologies.
11. Effective Patenting Requires "Why, What and When."
12. Effective Patents Need Participation and Perseverance.
13. Cutting Corners Results in Weak Patents.
14. Granted Patents Can Be Invalidated.
15. Using Your Patented Concept Can Infringe Other Patents.
16. You Can Influence the Speed of the Patent Process.
17. Big Companies Have Different Patent Goals.
18. What You Think About Patents Isn't Always the Point.
19. You Get to Decide Who Uses Your Patented Concept.
20. Monitoring Competitor Patents Provides Business Intelligence. ◀

[14] Based on extracts from Bailey (2024a, 2024b) and Scale AI (2025).

Takeaways Artificial Intelligence and Intellectual Property[15]

AI and patentability:

AI is considered a branch of computer science, and therefore, inventions involving AI are considered computer-implemented inventions (CII). However, CIIs are treated differently by patent offices in different regions of the world.

AI used to invent:

Widely accepted. AI-assisted inventions are patentable if a human can be identified as the inventor. From the perspective of inventorship, three categories of AI inventions may be identified:

1. Human-made inventions using AI for the verification of the outcome;
2. Inventions in which a human identifies a problem and uses AI to find a solution; and
3. AI-made inventions, in which AI identifies a problem and proposes a solution without human intervention.

In the first two categories, AI is used as a tool for human inventors, augmenting their capabilities. In the third category (AI-made inventions), scientists seem to agree that AI, which could invent independently of human direction, instruction, and oversight, is a matter of undefined future and thus science fiction. (See also Sect. 5.5 Generative Artificial Intelligence in Patent Management.)

AI as inventor:

Rejected in nearly all current jurisdictions. There is a common understanding that the inventor must be a human being: The person who created the invention by their own creative activity. (See also Dabus patent application example in Sect. 9.2.)

References

Bader, M. A. (2006). *Intellectual property management in R&D collaborations*. Physica.

Bader, M. A. (2007). Managing intellectual property in a collaborative environment: Learning from IBM. *International Journal of Intellectual Property Management, 1*(3), 206–225.

Bader, M. A. (2022). Innovationen im Handel nutzen und schützen. In M. Knoppe, S. Rock, & M. Wild (Eds.), *Der Zukunftsfähige Handel* (pp. 171–192). Springer Gabler.

Bader, M. A., & Stummeyer, C. (2019). The role of innovation and IP in AI-based business models. In R. Baierl, J. Behrens, & A. Brem (Eds.), *Digital entrepreneurship—Interfaces between digital technologies and entrepreneurship* (pp. 23–56). Springer.

[15] Based on extracts from EPO (2025c).

Bader, M. A., & Stummeyer, C. (2024). Innovation und geistiges Eigentum in KI-basierten Geschäftsmodellen. In L. Fend & J. Hofmann (Eds.), *Digitalisierung in Industrie-, Handels— und Dienstleistungsunternehmen* (4th ed., pp. 293–323). Springer Gabler.

Bailey, T. (2024a). *Intellectual property strategy foundations for artificial intelligence. A practical guide for founders, leaders and investors*. June 2024. Montréal: Scale AI. Retrieved September 26, 2025, from https://www.scaleai.ca/wp-content/uploads/2024/06/intellectual-property-strategy-foundations-for-artificial-intelligence.pdf

Bailey, T. (2024b). *Essential business principles for patenting in artificial intelligence. A practical guide for entrepreneurs, leaders and investors*. August 2024. Montréal: Scale AI. Retrieved September 26, 2025, from https://www.scaleai.ca/wp-content/uploads/2024/08/essential-business-principles-for-patenting-in-artificial-intelligence.pdf

Best, B. (2022). *Softwarepatente in Europa.* Conference: Software und Geschäftsmodelle patentieren?—So schützen Sie Ihre Software und Geschäftsmodelle. Munich: Bayern Innovativ.

BGW. (2019). *IP management in distributed ledger technology and in food technology*. BGW.

Boehm, B. W. (1976). Software engineering. *IEEE Transactions on Computers, C-25*(12), 1226–1241.

Bonakdar, A., Frankenberger, K., Bader, M. A., & Gassmann, O. (2017). Capturing value from business models: The role of formal and informal protection strategies. *International Journal of Technology Management, 73*(4), 151–175.

Carroll, J. T., Srinivasa, C. K., & Malaney, K. J. (2024). *Alice patent eligibility analysis divergence before USPTO and district court.* Foley and Lardner LLP. Retrieved July 7, 2025, from https://www.foley.com/insights/publications/2024/09/alice-patent-eligibility-analysis-divergance-before-uspto-and-district-court/

Chen, F. (2019). The investors' view. In WIPO (2019). In *WIPO technology trends 2019: Artificial intelligence* (p. 105). World Intellectual Property Organization.

Chen, H., Roco, M. C., Li, X., & Lin, Y. (2008). Trends in nanotechnology patents. *Nature Nanotechnology, 3*(3), 123–125.

Cohen, J. (2017). The birth of CRISPR. The American association for the advancement of science, license number 4803211490911. *Science, 355*(6326), 680–684. https://doi.org/10.1126/science.355.6326.680

Coriat, B., & Orsi, F. (2002). Establishing a new intellectual property rights regime in the United States: Origins, content and problems. *Research Policy, 31*(8–9), 1491–1507.

Costello-Caulkins, M. (2021). Nanotechnology patent law: A case study of the United States and European patent applications. *Santa Clara High Technology Law Journal, 37*(3), 337–386. https://digitalcommons.law.scu.edu/chtlj/vol37/iss3/3

Dutfield, G. (2003). *Intellectual property rights and the life science industries. A twentieth century history*. Ashgate.

EPO. (2007). *Scenarios for the future. How might IP regimes evolve by 2025? What global legitimacy might such regimes have?* European Patent Office.

EPO. (2013). *Nanotechnology and patents*. Munich: European Patent Office. Retrieved July 16, 2025, from https://www.epo.org/en/news-events/in-focus/classification/nanotechnology

EPO. (2018). *Patenting artificial intelligence. Conference summary*. Munich: European Patent Office. Retrieved July 7, 2025, from https://www.youtube.com/playlist?list=PLgDlswd0__eIqs4fl42UGeMNGrMdcYjGM

EPO. (2019). *Patents for software? European law and practice*. Munich: European Patent Office. Retrieved December 28, 2019, from https://www.epo.org/news-issues/issues/ict/hardware-and-software.html#tab1

EPO. (2020a). *Patents and the fourth industrial revolution. The inventions behind digital transformation*. Munich: European Patent Office. Retrieved June 27, 2025, from https://link.epo.org/web/patents_and_the_fourth_industrial_revolution_study_2020_en.pdf

EPO. (2020b). *The role of patents in an AI driven world*, virtual conference, 17./18.12.2020. Munich: European Patent Office. Retrieved July 7, 2025, from https://www.youtube.com/playlist?list=PLgDlswd0__eK5UHWAHnucwVI22O0pROdT

EPO. (2023). *Conference on AI technologies, regulation, inventorship and patenting*. Munich: European Patent Office. Retrieved July 7, 2025, from https://www.epo.org/en/news-events/in-focus/ict/artificial-intelligence

EPO. (2024). *Biotech patents*. Munich: European Patent Office. Retrieved July 10, 2025, from https://www.epo.org/en/news-events/in-focus/biotechnology-patents

EPO. (2025a). *Patent index 2024*. Munich: European Patent Office. Retrieved July 10, 2025, from https://www.epo.org/en/about-us/statistics/patent-index-2024

EPO. (2025b). *Guidelines for examination: Artificial intelligence and machine learning (G-II 3.3.1)*. Munich: European Patent Office. Retrieved July 7, 2025, from https://www.epo.org/en/legal/guidelines-epc/2025/g_ii_3_3_1.html

EPO. (2025c). *Artificial intelligence*. Munich: European Patent Office. Retrieved July 7, 2025, from https://www.epo.org/en/news-events/in-focus/ict/artificial-intelligence#collapsiblelang

EPO. (2025d). *Computer technology*. Munich European Patent Office. Retrieved August 11, 2025, from https://www.epo.org/en/about-us/statistics/statistics-centre/technologyfields?code=6

EPO and CNIPA. (2019). *Comparative study on computer implemented inventions/software related inventions—Report 2019 I EPO and CNIPA*. Munich: European Patent Office. Retrieved June 27, 2025, from http://documents.epo.org/projects/babylon/eponot.nsf/0/979CF38758D25C2CC12584AC004618D9/$File/comparative_study_on_computer_implemented_inventions_software_related_inventions_EPO_CNIPA_en.pdf

EPO and JPO. (2018). *Comparative study on computer implemented inventions/software related inventions—Report 2018 I EPO and JPO*. Munich: European Patent Office. Retrieved June 27, 2025, from http://documents.epo.org/projects/babylon/eponet.nsf/0/346e6018b0445380c12583cb002fdb34/$FILE/comparative_study_on_computer_implemented_inventions_software_related_inventions_EPO_JPO_en.pdf

European Commission. (2018). *Artificial intelligence for Europe*. Brussels: European Commission. Retrieved July 7, 2025, from https://eur-lex.europa.eu/legal-content/EN/TXT/?uri=COM:2018:237:FIN

European Commission. (2025). *AI continent action plan*. Brussels: European Commission. Retrieved July 7, 2025, from https://digital-strategy.ec.europa.eu/en/factpages/ai-continent-action-plan

Gassmann, O., & Bader, M. A. (2024). *Patentmanagement: Innovationen erfolgreich nutzen und schützen* (5th ed.). Springer Gabler.

Google. (2019). *Q3 earnings call*, October 31st.

GreyB (2025a). *Samsung faces a lawsuit every 5 days, pharma litigation booms, and NPEs stay highly active*. Retrieved August 16, 2025, from https://www.greyb.com/blog/patent-litigation-trends/

GreyB (2025b). *Inside anthropic's patent strategy: Filings, litigation trends, and licensing power.* Retrieved September 26, 2025, from https://www.greyb.com/blog/anthropics-patent-strategy/

Grosz, B. J., & Stone, P. (2018). *A century long commitment to assessing artificial intelligence and its impact on society*. December 2018. Communications of the ACM (CACM).

Hall, B. H., & MacGarvie, M. (2010). The private value of software patents. *Research Policy, 39*(7), 994–1009.

Huebner, S. R. (2008). The validity of European nanotechnology patents in Germany. *Nanotechnology Law and Business, 5*(3), 353–357.

IPStudies. (2019). *CRISPR patent landscape*. In *Les Paccots*. https://www.ipstudies.ch/

Jinek, M., Chylinski, K., Fonfara, I., Hauer, M., Doudna, J. A., & Charpentier, E. (2012). A programmable dual-RNA–guided DNA endonuclease in adaptive bacterial immunity. *Science, 337*(6096), 816–821.

Kallinger, C., Veefkind, V., Michalitsch, R., Verbandt, Y., Neumann, A., Scheu, M., & Forster, W. (2008). Patenting nanotechnology: A European patent office perspective. *Nanotechnology Law and Business, 5*(1), 95.

Ledford, H. (2016). Bitter fight over CRISPR patent heats up: Unusual battle among academic institutions holds key to gene-editing tool's future use. *Nature, 529*(7586), 265. Gale OneFile: Health and Medicine. Retrieved July 10, 2025, from https://doi.org/10.1038/nature.2015.17961

Littman, M. L., Ajunwa, I., Berger, G., Boutilier, C., Currie, M., Doshi-Velez, F., Hadfield, G., Horowitz, M. C., Isbell, C., Kitano, H., Levy, K., Lyons, T., Mitchell, M., Shah, J., Sloman, S., Vallor, S., & Walsh, T. (2021). *Gathering strength, gathering storms: The one hundred year study on artificial intelligence (AI100) 2021 study panel report*. Stanford, CA: Stanford University, September 2021. Retrieved July 10, 2025, from http://ai100.stanford.edu/2021-report

Mertens, A., & Scheufen, M. (2024). Intellectual property and fourth industrial revolution technologies: How the patent system is shaping the future in the data-driven economy. *European Journal of Law and Economics, 57*, 275–310. https://doi.org/10.1007/s10657-023-09789-2

MGI (McKinsey Global Institute). (2015). *The internet of things: Mapping the value beyond the hype*.

Miller, C., Serrato, R. M., Repressas-Cardenas, J. M., & Griffith, A. K. (2005). *The handbook of nanotechnology: Business, policy, and intellectual property law*. Wiley.

Nanosys. (2009). *Nanoco settles patent infringement lawsuit with nanosys, inc. for quantum dot technology*. Manchester: Nanosys. Retrieved July 10, 2025, from https://www.nanocotechnologies.com/nanoco-settles-patent-infringement-lawsuit-with-nanosys-inc-for-quantum-dot-technology/

OECD. (2003). *Genetic inventions, iprs and licensing practices: Evidence and policies*. OECD.

OECD. (2009). *Nanotechnology: An overview*. OECD.

OECD. (2017). *Key issues for digital transformation in the G20. Report prepared for a joint G20 German presidency/OECD conference*. OECD.

Ouellette, L. L. (2015). Nanotechnology and innovation policy. *Harvard Journal of Law and Technology, 29*(1), 33. Fall.

PERA. (2025). *Patent eligibility restoration act of 2025*. S.1546, 119th Cong. (2025–2026). Congress.gov. Retrieved July 7, 2025, from https://www.congress.gov/bill/119th-congress/senate-bill/1546

Reidenberg, J. R., Cammeron Russel, N., Price, M., & Mohand, A. (2015). *Patents and the small participants in the smartphone industry*. Fordham Center on Law and Information Policy & the World Intellectual Property Organization.

Scale AI. (2025). *Who we are*. Retrieved September 26, 2025, from https://www.scaleai.ca/about-us/

SCBT. (2024). *CRISPR technology: Patent & license landscapes*. N° 20231386. Neuchatel: Swiss Center for Business & Technology Intelligence–Centredoc. Retrieved July 10, 2025, from https://www.ige.ch/fileadmin/user_upload/recht/national/e/20231388_IPI_CRISPR_Patent_License_Landscape_revised_Final_16_02_24.pdf

Schwab, K. (2017). *The fourth industrial revolution*, 1st edition, New York Crowne Business (2017). Originally published by World Economic Forum, Geneva, Switzerland 2016.

ScienceMag. (2017). *How the battle lines over CRISPR were drawn*. Retrieved December 27, 2019, from https://www.sciencemag.org/news/2017/02/how-battlelines-over-crispr-were-drawn

Sherkow, J. S. (2015). Law, history and lessons in the CRISPR patent conflict. *Nature Biotechnology, 33*, 256–257.

Sherkow, J. S. (2018). The CRISPR patent landscape: Past, present, and future. *The CRISPR Journal, 1*(1), 5–9. https://doi.org/10.1089/crispr.2017.0013

Smalley, L. W. (2014). Will nanotechnology products be impacted by the federal courts' 'product of nature' exception to subject-matter eligibility under 35 U.S.C. 101? *Marshall Review of Intellectual Property Law, 13*, 397.

Spiegel Online. (2009). *Microsoft-Bezwinger greift Web-Wirtschaft an*. Retrieved June 27, 2025, from http://www.spiegel.de/netzwelt/netzpolitik/software-firma-eolas-microsoft-bezwinger-greift-web-wirtschaft-an-a-653659.html

Šrámek, P. (2019). AI startups in Europe. In *WIPO technology trends 2019: Artificial intelligence* (p. 108). World Intellectual Property Organization.

Statnano. (2024). *Top 10 countries by EPO nanotechnology patents in 2023*. Lund, Jiangsu, Teheran: StatNano. Retrieved July 16, 2025, from https://statnano.com/news/73567/Top-10-Countries-by-EPO-Nanotechnology-Patents-in-2023

Stellbrink. (2016). *Life after Alice*. Stellbrink & Partner on X: Retrieved June 27, 2025, from https://x.com/sp_patent/status/742705881851252737

Stiftung Science et Cité. (2004). *Streitfall biotechpatente*. Stiftung Science et Cité.

Stone, P., Brooks, R., Brynjolfsson, E., Calo, R., Etzioni, O., Hager, G., Hirschberg, J., Kalyanakrishnan, S., Kamar, E., Kraus, S., Leyton-Brown, K., Parkes, D., Press, W., Saxenian, A. L., Shah, J., Tambe, M., & Teller, A. (2016). *'Artificial intelligence and life in 2030.' One hundred year study on artificial intelligence: Report of the 2015–2016 study panel*. Stanford, CA: Stanford University, September 2016. Retrieved July 10, 2025, from http://ai100.stanford.edu/2016-report

Straus, J. (2003). *An updating concerning the protection of biotechnological inventions including the scope of patents for genes*. Munich: Special edition of the Official Journal of the European Patent Office on Gene Patenting.

Thumm, N. (2001). Management of intellectual property rights in European biotechnology firms. *Technological Forecasting and Social Change, 67*, 259–272.

Thumm, N. (2003). *Research and patenting in biotechnology—A survey in Switzerland*. Swiss Federal Institute of Intellectual Property.

USPTO. (2017). *Patent eligible subject matter: Report on views and recommendations from the public*. Alexandria, VA: United States Patent and Trademark Office. Retrieved July 7, 2025, from https://www.uspto.gov/sites/default/files/documents/101-Report_FINAL.pdf

USPTO. (2024). *2024 guidance update on patent subject matter eligibility, including on artificial intelligence*. Retrieved July 7, 2025, from https://www.federalregister.gov/documents/2024/07/17/2024-15377/2024-guidance-update-on-patent-subject-matter-eligibility-including-on-artificial-intelligence

Wang, B., Vuković, L., & Král, P. (2008). Nanoscale rotary motors driven by electron tunneling. *Physical Review Letters, 101*, 186808.

WIPO. (2019). *WIPO technology trends 2019: Artificial intelligence*. Geneva: World Intellectual Property Organization. (The user is allowed to reproduce, distribute, adapt, translate and publicly perform this publication, including for commercial purposes, without explicit permission, provided that the content is accompanied by an acknowledgement that WIPO is the source and that it is clearly indicated if changes were made to the original content.)

WIPO. (2025). *PATENTSCOPE artificial intelligence index*. Geneva: World Intellectual Property Organization. Retrieved July 16, 2025, from https://www.wipo.int/en/web/technology-trends/artificial_intelligence/patentscope

WSJ. (2019). *Can an AI system be given a patent?* New York City: The Wall Street Journal. Retrieved July 7, 2025, from https://www.wsj.com/articles/can-an-ai-system-be-given-a-patent-11570801500

Youtie, J., Porter, A., Shapira, P., & Newman, N. (2016). *Lessons from ten years of nanotechnology bibliometric analysis*. Paris: OECD. http://www.oecd.org/sti/080%20-%20Blue%20Sky%20STIP%20final%20submission.pdf

Zhu, S., Meng, H., Gu, Z., & Zhao, Y. (2021). Research trend of nanoscience and nanotechnology—A bibliometric analysis of Nano Today. *NanoToday, 39*, 101233. https://doi.org/10.1016/j.nantod.2021.101233

Patent Management in VUCA Environments

8

In dynamic environments, patent management must be adapted accordingly. We provide an overview of some further specific aspects of patent management under "VUCA" conditions, which are characterized by Volatility, Uncertainty, Complexity, and Ambiguity:

1. Inventor Culture as a Catalyst
2. Need for Action at SMEs
3. Challenges for Start-ups
4. Measures Against Product Piracy

8.1 Inventor Culture as a Catalyst

An essential component of the innovation culture is the ability of a company's employees to develop ideas and translate them into marketable technologies, products, and services. In order to implement the patent strategy, inventive activities are therefore shaped by business interests. An incentive system that rewards significant contributions is particularly suitable for this purpose. Appropriate measures can be taken to create an inventor culture:

- Ensuring broad access to all sources of information;
- Clarification of communication responsibilities and roles;
- Development of a common team code;
- Regular feedback and reviews;
- Promotion of social events for personal exchange;
- Active communication of success stories;
- Project debriefings at the end of the project;
- Break-out sessions to distance people from day-to-day business; and
- Establishment of experimental rooms to promote experiments.

M. A. Bader et al., *Patent Management*, Management for Professionals,
https://doi.org/10.1007/978-3-032-12030-4_8

Example—Georg Fischer Runs a Purely Monetary Incentive System

The Swiss industrial firm, *Georg Fischer*, has opted for a purely monetary incentive system to stimulate inventions that take account of national obligations, such as employee inventor remuneration. It is important that the incentive system is perceived as fair by those involved. This applies when employees from different areas and locations of the company work together as a team on projects. A relevant starting point for comparisons is the average salaries of the locations. Furthermore, transparency, broad communication, and appropriate training are required. Support must be provided by the R&D management or a technical board if the program is to be perceived and accepted as serious and sustainable. ◄

Example—Swiss Re Runs a Mixed Monetary and Non-Monetary Incentive System

The reinsurance company *Swiss Re* has introduced an incentive system for inventions with monetary and non-monetary components. The inventors are listed and honored in a *Hall of Fame* on the Intranet. This is accompanied by a letter of recognition from a member of the Executive Board and, if necessary, by small gifts. ◄

Example—Endress+Hauser Runs a Non-Monetary Incentive System

The process automation solution and services provider *Endress+Hauser* published an annual report, the cover of which had the portraits of all the company's inventors—a strong signal, on the one hand, to inventors and employees within the company and, on the other, to customers outside the company. ◄

"Innovate or Perish"

Although it is financially in decline, *Eastman Kodak* had a strong inventor culture, one that was initiated by its inventor-founder George Eastman in the nineteenth century; four main awards got established, three of which relate to patents:

First CTO first Patent Award:

- Award for the first patent granted, including a copy of the patent certificate issued and a letter signed by the CTO.

Second 20th Kodak Patent:

- Award for the 20th patent granted, including a cash prize and an invitation to an annual dinner hosted by the CEO and the CTO.

Third 100th Kodak Patent:

- CTO Century award, including a cash prize and an invitation to the annual dinner.

Fourth Eastman Innovation Award:

- Annual award related to important inventions, but not necessarily patents. However, the patent awards were not enough to prevent the eventual downfall of the Kodak corporation; Kodak did not promote enough disruptive innovation internally.

"Culture Eats Strategy for Breakfast"

Due to pressure on margins, and fierce competition, companies are facing pressure to innovate. While there are already many good solutions to the strategy and business model levels, the human factor of innovation is often overlooked. Yet, corporate culture can often be a key resource, enabling companies to use their employees as a key success factor for innovation (Gassmann et al., 2018).

An innovative corporate culture acts as a central factor in driving sustainable growth and attracting young talent. According to studies by the sociologist *Richard Florida*, young people can no longer be recruited and retained with a high salary and good career perspectives alone. What is more important in the competition for the world's best talent is a strong and positive organizational culture.

By looking at highly innovative companies, we focused not only on the leaders, as these mostly do not innovate, but also on the people that actually generate the innovation. We tried to identify successful practices of how to develop and promote a highly innovative company culture. In our research, we identified seven cultural aspects of innovative companies, which we call the *ANIMATE* model (see Fig. 8.1):

- ***A*gile implementation:** Act in fast, iterative learning cycles.
- ***N*urturing:** Develop measures to stimulate employees and external partners to think outside the box.
- ***I*nspire:** Give employees a purpose and inspire them.
- ***M*otivate:** Make employees go the extra mile by motivating them.
- ***A*lign teams:** Arrange teams to achieve goals together.
- ***T*ransparency:** Communicate openly so that all employees can contribute to the set goals in the most effective way.

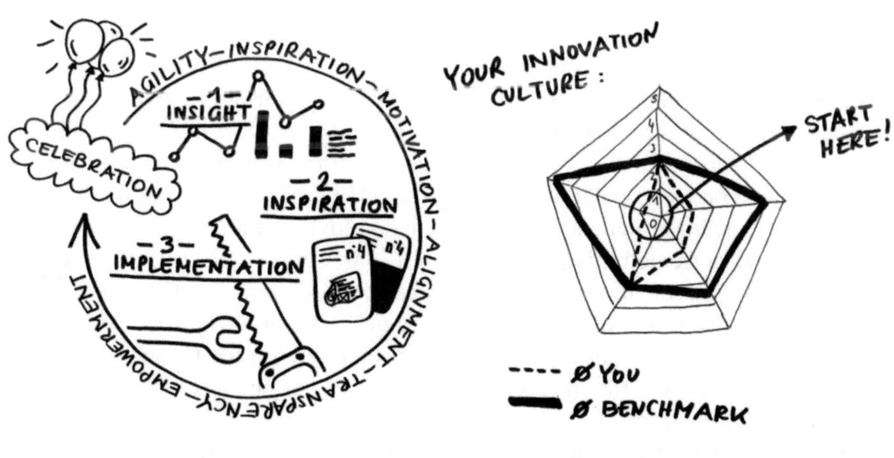

Fig. 8.1 Managing inventor culture: The St. Gallen Innovation Culture Navigator (Gassmann et al., 2018) (Used with kind permission by Carl Hanser Verlag GmbH. All rights reserved.)

- ***Empowerment:*** Create the feeling of being competent and in charge of one's own actions, and create confidence on all hierarchical levels. This will catalyze entrepreneurship.

To address cultural innovation, we created the St. Gallen Innovation Culture Navigator, which outlines 66 practices of highly successful organizations supporting their pursuit of company innovation. Linked to an online self-assessment on www.innovationculturenavigator.com, the Innovation Culture Navigator represents a playful way of developing your organizational culture by learning from practices from leading innovation players.

A strong innovation culture is not only enabling more patents and innovation but also, as a side effect, has led to 36% more profits and 45% more sales, as Michaelis found out in 2018. The ANIMATE framework supports specific practices concerning innovation culture. It is important to understand that culture is not God-given but can be developed and designed similarly to the business model itself. It takes time, but there are practices within the seven dimensions of ANIMATE that help leaders to create a dynamic environment for a vibrant, sparkling, and energetic corporate culture—the humus for innovation in every company.

Knowledge leaves when people do. In spite of digitization, immense efforts in the field of knowledge management, and the availability of new and innovative tools such as artificial intelligence, people remain the key drivers of innovation. It is widely accepted in software engineering that a good developer can be almost a hundred times more productive than an average developer. The cause of this productivity gap has less to do with training in technology, mathematics, or programming and more to do with specific skills of intelligent assessment and reflection. The best and most innovative software developers are becoming increasingly less likely to be employed in traditional industries such as banking, industry, or commerce. Instead, most of them end up at *Google*, *Amazon,* or *IBM*. Even more commonly, many of them apply their skills in open-source projects outside of their jobs, because that is where they find what is lacking in their workplaces: agility, diversity, inspiration, motivational feedback, high levels of transparency, and self-development.

Successful products, such as *Sony's PlayStation*, *Gmail* from *Google*, the first *Apple Macintosh*, or *Facebook's* famous "Like" button, were developed by innovative employees on their own initiative. The first *BMW* 3 Series' Touring was a model the company's management never wanted. An employee acting on his own initiative developed and presented this product himself. *3M's* famous *Post-it®s* were a by-product of an experiment with adhesives that did not work out. Even *Teflon* was developed as a "spin-off" after searching for a new type of refrigerant. The famous *tesafilm®* (adhesive tape) from *Beiersdorf,* which today (in the German language) is used synonymously for an entire product class, is actually an unsuccessful *Hansaplast®* (band-aid).

None of these products would exist if it had not been for the tremendous commitment of creative employees, some of whom encountered a lot of resistance within and outside their organization.

It is often claimed that innovation is pure luck. Indeed, the random screening of every conceivable active substance is in fact a common method in pharmaceutical research. That is how the transplant drug *Cyclosporin* from *Sandoz*, now part of *Novartis*, was developed, for example. However, it is often forgotten that large amounts of determination, perseverance, and teamwork are required in order to successfully identify and develop an active ingredient. There are companies that are constantly searching for and encouraging these curious pioneers. Innovation must not only be desired but must first and foremost as a precondition be permitted and encouraged. This is not always easy, because it also means going down many dead ends and accepting many failures. How do you measure this kind of innovation? One thing is certain: Linear innovation processes, such as stage-gate processes, are not going to take you all the way. You also have to take a chance. In the end, what matters is beating the failure rate statistics for innovation projects. In other words: You have to kiss a lot of frogs to find a prince.

In retrospect, companies often mythologize their innovations and founders. There are numerous stories and legends built up around *IBM* founder and inventor *Thomas Watson*, and the same is true of *Wilhelm Conrad Röntgen*. Often employees and colleagues are left forgotten and in the background—only the lonely, heroic warriors remain. Reality, however, is characterized by team efforts, and that is all the truer of a modern innovation organization. Without teams, most innovations would never have emerged. It is important for managers to be aware of this. You are hardly going to create an innovative organization by building a culture around silos.

A strong innovation culture also clearly supports the implementation of an innovation strategy: In a study of 1000 companies, it was shown that companies, the innovation strategy of which was supported by a suitable innovation culture, experienced 33% more growth in company value and a growth increase by one-sixth in net profit over a period of 5 years than companies that did not have a suitable innovation culture. It is not just Silicon Valley that offers successful examples of this. There are many regional hidden champions as well, such as the German multinational industrial control and automation company *Festo,* and the Swiss world-class screen printing, filtration, and architectural solutions provider *Sefar*, which manage to achieve sustainable innovation thanks to their systematic striving for an innovative and inventive culture.

Nevertheless, many of our industry partners, whose innovations we have supported in recent years, view culture as an intangible construct that cannot be managed systematically. Engineers work on designing and developing products and processes but view company culture as a given historical construct. The introduction of an incentive system that rewards significant contributions is particularly suitable for this purpose.

This fatalistic view is dangerous because it puts the spark of inspiration and innovation at risk. Executives and managers are especially responsible for implementing an innovative corporate culture. This can be done at all company levels and does not necessarily have to come from the executive—even though it might work better that way.

Seven Dimensions of Innovation Culture
"ANIMATE":

- **A**gile implementation;
- **N**urture and develop measures to stimulate thinking outside the box;
- **I**nspire employees, due to diverse perspectives;
- **M**otivate employees to go the extra mile;
- **A**lign teams in order to achieve goals together;
- **T**ransparency, so that all employees can contribute in the most effective way; and
- **E**mpower employees so that they can use their innovation potential.

Example— The St. Gallen Innovation Culture Navigator
The Swiss *Institute of Technology Management* at the renowned *University of St. Gallen (ITEM-HSG)* has been researching the management of innovation and has also been investigating the success factors of the most successful innovative organizations for almost 20 years. The Institute has also made numerous contributions to the rankings of the most innovative companies.

A central lever is considered to be the corporate culture, which allows to capitalize on employees as a success factor for innovation. Successful products such as Liechtenstein's multinational *Hilti's* Fleet Management were initiated by innovative employees on their own initiative. However, a culture of innovation also influences the success of strategic innovation from top management, which depends on the willingness and ability of employees to implement it. At the same time, many of our industrial partners see culture as too intangible a construct to be managed systemically. Based on this feedback, the *St. Gallen Innovation Culture Navigator* allows for a systematic management of innovation culture (see Fig. 9.1):

1. *Insight:* Learning what is missing;
2. *Inspiration:* Seeing what is working; and
3. *Implementation:* Doing what is fitting.

1. Insight Good management needs good data. Even an innovation culture cannot be designed efficiently on the basis of mere instinct. A precise assessment of your innovation culture will identify both the cultural strengths and the cultural possibilities, which your company can encounter if suitable cultural practices are selected. You can start developing your innovation culture by determining the most efficient drivers: Is your biggest challenge that your employees do not produce enough innovative ideas? Does your company lack the right channels to process and test ideas quickly and efficiently? Or do your employees perhaps have very little incentive to implement their innovative ideas within your company and therefore implement them externally? Systematically measuring your innovation culture and knowing your status quo both enable you to focus. You can direct your energy and time into the identified possibilities and thus achieve maximum impact. In addition, your employees can already get involved, aware of innovation culture being an important topic. To then give employees an active role as co-shapers of the company's future is a practical step toward a successful innovation culture.

We assess the seven dimensions of your innovation culture by using a standardized measurement tool.[1] You should, however, involve employees from different departments and hierarchical levels. This is the only way to guarantee a truly valid and representative measurement of your innovation culture. In order to make employee data directly interpretable and action-relevant, your data can be compared to a benchmark. Without such a context, it is difficult to interpret a "four" in the area of agility. First, you can have internal benchmarking in which different business areas are compared with each other. Second, we enable comparisons among companies, which form part of our growing research database. We ultimately recommend using internal time-based benchmarking, whereby a new measurement is performed cyclically (about every 12 or 24 months) so that trends can be tracked within the company. These three reference points—especially when combined—enable us to interpret the assessment results and to select specifically those goals for the second phase *Inspiration*, which promise the greatest impact.

2. Inspiration Learn from the best and be inspired by the innovation champions' 66 cultural practices.

The advantage of designing an innovation culture with concrete cultural practices is that tangible and visible developments quickly reach employees. The rich and varied perspectives within the 66 cultural practices help break out of familiar thinking patterns and old discussions in order to then consider completely new options for action. Numerous company examples help enliven the cultural practices and provide reference points that help convince colleagues. The cultural practices cover a very broad spectrum and let you decide how courageously the culture is to be developed: The *Heroic Failure Award*, which *Grey* symbolically bestows to improve the way in which failure is handled in a company, is not likely to be controversial—even in conservative companies. The payment service, *Stripe*, implemented the cultural practice known as *Zero Barriers* to *Users*, whereby product developers are assigned to customer support for 1 day a week to bring more empathy and customer centricity into product development. This is a practice with great impact requiring, for many CTOs, a lot of persuasion.

We recommend a workshop setting, which involves employees from different departments and an experienced (possibly external) facilitator. You should start with the results of stage 1 *Insight*. Present these results and reflect upon them: For example, which interpretation results from the comparisons within the benchmarking

[1] Self-assessment available under https://innovationskulturnavigator.ch/en

categories? Based on the analyses, the group should set a focus. Then you tackle the Innovation Culture Navigator's cultural practices, those which fit the selected focus goals and framework conditions. Yet, it is crucially important not to impulsively reject or to approve of a practice. Work through them in concrete terms: How would specifically this be understood in my company? Who would be affected? What possibilities and challenges arise? Remember that although the 66 cultural practices are excellent material for inspiration, they must often be adapted to the concrete conditions of the company. The cultural practices that are implemented must match the DNA of the company—do not merely follow just any trend. *Bosch* is a good example of this. They were inspired by *Google's* well-known 20% regulation, which allowed employees to work on their innovation projects every Friday. However, in the German corporate culture, it was more appropriate to allocate innovation time slots to Tuesday mornings.

3. Implementation You have to continuously deal with your own innovation culture. It is not just a once in a lifetime operation and far from being a static element. That is why you have to anchor innovation culture in concrete routines—routines for how your employees do their work, how they adjust, how they interact with each other, and what they celebrate. We design these routines according to the results in stage 2 *Inspiration*. Now it is time to implement and iteratively optimize the cultural practices, which you have selected and adapted. The iterative character of the process is particularly important here. Although it is becoming more and more widespread in product design, it is still not used frequently enough in organizational and cultural designs. The effectiveness of the practice can be optimized step by step via close feedback loops. Simply continue adapting them to the concrete needs and profiles of your employees. At the same time, this design integrates two important success factors of cultural development: transparency for employees and participation of employees.

Sweet spot thinking: We recommend that you identify and use simple, as well as promising, opportunities to create visible success stories before iteratively rolling out the practice any further. These success stories and the people behind them can play an important role, the people acting as ambassadors while the cultural practices are instantiated. An iterative rolling-out process offers several advantages (if it is organizationally feasible): On the one hand, you can simultaneously implement, learn through employee feedback, and further develop your cultural practice. On the other hand, it directly turns a short glimpse on innovation culture into an ongoing process of cultural design and development. In our experience, this enables an organic transition back to the first stage, *Insight*, which is both a measure of success and the kick-off for the next cycle of cultural design. You will have a permanent process of actively shaping your own innovation culture and constantly developing yourself as a company.

Three Steps Toward an Innovation Culture Plan

1. **Insight** (first stage): In order to identify the most efficient levers for action, get a clear assessment of your organization's innovation culture.
2. **Inspiration** (second stage): Taking your assessment results into consideration, the cultural practices that fit the company's profile best are examined. Obviously, these practices also have to be adapted for your specific organizational context.
3. **Implementation** (third stage): Roll out and test the adapted cultural practices.

Source: St. Gallen Innovation Culture Navigator (2025).

8.2 Need for Action at SMEs

In contrast to large companies, SMEs across industries have no differentiated processes, fewer research activities, and often no software tools to manage their patents. SMEs often focus on clear cost/benefit aspects of a patent. As a consequence, small companies apply more stringent criteria when selecting inventions for patent applications. They usually have a widely networked but very lean internal structure. Frequently, the managing director or the R&D manager coordinates all patent-management-related activities. The patent filing process, including file management and search activities, therefore usually involves a high degree of outsourcing to external patent law firms and consultants. In addition, the problem of patent enforceability may arise with regard to available resources and high costs. In contrast to large companies, small companies are often disadvantaged and therefore generally prefer to keep a patent application confidential.

However, the creation and use of industrial property rights also have advantages for SMEs (see Fig. 8.2):

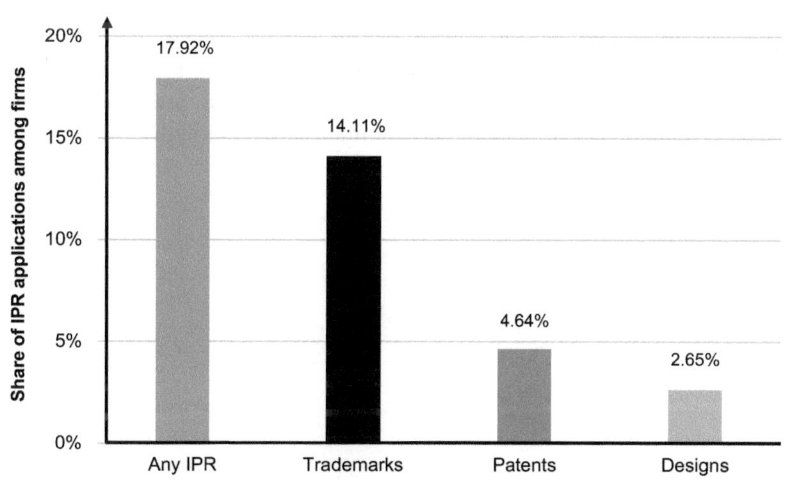

Fig. 8.2 Frequency of IPR use by European SMEs (based on EPO & EUIPO, 2019)

Strengthening the Negotiating Position

SMEs are more active in the business-to-business sector, where large companies dominate as customers. Without patent protection, their bargaining position vis-à-vis their large corporate customers would be extremely weak, as they can often adopt an innovation themselves or have it produced more cheaply by third parties. Patent protection can make a significant contribution to securing follow-up orders that are needed to amortize previous R&D investments.

Raising Capital

Venture capitalist firms often require collateral for their investments. Patents, patent applications, utility models, and trademarks are increasingly accepted as indicators for the business plan and as some measure of protection for innovations against imitators. Patents can now even be used directly as collateral for loans.

Particularly in the case of SMEs, which have so far had a not very consistent patent management, the core tasks of IP rights often still lie with the managing director. In some cases, the coordination of patent activities is delegated to a member of the development department, who is supposed to perform this task alongside other activities. The consequences of this type of informal arrangement are:

- Little strategic orientation of patent management;
- Little time for questions of industrial property rights;
- Few systematic methods of evaluation or valuation;
- Little or no structure or formalization;
- No official contact person; and
- Lack of technical or legal expertise.

There is a risk that patenting is not completed on time and that there is little overview of the many different procedures involved—payment of fees, examination deadlines, international filing, etc. On the other hand, there are SMEs that have grown rapidly in a short time and are globally active based on patenting activity. Our research on these so-called "*Born Globals*" has shown that very often patent management has played a central role in their rapid growth. Strategic patents were generated, systematically defended, and commercialized globally.

Practical Tips for Patent Management in SMEs

1. Carrying out patent searches at the beginning for each invention is the best way to protect yourself against surprises later on.
2. In the case of being blocked by a patent of a competitor, it is useful to develop workarounds.
3. Effective protection is often not provided by individual patents. Innovative SMEs should, therefore, set up a systematic patent cluster to secure their competitive advantages.
4. Broad patents have a greater impact but are also easier to attack. The application for broad patents should therefore be considered, especially at the beginning of a technology cycle.
5. In addition to basic patents, various concrete design variants can be patented.
6. The own negotiating basis can be improved in the event of a dispute if an improvement solution is filed based on a systematic analysis and evaluation of competing products, as this makes further development more difficult for the competitor.
7. In-licensing or patent cross-licensing enables the use of foreign, already patented inventions.
8. In patent law steps, such as opposition or nullity proceedings, it is advisable to engage a patent attorney, since technical knowledge is not sufficient in such cases.
9. A consistent and rigorous approach to patent infringers acts as a deterrent and increases the barriers to imitation.
10. Another option for action is the trade in patent rights: Patents are regarded as real products that are traded on a marketplace, including options such as barter, sale, or licensing.

Source: Gassmann and Bader (2024).

8.3 Challenges for Start-Ups

This section delves into the essentials what founders and their stakeholders need to know to navigate the multifaceted landscape of IP management, laying a solid foundation for sustainable growth and mitigated risks[2]:

[2] A selected portion of this chapter is based on Bader, M. A., & Süzeroglu-Melchiors, S. (2023). *Intellectual property management for start-ups—Value-enhancing approaches and practices for leveraging the potential.* Cham: Springer Nature. It also has been previously published in a conference article post the LESI Annual Conference 2024, Madrid: Bader, M. A., Süzeroglu-Melchiors, S., Kleyn, M., London, S., Schaberg, U. G., & Wilkinson, D. L. (2024). Navigating the Intellectual Property Maze: A Guide for Startups and Stakeholders. *LES Nouvelles*, June 2024, 113–117. Used with permission.

The Untapped Potential of Intellectual Property
For many start-ups, IP is the linchpin that holds the potential to catapult an innovative idea into a market-leading position. Yet, its role in value creation and risk mitigation is frequently underestimated or misunderstood. Intellectual property does more than just protect ideas; it serves as a key differentiator in the market, a barrier to entry for competitors, and a critical asset in negotiations with partners and investors.

Navigating Challenges and Mitigating Risks
Start-ups face common challenges and risks associated with IP management, such as unclear IP ownership, the complexities of global IP protection, and the potential for infringement disputes. Bader and Süzeroglu-Melchiors (2023) offer guidance on preemptive strategies to mitigate these risks, including conducting a thorough IP due diligence, developing a robust IP portfolio, and engaging in proactive IP education and training.

A Wide Spectrum of Perspectives
Within the entrepreneur's ecosystem, perspectives on the role of IP span a wide spectrum. Some stakeholders underestimate IP's relevance, viewing it as a secondary concern to product development and market entry strategies. Others may overestimate its power, believing that IP alone can ensure business success without robust business models and market strategies. Bridging this gap in understanding is crucial for start-ups and their stakeholders, including investors, established corporations (for partnering, as clients, or as future exit targets), universities, and transfer centers.

Strategies for Different Stakeholders
For start-ups, the path to effective IP management involves aligning their IP strategy with their overall business goals, ensuring clarity in IP ownership, and leveraging their IP for growth and investment. Investors, on the other hand, must evaluate a start-up's IP strategy as a key indicator of its potential for value creation and risk mitigation. Established corporations considering partnerships or acquisitions must assess the strategic value of a start-up's IP in the context of their global business strategies. Universities and technology transfer offices need to navigate the balance between protecting academic innovations and fostering its commercialization.

The Importance of an Expert Network
Engaging with a network of IP experts—patent attorneys, IP strategists, and consultants—is not just beneficial; it is imperative for start-ups aiming to navigate the IP landscape successfully. These experts bring a wealth of knowledge and experience, guiding start-ups through the complexities of IP management, from patent filing and strategy development to licensing and defense against infringement. Their insights can help transform IP from a mere legal requirement into a strategic asset that propels the company forward.

A Framework for Managing Intellectual Property

The framework of Bader and Süzeroglu-Melchiors (2023) is anchored in a project of remarkable scope and depth, drawing together over 40 esteemed authors from across the globe, each contributing their unique perspectives shaped by extensive experience in their respective fields. From the technological heartlands of *Silicon Valley* to the innovation hubs of *Israel*, *Switzerland*, *Germany*, and beyond, these experts bring to the table a wealth of knowledge from a diverse array of industries, including information and communication technology, artificial intelligence, machine learning, cybersecurity, and more. The essence of their concept is a collaborative approach to weaving together a rich spectrum of insights from six key stakeholder groups that form the backbone of the start-up ecosystem:

I. Start-ups themselves and their founders;
II. Investors looking for scalable and back-paying investments;
III. Established companies looking for innovation;
IV. Academic institutions and universities fostering groundbreaking research;
V. Global IP offices providing information, training and various services; and
VI. Specialized IP advisors guiding the strategic navigation of IP rights.

The collective wisdom of these contributors illuminates the vast spectrum of experiences and viewpoints on IP management, offering a panoramic view of its role in the life cycle of innovation—from ideation to commercialization.

The comprehensive examination by Bader and Süzeroglu-Melchiors (2023) seeks to catalyze engaging discussions among entrepreneurs, their advisors, and stakeholders, shedding light on the nuanced strategies and challenges of IP management. They aspire to inspire investors to adopt an IP-centric lens when evaluating their portfolios, recognizing the intrinsic value and potential of intellectual assets. For start-up founders, they invite you to deepen your understanding of IP management and strategy, not just as a legal necessity but as a pivotal element of business acumen that signals credibility and potential to partners and investors alike.

Moreover, Bader and Süzeroglu-Melchiors (2023) endeavor to bridge the communication gap between diverse entities in the ecosystem, facilitating meaningful dialogs on the strategic management of IP among institutions, companies, and entrepreneurs who place a premium on the commercialization of innovative technology. The underlying message is clear and compelling: The proactive incorporation of IP management into the strategic framework of a start-up or an established company is not merely advantageous—it is imperative for sustained competitiveness and success.

The Reality: "It Starts with IP, and It Ends with IP"[3]

Understanding the IP landscape within one's industry, recognizing potential competitive advantages, leveraging the innovations of peers without infringing on their IP rights, and utilizing patents as shields and swords in the market—all these aspects form the crux of strategic IP management. Yet, the journey of IP management is fraught with complexities and challenges that can daunt even the most seasoned entrepreneurs and innovators. It is important to demystify these complexities, offering actionable insights and guidance to navigate the IP maze with confidence and strategic acumen.

I. The Perspective of Start-Ups

From the perspective of start-ups, experts address the most frequent questions and concerns of founders about protecting their intellectual property, avoiding infringement of others' intellectual property, exploiting existing intellectual property, and acquiring and expanding assets for valuation and exit. Readers will learn about best practices for handling intellectual property in *Israel*, *Germany*, *Australia*, and *Brazil* and gain insights into the *cybersecurity* industry, information technology and software sector, technology services for mining equipment, and the sustainability and climate technologies sector.

The "holy trinity" of the world of start-up investments consists of:

- *Market and IP landscape:* Know your addressable market and how your value proposition fits.
- *Founding team and IP savviness:* Skills, capability, and awareness are important.
- *Technology and associated IP:* These factors will significantly determine your success.

II. The Perspective of Investors

From the perspective of investors, experts evaluate intellectual property as a proxy for value creation and future growth and discuss how to manage IP during due diligence and valuation processes. Readers gain insights from *US*, *Canadian*, *Swiss*, and *Israeli* investors who consider intellectual property as an important asset class in their investment decisions, along with insights into non-equity-based financing options in the form of IP-backed financial services. Selected insights from the investor perspective include:

- The IP strategy must go hand in hand with the business strategy.
- Intellectual property is the third most important consideration in early financing decisions and becomes even more important at exit.

[3] Quote from: Schaberg, U. G. (2023). "IP is paramount:" The significance of IP in early-stage startup investment decisions. In M. A. Bader, & S. Süzeroglu-Melchiors (Eds.), *Intellectual property management for start-ups—Value-enhancing approaches and practices for leveraging the potential*. Cham: Springer Nature.

- Founders should consider intellectual property early on.
- Unclear ownership and usage rights of intellectual property set off alarm bells.
- For digital start-ups, speed is of the essence.
- Brands are of minor importance to investors in the initial stages.

III. The Perspective of Established Companies

From the perspective of established companies, experts explore the innovation and growth strategies of established companies through start-ups that provide access to innovative technologies and markets. Established international companies like *Siemens*, *Nokia*, and *Bayer* evaluate and manage intellectual property in partnerships with start-ups, considering their global business perspectives, and *Japanese* companies bridge the cultural gap between start-ups and corporations. Selected insights from the investor perspective here include:

- Intellectual property has become an important value driver in partnership strategies.
- Strategic use of intellectual property enables companies to increase corporate value by securing optimal freedom of action in the relevant market and a favorable position against competitors.
- Implementing IP strategies for start-ups requires considering various value creation and risk mitigation options.
- It must be ensured that the rights to intellectual property clearly belong to the start-up or university spin-off and that employee invention rights are taken into account.

IV. The Perspective of Universities

Experts analyze how technology transfer and licensing of intellectual property function from a university's perspective. Readers learn about the commercialization of academic technologies at the American-Israeli *Jacobs Technion-Cornell Institute NYC*; gain insights into the technology transfer of *Stellenbosch University* in *South Africa*; learn about Swiss *ETH Zurich's* suggestions for managing tensions between universities and their spin-offs; and learn how the technology transfer office handles research spin-offs and commercialization of innovation, and investments in Europe's largest entrepreneurship center *TUM* in Munich, Germany.

The biggest challenges for technology transfer offices (TTOs), especially for spin-offs, are:

- Extracting the disclosures of innovation from researchers and the challenges of managing the drive to publish vs. the drive for IP protection (especially patents).
- Effectively managing the innovation processes and commercialization opportunities.
- Not all TTOs are professional advisors for intellectual property protection.
- There is a need for standardized yet tailored processes.
- Independence of the spin-off but continued dependence on the university due to legislation that governs IP emanating from publicly funded research institutions.

- Red Flag 1: IPRs held in private ownership by students or researchers.
- Red Flag 2: IPRs held in private ownership by shareholders or founders.

V. The Perspective of Global IP Offices
From the perspective of IP offices, experts examine current developments and emerging institutional programs supporting the IP activities of start-ups. Readers learn about the patent and trademark work of *IP Australia*, which supports Australians in utilizing their intellectual property in *China*; the European Patent Office's *Patent Academy*, which offers training programs to facilitate the commercialization of technology and high growth; and how the French Patent and Trademark Office views the international start-up landscape with a *United Nations* perspective on IP management. Selected insights from an investor's perspective include:

- It is typically a warning sign for investors if founders are not familiar with their IP situation and do not know how to handle it.
- Intellectual property offices offer services with low barriers to entry to improve knowledge of intellectual property.
- Utilize the free search and consulting services of local, regional, and international intellectual property offices (also available online), including their IP consulting centers worldwide, e.g., in China (IP Australia).

VI. The Perspective of IP Advisors
From the perspective of consultants, experts examine the most common types of protection rights and provide an introduction to the complementary use of formal and informal protection strategies for start-ups to gain and maintain competitive advantages. Readers learn how to capture the value of innovations, secure intellectual property in technology- and science-oriented start-ups, use patent searches and analyses, and navigate around patents. Selected lessons from an investor's perspective are:

- As long as there are no direct performance signals, investors must use IP and IA (Intellectual Assets) as proxy signals for future success.
- As a general rule of thumb, best practice is to allocate resources for intellectual property protection as early as possible.
- IP is not an end in itself: Link both business and IP strategies.
- Prevention is better than cure.

Conclusion: "Take IP Very Seriously. Therefore, Do Invest in It"[4]

To summarize the findings from the investors' perspective in relation to the six stakeholder views: Investors start with the realization of their investment as a goal

[4] Quote from: Thomaier, J. (2023). How the life sciences industry handles IP in start-ups. In M. A. Bader, & S. Süzeroglu-Melchiors (Eds.), *Intellectual property management for start-ups—Value-enhancing approaches and practices for leveraging the potential*. Cham: Springer Nature.

in mind. They pursue the way in which the investment can later be successfully monetized, e.g., through follow-up investments or typically through a sale (exit) or initial public offering (IPO).

Outlook: The Path Forward

As start-ups continue to drive innovation and economic growth, the strategic management of intellectual property will remain a cornerstone of their success. By engaging a network of experts, founders can demystify the complexities of IP management, unlocking its full potential as a source of value creation and competitive advantage. In doing so, they not only secure their own future but also contribute to a vibrant, innovation-driven economy.

Key messages and lessons for all start-ups include:

- Start with the end in mind: Ask where you will be in 5 years and work back from there!
- Speed and focus are a key philosophy for all start-ups to stay focused and move fast!
- Stay agile and nimble to deliver speed and create value.
- Cash is king: Cash burn rates and cash runway will define your success. Manage cash carefully, spend wisely, and plan your future based on cash generation and spending.
- Model your finance and run scenarios to highlight the best approach to success.
- IP is important to your future—understanding your strategy and investing now in the future.
- Strategic options to be considered:
  - What is your IP? It is valuable for investors and future enterprise value.
  - Internationalization or local?
  - Decide the best ways to protect your IP: Trade secret or patenting or combination:
    - Trade secrets: Low investment but harder to protect and grow the business.
    - Patents: Tangible value, which creates long-term legacy; costly to create but benefits, e.g., easier to license.
- Develop an IP strategy that should fit with overall business strategy.
- IP must reinforce customer value proposition and market differentiation.
- Surround yourself with a good team who understands IP and how it fits with the strategy. ◀

Practical Tips for Patent Management in Start-Ups
The key value drivers for value development are:

- *The market*, including the intellectual property landscape;
- *The team*, including their IP savviness; and
- *The technology*, including the associated intellectual property!

The main mistakes, risks, and undesirable value differentiators that damage investments are:

- Unaligned business and IP strategy;
- Unclear IP ownership and/or usage rights;
- Unresolved employee invention rights; and
- Ongoing license obligations or other ongoing dependencies, e.g., on universities.

8.4 Measures Against Product Piracy

Counterfeit goods not only pose a risk of loss of profit but can also damage a company's image, cause an outflow of know-how, lead to a loss of market share, and inhibit growth potential. In a report, the OECD has been tracking trade in counterfeit goods (OECD, 2019); given the importance of luxury goods to Europe, the OECD's work has been continued by the EUIPO in its 2025 report (OECD & EUIPO, 2025; see Fig. 8.3). The major goods remained largely the same with a bit of a decline in pharmaceutics and headwear; a new counterfeit area is vehicle (parts).

The renowned chainsaw manufacturer *Andreas Stihl* has been actively fighting against brand and product piracy from Asia for years. However, the company only became aware of product piracy after losing about 40% in sales in Indonesia. The company noticed not only that spare parts for outdated models were being copied, but that complete models of the current series were also being pirated.

The case serves as a lesson showing the potential risks of why a product portfolio must consequently be safeguarded at an early stage in order to identify the causes of piracy and to counteract them. Potential risks from product piracy, which lead to considerable loss of financial returns, are:

- Loss of market share and growth potential;
- Know-how outflow;
- Loss of image;
- Reduced product quality; and
- Danger of product liability.

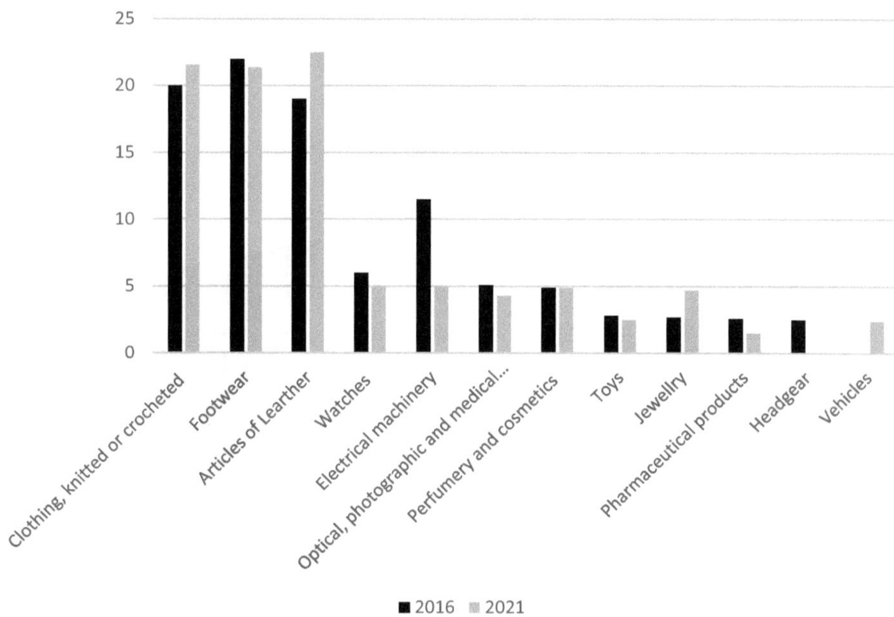

Fig. 8.3 Share of seizures of counterfeit and pirated goods: Top industries by Harmonized System (HS) code, 2016 and 2021 (OECD, 2019; OECD & EUIPO, 2025)

In emerging markets such as *China*, external factors such as uncertain legal certainty, cultural differences, language barriers, and lack of transparency (flow of information, provision of information, responsibilities, corruption, and geographical reach) are also very important (Prud'homme et al., 2018; Thraen & Bader, 2026). In order to identify possible effects in good time, the risk portfolio of individual products or product groups should be assessed. This assessment is based on the probability of imitation on the one hand and on the potential business damage of a counterfeit on the other. The imitation probability results from the significance and image of the product in the market. The potential business damage results from the significance of the product for the company, for example, margin, market penetration, and degree of awareness, complexity of the product, and then also the phase of the product life cycle (Gassmann & Bader, 2024).

If, for example, the question arises whether a patent should be applied for in China, always keeping an eye on the knowledge to be thereby completely protected is important. Legal measures, such as patent, design, and trademark protection, alone are not sufficient to protect against piracy and the outflow of know-how. Just as important are technological business, marketing, and personnel measures. Only a holistic approach that combines both legal and factual strategies can comprehensively optimize protection against product piracy and IP infringement (see Sect. 1.2).

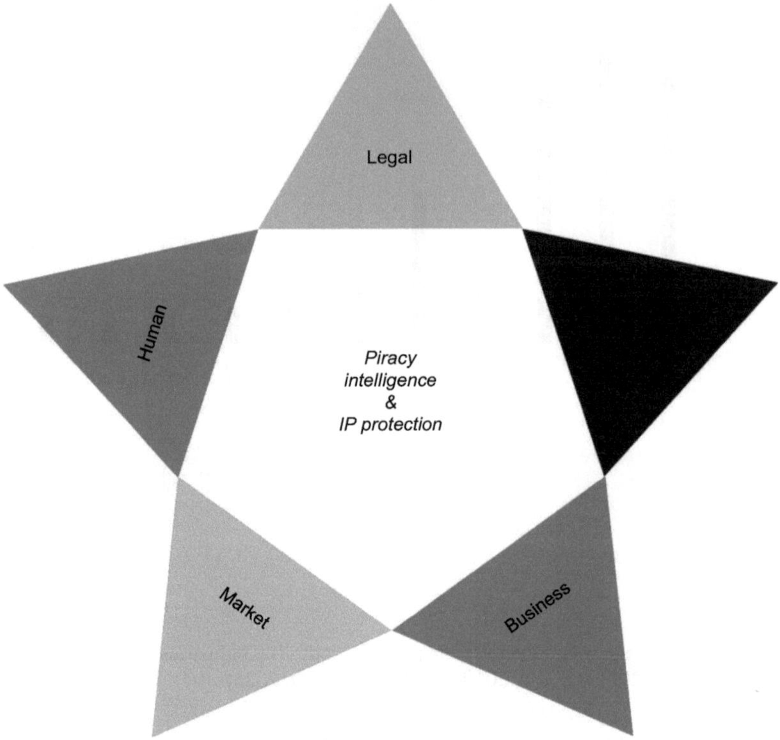

Fig. 8.4 Comprehensive protection strategy against piracy (Gassmann et al., 2012)

Example—Siemens in China

In China, the multinational engineering and electronics company *Siemens* succeeded in reducing the leaving rate of its R&D employees to less than 10% with both monetary and non-monetary incentives. For example, employees are tied to the *Western Group* through international training and development opportunities. Local values and standards also play an important role, since, for example, job descriptions and corresponding titles are particularly important for the function of employees. ◀

One example of such a holistic approach is the *IP-Protection Star* (Gassmann et al., 2012). In this model, five dimensions of IP protection are addressed: *Legal, Technology, Business, Market,* and *Human* (see Fig. 8.4). To establish a holistic perspective of IP management, the same importance must be attached to each of these five dimensions, as this is the only way to avoid blind spots. The following describes and explains these individual dimensions:

Legal

Intellectual property must be protected legally by the application of various types of intellectual property rights, such as patents, and trade secrets. This can be supplemented by contractual protective measures, such as confidentiality agreements made with employees or confidentiality agreements made with suppliers. The legal enforcement of these protective measures is central to this: If violations are ignored and thus have no consequences for infringers, the legal protective measures lose their deterrent effect.

Technology

The aim is to prevent infringement in advance by means of various technical measures. Products can be protected with the help of various technical aids: Both in a visible way, such as with holograms or security labels, and in an invisible way, such as through isotopes that can only be recognized with the help of technological devices. The complexity of the product also plays a decisive role here: The higher the complexity of a product, the more difficult it is to copy it and the higher the barriers for possible imitators. The degree of complexity is influenced by various factors, such as the degree of standardization or the number of process steps. The degree of customization can also support the protection efforts, as it is much more difficult to copy a highly individualized product. A further measure is the distribution of production to different development and production sites. In accordance with the "need-to-know" principle, only the necessary part of the know-how is passed on to the sites, thus preventing the outflow of production knowledge.

Business

In this context, the protection of competitive advantages is of central importance, such as through a unique business model or by means of targeted differentiation strategies. Possible differentiation strategies include strong corporate branding, quality, price, or product differentiation as well as an established brand. Such competitive advantages can better protect innovations, as they represent barriers for possible imitators. It also makes sense to control corporate processes. Violations often occur at certain points in the value chain, which is why monitoring and tracking products are very effective. Close cooperation with customs can also prevent the import or export of imitations. The use of your own sales staff can also play a protective role along with educating customers by convincing them of the added value of the original product. In addition, qualified sales personnel create a general added value for customers that imitation cannot offer.

Market

In order to detect or even prevent possible infringement of IP rights by competitors or suppliers at an early stage, continuous monitoring of market activities and key technologies is just as necessary as an active search for products that infringe IP rights. An additional de facto measure is to convince customers of the value of the company and its product portfolio. On the one hand, this can reduce the risk of customers unknowingly acquiring copies, and on the other hand, it can strengthen customer loyalty, as they also become familiar with the long-term advantages of the product, differentiating it from imitation products.

Human

This dimension concerns measures against the direct or indirect outflow of know-how. In addition to controlling access to facilities and data, it is important to create awareness among employees for the responsible handling of confidential information, for example, through internal training. Cooperation with universities can also be useful in developing the skills of employees at the local level. For example, *Philips* entered into partnerships with several Chinese universities and offered events for students on intellectual property as part of its *Philips IP Academy*. Loyalty and identification with the company, which can be promoted through career opportunities or reward systems, can also be an effective means of preventing know-how loss.

References

Bader, M. A., & Süzeroglu-Melchiors, S. (2023). *Intellectual property management for start-ups—Value-enhancing approaches and practices for leveraging the potential*. Springer Nature.

Bader, M. A., Süzeroglu-Melchiors, S., Kleyn, M., London, S., Schaberg, U. G., & Wilkinson, D. L. (2024). Navigating the intellectual property maze: A guide for start-ups and stakeholders. *LES Nouvelles, June 2024*, 113–117.

EPO & EUIPO. (2019). High-growth firms and intellectual property rights. IPR profile of high-potential SMEs in Europe, May 2019. A joint project between the European Patent Office and the European Union. European Patent Office and Alicante: European Union Intellectual Property Office. Accessed August 18, 2025, from https://link.epo.org/web/high_growth_firms_study_en.pdf

Gassmann, O., Beckenbauer, A., & Friesike, S. (2012). *Profiting from innovation in China*. Heidelberg: Springer.

Gassmann, O., & Bader, M. A. (2024). *Patentmanagement: Innovationen erfolgreich nutzen und schützen* (5th ed.). Springer Gabler.

Gassmann, O., Wecht, C. H., Meister, C., & Boemelburg, R. (2018). *Exploit the hidden success factor of innovation culture. Munich: Innovationskulturnavigator*. Carl Hanser.

OECD. (2019). *Trends in trade in counterfeit and pirated goods*. OECD Publishing. https://doi.org/10.1787/g2g9f533-en

OECD & EUIPO. (2025). *Mapping global trade in fakes 2025: Global trends and enforcement challenges, illicit trade*. OECD Publishing. https://doi.org/10.1787/94d3b29f-en

Prud'homme, D., von Zedwitz, M., Thraen, J. J., & Bader, M. A. (2018). Forced technology transfer policies: Workings in China and strategic implications. *Technological Forecasting and Social Change, 134*, 150–168.

Schaberg, U. G. (2023). "IP is paramount:" The significance of IP in early-stage start-up investment decisions. In M. A. Bader & S. Süzeroglu-Melchiors (Eds.), *Intellectual property management for start-ups—Value-enhancing approaches and practices for leveraging the potential*. Cham.

St. Gallen Innovation Culture Navigator. (2025). Accessed June 20, 2025, from https://innovationskulturnavigator.ch/en

Thomaier, J. (2023). How the life sciences industry handles IP in start-ups. In M. A. Bader & S. Süzeroglu-Melchiors (Eds.), *Intellectual property management for start-ups—Value-enhancing approaches and practices for leveraging the potential*. Cham.

Thraen, J. J., & Bader, M. A. (2026). Key success factors in nurturing and sustaining 21st-century technology clusters. In J. J. Thraen & C. H. Hoffmann (Eds.), *Successful technology clusters in the 21st century*. Walter de Gruyter.

Useful Information for Practitioners 9

The following section provides useful information, facts, and trends for the practitioner:

1. Patent Growth Worldwide
2. Structure of a Patent
3. Patent Document Codes
4. Patent Classification
5. Notes on Patent Search
6. Member States of the European Patent Organisation
7. EUIPO/Unitary Patent/Unified Patent Court
8. IP Tax Regimes
9. Brief Comparison of Patent Legislations
10. The World Intellectual Property Day

9.1 Patent Growth Worldwide

The request for commercial IP rights has increased dramatically in the last two decades. A growing number of companies have recognized the advantage that formal IP rights can bring. The five largest intellectual property offices—the so-called *IP5 Offices*—namely the European Patent Office (EPO), the Japan Patent Office (JPO), the Korean Intellectual Property Office (KIPO), the China National Intellectual Property Administration (CNIPA), and the United States Patent and Trademark Office (USPTO) count the following statistics (Five IP Offices, 2024a):

- At the end of 2017, 13.6 million patents were in force in the world (+15.9%).
- Ninety-one percent of these patents were in force in one of the IP5 Office jurisdictions.
- In 2017, 2.8 million patent applications were filed worldwide, as direct national, direct regional, or international phase PCT applications, of which 94% originated from the IP5 regions.

M. A. Bader et al., *Patent Management*, Management for Professionals,
https://doi.org/10.1007/978-3-032-12030-4_9

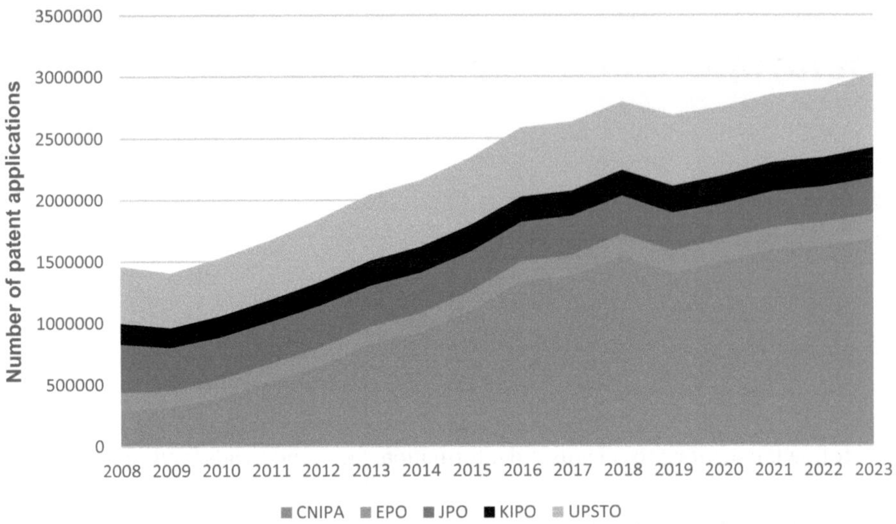

Fig. 9.1 Patent applications worldwide at the IP5 Offices (Five IP Offices, 2024a, 2024b)

- In 2017, 89% of the worldwide patent applications were filed as direct national applications. The proportion of applications filed via the PCT remained stable.
- In 2018, 2.8 million patent applications were filed at the IP5 Offices (+6.0%).
- Together, the IP5 Offices granted 1.2 million patents in 2018 (+1.4%).

In the wake of the 2009 recession, there was a strong decline in the number of patent applications worldwide. In the meantime, this trend has reversed into a continual increase. It is especially noticeable that China (CNIPA) and South Korea (KIPO) have established themselves among the five largest application countries (Five IP Offices, 2024b); *China* now finds itself in the pole position (see Fig. 9.1).

9.2 Structure of a Patent

A *patent document* typically has the following structure and content:

I. Title page (example, see Fig. 9.2):

- Country
- Publication number
- Classification
- Bibliographic data (priority date, application date, publication date, grant date, and evaluated state of the art)
- Applicant, inventor, and representative/agent
- Title/description
- Summary

(19) Europäisches Patentamt / European Patent Office / Office européen des brevets

(11) **EP 3 564 144 A1**

(12) **EUROPEAN PATENT APPLICATION**

(43) Date of publication:
06.11.2019 Bulletin 2019/45

(21) Application number: **18275163.6**

(22) Date of filing: **17.10.2018**

(51) Int Cl.:
B65D 6/02 (2006.01) ***B65D 8/00*** (2006.01)
B65D 6/00 (2006.01) ***B65D 13/02*** (2006.01)
B65D 21/02 (2006.01) ***B65D 1/02*** (2006.01)

(84) Designated Contracting States:
AL AT BE BG CH CY CZ DE DK EE ES FI FR GB GR HR HU IE IS IT LI LT LU LV MC MK MT NL NO PL PT RO RS SE SI SK SM TR
Designated Extension States:
BA ME
Designated Validation States:
KH MA MD TN

(71) Applicant: **Thaler, Stephen L.**
St. Charles MO 63303 (US)

(72) Inventor: **The designation of the inventor has not yet been filed**

(74) Representative: **Williams Powell**
11 Staple Inn
London WC1V 7QH (GB)

Remarks:
•The designation of inventor does not meet the requirements laid down in Article 81 and Rule 19 EPC.
•Amended claims in accordance with Rule 137(2) EPC.

(54) **FOOD CONTAINER**

(57) A container (10) for use, for example, for beverages, has a wall (12) with and external surface (14) and an internal wall (16) of substantially uniform thickness. The wall (12) has a fractal profile which provides a series of fractal elements (18-28) on the interior and exterior surfaces (14-16), forming pits (40) and bulges (42) in the profile of the wall and in which a pit (40) as seen from one of the exterior or interior surfaces (12, 14) forms a bulge (42) on the other of the exterior or interior surfaces (12, 14). The profile enables multiple containers to be coupled together by inter-engagement of pits and bulges on corresponding ones of the containers. The profile also improves grip, as well as heat transfer into and out of the container.

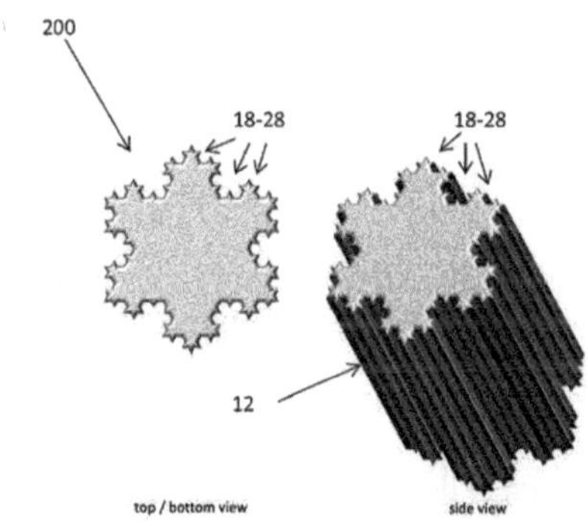

EP 3 564 144 A1

Fig. 9.2 Example of patent application title page (EP 3564144) ["EPO refuses *DABUS patent applications* designating a machine inventor: The EPO has refused two European patent applications in which a machine was designated as inventor. Both patent applications indicate 'DABUS' as inventor, which is described as 'a type of connectionist artificial intelligence'. The applicant stated that they acquired the right to the European patent from the inventor by being its successor in title. After hearing the arguments of the applicant in non-public oral proceedings on 25 November the EPO refused EP 18275163 (published as EP 3564144) and EP 18 275 174 on the grounds that they do not meet the requirement of the EPC that an inventor designated in the application has to be a human being, not a machine." (EPO, 2019)]

II. Description:

- Circumscription of the technical field
- Discussion of the state of the art and its disadvantages
- Task
- Presentation of the invention (generally the first claim), including a description of the advantages; various solutions
- Captions for drawings
- Description of the invention referencing the drawings

III. Independent and dependent claims,[1] written in unitary or two-part[2] claim form ("characterized in that" or "characterized by")

IV. Drawings

Example of a *title page* of a patent document (see Fig. 9.2)

- Country, publication number (19), (10)
- IPC classification (51)
- Priority date (30)
- Application date (22)
- Publication date/Grant date (43), (45)
- Applicant, Inventor, Representative (71), (72), (74)
- Title/Description (54)
- Summary (57)
- Drawing ◄

9.3 Patent Document Codes

EP 3 564 144A1

For the unique identification of different types of patent documents, e.g., publications, patents, utility patents, the World Intellectual Property Organization (WIPO)

[1] "*Independent claim:* A claim that does not rely on any other claim for its content, structure, or validity and is usually considered on its own for purposes of determining validity or infringement. The opposite type of claim is a *dependent claim*. One factor in evaluating independent claims that does relate them to other claims is the doctrine of claim differentiation." (source: www.ipglossary.com).

[2] "*Two-part claim:* A type of patent claim common in Europe, where the first part of the claim describes what is recognized as existing in the prior art or as being obvious and the second part, following the use of the terms of art "characterized in that" or "characterized by" constitutes the claimed invention. In the US such a claim is known as a *Jepson Claim*" (source: www.ipglossary.com).

has developed a standard (ST.16) way of classifying such documents.[3] The codes consist of a letter and often a number, which is printed along with the document number. Unfortunately, not all countries adhere to this standard, and such codes have changed in various countries over time. It is important to know that each jurisdiction employs its own variant of the standard. Here are some of the more common codes:

- **A1** Patent application with search report (EPO)
- **A2** Patent application without search report (EPO)
- **A3** Search report (EPO)
- **B1** Granted patent (EPO)
- **B2** Granted patent (USPTO)
- **B2** Modified patents (typically after opposition) (EPO)
- **C** Reexamination documents (USPTO)
- **E, F, G** Other sui generis rights and documents (rare)
- **M** Medical claims and patent documents
- **L** Bibliographic, figures, drawings, claims, etc. (rare)
- **N** Non-patent literature documents
- **H, I** Special requirement documents (rare)
- **P** Plant breeders' rights and patents
- **R** Separately published search reports
- **S** Design patent documents
- **T** Translation documents of applications, granted patents, etc.
- **U, W, Y, Z** Utility model documents
- **X** Restricted documents, documents for country-specific usage

9.4 Patent Classification

The entire worldwide patent literature comprises more than 115 million documents issued by more than 60 worldwide patent-issuing authorities. A structured categorization of the documents allows a simplified search. To that end, the International Patent Classification (IPC) has established itself as a taxonomy for patents and utility models based on their field of application. It is used by patent offices in over 100 countries. The USPTO and EPO have developed a more refined classification, called the Common Patent Classification (CPC), but it retains the structure of the IPC. Patent classifications are organized hierarchically (see Tables 9.1 and 9.2).

[3] WIPO-Standard ST.16 und ST.50: www.wipo.int/standards/en/part_03_standards.html.

Table 9.1 Sections from the CPC (https://www.wipo.int/classifications/ipc/ipcpub)

CPC section	Description
Section A	Human necessities
Section B	Performing operations; transporting
Section C	Chemistry; metallurgy
Section D	Textiles; paper
Section E	Fixed constructions
Section F	Mechanical engineering; lighting; heating; weapons; blasting engines or pumps
Section G	Physics
Section H	Electricity
Section Y	General tagging of new technological developments; general tagging of cross-sectional technologies spanning over several sections of the CPC; technical subjects covered by former USPC cross-reference art collections (XRACs) and digests.

Table 9.2 Example of CPC classification for B65D1/0223 (EP) (B65D1/02—IPC)

Section	Letter	B	TRANSPORTING
Subsection	Number (2-digit)	65	PACKING; STORING
Class	Letter	D	CONTAINERS FOR STORAGE OR TRANSPORT OF ARTICLES OR MATERIALS
Subclass	Number	1	Containers having bodies formed in one piece
Main group	Number	/02	… bottles or similar containers with necks or like restricted apertures
Sub-group	Number	23	… characterized by shape

9.5 Notes on Patent Search

When is a patent search using the Internet possible?

- Finding a single document.
- Looking up specific information. When was this document published?
- Answering simple questions, e.g., is there a JP application for this US patent?

When is a patent search with a professional advisable?

- When you need to ensure freedom to operate.
- When the patent technology comprises multiple subdomains.
- When a specific competitor or technology is not known (Tables 9.3 and 9.4).

Table 9.3 Overview of free internet search webpages (table compiled by authors)

Patents	Address
Canadian Patents Database	https://www.ic.gc.ca/opic-cipo/cpd/eng/searchMenu.html
Australia *(AusPat)*	https://ipsearch.ipaustralia.gov.au/patents/
Austria *(see.ip)*	https://seeip.patentamt.at/
Switzerland *(Swissreg)*	https://www.swissreg.ch/
Germany *(DEPATISnet)*	https://depatisnet.dpma.de/
Germany *(DPINFO)*	https://register.dpma.de/
EPO *(esp@cenet)*	https://worldwide.espacenet.com/
Asian patent information from EPO (incl. e.g. China, Chinese Taipei, Gulf Cooperation Council, India, Japan, Korea, Russian Federation)	https://www.epo.org/en/searching-for-patents/helpful-resources/asian
USPTO *(PatFT/AppFT)*	patft.uspto.gov
Google Patent Search	google.com/patents

Last updated: September 2025

Table 9.4 Other useful IP links (table compiled by authors)

Subject	Address
IP glossary (WIPO)	https://www.wipo.int/tk/en/resources/glossary.html
Patent glossary (IP5)	https://link.epo.org/ip5_Glossary_PRT
IP glossary	http://www.ipglossary.com/
IP portal WIPO	https://ipportal.wipo.int/
IPI SME portal (E, DE, FR, IT)	https://www.ige.ch/en/intellectual-property/sme-portal.html
IP management advisory	https://www.bgw-ip.com/

Last updated: September 2025

esp@cenet

Strengths:

- CPC classification → also via Internet.
- Most comprehensive collection (including technical non-patent literature).
- Documents available relatively soon after publication (often the next workday).
- Good for monitoring rights.
- Simple search with keyword or word stem.
- PDF download of documents, easy and fast.
- Possibility of simultaneous search in the three official languages in full text.
- Direct link from individual documents to the family members, legal status, machine translations, and citing and cited documents.

Weaknesses:

- Limited statistical evaluations.
- Maximum of 20 search items per query and 10 terms in the same search field.
- Neither full text nor abstracts are available for some countries. ◀

DEPATISnet

Strengths:

- Documents available within 1 week of publication.
- Ideal for monitoring.
- Second biggest collection (about 28 m documents).
- Combines Boolean search with more than 40 search fields, including full text.
- Search by word stem possible.
- Free arrangement of search result lists (e.g., by applicant and IPC).
- Multilingual search possible.
- Complete PDF files for saving and printing.

Weaknesses:

- Relations are not as wide as Espacenet's word search and sometimes limited (to title, abstract, or IPC).
- Complex query language when using advanced or Ikofax mode. ◀

9.6 Member States of the European Patent Organisation

European patents provide protection in the 39 member states of the European Patent Organisation but also in one extension state and six validation states. This represents an area with some 700 million inhabitants (as of January 15, 2025; see Fig. 9.3).

9.7 EUIPO/Unitary Patent/Unified Patent Court

European Union Intellectual Property Office

The European Union Intellectual Property Office (EUIPO), formerly known as the Office for Harmonization in the Internal Market (OHIM) until March 23, 2016, is a

Fig. 9.3 Jurisdictional scope of European patent protection (EPO, 2025)

decentralized agency of the European Union established to provide IP rights protection across the EU's 27 member states. Since its founding in 1994, it has been based in Alicante, Spain, where it manages European Union trademarks (EUTMs), registered EU designs (REUDs), and geographical indications (GIs) for craft and industrial products. The EUIPO plays a central role in coordinating European and international cooperation in the IP field. It acts as a key facilitator of the European Union Intellectual Property Network (EUIPN) and participates in numerous EU-funded projects under contribution agreements with the European Commission. The Office also oversees the European Observatory on Infringements of Intellectual Property Rights, which works to raise public awareness, provide training, develop enforcement tools, and produce evidence-based research. Furthermore, the EUIPO is responsible for managing the EU orphan works database and the public single online portal for out-of-commerce works (EUIPO, 2025).

Unitary Patent

European patents with unitary effect registered by the EPO on or after September 1, 2024, will take effect in the 18 EU Member States participating in enhanced cooperation and having ratified the Agreement on a Unified Patent Court (UPCA) by that date. It is expected that more EU Member States will ratify the UPCA in the coming years, so that eventually Unitary Patents will make it possible to get patent protection in up to 25 EU Member States by submitting a single request to the EPO.

The new Unitary Patent is based on the European patent granted by the EPO under the rules of the European Patent Convention (EPC), so nothing changes in the pre-grant phase and the same high standards of quality search and examination apply. After a European patent is granted, the patent proprietor can request unitary effect, thereby getting a European patent with unitary effect (Unitary Patent) that provides uniform patent protection in 18 EU Member States (extracted from EPO, 2024a).

Unified Patent Court

The Unified Patent Court (UPC) is an international court set up by 25 EU member states. The UPC deals with the infringement and validity of both Unitary Patents and European patents. Its rulings apply to all those EU member states that have ratified the UPCA. Currently, 18 EU member states have done so (extracted from EPO, 2024b).

Its Court of First Instance has a decentralised structure. It comprises a both central division in Paris, France, with a section in Munich, Germany, and Milan, Italy, and various local divisions and a regional division located all over Europe. The Court of Appeal has its seat in Luxembourg, the Patent Mediation and Arbitration Centre (PMAC) operates with two seats in Ljubljana, Slovenia, and Lisbon, Portugal (UPC, 2025).

9.8 IP Tax Regimes

Intellectual Property (IP) regimes—also known as "*Patent Box*," "*IP Box*," or "*Innovation Box*"—allow income from the exploitation of IP to be taxed at a lower rate than the standard statutory tax rate. IP regimes can be regimes that exclusively provide benefits to income from IP, but some preferential regimes categorized as IP regimes are "dual category" regimes. These regimes also provide benefits to income from other geographically mobile activities or provide benefits to a wide range of activities and do not necessarily exclude income from IP. The so-called "*Nexus Approach*" is the substantial activity requirement developed for IP regimes. The nexus approach requires a link between the income benefiting from the IP regime and the extent to which the taxpayer has undertaken the underlying R&D that generated the IP asset (extracted from OECD, 2020).

Table 9.5 Patent boxes (selected extract; table compiled by authors)

Country	Patent box tax rate (standard statutory tax rate)	Regime name/comment (type of IP)
Belgium	3.8% (25%)	IP income (software if copyright, patents, SPCs, plant varieties); since 2020
France	10% (25.83%)	IP income (patents, SPCs, plant varieties, topography); since 2020
Greece	10% (22%)	Tax patent incentives (patents)
Hungary	0%/4.5% (9%)	IP regime for royalties and capital gains (patents, software)
Ireland	6.25% (12.5%)	Knowledge development box (patents); since 2016
Israel	6%/7.5%/12% (23%)	Preferred technological enterprise regime (patents, software)
Luxemburg	4.99% (24.94%)	IP regime: IP income (patents, software); since 2019
Netherlands	7% (20–25%)	Innovation box: IP income; IP: software, patents, SPCs, plant varieties, utility models, …; since 2019
Poland	5% (19%)	IP box: Patents, software
Portugal	10.5% (21%)	Only patents and industrial designs or models; since 2019
Slovak Republic	10.5% (21%)	Patent-box: Patents, software
Spain	10% (25%)	Patents, software; since 2019
Switzerland	As of 9%	Canton specific (max. tax advantages of box are limited to 70%); since 2020
UK	10% (19%)	Patent box: IP income (patents, SPCs, plant varieties); since 2013
USA	13.13% (21%)	FDII (in the process of being eliminated)
China	15% (25%)	Reduced rate for high- and new tech enterprises (patents)
India	10.3–11.85% (30.91–35.54%)	Tax on income from patent (patents)
Korea	5–12.5%/7.5 18.75% (10–27.5%)	Special taxation for transfer, acquisition, etc. of technology
Singapore	5%/10% (17%)	IP development incentive (patents, software)

Last updated: July 2025 (Sources: Botschaft STAF, 2018; King & Zhu, 2019; Mengden, 2023; OECD, 2025)

IP regimes are used to incentivize research and development by taxing patent revenues differently from other commercial revenues. However, they have also been used as so-called *base erosion and profit shifting (BEPS)* tools, to avoid corporate taxes and have therefore been investigated by the OECD (2017, 2025). Table 9.5 gives an overview of different patent boxes currently being installed in Europe and beyond.

9.9 Brief Comparison of Patent Legislations

A brief comparison of patent legislations is shown in Table 9.6.

Table 9.6 Comparison of different patent jurisdictions (table compiled by authors)

	Europe (EPO)	USA
Priority	First-to-file	First-to-file/first-to-invent—*Leahy-Smith America Invents Act (AIA):* Since the 16th of March 2013 the USA underwent a comprehensive patent reform. This caused, inter alia, the following changes: (a) change to first-to-file scheme, (b) change to the publication conditioned grace period practiced since 1952, (c) opposition (new: inter partes review/post-grant review/ covered business method; old and new: *ex parte* reexamination)
Grace period	No—Exceptions: in case of abuse or officially recognized exhibition up to a max. of 6 months before the national application day (Art. 55 EPC)	Up to a year before filing a national application
Publication	18 months from priority date	18 months from priority date—For US patent applications filed after 1999-11-28 applicants can elect to file a non-publication request if no foreign application is filed *(American Inventor Protection Act, 1999)*
Duration	Max. 20 years from filing	Max. 20 years from filing—For patent applications filed on or after June 8, 1995; applicants filed before that date have a 17 years term as of the issue date
Examination request	Up to 6 months after publication of search report	No separate request possible (already included when filing the application)
Language	German, English, French as the official languages of the EPO; patents can be filed in the official languages of member states, but translations must be submitted later (Art. 14(2) EPC)	English

(continued)

Table 9.6 (continued)

	Australia	**Canada**
Priority	First "real and reasonably clear disclosure of the subject matter of the claim"	First-to-file
Grace period	12 months for pre-April 2002 applications	1 year, from Canadian or PCT (designating Canada) filing date
Publication	18 months from priority date	Open to public inspection after 18 months from the priority date
Duration	Max. 20 years from filing	20 years from filing
Examination request	Within 5 years of filing	Yes, 4 years from filing
Language	English	English and French
	Japan	**Korea**
Priority	First-to-file	First-to-file
Grace period	Max. 6 months before national application	6 months before application
Publication	18 months from priority date	18 months from priority date
Duration	Max. 20 years from filing	Max. 20 years from filing
Examination request	Up to 3 years from filing—For all JP patent applications since October 1, 2001; earlier applications had a period of 7 years	3 years from filing
Language	Japanese, English	Korean
	China / Hong Kong	**Taiwan**
Priority	First-to-file	First-to-file
Grace period	No	No—Exceptions: Publications for the purpose of research and experimentation, or at international trade fair, until max. 6 months before the date of application
Publication	18 months from priority date	18 months from priority date
Duration	Max. 20 years from filing	Max. 20 years from filing
Examination	Up to 3 years from priority date	Up to 3 years from filing
Language	Chinese—Limited application for Chinese text from Taiwan	Taiwanese, English—Taiwanese translation must be delivered within 60 days
	Russian Federation	**Eurasia (EAPO)**
Priority	First-to-file	First-to-file
Grace period	6 months before application	12 months before priority
Publication	18 months from filing	18 months from filing
Duration	Max. 20 years from filing	Max. 20 years from filing
Examination request	Up to 3 years from filing	Up to 6 months after search
Language	Russian	Russian

Sources: Gassmann and Bader (2024), BCF (2020), Slater and Matsil (2020)

9.10 The World Intellectual Property Day

Every **April 26**, the World Intellectual Property Organization (WIPO) celebrates the World Intellectual Property Day to learn about the role that intellectual property (IP) rights play in encouraging innovation and creativity (see Fig. 9.4):

- #worldipday
- wipo.int/ipday
- youtube.com/wipo

Fig. 9.4 The World Intellectual Property Day: April 26th (WIPO, 2025)

References

BCF. (2020). Montréal: BCF Business Law.

Botschaft STAF. (2018). *Botschaft zum Bundesgesetz über die Steuervorlage 17 (SV17).* Schweizerische Eidgenossenschaft.

EPO. (2019). *EPO refuses DABUS patent applications designating a machine inventor.* News, 20 December 2019. Munich: European Patent Office. Accessed July 3, 2020, from https://www.epo.org/news-issues/news/2019/20191220.html

EPO. (2024a). *Unitary Patent.* Munich: European Patent Office. Accessed July 17, 2025, from https://www.epo.org/en/applying/european/unitary/unitary-patent

EPO. (2024b). *Unified Patent Court (UPC).* Munich: European Patent Office. Accessed July 17, 2025, from https://www.epo.org/en/applying/european/unitary/upc

EPO. (2025). *The EPO at a glance.* Accessed July 17, 2025, from https://www.epo.org/en/about-us/at-a-glance

EUIPO. (2025). *About EUIPO.* Alicante: European Union Intellectual Property Office. Accessed July 17, 2025, from https://www.euipo.europa.eu/en/about-us/the-office

Five IP Offices. (2024a). *IP5 statistics report 2023 edition.* Seoul: Korean Intellectual Property Office. Accessed July 17, 2025, from https://www.fiveipoffices.org/statistics/statisticsreports/2023edition

Five IP Offices. (2024b). *IP5 statistical tables 2023.* Seoul: Korean Intellectual Property Office. Accessed July 17, 2025, from https://link.epo.org/ip5_table2023

Gassmann, O., & Bader, M. A. (2024). *Patentmanagement: Innovationen erfolgreich nutzen und schützen* (5th ed.). Springer Gabler.

King, C. C., & Zhu, S. (2019). *Patentboxen im Europäischen Vergleich und steuerliche Forschungsförderung in Deutschland.* In: VPP-Rundbrief No. 4/2019. Frankfurt/Main and Ludwigshafen: VCI und BASF.

Mengden, A. (2023). *Patent box regimes in Europe, 2023.* Tax Foundation Europe. Accessed July 17, 2025, from https://taxfoundation.org/data/all/eu/patent-box-regimes-europe-2023/

OECD. (2017). Harmful tax practices—2017 Progress report on preferential regimes. In *OECD/G20 base erosion and profit shifting project.* Paris: Organisation for Economic Co-operation and Development.

OECD. (2020). *Intellectual property regimes.* Paris: Organisation for Economic Co-operation and Development. Accessed January 7, 2020, from https://qdd.oecd.org/subject.aspx?Subject=IP_Regimes

OECD. (2025). *Intellectual properties regimes—Corporate tax statistics 2024.* Paris: Organisation for Economic Co-operation and Development. Accessed July 17, 2025, from https://data-viewer.oecd.org/?chartId=ff7c45ac-6d39-4a1e-9d17-45415e239553

Slater & Matsil. (2020). Dallas: Slater and Matsil.

UPC. (2025). *Unified Patent Court Structure.* Unified Patent Court. Accessed January 9, 2026, from https://www.unifiedpatentcourt.org/en/court/presentation

WIPO. (2025). *World intellectual property day.* Geneva: World Intellectual Property Organization. Accessed July 17, 2025, from https://www.wipo.int/en/web/ipday/2025/index

Glossary

Abbreviations

4IR	Fourth Industrial Revolution
AI	Artificial Intelligence
AIA	Leahy-Smith America Invents Act
AOP	Protected Appellations of Origin
B2B	Business-to-Business
BEPS	Base Erosion and Profit Shifting
BSE	Bovine Spongiform Encephalopathy
BVM	Backward Valuation Method
CAPM	Capital Asset Pricing Model
CDMA	Code Division Multiple Access
CII	Computer-Implemented Inventions
COI	Conflict of interest
CPC	Common Patent Classification
CRISPR	Clustered Regularly Interspaced Short Palindromic Repeats
CT	Computed Tomography
CTM	Community Trade Mark
DABUS	Device for the Autonomous Bootstrapping of Unified Sentience
DCF	Discounted Cash Flows
DLT	Distributed Ledger Technology
DNA	DeoxyriboNucleic Acid
DNS	Domain Name System
DRM	Digital Rights Management
EBITDA	Earnings Before Interest, Taxes, Depreciation, and Amortization
ECLA	European Classification
EPC	European Patent Convention
EPUE	European Patent with Unitary Effect
EUTM	EU Trade Mark

M. A. Bader et al., *Patent Management*, Management for Professionals,
https://doi.org/10.1007/978-3-032-12030-4

EV	Enterprise Value
FCEV	Fuel Cell Electric Vehicle
FDII	Foreign Derived Intangible Income
FOA	Freedom-of-Action
FRAND	Fair, Reasonable and Non-Discriminatory
FTO	Freedom-to-Operate
GANs	Generative Adversarial Networks
GDPR	General Data Protection Regulation
GenAI	Generative Artificial Intelligence
GI	Geographical Indication
GPS	Global Positioning System
GSM	Global System for Mobile Communications
HMA	Hague Model Convention
HS	Harmonized System code
IA	Intellectual Asset
IANA	Internet Assigned Numbers Authority
ICANN	Internet Corporation for Assigned Names and Numbers
ICT	Information and Communication Technology
IGP	Protected Geographical Indications
IOT	Internet of Things
IP	Intellectual Property
IPC	International Patent Classification
IPF	International Patent Family
IPO	Initial Public Offering
IPPM	Intellectual Property Protection Mechanism
IPR	Intellectual Property Right
IT	Information Technology
KPI	Key Performance Indicator
LAN	Local Area Network
LCD	Liquid Crystal Display
LED	Light Emitting Diode
LLMs	Large Language Models
M&A	Mergers and Acquisitions
MPEP	USPTO Manual of Patent Examining Procedure
MRI	Magnetic Resonance Imaging
NDA	Non-Disclosure Agreement
NIE	New Institutional Economics
NLG	Natural Language and Generation
NLU	Natural Language Understanding
NPE	Non-Practicing Entity
NPV	Net Present Value
OEMs	Original Equipment Manufacturers
OTC	Over-The-Counter drug
PAE	Patent Assertion Company
PBR	Plant Breeders' Right

PCIP	Paris Convention for the Protection of Industrial Property
PCR	Polymerase Chain Reaction
PCT	Patent Cooperation Treaty
PERA	US Patent Eligibility Restoration Act
PVR	Plant Variety Right
R&D	Research and Development
RCD	Registered Community Design
REUD	European Union Design
RFID	Radio-Frequency IDentification
RIV	Residual Income Valuation
RLHF	Reinforcement Learning from Human Feedback
RNA	Ribonucleic Acid
ROA	Real Options Analysis
ROCE	Return On Capital Employed
ROI	Return On Investment
SDRAM	Synchronous Dynamic Random-Access Memory
SEPs	Standard Essential Patents
SGPI	St. Gallen Patent Index
SME	Small and Medium-sized Enterprise
SOTP	Sum-of-the-Parts
SPC	Supplementary Protection Certificate
TTO	Technology Transfer Office
ULR	Unit License Rights
UMTS	Universal Mobile Telecommunications System
UPCA	Agreement on a Unified Patent Court
USPC	United States Patent Classification
VC	Venture Capital
VUCA	Volatility, Uncertainty, Complexity, Ambiguity
WACC	Weighted Average Cost of Capital
XRAC	Cross-Reference Art Collection

Institutions and Associations

ARIPO	African Regional Intellectual Property Organization
BPAI	United States Board of Patent Appeals and Interferences
CAFC	United States Court of Appeals for the Federal Circuit
CNIPA	China National Intellectual Property Administration
CPVO	Community Plant Variety Office
EAPO	Eurasian Patent Organization
EBSI	European Blockchain Services Infrastructure
EPO	European Patent Office
ETH Zurich	Federal Institute of Technology Zurich, Switzerland
EU	European Union
EUIPN	European Union Intellectual Property Network

EUIPO	European Union Intellectual Property Office
FTC	US Federal Trade Commission
GWF	Group for Science and Research
HIMPP	Hearing Instrument Manufacturers Patent Partnership
HSG	University of St. Gallen
INATBA	International Association for Trusted Blockchain Applications
INPI	French Patent and Trademark Office
IPI	Swiss Federal Institute of Intellectual Property
ITEM-HSG	Institute of Technology Management at HSG
JPO	Japan Patent Office
KIPO	Korean Intellectual Property Office
NIST	US National Institute of Standards and Technology
OAPI	Organisation Africaine de la Propriété Intellectuelle
OECD	Organisation for Economic Co-operation and Development
OFCOM	Swiss Federal Office of Communications
OHIM	Office for Harmonization in the Internal Market
SACEM	Society of Music Authors, Composers, and Publishers
SCBT	Swiss Center for Business and Technology Intelligence (formerly Centredoc).
SEC	US Securities and Exchange Commission
TUM	Technical University of Munich
UKIPO	Intellectual Property Office of the United Kingdom
UN	United Nations
UPC	Unified Patent Court
USPTO	United States Patent and Trademark Office
WIPO	World Intellectual Property Organization
WTO	World Trade Organization

References

Aboy, M., Liddell, K., & Lath, A. (2025). Inventorship in the age of AI: Examining the USPTO Guidance on AI-assisted inventions. *Journal of Intellectual Property Law and Practice, 20*(7), 495–502. https://doi.org/10.1093/jiplp/jpaf019

AIPLA. (2024). *Report of the economic survey*. AIPLA American Intellectual Property Law Association.

Alpana Ventures. (2021). *IBM and IPwe team up to disrupt the patent ecosystem with blockchain and AI*. Alpana Ventures. Accessed July 16, 2025, from https://alpana-ventures.ch/ibm-ans-ipwe-team-up-to-disrupt-the-patent-ecosystem-with-blockchain-and-ai/

Amara, N., Landry, R., & Traoré, N. (2008). Managing the protection of innovations in knowledge intensive business services. *Research Policy, 37*(9), 1530–1547.

Amit, R., & Zott, C. (2001). Value creation in e-business. *Strategic Management Journal, 22*(6/7), 493.

Aplin, T., Radauer, A., Bader, M. A., & Searle, N. (2023). The role of EU trade secrets law in the data economy: An empirical analysis. *International Review of Intellectual Property and Competition Law, 54*, 826–858. https://doi.org/10.1007/s40319-023-01325-8

Arora, A., & Ceccagnoli, M. (2006). Patent protection, complementary assets, and firms incentives for technology licensing. *Management Science, 52*(2), 293–308.

Arundel, A. (2001). The relative effectiveness of patents and secrecy for appropriation. *Research Policy, 30*(4), 611–624.

Ashrafi, A., Constantinides, P., Mehandjiev, N., & Thatcher, J. B. (2024). Mobilising new frontiers in digital transformation research: A problematization review. *Information Systems Journal, 35*(1), 97–139. https://doi.org/10.1111/isj.12531

Athreye, S., & Fassio, C. (2018). *When do firms not use patents and trademarks to protect valuable innovations? Evidence from the SIPU 2015 survey*. Intellectual Property Office.

Bader, M. A. (2006). *Intellectual property management in R&D collaborations*. Physica.

Bader, M. A. (2007a). Extending legal protection strategies to the service innovations area: Review and analysis. *World Patent Information, 29*, 122–135.

Bader, M. A. (2007b). Managing intellectual property in a collaborative environment: Learning from IBM. *International Journal of Intellectual Property Management, 1*(3), 206–225.

Bader, M. A. (2008). Managing intellectual property in the financial services industry sector: Learning from Swiss Re. *Technovation, 28*(4), 196–207.

Bader, M. A. (2022). Innovationen im Handel nutzen und schützen. In M. Knoppe, S. Rock, & M. Wild (Eds.), *Der Zukunftsfähige Handel* (4th ed., pp. 171–192). Springer Gabler.

M. A. Bader et al., *Patent Management*, Management for Professionals,
https://doi.org/10.1007/978-3-032-12030-4

Bader, M. A. (2023). An introduction to intellectual property rights and formal and informal protection strategies. In M. A. Bader & S. Süzeroglu-Melchiors (Eds.), *Intellectual property management for start-ups – Value-enhancing approaches and practices for leveraging the potential*. Springer Nature.

Bader, M. A., Beckenbauer, A., Gassmann, O., König, T., Lohwasser, E., & Menninger, J. (2008). *One valuation fits all? – How Europe's most innovative companies valuate technologies and patents*. PricewaterhouseCoopers.

Bader, M. A., & Bischof, D. (2005). Intellectual Property Management in der Finanzdienstleistungsbranche. In O. Gassmann & S. Albers (Eds.), *Handbuch Technologie- und Innovationsmanagement*. Gabler.

Bader, M. A., & Cuypers, F. (2008). Swiss Re: Global intellectual property management in the financial services industry. In R. Boutellier, O. Gassmann, & M. von Zedtwitz (Eds.), *Managing global innovation* (3rd ed.). Springer.

Bader, M. A., & Gassmann, O. (2022a). Patents in the biomedical sciences and industry – The case of the Swiss life science company Prionics. In M. Hinder, A. Schuhmacher, J. Goldhahn, & D. Hartl (Eds.), *Principles of biomedical sciences and industry*. Wiley-VCH.

Bader, M. A., & Gassmann, O. (2022b). Patent strategies in the networked economy. In O. Gassmann & F. Ferrandina (Eds.), *Connected business* (pp. 247–264). Springer Nature.

Bader, M. A., Gassmann, O., Jha, P., Liegler, F., Maicher, L., Posselt, T., Preissler, S., Rüther, F., Tonisson, L., & Wabra, S. (2012a). Creating an organised IP rights market in Europe. *Intellectual Asset Management Magazine, 26*, 33–38.

Bader, M. A., Gassmann, O., Jha, P., Liegler, F., Maicher, L., Posselt, T., Preissler, S., Rüther, F., & Wabra, S. (2012b). *Creating a financial market for IPR*. European Commission.

Bader, M. A., & Hofmann, E. (2006). Intellectual Property Management in der Logistik. *Supply Chain Management, 6*(4), 7–13.

Bader, M. A., & Liegler, F. (2013). Ein europäischer (Finanz-)Markt für Geistiges Eigentum? *Mitteilungen der deutschen Patentanwälte, 104*(1), 25–26.

Bader, M. A., & Mohr, C. A. (2025). Patentanwalt und Patentmanager – zwei Rollen im Wandel der Zeit. In U. Fitzner (Ed.), *Festschrift zum 125-jährigen Bestehen des Patentanwaltsberufs* (pp. 131–152). Wolters Kluwer.

Bader, M. A., & Stummeyer, C. (2019). The role of innovation and IP in AI-based business models. In R. Baierl, J. Behrens, & A. Brem (Eds.), *Digital entrepreneurship – interfaces between digital technologies and entrepreneurship* (pp. 23–56). Springer.

Bader, M. A., & Stummeyer, C. (2024). Innovation und geistiges Eigentum in KI-basierten Geschäftsmodellen. In L. Fend & J. Hofmann (Eds.), *Digitalisierung in Industrie-, Handels- und Dienstleistungsunternehmen* (4th ed., pp. 293–323). Springer Gabler.

Bader, M. A., & Süzeroglu-Melchiors, S. (2023). *Intellectual property management for start-ups – Value-enhancing approaches and practices for leveraging the potential*. Springer Nature.

Bader, M. A., Süzeroglu-Melchiors, S., Kleyn, M., London, S., Schaberg, U. G., & Wilkinson, D. L. (2024, June). Navigating the intellectual property maze: A guide for start-ups and stakeholders. *LES Nouvelles*, 113–117.

Bader, M. A., Vogel, H., Tobias, M., Rüther, F., & Gassmann, O. (2012). *Intellectual property right valuation index and a method and a system for creating such an index*. US 2012/0303537 A1.

Bailey, T. (2024a). *Intellectual property strategy foundations for artificial intelligence. A practical guide for founders, leaders and investors*. Scale AI. Accessed September 26, 2025, from https://www.scaleai.ca/wp-content/uploads/2024/06/intellectual-property-strategy-foundations-for-artificial-intelligence.pdf

Bailey, T. (2024b). *Essential business principles for patenting in artificial intelligence. A practical guide for entrepreneurs, leaders and investors*. Scale AI. Accessed September 26, 2025, from https://www.scaleai.ca/wp-content/uploads/2024/08/essential-business-principles-for-patenting-in-artificial-intelligence.pdf

Bar-Shalom, A., & Cook-Deegan, R. (2002). Patents and innovation in cancer therapeutics: Lessons from CellPro. *The Milbank Quarterly, 80*(4), 637–676.

Bartenbach, K., Jung, I., & Renvert, A. (2013). Apple vs. Samsung – Zu den Grenzen von Geschmacksmusterschutz und ergänzendem wettbewerbsrechtlichen Leistungsschutz. *Mitteilungen der deutschen Patentanwälte, 104*(1), 18–24.

BCF. (2020). BCF Business Law.

Bekkers, R., Duysters, G., & Verspagen, B. (2002). Intellectual property rights, strategic technology agreements and market structure: The case of GSM. *Research Policy, 31*(7), 1141–1161.

Bertolotti, N. (1996). *The valuation of intellectual property*. World Intellectual Property Organization (WIPO).

Bessen, J., & Meurer, M. J. (2013). Direct costs from NPE disputes. *The Cornell Law Review, 99*, 387.

Bessler, W., Bittelmeyer, C., & Lipfert, S. (2003). Zur Bedeutung von wissensbasierten immateriellen Vermögensgegenständen für die Bewertung und Finanzierung von kleinen und mittleren Unternehmen. In J.-A. Meyer (Ed.), *Unternehmensbewertung und Basel II in kleinen und mittleren Unternehmen* (pp. 309–334). EUL.

Best, B. (2022). *Softwarepatente in Europa*. Conference: Software und Geschäftsmodelle patentieren? – So schützen Sie Ihre Software und Geschäftsmodelle". Bayern Innovativ.

BGW. (2019). *IP management in distributed ledger technology and in food technology*. BGW.

Block, J. H., De Vries, G., Schumann, J. H., & Sandner, P. (2014). Trademarks and venture capital valuation. *Journal of Business Venturing, 29*(4), 525–542. https://doi.org/10.1016/j.jbusvent.2013.07.006

BMWFJ. (2013). *Immaterielle Vermögenswerte – geistiges Eigentum als Wachstumstreiber*. Bundesministerium für Wirtschaft, Familie und Jugend.

Boehm, B. W. (1976). Software engineering. *IEEE Transactions on Computers, C-25*(12), 1226–1241.

Bogdan, B., & Villiger, R. (2010). *Valuation in life sciences*. Springer.

Bonakdar, A., Frankenberger, K., Bader, M. A., & Gassmann, O. (2017). Capturing value from business models: The role of formal and informal protection strategies. *International Journal of Technology Management, 73*(4), 151–175.

Bördin, J. (2019). Born from business need. *iam magazine*, autumn 2019. Accessed July 1, 2025, from https://www.iam-media.com/patents/born-business-need

Bosworth, D., & Rogers, M. (2001). Market value, R&D and intellectual property: An empirical analysis of large Australian firms. *The Economic Record, 77*(239), 323–337.

Botschaft, S. T. A. F. (2018). *Botschaft zum Bundesgesetz über die Steuervorlage 17 (SV17)*. Schweizerische Eidgenossenschaft.

Boutellier, R., Gassmann, O., & von Zedtwitz, M. (2008). *Managing global innovation* (3rd ed.). Springer.

Boutellier, R., Hallbauer, S., & Locker, A. (1995). *Technologiestrategie für kleinere und mittlere Unternehmen*. University of St. Gallen (HSG).

Brealey, R. A., & Myers, S. C. (2003). *Principles of corporate finance* (7th ed.). McGraw-Hill.

Brem, A., Maier, M., & Wimschneider, C. (2016). Competitive advantage through innovation: The case of Nespresso. *European Journal of Innovation Management, 19*(1), 133–148.

Brockhoff, K. (1999). *Forschung und Entwicklung: Planung und Kontrolle* (5th ed.). Oldenburg.

Buchholz, K. (2019). Who is leading the 5G patent race? Companies which have filed the most patents for 5G technology as of November 2019. *Statista*. Accessed July 1, 2025, from https://www.statista.com/chart/20095/companies-with-most-5g-patent-families-and-patent-families-applications/

Buckminster Fuller, R. (1982). *Critical path*. St. Martin's Press.

Carroll, J. T., Srinivasa, C. K., & Malaney, K. J. (2024). *Alice patent eligibility analysis divergenc before USPTO and district court*. Foley and Lardner LLP. Accessed July 7, 2025, from https://www.foley.com/insights/publications/2024/09/alice-patent-eligibility-analysis-divergance-before-uspto-and-district-court/

Castellion, G., & Markham, S. K. (2012). Business model innovation: It's not just about technology anymore. *Journal of Product Innovation Management, 30*(5), 976–979.

Chang, Y., Wang, X., Wang, J., Wu, Y., Yang, L., Zhu, K., Chen, H., Yi, X., Wang, C., Wang, Y., Ye, W., Zhang, Y., Chang, Y., Yu, P. S., Yang, Q., & Xie, X. (2024). A survey on evaluation of large language models. *ACM Transactions on Intelligent Systems and Technology, 15*(3), 39. https://doi.org/10.1145/3641289

Chen, F. (2019). The investors' view. In *WIPO (2019) WIPO technology trends 2019: Artificial intelligence* (p. 105). World Intellectual Property Organization.

Chen, H., Roco, M. C., Li, X., & Lin, Y. (2008). Trends in nanotechnology patents. *Nature Nanotechnology, 3*(3), 123–125.

Chesbrough, H. (2007). Business model innovation: It's not just about technology anymore. *Strategy and Leadership, 35*(6), 12–17.

Chesbrough, H., Birkinshaw, J., & Teubal, M. (2006). Introduction to the research policy 20th anniversary special issue of the publication of 'profiting from innovation by DavidJ. Teece'. *Research Policy, 35*(8), 1091–1099.

Chesbrough, H., & Rosenbloom, R. S. (2002). The role of the business model in capturing value from innovation: Evidence from Xerox Corporation's technology spin-off companies. *Industrial and Corporate Change, 11*(3), 529–555.

Chimuka, G. (2019). Impact of artificial intelligence on patent law. Towards a new analytical framework – [the multi-level model]. *World Patent Information, 59*, 101926. https://doi.org/10.1016/j.wpi.2019.101926

Chu, J., Lo, H., Hsiang, J., & Cho, C. (2024). From Paris to Le-Paris: Toward patent response automation with recommender systems and collaborative large language models. *Artificial Intelligence and Law*, 1–27. https://doi.org/10.1007/s10506-024-09409-7

Clark, B., & Burstall, R. (2018). Blockchain, IP and the pharma industry—How distributed ledger technologies can help secure the pharma supply chain. *Journal of Intellectual Property Law and Practice, 13*(7), 531–533.

Coase, R. H. (1937). The nature of the firm. *Economica, 4*(16), 386–405.

Cockburn, I., & Griliches, Z. (1987). Industry effects and appropriability measures in the stock market's valuation of R&D and patents. *American Economic Review, 78*, 419–423.

Cohen, J. (2017). The birth of CRISPR. The American Association for the Advancement of Science, License Number 4803211490911. *Science, 355*(6326), 680–684. https://doi.org/10.1126/science.355.6326.680

Cohen, W. M., Goto, A., Nagata, A., Nelson, R. R., & Walsh, J. P. (2002). R&D spillovers, patents and the incentives to innovate in Japan and the United States. *Research Policy, 31*(8–9), 1349–1367.

Cohen, W. M., Nelson, R. R., & Walsh, J. P. (2000). *Protecting their intellectual assets: Appropriability conditions and why US manufacturing firms patent or not*. NBER Working Paper, No. 7552.

Columbus, L. (2019). *10 Charts that will change your perspective ofAmazon's patent growth*. Forbes. Accessed July 1, 2025, from https://www.forbes.com/sites/louiscolumbus/2019/07/21/10-charts-that-will-change-your-perspective-of-amazons-patent-growth/

Connolly, R. A., & Hirschey, M. (1988). Market value and patents: A Bayesian approach. *Economics Letters, 27*, 83–87.

Coriat, B., & Orsi, F. (2002). Establishing a new intellectual property rights regime in the United States: Origins, content and problems. *Research Policy, 31*(8–9), 1491–1507.

Costello-Caulkins, M. (2021). Nanotechnology patent law: A case study of the United States and European patent applications. *Santa Clara High Technology Law Journal, 37*(3), 337–386. https://digitalcommons.law.scu.edu/chtlj/vol37/iss3/3

Cotropia, C. A., Kesan, J. P., Rozema, K., & Schwartz, D. L. (2017). *Endogenous litigation costs: An empirical analysis of patent disputes* (January 3, 2017). Northwestern Law & Econ Research Paper 17-01; University of Illinois College of Law Legal Studies Research Paper No. 17-14. Available at SSRN: https://ssrn.com/abstract=2893503 or https://doi.org/10.2139/ssrn.2893503.

Deng, Z., Lev, B., & Narin, F. (1999). Science and technology as predictors of stock performance. *Financial Analysts Journal, 55*(5), 20–32.

Desyllas, P., & Sako, M. (2013). Profiting from business model innovation: Evidence from pay-as-you-drive auto insurance. *Research Policy, 42*(1), 101–116.

DIN 77100. (2011). *Patentbewertung – Grundsätze der monetären Patentbewertung*. DIN Deutsches Institut für Normung e.V.

Dosi, G., Marengo, L., & Pasquali, C. (2006). How much should society fuel the greed of innovators? On the relations between appropriability, opportunities and rates of innovation. *Research Policy, 35*(8), 1110–1121.

Dressler, A. (2006). *Patente in technologieorientierten Mergers & Acquisitions. Nutzen, Prozessmodell, Entwicklung und Interpretation semantischer Patentlandkarten*. DUV.

Dutfield, G. (2003). *Intellectual property rights and the life science industries. A twentieth century history*. Ashgate.

Econsight. (2020). Difference between quantitative and qualitative patent analysis – Citation of Swatch patents by third parties (number of cited patents vs. cumulative value of cited patents), 2000–2017. In *Green technologies – A new approach for investment strategies*.

Ehrat, M. (1997). *Kompetenzorientierte, analysegestützte Technologiestrategieerarbeitung*. Dissertation University of St. Gallen (HSG), St. Gallen, No. 1981.

Engberg, E., Koch, M., Lodefalk, M., & Schroeder, S. (2025). Artificial intelligence, tasks, skills, and wages: Worker-level evidence from Germany. *Research Policy, 54*(8), 105285. https://doi.org/10.1016/j.respol.2025.105285

Ensthaler, J., & Strübbe, K. (2006). *Patentbewertung. Ein Praxisleitfaden zum Patentmanagement*. Springer.

EPO. (2007). *Scenarios for the future. How might IP regimes evolve by 2025? What global legitimacy might such regimes have?* European Patent Office.

EPO. (2013). *Nanotechnology and patents*. European Patent Office. Accessed July 16, 2025, from https://www.epo.org/en/news-events/in-focus/classification/nanotechnology

EPO. (2017). *Patents and the fourth industrial revolution. The inventions behind digital transformation*. European Patent Office. Accessed July 1, 2025, from https://www.epo.org/en/news-events/in-focus/ict/fourth-industrial-revolution

EPO. (2018a). *Information and communications technology patents at the EPO*. European Patent Office. Accessed July 1, 2025, from https://www.epo.org/en/news-events/in-focus/ict/about-ict

EPO. (2018b). *Patenting artificial intelligence. Conference summary*. European Patent Office. Accessed July 7, 2025, from https://www.youtube.com/playlist?list=PLgDlswd0__eIqs4fl42UGeMNGrMdcYjGM

EPO. (2019a). *Annual report 2018*. European Patent Office.

EPO. (2019b). *EPO refuses DABUS patent applications designating a machine inventor*. News, 20 December 2019. Munich: European Patent Office. Accessed July 3, 2020, from https://www.epo.org/news-issues/news/2019/20191220.html

EPO. (2019c). *Patenting biotechnological inventions at the EPO*. Dr. Harald Schmidt-Yodlee. European Patent Office.

EPO. (2019d). *Patents for software? European law and practice*. European Patent Office. Accessed December 28, 2019, from https://www.epo.org/news-issues/issues/ict/hardware-and-software.html#tab1

EPO. (2020a). *Patents and the fourth industrial revolution. The inventions behind digital transformation*. European Patent Office. Accessed June 27, 2025, from https://link.epo.org/web/patents_and_the_fourth_industrial_revolution_study_2020_en.pdf

EPO. (2020b). *The role of patents in an AI driven world, virtual conference, 17./18.12.2020*. European Patent Office. Accessed July 7, 2025, from https://www.youtube.com/playlist?list=PLgDlswd0__eK5UHWAHnucwVI22O0pROdT

EPO. (2023). *Conference on AI technologies, regulation, inventorship and patenting*. European Patent Office. Accessed July 7, 2025, from https://www.epo.org/en/news-events/in-focus/ict/artificial-intelligence

EPO. (2024a). *Biotech patents*. European Patent Office. Accessed July 10, 2025, from https://www.epo.org/en/news-events/in-focus/biotechnology-patents

EPO. (2024b). *Services and activities – Quality – Statistics – Examination*. Accessed July 30, 2025, from https://www.epo.org/en/about-us/services-and-activities/quality/statistics/examination

EPO. (2024c). *Statistics reported to the Administrative Council (CA/F 5)*. European Patent Office.

EPO. (2024d). *Unified Patent Court (UPC)*. European Patent Office. Accessed July 17, 2025, from https://www.epo.org/en/applying/european/unitary/upc

EPO. (2024e). *Unitary Patent*. European Patent Office. Accessed July 17, 2025, from https://www.epo.org/en/applying/european/unitary/unitary-patent

EPO. (2025a). *Artificial intelligence*. European Patent Office. Accessed July 7, 2025, from https://www.epo.org/en/news-events/in-focus/ict/artificial-intelligence#collapsiblelang

EPO. (2025b). *Computer technology*. European Patent Office. Accessed August 11, 2025, from https://www.epo.org/en/about-us/statistics/statistics-centre/technologyfields?code=6

EPO. (2025c). *Guidelines for examination: Artificial intelligence and machine learning (G-II 3.3.1)*. European Patent Office. Accessed July 7, 2025, from https://www.epo.org/en/legal/guidelines-epc/2025/g_ii_3_3_1.html

EPO. (2025d). *Patent Index 2024*. European Patent Office. Accessed July 10, 2025, from https://www.epo.org/en/about-us/statistics/patent-index-2024

EPO. (2025e). *Statistics and Trends Centre*. Accessed August 17, 2025, from https://www.epo.org/en/about-us/statistics/statistics-centre

EPO. (2025f). *The EPO at a glance*. Accessed July 17, 2025, from https://www.epo.org/en/about-us/at-a-glance

EPO & CNIPA. (2019). *Comparative study on computer implemented inventions/software related inventions – Report 2019 I EPO and CNIPA*. European Patent Office. Accessed June 27, 2025, from http://documents.epo.org/projects/babylon/eponot.nsf/0/979CF38758D25C2CC12584AC004618D9/$File/comparative_study_on_computer_implemented_inventions_software_related_inventions_EPO_CNIPA_en.pdf

EPO & EUIPO. (2019). *High-growth firms and intellectual property rights. IPR profile of high-potential SMEs in Europe, May 2019. A joint project between the European Patent Office and the European Union*. European Patent Office and Alicante: European Union Intellectual Property Office. Accessed August 18, 2025, from https://link.epo.org/web/high_growth_firms_study_en.pdf

EPO & JPO. (2018). *Comparative study on computer implemented inventions/software related inventions – Report 2018 I EPO and JPO*. European Patent Office. Accessed June 27, 2025, from http://documents.epo.org/projects/babylon/eponet.nsf/0/346e6018b0445380c12583cb002fdb34/$FILE/comparative_study_on_computer_implemented_inventions_software_related_inventions_EPO_JPO_en.pdf

Ericsson. (2019). *The internet of things: Challenges for IP and best practices (Dr. C. Tapia)*. Management Circle IP Service World: Munich, November 2019.

Ericsson. (2023). *Ericsson and Huawei renew global patent license agreement*. Accessed June 26, 2025, from https://www.ericsson.com/en/press-releases/2023/8/ericsson-and-huawei-renew-global-patent-license-agreement

Ernst, H. (1996). *Patentinformationen für die strategische Planung von Forschung und Entwicklung*. Gabler.

Ernst, H. (1998). Patent portfolios for strategic R&D planning. *Journal of Engineering and Technology Management, 15*(4), 279–308.

Ernst, H. (1999). Evaluation of dynamic technological developments by means of patent data. In K. Brockhoff, A. K. Chakrabarti, & J. Hauschildt (Eds.), *The dynamics of innovation. Strategic and managerial implications* (pp. 107–132). Springer.

Ernst, H. (2001). Patent applications and subsequent changes of performance: Evidence from time-series cross-section analyses on the firm level. *Research Policy, 30*, 143–157.

Ernst, H. (2002). Patentmanagement. In D. Specht & M. G. Möhrle (Eds.), *Lexikon Technologiemanagement* (pp. 214–218). Gabler.

Ernst, H., & Omland, N. (2010). The patent asset index – A new approach to benchmark patent portfolios. *World Patent Information, 33*(1), 34–41.

EUIPO. (2018). *2017 situation report on counterfeiting and piracy in the European Union*. European observatory on infringements of intellectual property rights. Accessed July 7, 2025, from https://euipo.europa.eu/ohimportal/en/web/observatory/observatory-publications

EUIPO. (2025). *About EUIPO*. European Union Intellectual Property Office. Accessed July 17, 2025, from https://www.euipo.europa.eu/en/about-us/the-office

European Commission. (2018). *Artificial Intelligence for Europe*. European Commission. Accessed July 7, 2025, from https://eur-lex.europa.eu/legal-content/EN/TXT/?uri=COM:2018:237:FIN

European Commission. (2025a). *AI continent action plan*. European Commission. Accessed July 7, 2025, from https://digital-strategy.ec.europa.eu/en/factpages/ai-continent-action-plan

European Commission. (2025b). *The European Union Intellectual Property Office (EUIPO) and European Blockchain Services Infrastructure (EBSI) have joined forces to undertake the EBSI-ELSA project*. European Commission. Accessed August 20, 2025, from https://ec.europa.eu/digital-building-blocks/sites/display/EBSI/EBSI-ELSA+EUIPO

Ewing, T., & Feldman, R. (2012). The giants among us. *Stanford Technology Law Review, 1*, 1–61.

Faix, A. (2001). Die Patentportfolio-Analyse – Methodische Konzeption und Anwendung im Rahmen der strategischen Patentpolitik. *Zeitschrift für Planung, 2*, 185–208.

Fedorenko, I., Berthon, P., & Edelman, L. (2023). Top secret: Integrating 20 years of research on secrecy. *Technovation, 123*, 102691. https://doi.org/10.1016/j.technovation.2023.102691

Five IP Offiecs. (2024a). *IP5 statistics reports 2023 edition*. Seoul: Edited by Korean Intellectual Property Office. Accessed July 30, 2025, from https://www.fiveipoffices.org/statistics/statisticsreports/2023edition

Five IP Offices. (2024b). *IP5 statistical tables 2023*. Seoul: Korean Intellectual Property Office. Accessed July 17, 2025, from https://link.epo.org/ip5_table2023

Frost & Sullivan. (2025). Global automotive outlook 2025. Retrieved January 9, 2026, from https://automotive.messefrankfurt.com/content/dam/messefrankfurt-redaktion/automotive/documents/exl/globalautomotive-outlook-july-2025.pdf

Galetovic, A., Haber, S., & Zaretzki, L. (2018). An estimate of the average cumulative royalty yield in the world mobile phone industry: Theory, measurement and results. *Telecommunications Policy, 42*(3), 263–276. https://doi.org/10.1016/j.telpol.2018.02.002

Gallié, E. P., & Legros, D. (2012). French firms' strategies for protecting their intellectual property. *Research Policy, 41*(4), 780–794.

Gambardella, A., Giuri, P., & Luzzi, A. (2007). The market for patents. *Europe Research Policy, 39*, 1163–1183.

Gans, J., Hsu, D. H., & Stern, S. (2002). When does start-up innovation spur the gale of creative destruction? *RAND Journal of Economics, 33*(4), 571–586.

Garcia, M. B., Rosak-Szyrocka, J., & Bozkurt, A. (Eds.). (2025). *Pitfalls of AI Integration in education: Skill obsolescence, misuse, and bias: skill obsolescence, misuse, and bias*. IGI Global. https://doi.org/10.4018/979-8-3373-0122-8

Gassmann, O., & Bader, M. A. (2024). *Patentmanagement: Innovationen erfolgreich nutzen und schützen* (5th ed.). Springer Gabler.

Gassmann, O., Beckenbauer, A., & Friesike, S. (2012). *Profiting from innovation in China*. Springer.

Gassmann, O., & Frankenberger, K. (2025). *The business model navigator* (3rd ed.). FT Publishing.

Gassmann, O., Krech, C.-A., Bader, M. A., & Reepmeyer, G. (2016). Out-licensing in pharmaceutical research and development. In A. Schuhmacher, M. Hinder, & O. Gassmann (Eds.), *Value creation in the pharmaceutical industry – The critical path to innovation* (pp. 363–380). Wiley-VCH.

Gassmann, O., Schuhmacher, A., Reepmeyer, G., & von Zedtwitz, M. (2018). *Leading pharmaceutical innovation – How to win the life science race* (3rd ed.). Springer.

Gassmann, O., Wecht, C. H., Meister, C., & Boemelburg, R. (2018). *Exploit the hidden success factor of innovation culture. Innovationskulturnavigator*. Carl Hanser.

Gassmann, O., Ziegler, N., Bader, M. A., & Nowak, R. (2010). *IP management in practice*. University of St. Gallen (ITEM-HSG).

Ghapar, F., Brooks, R., & Smyth, R. (2014). The impact of patenting activity on the financial performance of Malaysian firms. *Journal of the Asia Pacific Economy, 19*(3), 445–463.

Glazier, S. C. (2003). *E-patent strategies*. LBI Law & Business Institute.

Google. (2019). *Q3 earnings call*, October 31st.

Granstrand, O. (1999). *The economics and management of intellectual property. Towards intellectual capitalism*. Edward Elgar.

Granstrand, O. (2018). *Evolving properties of intellectual capitalism: Patents and innovations for growth and welfare*. Edward Elgar.

Grey, B. (2020). *Who owns core 5G patents? – Essentiality check on 5G declared patents*. Accessed August 17, 2025 from https://info.greyb.com/hubfs/5G%20Report%20-%201st%20Release.pdf

Grey, B. (2025a). *Samsung faces a lawsuit every 5 days, Pharma Litigation Booms, and NPEs stay highly active*. Accessed August 16, 2025, from https://www.greyb.com/blog/patent-litigation-trends/

Grey, B. (2025b). *Inside Anthropic's patent strategy: Filings, litigation trends, and licensing power*. Accessed September 26, 2025, from https://www.greyb.com/blog/anthropics-patent-strategy/

Griliches, Z. (1981). Market value, R&D, and patents. *Economic Letters, 7*, 183–187.

Grindley, P. C., & Teece, D. J. (1997). Managing intellectual capital: Licensing and cross-licensing in semiconductors and electronics. *California Management Review, 39*(2), 8–41.

Grosz, B. J., & Stone, P. (2018, December). *A century long commitment to assessing artificial intelligence and its impact on society*. Communications of the ACM (CACM).

Grünecker. (2013). *E-Auto-Patentindex 2013*. Grünecker Patent- und Rechtsanwälte.

Hall, B. H. (2003). *Business method patents, innovation and policy*. NBER Working Paper, No. 9717.

Hall, B., Helmers, C., Rogers, M., & Sena, V. (2014). The choice between formal and informal intellectual property: A review. *Journal of Economic Literature, 52*, 375–423.

Hall, B., Jaffe, A., & Trajtenberg, M. (2005). Market value and patent citations. *RAND Journal of Economics, 36*(1), 16–38.

Hall, B. H., & MacGarvie, M. (2010). The private value of software patents. *Research Policy, 39*(7), 994–1009.

Hall, B. H., & Mairesse, J. (2007). Empirical studies of innovation in the knowledge-driven economy. *Economics of Innovation and New Technology, 15*(4–5), 289–299.

Hall, B. H., von Graevenitz, G., & Helmers, C. (2021). Technology entry in the presence of patent thickets. *Oxford Economic Papers, 73*(2), 903–926.

Hall, B. H., & Ziedonis, R. H. (2001). The patent paradox revisited: An empirical study of patenting in the US semiconductor industry 1979–1995. *RAND Journal of Economics, 32*(1), 101–128.

Hannah, D., Parent, M., Pitt, L., & Berthon, P. (2018). Secrets and knowledge management strategy: The role of secrecy appropriation mechanisms in realizing value from firm innovations. *Journal of Knowledge Management, 23*, 297–312.

Hellebrand, O., Kaube, G., & Falckenstein, R. (2007). *Lizenzsätze für technische Erfindungen* (3rd ed.). Carl Heymanns.

Heller, M. A., & Eisenberg, R. S. (1998). Can patents deter innovation? The anticommons in biomedical research. *Science, 280*(5364), 698–701.

Hess-Blumer, A. (2009). Patent trolls – Eine Analyse nach Schweizer Recht. *sic!*, 851–865.

Hofinger, S. (1997). Portfolio-Analyse als Instrument unternehmerischer Patentpolitik. *EPI Information, 4*, 100–104.

Howell, S., Stark, A., Newton, D., Paxson, D., Cavus, M., Pereira, J., & Patel, K. (2001). *Realoptions. Evaluating corporate investment opportunities in a dynamic world*. Financial Times Prentice Hall.

Huebner, S. R. (2008). The validity of European nanotechnology patents in Germany. *Nanotechnology Law and Business, 5*(3), 353–357.

Hyundai. (2018). *Hyundai motor group and Audi partner in fuel cell technology*. Accessed June 26, 2025, from https://www.hyundainews.com/en-us/releases/2557

iam. (2015). *In search of the next patent war*. Accessed July 1, 2025, from https://www.iam-media.com/litigation/search-next-patent-war

iam. (2016). *Innovation and survival: Lessons from the smartphone wars*. Accessed July 1, 2025, from https://www.iam-media.com/innovation-and-survival-lessons-smartphone-wars

IBM. (2006). *The toxic terabyte: How data-dumping threatens business efficiency*. IBM Global Technical Services white paper. Accessed July 1, 2025, from https://archive.org/stream/TheToxicTerabyte/The%20Toxic%20Terabyte_djvu.txt

IBM. (2021). *IPwe creates world's first blockchain-powered patent platform*. IBM Corporation. Accessed July 16, 2025, from https://www.ibm.com/case-studies/ipwe

IDW S 5. (2013). *IDW Standard: Principles of the valuation of intangible assets (IDW S 5) (5/2011)*. IDW.

Internet of Business. (2021a). *New Walmart patents signal a push towards Retail 2.0*. Accessed April 30, 2021, from https://internetofbusiness.com/walmart-patents-retail-2-0/

Internet of Business. (2021b). *Bee robotic: Walmart files patents on automating agriculture*. Accessed April 30, 2021, from https://internetofbusiness.com/walmart-files-patent-autonomous-bees/

IP Watchdogs. (2013). *Why bash individual inventor owned or controlled companies?*http://www.ipwatchdog.com/2013/06/30/why-bash-individual-inventor-owned-or-controlled-companies/id=42613/

IPI. (2019). *Pulling no punches – How Prionics, a life science company in Zurich, defends its intellectual property*. Accessed July 1, 2025, from https://www.ige.ch/en/intellectual-property/sme-portal/smes-report/detailseiten/prionics-ag.html

IPI. (2024). *Envisioned. Created. Protected. A concise guide to trade marks, patents and co* (13th ed.). IPI Swiss Federal Institute of Intellectual Property.

IPI/PatentSight. (2020). *Patent analytics as a support to business decisions*. IPI.

IPStudies. (2019). *CRISPR patent landscape*. In *Les Paccots*. https://www.ipstudies.ch/

IPXI. (2015). *Corporate announcement*. Intellectual Property Exchange International. https://www.ipxi.com/corporate-announcement.html

Jaffe, A. B., & Lerner, J. (2004). *Innovation and its discontents: How our broken patent system is endangering innovation and progress, and what to do about it*. Princeton University Press.

Jinek, M., Chylinski, K., Fonfara, I., Hauer, M., Doudna, J. A., & Charpentier, E. (2012). A programmable dual-RNA–guided DNA endonuclease in adaptive bacterial immunity. *Science, 337*(6096), 816–821.

Juve. (2020). *Collision course set for Nokia and Daimler.* Accessed July 1, 2025, from https://www.juve-patent.com/news-and-stories/cases/collision-course-set-for-nokia-and-daimler/ & *Hopes dwindle for peaceful settlement between Nokia and Daimler.* Accessed July 1, 2025, from https://www.juve-patent.com/news-and-stories/cases/hopes-dwindle-for-peaceful-settlement-between-nokia-and-daimler/

Kallinger, C., Veefkind, V., Michalitsch, R., Verbandt, Y., Neumann, A., Scheu, M., & Forster, W. (2008). Patenting nanotechnology: A European patent office perspective. *Nanotechnology Law and Business, 5*(1), 95.

Kamiyama, S., Sheehan, J., & Martinez, C. (2006). *Valuation and exploitation of intellectual property. OECD science, technology and industry Working Papers, No. 5*. OECD.

King, C. C., & Zhu, S. (2019). *Patentboxen im Europäischen Vergleich und steuerliche Forschungsförderung in Deutschland*. In: VPP-Rundbrief No. 4/2019. VCI und BASF.

Köllner, M. (2009, March). Due diligence or discount monetary effect of legal aspects in patent valuation. *LES Nouvelles*, 24–37.

Krech, C.-A., Rüther, F., & Gassmann, O. (2015). Profiting from invention: Business models of patent aggregating companies. *International Journal of Innovation Management, 19*(3), 1–26.

Kuckartz, M. (2007). *IPC-Patentportfolio-Bewertung: Patentmanagement speziell* für *den Mittelstand*. 5. Patentforum Nordbayern 2007.

Landes, W. M., & Posner, R. A. (2003). *The economic structure of intellectual property law*. Belknap Press of Harvard University Press.

Ledford, H. (2016). Bitter fight over CRISPR patent heats up: Unusual battle among academic institutions holds key to gene-editing tool's future use. *Nature, 529*(7586), 265. Gale OneFile: Health and Medicine. Accessed July 10, 2025, from. https://doi.org/10.1038/nature.2015.17961

Lepak, D. P., Smith, K. G., & Taylor, M. S. (2007). Value creation and value capture: A multilevel perspective. *Academy of Management Review, 32*(1), 180–194.

Lerner, J. (1994). The importance of patent scope: An empirical analysis. *RAND Journal of Economics, 25*(2), 319–332.
Lerner, J., Strojwas, M., & Tirole, J. (2007). The design of patent pools: The determinants of licensing rules. *The RAND Journal of Economics, 38*(3), 610–625.
LexisNexis PatentSight. (2020a). *Number of Alibaba patent families worldwide by filing year from 1999 to 2019, by legal status.* Statista. Accessed July 9, 2025, from https://www.statista.com/statistics/1033899/number-of-alibaba-patents-by-filing-year-and-status-worldwide/
LexisNexis PatentSight. (2020b). *Number of Amazon patent families worldwide by filing year from 1999 to 2019, by legal status.* Statista. Accessed July 9, 2025, from https://www.statista.com/statistics/1033929/number-of-amazon-patents-by-filing-year-and-status-worldwide/
LexisNexis PatentSight. (2020c). *Number of Walmart patent families worldwide by filing year from 1999 to 2019, by legal status.* Statista. Accessed July 9, 2025, from https://www.statista.com/statistics/1034115/number-of-walmart-patents-by-filing-year-and-status-worldwide/
Littman, M. L., Ajunwa, I., Berger, G., Boutilier, C., Currie, M., Doshi-Velez, F., Hadfield, G., Horowitz, M. C., Isbell, C., Kitano, H., Levy, K., Lyons, T., Mitchell, M., Shah, J., Sloman, S., Vallor, S., & Walsh, T. (2021). *Gathering strength, gathering storms: The One Hundred Year Study on Artificial Intelligence (AI100) 2021 Study Panel Report.* Stanford University. Accessed July 10, 2025, from https://ai100.stanford.edu/2021-report
Lloyd, R. (2018). Uber's patent transactions head explains how the company built its portfolio through savvy deal-making. *Intellectual Asset Management (IAM).*
LobbyFacts. (2025). *LobbyControl.* Corporate Europe Observatory & LobbyControl. Retrieved August 8, 2025, from https://lobbyfacts.eu/datacard/lobbycontrol?rid=6314918394-16
Loebbert, M. (2000). Interne Dienstleister: Was sie alles können müssen. *Harvard Business Manager, 3*, 49–57.
London, S. (2023). Strategic uses of IP: Applying learnings from large companies to start-ups. In M. A. Bader & S. Süzeroglu-Melchiors (Eds.), *Intellectual property management for start-ups – Value-enhancing approaches and practices for leveraging the potential.* Springer Nature.
Mangubat, J. C., Mangubat, M. R., Uy, T. B. L., Acut, D. P., & Garcia, M. B. (2025). Safeguarding educational innovations amid AI disruptions: A reassessment of patenting for sustained intellectual property protection. In *Pitfalls of AI integration in education skill obsolescence misuse and bias* (pp. 297–318). IGI Global Scientific Publishing. https://doi.org/10.4018/979-8-3373-0122-8.ch013
McGahan, A. M., & Silverman, B. S. (2006). Profiting from technological innovation by others: The effect of competitor patenting on firm value. *Research Policy, 35*(8), 1222–1242.
Megna, P., & Klock, M. (1993). The impact of intangible capital on Tobin's q in the semiconductor industry. *The American Economic Review, 83*(2), 265–269.
Mengden, A. (2023). *Patent box regimes in Europe, 2023.* Tax Foundation Europe. Accessed July 17, 2025, from https://taxfoundation.org/data/all/eu/patent-box-regimes-europe-2023/
Meutens, A., & Scheufen, M. (2024). Intellectual property and fourth industrial revolution technologies: how the patent system is shaping the future in the data-driven economy. *European Journal of Law and Economics, 57*, 275–310. https://doi.org/10.1007/s10657-023-09789-2
MGI (McKinsey Global Institute). (2015). *The internet of things: Mapping the value beyond the Hype.*
Microsoft. (2004). *Siemens and Microsoft to cross-license patent holdings.* Accessed June 11, 2025, from https://news.microsoft.com/source/2004/05/03/siemens-and-microsoft-to-cross-license-patent-holdings/
Miller, C., Serrato, R. M., Represas-Cardenas, J. M., & Griffith, A. K. (2005). *The handbook of nanotechnology: Business, policy, and intellectual property law.* Wiley.
Mintzberg, H., Ahlstrand, B., & Lampel, J. (2005). *Strategy safari: A guided tour through the wilds of strategic management.* Simon and Schuster.
Moeller, A., & Moehrle, M. G. (2015). Completing keyword patent search with semantic patent search: Introducing a semiautomatic iterative method for patent near search based on semantic similarities. *Scientometrics, 102*(1), 77–96. https://doi.org/10.1007/s11192-014-1446-9

Möhrle, M. G., & Walter, L. (2009). *Patentierung von Geschäftsprozessen. Monitoring – Strategien – Schutz*. Springer.

Moser, U., & Goddar, H. (2007). Grundlagen der Bewertung immaterieller Vermögenswerte am Beispiel der Bewertung patentgeschützter Technologien. *Finanzbetrieb, 10*, 594–609.

Nanosys. (2009). *Nanoco Settles Patent Infringement Lawsuit with Nanosys, Inc. for Quantum Dot Technology*. Nanosys. Accessed July 10, 2025, from https://www.nanocotechnologies.com/nanoco-settles-patent-infringement-lawsuit-with-nanosys-inc-for-quantum-dot-technology/

Niemann, H. (2014). *Corporate Foresight mittels Geschäftsprozesspatenten: Entwicklungsstränge der Automobilindustrie*. Springer.

Niemann, H., Moehrle, M. G., & Walter, L. (2013). The development of business method patenting in the logistics industry—Insights from the case of intelligent sensor networks. *International Journal of Technology Management, 61*(2), 177–197.

Obschonka, M., Grégoire, D. A., Nikolaev, B., Ooms, F., Lévesque, M., Pollack, J. M., & Behrend, T. S. (2025). Artificial intelligence and entrepreneurship: A call for research to prospect and establish the scholarly AI frontiers. *Entrepreneurship Theory and Practice, 49*(3), 620–641. https://doi.org/10.1177/10422587241304676

OECD. (2003). *Genetic inventions, IPRS and licensing practices: Evidence and policies*. OECD Publishing.

OECD. (2004). *Patents and innovation: Trends and policy challenges*. OECD Publishing.

OECD. (2009). *Nanotechnology: An overview*. OECD Publishing.

OECD. (2017a). Harmful tax practices – 2017 Progress report on preferential regimes. In *OECD/G20 base erosion and profit shifting project*. OECD Publishing.

OECD. (2017b). *Key issues for digital transformation in the G20. Report prepared for a joint G20 German Presidency/OECD conference*. OECD Publishing.

OECD. (2019a). *Licensing of IP rights and competition law*. OECD Publishing.

OECD. (2019b). *Trends in trade in counterfeit and pirated goods*. OECD Publishing. https://doi.org/10.1787/g2g9f533-en

OECD. (2020). *Intellectual property regimes*. Paris: Organisation for Economic Co-operation and Development. Accessed January 7, 2020, from https://qdd.oecd.org/subject.aspx?Subject=IP_Regimes

OECD. (2025). *Intellectual properties regimes—Corporate tax statistics 2024*. Paris: Organisation for Economic Co-operation and Development. Accessed July 17, 2025, from https://data-viewer.oecd.org/?chartId=ff7c45ac-6d39-4a1e-9d17-45415e239553

OECD & EUIPO. (2025). *Mapping global trade in fakes 2025: Global trends and enforcement challenges, illicit trade*. OECD Publishing. https://doi.org/10.1787/94d3b29f-en

Osram. (2013). *Osram GmbH und Sharp Corporation schließen Patentlizenzaustauschvertrag*. Osram. Press release dated 2013-08-26. Accessed July 17, 2025, from https://ams-osram.com/de/news/press-releases/pr-26-08-2013

Otto Toivanen, P. S., & Bosworth, D. (2002). Innovation and the market value of UK firms, 1989–1995. *Oxford Bulletin of Economics and Statistics, 64*(39), 0305–9049.

Ottoz, E., & Cugno, F. (2008). Patent–secret mix in complex product firms. *American Law and Economics Review, 10*, 142–158.

Ouellette, L. L. (2015). Nanotechnology and innovation policy. *Harvard Journal of Law and Technology, 29*(1), 33.

Ozcan, O., Pickernell, D., & Trott, P. (2023). A trade secrets framework and strategic approaches. *IEEE Transactions on Engineering Management, 71*, 1–17. https://doi.org/10.1109/TEM.2023.3285292

Parr, R. L. (1999). *IP valuation issues and strategies*. World Intellectual Property Organization (WIPO).

Parr, R. L., & Sullivan, P. H. (1996). *Technology licensing. Corporate strategies for maximizing value*. Wiley.

Pepe, S., & Post, K. J., & Middleton, A. (2019). Continental Automotive v. Avanci: Wireless SEP licensing presents challenges for automotive industry. Ropes and Gray LPP on *Lexology*.

Accessed July 1, 2025, from https://www.lexology.com/library/detail.aspx?g=2e0a83b4-6e78-4faa-8311-9b6e4a0c945f

PERA. (2025). *Patent Eligibility Restoration Act of 2025.* S.1546, 119th Cong. (2025–2026). Congress.gov. Accessed July 7, 2025, from https://www.congress.gov/bill/119th-congress/senate-bill/1546

Pfeiffer, W., Schäffner, G. J., Schneider, W., & Schneider, H. (1989). *Studie zur Anwendung der Portfolio-Methode auf die strategische Analyse und Bewertung von Patentinformationen.* Nürnberg.

Picanço-Castro, V., Pereira, C., Covas, D. T., Porto, G., Athanassiadou, A., & Figueiredo, M. L. (2020). Emerging patent landscape for non-viral vectors used for gene therapy. *Nature: Biotechnology, 38*, 151–157. Graphic released to public by Purdue University. Accessed July 1, 2025, from https://www.purdue.edu/newsroom/releases/2020/Q1/novel-techniques-for-mining-patented-gene-therapies-offer-promising-treatment-options-for-cancers,-other-diseases.html

Pichler, R., & Kastler, H. A. (2019). FRAND Case Law in Europe after Huawei vs. ZTE. Morrison Foerster LLP on *Lexology*. Accessed July 1, 2025, from https://www.lexology.com/library/detail.aspx?g=f4c5633a-21ed-4aec-a1d2-23803d5d1806

Pisano, G. (2006). Profiting from innovation and the intellectual property revolution. *Research Policy, 35*(8), 1122–1130.

Pitkethly, R. (1997). *The valuation of patents.* Working paper. University of Oxford, Said Business School.

Pohlmann, T., Blind, K., & Heß, P. (2020). *Studie zur Untersuchung undAnalyse der Patentsituation bei der Standardisierung von 5G.* Study on behalf of the German Bundesministerium für Wirtschaft und Energie.

Poredda, A., & Wildschütz, S. (2004). Patent valuation – A controlled market share approach. *Les Nouvelles – Journal of the Licensing Executives Society, 34*(2), 77–85.

PricewaterhouseCoopers. (2018). *2018 Patent litigation study.* https://www.pwc.com/us/en/forensic-services/publications/assets/2018-pwc-patent-litigation-study.pdf

Prud'homme, D., von Zedwitz, M., Thraen, J. J., & Bader, M. A. (2018). Forced technology transfer policies: Workings in China and strategic implications. *Technological Forecasting and Social Change, 134*, 150–168.

Radauer, A., Bader, M. A., Aplin, T., Konopka, U., Searle, N., Altenburger, R., & Bachner, C. (2022). *Study on the legal protection of trade secrets in the context of the data economy.* European Innovation Council and SMEs Executive Agency (European Commission). Accessed July 1, 2025, from https://op.europa.eu/publication-detail/-/publication/c0335fd8-33db-11ed-8b77-01aa75ed71a1

Radauer, A., Bader, M. A., Aplin, T., Konopka, U., Searle, N., Altenburger, R., & Bachner, C. (2025). Trade secrets as a complementary tool to patenting in the data economy of the 21st century. In N. Thumm & K. Blind (Eds.), *A modern guide to patenting; challenges of patenting in the 21st century.* Elgar Publishing.

Radauer, A., Searle, N., & Bader, M. A. (2023). The possibilities and limits of trade secrets to protect data shared between firms in agricultural and food sectors. *World Patent Information, 73*, 102183. https://doi.org/10.1016/j.wpi.2023.102183

Razgaitis, R. (2003a). *Dealmaking using real options and Monte Carlo analysis.* Wiley Finance.

Razgaitis, R. (2003b). *Valuation and pricing of technology-based intellectual property.* Wiley.

Reidenberg, J. R., Cammeron Russel, N., Price, M., & Mohand, A. (2015). *Patents and the small participants in the smartphone industry.* Fordham Center on Law and Information Policy & the World Intellectual Property Organization.

Reitzig, M. (2002). *Die Bewertung von Patentrechten. Eine theoretische und empirische Analyse aus Unternehmenssicht.* DUV.

Reuters.(2014).*RPXbuysApple-backedRockstarpatentsfor$900million.*AccessedJuly17,2025,from https://www.reuters.com/article/2014/12/23/us-rpx-rockstar-ip-idUSKBN0K11AI20141223/

Reuters. (2018). *Alexandria Sage, Dan Levine, Heather Somerville.*

Rings, R. (2000). Patentbewertung – Methoden und Faktoren zur Wertermittlung technischer Schutzrechte. *GRUR, 10*, 839–848.

Rivette, K. G., & Kline, D. (2000). Discovering new value in intellectual property. *Harvard Business Review, 79*(1), 54–66.

Rudolf, M., & Witt, P. (2002). *Bewertung von Wachstumsunternehmen: Traditionelle und innovative Methoden im Vergleich*. Gabler.

Sacem. (2019). *ASCAP, SACEM, and PRS for music initiate blockchain project to improve data accuracy for rightsholders*, press release dated 2019-03-12.

Scale AI. (2025). *Who we are*. Accessed September 26, 2025, from https://www.scaleai.ca/about-us/

SCBT. (2024). *CRISPR technology: Patent & License landscapes. N° 20231386*. Swiss Center for Business & Technology Intelligence–Centredoc. Accessed July 10, 2025, from https://www.ige.ch/fileadmin/user_upload/recht/national/e/20231388_IPI_CRISPR_Patent_License_Landscape_revised_Final_16_02_24.pdf

Schaberg, U. G. (2023). "IP is paramount:" The significance of IP in early-stage start-up investment decisions. In M. A. Bader & S. Süzeroglu-Melchiors (Eds.), *Intellectual property management for start-ups – Value-enhancing approaches and practices for leveraging the potential*. Cham.

Schuhmacher, A., Gassmann, O., McCracken, N., & Hinder, M. (2018). Open innovation and external sources of innovation. An opportunity to fuel the R&D pipeline and enhance decision making? *Journal of Translational Medicine, 119*(16), 1–14.

Schulze, A. (2005). Patent-Portfoliomanagement für große Unternehmen. *Mitteilung der deutschen Patentanwälte, 9*(10), 416–421.

Schumpeter, J. A. (1934). *Theorie der wirtschaftlichen Entwicklung* (8th ed.). Dunker und Humblot.

Schwab, K. (2017). *The fourth industrial revolution* (1st ed.). Crowne Business. Originally published by World Economic Forum, Geneva, Switzerland 2016.

ScienceMag. (2017). *How the battle lines over CRISPR were drawn*. Accessed December 27, 2019, from https://www.sciencemag.org/news/2017/02/how-battlelines-over-crispr-were-drawn

Searle, N., Bader, M. A., Radauer, A., & Aplin, T. (2026). Intellectual property protection mechanisms and secrecy. Based on: Searle, N., Bader, M. A., Radauer, A, Aplin, T. (2024). Degrees of secrecy: Factual secrets and trade secrets in data; EPIP 2024 (European Policy for Intellectual Property); 09/2024. Forthcoming.

Shane, S. (2001). Technological opportunities and new firm creation. *Management Science, 47*(2), 205–220.

Sheehan, J., Guellec, D., & Martinez, C. (2003). Business patenting and licensing: Results from the OECD/BIAC survey. In *Proceedings of the OECD Conference on IPR, Innovation and Economic Performance, 28–29 August 2003*. OECD.

Sherkow, J. S. (2015). Law, history and lessons in the CRISPR patent conflict. *Nature Biotechnology, 33*, 256–257.

Sherkow, J. S. (2018). The CRISPR patent landscape: Past, present, and future. *The CRISPR Journal, 1*(1), 5–9. https://doi.org/10.1089/crispr.2017.0013

Singh, S. (2025). *Germany fast moving consumer goods market research report. ID: MRFR/CR/42607-HCR*. Market Research Future, WantStats Reasearch And Media. Accessed July 1, 2025, from https://www.marketresearchfuture.com/reports/germany-fast-moving-consumer-goods-market-44286#

Slater & Matsil. (2020). Slater and Matsil.

Smalley, L. W. (2014). Will nanotechnology products be impacted by the federal courts' 'Product of nature' exception to subject-matter eligibility under 35 U.S.C. 101? *Marshall Review of Intellectual Property Law, 13*, 397.

Smith, G. V., & Parr, R. L. (2019). *Intellectual property. Valuation, exploitation and infringement damages* (5th ed.). Wiley.

Spiegel Online. (2009). *Microsoft-Bezwinger greift Web-Wirtschaft an*. Accessed June 27, 2025, from http://www.spiegel.de/netzwelt/netzpolitik/software-firma-eolas-microsoft-bezwinger-greift-web-wirtschaft-an-a-653659.html

Squicciarini, M., Dernis, H., & Criscuolo, C. (2013). *Measuring patent quality*. OECD.

Šrámek, P. (2019). *AI startups in Europe*. In *WIPO technology trends 2019: Artificial intelligence* (p. 108). World Intellectual Property Organization.

St. Gallen Innovation Culture Navigator. (2025). Accessed June 20, 2025, from https://innovationskulturnavigator.ch/en

Statista. (2015). *The companies sued the most over patents in 2015. Number of US patent litigation cases against companies in the first half of 2015*. Accessed June 27, 2025, from https://www.statista.com/chart/3699/the-companies-sued-the-most-over-patents-in-2015/

Statnano. (2024). *Top 10 countries by EPO nanotechnology patents in 2023*. Lund, Jiangsu, Teheran: StatNano. Accessed July 16, 2025, from https://statnano.com/news/73567/Top-10-Countries-by-EPO-Nanotechnology-Patents-in-2023

Stellbrink. (2016). *Life after Alice*. Stellbrink & Partner on X. Accessed June 27, 2025, from https://x.com/sp_patent/status/742705881851252737

Stevens, G. A., & Burley, J. (1997). 3,000 raw ideas = 1 commercial success! *Research-Technology Management, 40*(3), 16–27.

Stiftung Science et Cité. (2004). *Streitfall biotechpatente*. Stiftung Science et Cité.

Stone, P., Brooks, R., Brynjolfsson, E., Calo, R., Etzioni, O., Hager, G., Hirschberg, J., Kalyanakrishnan, S., Kamar, E., Kraus, S., Leyton-Brown, K., Parkes, D., Press, W., Saxenian, A. L., Shah, J., Tambe, M., & Teller, A. (2016). *'Artificial intelligence and life in 2030.' One hundred year study on artificial intelligence: Report of the 2015-2016 study panel*. Stanford University. Accessed July 10, 2025, from https://ai100.stanford.edu/2016-report

Straus, J. (2003). *An updating concerning the protection of biotechnological inventions including the scope of patents for genes*. Special edition of the Official Journal of the European Patent Office on Gene Patenting.

TechInsights. (2018). *What does Uber's patent landscape look like?*https://www.techinsights.com/blog/what-does-ubers-patent-landscape-look

Teece, D. J. (1986). Profiting from technological innovation: Implications for integration, collaboration, licensing and public policy. *Research Policy, 15*(6), 285–305.

Teece, D. J. (2006). Reflections on "profiting from innovation". *Research Policy, 35*(8), 1131–1146.

Teece, D. J. (2010). Business models, business strategy and innovation. *Long Range Planning, 43*(2), 172–194.

Thomä, J., & Bizer, K. (2013). To protect or not to protect? Modes of appropriability in the small enterprise sector. *Research Policy, 42*(1), 35–49. https://doi.org/10.1016/j.respol.2012.04.019

Thomaier, J. (2023). How the life sciences industry handles IP in start-ups. In M. A. Bader & S. Süzeroglu-Melchiors (Eds.), *Intellectual property management for start-ups – Value-enhancing approaches and practices for leveraging the potential*. Springer Nature.

Thommen, J.-P., Achleitner, A.-K., Gilbert, D. U., Hachmeister, D., & Kaiser, G. (2023). *Allgemeine Betriebswirtschaftslehre* (10th ed.). Springer Gabler.

Thompson, M. J. (2013). Costs of Swiss patent litigation. *Sic!* June, 6|2013, 332–345.

Thompson, M. J. (2016). Estimating global patent rents from public market data. Paper presented *IP Statistics for Decision Makers*, OECD, Sydney 2016.

Thompson, M. J. (2017). The cost of patent protection: Renewal propensity. *World Patent Information, 49*, 22–33.

Thraen, J. J., & Bader, M. A. (2026). Key success factors in nurturing and sustaining 21st-century technology clusters. In J. J. Thraen & C. H. Hoffmann (Eds.), *Successful technology clusters in the 21st century*. Walter de Gruyter. Forthcoming.

Thumm, N. (2001). Management of intellectual property rights in European biotechnology firms. *Technological Forecasting and Social Change, 67*, 259–272.

Thumm, N. (2003). *Research and patenting in biotechnology – A survey in Switzerland*. Swiss Federal Institute of Intellectual Property.

Thumm, N., & Blind, K. (2025). *A modern guide to patenting; challenges of patenting in the 21st century*. Elgar Publishing.

Treija. (2016). Uber, what? Taxify is the most popular taxi startup in the Baltics. *EU Start-Ups*.

Tseng, Y., Lin, C., & Lin, Y. (2007). Text mining techniques for patent analysis. *Information Processing and Management, 43*(5), 1216–1247. https://doi.org/10.1016/j.ipm.2006.11.011

Turner, J. (2000). *Valuation of intellectual property assets; valuation techniques: Parameters, methodologies and limitations*. World Intellectual Property Organization (WIPO).

UPC. (2025). *Unified Patent Court Structure*. Unified Patent Court. Accessed January 9, 2026, from https://www.unifiedpatentcourt.org/en/court/presentation

UKIPO. (2013). *A study of patent thickets*. The Intellectual Property Office.

USPTO. (2017). *Patent eligible subject matter: Report on views and recommendations from the public*. United States Patent and Trademark Office. Accessed July 7, 2025, from https://www.uspto.gov/sites/default/files/documents/101-Report_FINAL.pdf

USPTO. (2024). *2024 guidance update on patent subject matter eligibility, including on artificial intelligence*. Accessed July 7, 2025, from https://www.federalregister.gov/documents/2024/07/17/2024-15377/2024-guidance-update-on-patent-subject-matter-eligibility-including-on-artificial-intelligence

von Zedtwitz, M., & Gassmann, O. (2002). Market versus technology drive in R&D internationalization: Four different patterns of managing research and development. *Research Policy, 31*(4), 569–588.

Wagner, R. (2015). Wichtige Trends in der Automobilindustrie. In R. Wagner & G. Hab (Eds.), *Projektmanagement in der Automobilindustrie* (pp. 3–9). Springer Fachmedien.

Wallstreet Journal. (2019). *Qualcomm's practices violate antitrust law, judge rules*, 2019-05-22.

Wang, B., Vuković, L., & Král, P. (2008). Nanoscale rotary motors driven by electron tunneling. *Physical Review Letters, 101*, 186808.

Warraich, M. K. S., Usman, H., Zakir, S., & Mehboob, M. (2025). Ethical governance of artificial intelligence hallucinations in legal practice. *Social Sciences Spectrum, 4*(2), 603–615. https://doi.org/10.71085/sss.04.02.297

Winterhalter, S., Zeschky, M., Neumann, L., & Gassmann, O. (2017). Business models for frugal innovation in emerging markets: The case of the medical device and laboratory equipment industry. *Technovation*, 66–67.

WIPO. (2017). *Patent office operations: Application processing times, examination capacity and examination outcomes. World Intellectual Property Indicators 2017*. WIPO. Accessed July 1, 2025, from https://www.wipo.int/edocs/pubdocs/en/wipo_pub_941_2017-chapter1.pdf

WIPO. (2019). *WIPO technology trends 2019: Artificial intelligence*. World Intellectual Property Organization. (The user is allowed to reproduce, distribute, adapt, translate and publicly perform this publication, including for commercial purposes, without explicit permission, provided that the content is accompanied by an acknowledgement that WIPO is the source and that it is clearly indicated if changes were made to the original content.)

WIPO. (2020). *What is a trade secret?* World Intellectual Property Organization. Accessed January 8, 2020, from https://www.wipo.int/sme/en/ip_business/trade_secrets/trade_secrets.htm

WIPO. (2022). *World intellectual property report 2022: The direction of innovation*. World Intellectual Property Organization. Accessed August 11, 2025, from. https://doi.org/10.34667/tind.45356

WIPO. (2025a). *PATENTSCOPE artificial intelligence index*. World Intellectual Property Organization. Accessed July 16, 2025, from https://www.wipo.int/en/web/technology-trends/artificial_intelligence/patentscope

WIPO. (2025b). *World intellectual property day*. Geneva: World Intellectual Property Organization. Accessed July 17, 2025, from https://www.wipo.int/en/web/ipday/2025/index

Wolfe, J. (2019). *Bristol-Myers wins $752 million in US patent case against Gilead Reuters*.

WSJ. (2019). *Can an AI system be given a patent?* The Wall Street Journal. Accessed July 7, 2025, from https://www.wsj.com/articles/can-an-ai-system-be-given-a-patent-11570801500

Wu, M., & Tseng, C. (2006). Valuation of patent – A real options perspective. *Applied Economics Letters, 13*(5), 313–318.

Wurzer, A. (2005). Wertorientiertes Patentportfolio. *Mitteilung der deutschen Patentanwälte, 9*(10), 430–439.

Wurzer, A., & Reinhardt, D. F. (2010). *Handbuch der Patentbewertung* (2nd ed.). Carl Heymanns.

Yaga, D., Mell, P., Roby, N., & Scarfoneet, K. (2018). *Blockchain technology overview*. National Institute of Standards and Technology, U.S. Department of Commerce. https://doi.org/10.6028/NIST.IR.8202

Yakubovich, V., & Wu, S. (2025). Orgtech: Evidence of organizational innovations in patent data. *Research Policy, 54*(5), 105209. https://doi.org/10.1016/j.respol.2025.105209

Yanisky-Ravid, S., & Kim, E. (2019). Patenting blockchain: Mitigating the patent infringement war. *Albany Law Review, 83*(2), 603–630.

Youn, H., Strumsky, D., Bettencourt, L. M. A., & Lobo, J. (2015). Invention as combinatorial process: Evidence from US patents. *Journal of the Royal Society Interface, 12*(20150272), 1–15.

Youtie, J., Porter, A., Shapira, P., & Newman, N. (2016). *Lessons from ten years of nanotechnology bibliometric analysis*. OECD. http://www.oecd.org/sti/080%20-%20Blue%20Sky%20STIP%20final%20submission.pdf

Zeschky, M., Widenmayer, B., & Gassmann, O. (2014). Organizing for reverse innovation in Western MNCs: The role of frugal product innovation capabilities. *International Journal of Technology Management, 64*(2–4), 255–275.

Zhu, S., Meng, H., Gu, Z., & Zhao, Y. (2021). Research trend of nanoscience and nanotechnology – A bibliometric analysis of Nano Today. *Nanotoday, 39*, 101233. https://doi.org/10.1016/j.nantod.2021.101233

Ziegler, N., Bader, M. A., & Rüther, F. (2011). *Handbook: External patent exploitation: Motives, forms, the role of intermediaries, and a guideline*. University of St. Gallen (ITEM-HSG).

Zott, C., Amit, R., & Massa, L. (2011). The business model: Recent developments and future research. *Journal of Management, 37*(4), 1019–1042.

Index

A
ABB, 20, 176
Abbott Laboratories, 56
AbbVie, 158
Acacia, 112, 194
Acacia Research, 111
Access to finance, 107
Accounting, 63, 66
Acquisition strategy, 108
Actavis, 228
Actelion, 105
Additional profit, 70
Adobe, 29
Advair, 158
African Regional Intellectual Property Organization (ARIPO), 40
Agent, 125
AI safety, 248
Alcatel-Lucent, 35, 189
Algorithms, 244
Alibaba, 1, 3, 169
Alice, 199, 236, 240, 244
Aliskiren, 106
Allied Security Trust, 111
Allocation, 129
Alphabet, 56, 195, 200, 245
Alternative techniques of value appropriation, 49
Amadeus, 183
Amazon, 1, 3, 5, 108, 149, 169, 195, 200, 226–228, 235, 246, 260
Amazon IP Accelerator, 201
Amazon Web Services (AWS), 200
America Invents Act (AIA), 17, 211
American Express Travel, 183
American Steel and Wire Company, 102
American Tobacco Company, 102
Amgen, 158
Analog Devices, 56
Analogy method, 66
Andreas Stihl, 275
Andreessen Horowitz, 246
Android, 112, 181, 190, 227
Anheuser-Busch InBev, 167
Animals, 209–210
Annual fees, 41, 42
Anthropic, 248
Anti-commons, 221
AppFT, 287
Apple, 5, 18, 20, 37, 56, 183, 187, 190, 192, 195, 227, 228, 260
Arthur D. Little, 73
Artificial intelligence (AI), 188, 237–251
ASEA, 176
Asia, 42, 275
Asset-based method, 76
Assertion, 100
Aston Martin, 187
AstraZeneca, 158
Asus, 181
AT&T, 108, 228
AUDI, 20, 103
Audius, 147
AusPat, 287
Australia, 18, 67, 152, 270, 272, 293
Austria, 18, 19, 22, 40, 42
Automotive, 2, 102, 103, 182–188
Avanci, 186, 222
Aventis, 11
Award, 258

B
Backlog, 133, 139
Backward valuation method, 76
Bailey, Todd, 250

M. A. Bader et al., *Patent Management*, Management for Professionals,
https://doi.org/10.1007/978-3-032-12030-4

Ballmer, Steve, 228
Baltics, 109
Bank of America, 195, 198
Bank One, 195
Barclays, 195
Barnesandnoble, 226
Barr Laboratories, 32
BASF, 160, 215
Battery industry, 49
Bayer, 32, 114, 149, 163, 271
Bayer MaterialScience, 160
Bayer Pharma, 36
Bayesian method, 67
Baylor College of Medicine, 166
BBC, 176
Beiersdorf, 260
Belgium, 291
Benchmark Capital, 108
Benelux, 223
Berkus, Dave, 75
Berkus method, 75
Bezos, Jeff, 108
Billing, 129
Bilski, 195, 235
Bilski, Bernard, 235
Biomedical sector, 102
Biopatent directive, 209
Biotechnology, 8, 206–215, 242
Bivariate patent evaluation, 56
BlackBerry, 11
Black box, 45
Blockchain, 147–155, 196
Block Inc., 198
BMW, 91, 182, 260
BNP Paribas, 195
Bolt, 109
Book value, 67
Book value method, 76
Born globals, 266
Bosch, 56, 182, 184
Bosentan, 105
Brainstorming, 135
Brands, 271
Brand strategy, 168
Brash, Kurt, 108
Brazil, 18, 40, 270
Brin, Sergey, 36
Bristol-Myers Squibb, 158
British Telecom, 112
Broadcom, 194
Broccoli EPO ruling, 162
BT Exact, 112
Buehler, 48
Business methods, 225–237
Business models, 3–4, 15, 237–251
  license, 72
Business valuation methods, 75
BYD, 182, 187

C

Call-back option, 105, 106
Camp, Garrett, 107
Canada, 7, 42, 112, 162, 163, 229, 241, 270, 293
Capital asset pricing model (CAPM), 72
Capital One, 195, 198
Cash flows, 68–71, 73
Cash value, 70
Casio, 56
CeramTec, 90
Charpentier, Emmanuelle, 211
Checklist method, 76
Chemistry, 8, 32, 85, 160–162
China, 1–4, 11, 15, 18, 42, 48, 187, 215, 223, 231, 240, 245, 272, 275, 276, 282, 291, 293
Cie Richemont, 56
Cisco, 229
Citibank, 195
Citizen Watch, 56
ClaimMaster, 143
Climate technology, 270
Cloud computing, 200
CLS Bank, 236, 240
CN 118781682 A ('BYD'), 187
CNIPA, 231, 281
Coca-Cola, 5, 20, 46, 167
Code, 244
Code analysis, 141
Code division multiple access (CDMA), 101, 189
Code generation, 141
Collateral, 63
Commercialization, 39, 100, 179, 269
  access to finance, 107–110
  complex strategies, 112–114
  cross-licensing, 101–103
  guideline, 114–118
  joint venture, 106–107
  licensing, 100–101
  litigation, 110–112
  sale, 103–104
  spin-off, 105–106
  strategic alliance, 104–105
  success factors, 117
Common patent classification (CPC), 285
Commons, 185, 246

Competition, 8
Competitive advantage, 39, 62, 66
Complementary strategies, 43
Compliance, 123–128
Computer-implemented inventions (CII), 145, 234, 238
Computer vision, 245
Conflict of interest (COI), 125
Connectivity, 182–188
Consumer electronics, 8
Consumer goods, 6, 38, 167–169
Continental, 20, 182, 186
Controlling, 65
Conversant, 186
Cooperation, 183
Copyrights, 6, 16, 22, 244
Cornell, 271
Corporate governance, 121–123, 125
Corporate leadership, 126–128
Cost of capital, 64
Cost of patents, 40–43
Cost-oriented valuation, 64
Costs, 128–133
  patent department, 128–133
Costs of infringement, 42
Counterfeiting, 273
Countries, 15, 135
  Australia, 18, 67, 293
  Austria, 18, 19, 22, 42
  Belgium, 291
  Brazil, 18
  Canada, 7, 42, 163, 293
  China, 1–4, 15, 18, 42, 215, 231, 240, 245, 282, 291, 293
  Czech Republic, 18
  Denmark, 18
  European Union (EU), 19
  Finland, 18
  France, 18, 42, 291
  Germany, 18, 19, 22, 42, 241
  Great Britain, 42, 67, 291
  Greece, 291
  Hongkong, 293
  Hungary, 18, 291
  India, 2, 208, 215, 291
  Ireland, 291
  Israel, 291
  Italy, 18, 42
  Japan, 18, 19, 42, 49, 139, 210, 231, 240, 293
  Korea, 215, 240, 282, 291, 293
  Liechtenstein, 262
  Luxemburg, 43, 291
  Malaysia, 67
  Mexico, 18
  Netherlands, 291
  Poland, 18, 215, 291
  Portugal, 291
  Russia, 18, 293
  Singapore, 291
  Slovak Republic, 291
  South Africa, 241
  South Korea, 18, 42
  Spain, 18, 291
  Switzerland, 2, 18, 19, 22, 39, 42, 210, 291
  Taiwan, 42, 293
  USA, 1, 3, 13, 14, 17–19, 34, 35, 37, 42, 49, 139, 159, 210, 235–238, 245, 291, 292
Covestro, 160
CoViD, 197
CPA, 35
Credit Suisse, 195
Cree, 31
CRISPR-Cas9, 210–215
Crop science, 20, 162–164
Cross-licensing, 37, 47, 63, 90, 101–103
Cross-licensing agreement, 57
Crypto micropayments, 147
CSL Behring, 166
Culture, 14, 36, 257–265
Curevac, 166
CWS, 152
Cybersecurity, 270
Cyclosporin, 261
Czech Republic, 18

D

DABUS, 145, 241, 283
Daimler, 20, 93, 182, 186
Damages, 63
Danavox, 92
Data, 244
Data analysis, 141
Data security, 196
Dataset, 245
Data Treasury, 195
Debt and equity financing, 63
Decision-tree analysis, 74
Declarations of origin, 21
DeepIP, 142
Deep learning, 245
DeepMind, 241
Defensive disclosure, 45
Defensive patent exploiter, 112
Defensive publication, 43, 45
Delphi, 182

Denmark, 18
Dennemeyer, 43
DEPATISnet, 287, 288
Derwent, 35, 136
Design access, 36
Designed complexity, 48
Design patents, 16, 18, 289
Design rights, 6
DesignView, 153
Deutsche Bank, 195
Deutsche Post, 199
Deutsche Telekom, 20
DHL, 199
Differentiation, 168
Diffusion models, 141
Digital rights management (DRM), 228
Direct cash flow forecast, 69
Disclosure, 219, 220
Discounted cash flows (DCF), 68, 73
Distributed ledger technology (DLT), 147–155
Division of tasks, 126
Domain names, 21
Domain name system (DNS), 21
Doudna, Jennifer, 211
Dow Chemical, 73, 160
Doyle, Michael, 235
DPINFO, 287
DSM Nutrition, 88
Due diligence, 63, 270
DuPont, 162
Dynamit Nobel Group, 90

E

eBay, 227, 235
EBSI-ELSA, 153
EC Regulation No. 1768/92, 17
E-commerce, 169
Economics, 8
Edge, 143
Electronics, 4, 31, 47, 176–182
Elfakhri, Christine, 239
Eli Lilly, 158
Emch, 37
EMG Technology, 190
EMVCo, 198
Endress+Hauser, 29, 89, 258
Enforcement, 100, 229
Entrepreneurship, 260
Eolas, 235
EP 0 546 090 B2 ('Roundup'), 162
EP 0 888 687 B1 ('Philips PIP'), 181
EP 0 914 452 A2, 209
EP 1 069 819 B2 ('Broccoli'), 162
EP 1 211 926 B1 ('Wrinkled tomato'), 162
EP 1 330 522 A1, 209
EP 1 640 448 A2, 209
EP 2 771 468 ('CRISPR-void'), 212
EP 3 564 144 ('DABUS I'), 283
EP 4 000 000 A1 ('L'Oréal'), 239
EP 18 275 174 ('DABUS II'), 283
EPC, Art. 52, 16
EPO Patent Academy, 272
Epson, 56
Erbe Elektromedizin, 88
Ericsson, 193, 194, 198, 223
esp@cenet, 287
Ethereum, 147
Ethical standards, 126
Ethics, 209
ETH Zürich, 110, 271
Eurasia, 293
Eurasian Patent Organization (EAPO), 40
EUROPatfull, 35
Europe, 16, 30, 42, 67, 101, 137, 210, 223, 227, 230, 238, 244, 292
European patent application, 218
European Patent Convention (EPC), 17
European Patent Office (EPO), 7, 38, 40, 135, 138, 139, 230, 241, 281
  member states, 288
European Union (EU), 19, 159
European Union Intellectual Property Office (EUIPO), 20, 288–289
Evaluation, 12, 51, 52, 135
  bivariate, 56
  monovariate, 52, 53
  trivariate, 59
Exit, 273
Ex parte reexamination, 37
Exploitation, 12, 100
Exposure, 56

F

Facebook, 5, 246, 260
Fashion industry, 18
Federal Trade Commission (FTC), 37
FedEx, 199
Festo, 136, 261
Fiat, 182
Financial services, 195–198
Finland, 18
First Chicago method, 76
First Round Capital, 108
First-to-file principle, 17, 211, 292
First-to-invent principle, 17, 175, 211, 292
5G, 189, 193

Flat-rate, 129
Florida, Richard, 259
Food processing industries, 48
Ford, 56, 182
4G, 193
4IR, 220–225
Fourth industrial revolution, 220, 224
Foxconn, 56
France, 18, 42, 223, 272, 291
FRAND, 186, 190–192, 222
Fraunhofer Society, 110
Freedom-of-Action (FOA), 29, 34, 271
Freedom-to-Operate (FTO), 29, 32–34, 45, 46, 145, 179, 222, 248
Freedom of production, 62
Freeman-Walter-Abele test, 225, 236
Fuel cell electric vehicle (FCEV), 103
Fuel cell technologies, 103
Funk Bros., 236
Furniture industry, 31, 38, 40
Future cash flows, 70
Future valuation multiple approach, 77

G
Galaxy Tablet, 18
Gates, Bill, 228
GE, 112
Geberit, 32
Gebrauchsmuster, 18
General Data Protection Regulation (GDPR), 244
General Motors, 182
Generative adversarial networks (GANs), 140
Generative artificial intelligence (GenAI), 139–147, 248
Genetic plant engineering, 163
Genzyme, 166
Geographic designation of origin, 16
Georg Fischer, 258
GE Plastics, 160
Germany, 18, 19, 22, 42, 94, 131, 181, 223, 241, 269, 270
Gilead, 159
GitHub, 245
GlaxoSmithKline, 158
Global positioning system (GPS), 11
Global system for mobile communications (GSM), 11
Glossary, 287
Gmail, 260
Golden Rice, 111
Goldman Sachs, 108, 148, 195
Google, 5, 36, 108, 112, 181, 183, 190, 193, 194, 222, 227, 235, 245, 246, 260, 264
Google Patent Search, 287
Gore, 9, 12, 15, 39
Great Britain, 42, 67, 241, 291
Greece, 291
Greenpeace, 162
Grey, 263
GSM, 189

H
Hague Model Convention (HMA), 19
Haier, 5, 191
Hall of Fame, 258
Hansaplast, 260
Harmonized system code (HS), 274
Harvard, 211
Harvard Mouse, 210
HBSC, 195
Healthcare, 2
Hearing Instrument Manufacturers Patent Partnership (HIMPP), 92
Henkel, 20, 38, 91, 136, 167, 168
Heroic failure award, 263
Hettich, 31
Hewlett-Packard, 104, 215, 227–229
Hexagon, 11, 46
HGGC, 112
Hilti, 5, 8, 49, 262
Historical costs method, 64
Hoechst-Marion-Roussel, 32
Honda, 182
Hongkong, 293
HTC, 112, 190, 227
Huawei, 187, 190, 191, 193, 194, 223
Huga Optotech, 83
Human genes, 209–210
Humira, 158
Hungary, 18, 291
Huntsman, 160
Hydrogen mobility sector, 103
Hyundai, 103, 182

I
IBM, 2, 12, 13, 32, 36, 47, 104, 111, 149, 150, 183, 188, 194, 195, 200, 215, 229, 230, 260, 261
ICAP Patent Brokerage, 66
Iceland, 198
Ideation, 134, 269

i4i, 229
Immersion, 91
Incentive system, 257
Income-oriented valuation, 68
India, 2, 48, 208, 215, 291
Individualism, 123
Indonesia, 275
Industrial application, 18
Industrial property rights, 16
Industries, 14
 automotive, 2, 102, 182–188
 battery, 49
 biomedical, 102
 chemistry, 8, 32, 85, 160–162
 consumer electronics, 8
 consumer goods, 6, 38
 crop science, 20, 162–164
 cybersecurity, 270
 electronics, 4, 31, 47, 176–182
 fashion, 18
 financial services, 195–198
 food processing, 48
 healthcare, 2
 ICT, 188–195
 kitchen and furniture, 31, 38, 40
 life sciences, 160, 164–167
 machinery, 2, 4, 34, 46, 48, 172–176
 microelectronics, 19
 mining, 270
 optoelectronics, 31
 pharma, 4, 8, 17, 32, 36, 45, 73, 74, 86, 157–160
 retail, 169–172
 semiconductor, 19, 30, 31, 47, 67, 102
 telecommunications, 4, 35, 39, 102, 112
 textiles, 12
 toys, 4
 transport and logistics, 198–200
 watches, 12
Industry 4.0, 220
Infineon Technologies, 47, 130
Information and communication technology (ICT), 2, 102, 188–195, 238, 270
Infringement, 42
 costs, 42
Initial public offering (IPO), 36, 63, 108, 130, 273
Innovation, 1, 66, 269
 open innovation, 12, 247
 proprietary innovation, 247
 service innovation, 88
Innovation box, 290–292
Innovation culture, 257
Innovation organization, 261
Innovation patent, 18
Innovative step, 18
Inpadoc, 35
INPI, 272
In re Stepan Co., 212
Insolvency, 63
Institute of Technology Management (ITEM-HSG), 81
Integrity, 125
Intel, 56, 148
Intellectual Discovery, 111
Intellectual property protection mechanism (IPPM), 7
Intellectual property rights, 1
 copyrights, 22
 design patents, 18
 glossary, 287
 overview, 15
 patents, 15, 16
 plant breeders' rights, 20
 plant variety rights, 20
 supplementary protection certificates, 17
 topography, 19, 20
 trade dress, 22
 trademarks, 20
 trade secrets, 23
 utility models, 18
Intellectual Ventures, 111
InterDigital, 110, 194, 222
Interference proceeding, 211
Intermediary, 116
International patent classification (IPC), 285
Internet Assigned Numbers Authority (IANA), 21
Internet Corporation for Assigned Names and Numbers (ICANN), 21
Internet Explorer, 235
Internet of things (IoT), 220–225
Inter partes reexamination, 37
Inter Trust, 228
Invalidation, 37–38
Inventio, 55, 172
Invention, 11, 16, 134, 141, 236
Inventiveness, 16
Inventive step, 18, 219
Inventor culture, 257–265
Inventor remuneration, 63
Inventorship, 145, 241
Investor, 270
Iolab, 145
IOTA Foundation, 224
iPad, 18
IP Australia, 152, 272
IP-backed finance, 270

IP Box, 290–292
IPchain, 152
ip.com, 45
IP Copilot, 142
IP5 Offices, 281
IP protection star, 276
IPRally, 143
IPwe, 153
IPXI, 104
Ireland, 291
Israel, 269, 270, 291
Italy, 18, 42

J
Japan, 18, 19, 42, 49, 94, 139, 210, 231, 240, 271, 293
Japan Patent Office (JPO), 231, 281
Japan Science and Technology Agency, 215
Java, 190, 228
Jepson claim, 284
Johnson & Johnson, 56, 158
Joint venture, 63, 106–107
JP Morgan Chase, 104, 195
Julius Blum, 40
Juno, 159

K
Kaefer, David, 229
KAG Kugelfischer, 182
Kalanick, Travis, 107
Kalo Inoculant, 236
Keep-or-sell decision, 114, 115
Kern, 46
Kettering Cancer Center, 159
Kitchen industry, 38, 40
Kite, 159
Kleenex, 21
Know-how, 48, 49
Knowledge, 2, 9, 47, 112, 114, 208
Kodak, 54, 215, 258
Kone, 172
Korea, 215, 223, 240, 282, 291, 293
Korean Intellectual Property Office (KIPO), 281

L
La Poste, 199
Large language models (LLMs), 139–140
Leahy-Smith, *see* America Invents Act (AIA)
Leahy-Smith America Invents Act, 292
Lehman Brothers, 195
Leica Geosystems, 11
Levis, 20
LeWeb, 107
LG, 31, 56, 183, 190, 223
Library of Congress, 22
License business model, 72
License fees, 69
Licensing, 36, 39, 66, 100–101, 229
  assertion licensing, 101
  carrot licensing, 101
  cross-licensing, 37
  enablement licensing, 101
  enforcement licensing, 101
  fixed-term agreements, 102
  guillotine approach, 102
  open strategy, 36
  opportunity licensing, 101
  perpetual agreements, 102
  stick licensing, 101
Licensing price analogy, 69
Liechtenstein, 262
Life cycle, 84, 86, 114, 141–145, 159, 269
Life sciences, 160, 164–167
LinkedIn, 5
Linux, 227
Lipitor, 158
Liquidation, 63
Liquid crystal display (LCD), 222
Litigation, 35, 228
Lloyds, 20
LML Payment Systems, 195
L'Oréal, 167, 215, 239
Lotus Notes, 35
Louis Vuitton, 56
Luxemburg, 43, 291
Lyft, 108

M
Machine learning, 196, 241, 245
Machine-or-transformation test, 236
Machinery, 2, 4, 34, 46, 48, 172–176
Macintosh, 260
Macroeconomics, 8
Macromedia, 29
Make-or-buy decision, 66, 90, 114, 117
Malaysia, 67
Mammals, 210
Mann+Hummel, 182
Market capitalization, 67
Market-oriented valuation, 66
Market price method, 66
Massachusetts Institute of Technology (MIT), 211, 217

Mastercard, 196, 197
Matsushita, 215
Maturity, 14
Mayo, 236, 240
Memotech, 35
Menlo Ventures, 108
Mercedes, 20, 182
MercExchange, 227
Merrill Lynch, 195
Meta, 5
Mexico, 18
Microelectronics, 19
Micron, 215
MicroPatent, 136
Microsoft, 5, 31, 37, 103, 105, 190, 194, 195, 200, 227, 228, 235, 246
Microsoft IP Ventures, 229
Midtronics, 56
MILA, 245
Mining, 270
Misereor, 162
Mission, 81
MIT-IBM Watson AI Lab, 245
Mitsubishi, 172
Monovariate patent evaluation, 52
Monsanto, 162, 163
Monte Carlo method, 74
Morphological box, 135
Motorola, 189, 190, 193, 194
MPEG LA, 111
MTel, 199
Multimodal content generation, 141
Musk, Elon, 185
Myriad, 215

N

Nanoco, 217
Nanosys, 217
Nanotechnology, 215–220
  disclosure, 219
  inventive step, 219
  novelty, 218
Natural language generation (NLG), 141
Natural language understanding (NLU), 141
Nature of the firm, 123
Negotiation, 66
Nespresso, 3, 5, 6, 49, 167
Nestlé, 6, 21, 167
Netherlands, 291
NetMoneyIn, 195
Net present value (NPV), 73
Netscape, 228
Neural networks, 245
New institutional economics (NIE), 123
Nexus approach, 290
Nichia, 31
Nike, 21
Nissan, 182
NIST, 150
Nokia, 186, 190, 194, 198, 223, 271
Non-disclosure agreement (NDA), 49, 191
Non-practicing entities (NPEs), 31, 110, 248
Nordic countries, 223
Nortel, 112
North America, 42
Novartis, 105, 106, 241, 261
Novell, 227
Novelty, 16, 218
Novo Nordisk, 158
NTP, 11
Nullity procedure, 35, 38
NXP, 56

O

Ocean Tomo, 53, 66, 104
OC Oerlikon, 37
Oncomouse, 210
1-Click/Amazon (US 5,960,411), 226
Open innovation, 12, 247
OpenSecrets, 149
Open source, 49, 245
Operational patent committee, 139
Opportunities, 57, 72
Opportunity costs, 70
Opposition, 37–38, 138, 161
Optoelectronics, 31
Oracle, 190, 195, 227
Organisation Africaine de la Propriété Intellectuelle (OAPI), 40
Organisation for Economic Co-operation and Development (OECD), 8
Organization, 13, 121, 176, 178
Osram, 31
OTC drug, 159
Oticon, 92
OTIS, 172
Otto, 108
Outsourcing, 43, 123–128, 130–133
Overture, 36
Ownership, 73, 271, 274

P

Page, Larry, 36
Pannu, 145
Pasteur, Louis, 164

Patek Philippe, 56
Patentability, 16, 212, 238
  algorithms, 244
  business methods, 235–237
  code, 244
  data, 244
  two-hurdle approach, 238
  two-step test, 240
Patent application procedure, 137
Patent assertion companies (PAEs), 31, 110
Patent attorney
  agent, 125
  compliance, 123–128
  conflict of interest, 125
  division of tasks, 126
  ethical standards, 126
  integrity, 125
  remuneration, 126
  rule of conduct, 125
Patent box, 290–292
Patent classification, 285–286
Patent clearing, 34
Patent cluster, 86, 91, 92
Patent committee, 134, 139
Patent Cooperation Treaty (PCT), 17, 40
Patent department, 121–123
  compliance, 123–128
  costs, 128–133
  organization, 121–123
  outsourcing, 130–133
  performance indicators, 130
  processes, 133
Patent Eligibility Restoration Act (PER), 242
Patent-eligible subject matter, 238
Patent landscape, 102, 270
Patent liaison, 139
Patent management, 9, 11, 12
  alternative techniques of value appropriation, 49
  defensive publication, 45
  designed complexity, 48
  methods, 52
  secrecy, 46, 47
  speed, 47
Patent monitoring, 88, 90
Patent pool, 102, 186, 198, 222
Patent portfolio, 42
  growing, 91
  pruning, 91
Patent portfolio management, 81
Patent quality, 56, 61, 108
PatentRatings, 53
Patents, 6, 16
  alternatives, 43
  annual fees, 41, 42
  application procedure, 137
  circumvent, 6, 11
  classification, 285–286
  commercialization, 39
  complementary actions, 43
  core processes of patent management, 133–139
  costs, 40–43
  document codes, 284–285
  document structure, 282–284
  first filing, 135
  first-to-file principle, 17, 292
  first-to-invent principle, 17, 292
  generative AI, 140–141
  growth, 281–282
  industrial application, 18
  innovation patent, 18
  innovative step, 18
  invention, 134–135
  inventiveness, 16
  inventive step, 18
  legislations, 292–294
  licensing, 39
  litigation, 35
  maintenance, 137
  nanotechnology, 217–220
  novelty, 16
  opposition procedure, 37
  patentability, 16
  patent box, 290–292
  patent management, 9, 11, 12
  patent portfolio, 42
  prior art, 144
  priority date, 136
  prosecution, 135–139
  quality, 11
  reexamination, 37, 226
  searching, 286–288
  second application, 136
  strategic management, 12, 13
  unitary patent, 289–290
  validity, 45
Patent scanning, 88
Patent Select, 111
Patent strategy, 27–30, 229
Patent system, 8–9
Patent tactics, 30
Patent thicket, 92, 102
Patent troll, 31, 110, 193
PatFT, 287
Patlytics, 142
Payne, Bill, 78
Peculiarity, 18

Pediatric medicines, 159
Pepsi, 167
Performance indicators, 130
Persil, 20
Pete Invest, 111
Petty patents, 18
Pfizer, 158
Pharma, 4, 8, 17, 32, 36, 45, 73, 74, 86, 157–160
Phelps, Marshall, 230
Philips, 31, 32, 104, 105, 112, 181, 194, 223, 278
Philips IP Academy, 278
Phonak, 89, 92
Piracy, 161, 164, 273–278
Plant breeders' rights (PBRs), 16, 20
Plants, 209
Plant variety rights (PVRs), 16, 20
PlayStation, 260
Poland, 18, 40, 215, 291
Polymerase chain reaction (PCR), 207
Porsche, 92
Porter, Michael, 39
Portfolio
  differentiation, 38, 39
Portfolio evaluation, 136
Portfolio management, 173, 178
  The St. Gallen Patent Portfolio Management Model, 81, 86, 95
Portugal, 291
Post-it, 260
PQAI, 143
Precedent transactions method, 77
Preferences, 123
Price, 62, 73, 116
PricewaterhouseCoopers, 111
Principal, 125
Principal-agent dilemma, 123–128
Principal-agent theory, 124
Prionics, 164
Prior art, 17, 43, 45, 144
priorartpublishing.com, 45
Priority date, 16, 136
Processes, 128–133, 172, 177
  core processes, 133–139
  ideation, 173
  invention disclosure, 173
Procter & Gamble, 167
Product clearing, 34
Product piracy, 273–278
Prometheus, 215, 236, 240
Property rights, 124
Proprietary innovation, 247
Prosecution, 135–139
Protected appellations of origin, 21
Protected geographical indications, 21, 289
Protection strategies
  de facto, 4
  de jure, 4
  formal, 4, 6, 112, 237, 244
  informal, 4, 7, 8, 112, 237, 244
Prototypes, 85
PSA Peugeot Citroën, 182
Public comps method, 77
Publication, 45

Q
Qualcomm, 37, 56, 101, 148, 189, 193, 194
Qualitative evaluation, 51, 52
Quality management, 132
Quality of patents, 11, 56, 61, 108
Quantitative valuation, 51, 61
Quantum technologies, 242
Questel, 143
Quick-Place, 35

R
Radio Corporation of America, 102
Radio-frequency identification (RFID), 198
Rambus, 30
Rationality, 123
R&D budget, 2
Real options method, 73
Red Bull, 49
Reexamination, 37
Regions
  Asia, 42, 161, 275, 287
  Benelux, 223
  Eurasia, 293
  Europe, 16, 42, 67, 159, 210, 227, 230–234, 238, 244, 292
  Nordic, 223
  North America, 42
Register of agriculture, 21
Relief from royalty, 69
Remicade, 158
Remuneration, 126, 258
Reproduction costs, 65
Residual value, 71
ReSound, 92
Retail, 169–172
Return on investment (ROI), 92, 93
RIM, 11
Risk-adjustment, 67, 69–71
Risk factor summation method, 77
Risks, 57, 69, 72, 73, 116, 273

Road mapping, 88
Robotics, 245
Roche, 45, 88, 105
Rockstar Bidco, 112
Rolex, 56
Röntgen, Wilhelm Conrad, 261
Rospatent, 152
Roundup, 162
Royal Bank of Scotland, 195
Royalty rate, 66
RPX, 112
Ruby, 32
Rule of conduct, 125
Russia, 18, 48, 152, 293

S
Sabic, 160
Sacem, 150
Sahlmann, Bill, 78
Salesforce, 5
Samsung, 18, 30, 31, 56, 112, 183, 190, 192, 198, 215, 223, 228
Sandoz, 261
Sanofi, 36
SAP, 37, 225, 227, 229
Saudi Arabia, 108
Scale AI, 250
Scenario techniques, 88
Schaeffler, 184
Schäffler, 182
Schering-Plough, 158
Schindler, 12, 34, 46, 55, 172
Schumpeter, Joseph, 8
Scikit-learn, 245
Scope of use, 66
Scorecard method, 78
Searching, 144, 286–288
Secrecy, 7, 8, 43, 46, 47
Seeds, 20
see.ip, 287
Sefar, 261
Seiko, 56
Semiconductor Energy Lab, 56
Semiconductors, 19, 30, 31, 47, 67, 102
SenseIP, 143
Series B funding, 108
Service innovations, 88
1790 Analytics, 53
Share of profit method, 72
Sharp, 31, 186
Siemens, 11, 29, 31, 32, 37, 47, 103, 112, 130, 188, 189, 229, 271, 276
Silicon Valley, 3, 261
Singapore, 291
Sisvel, 191
6-3-5 method, 135
Skype, 3
Sloan Kettering, 159
Slovak Republic, 291
Small and Medium Enterprises (SMEs), 139, 164, 265–267
Smartphone patent wars, 190
Software, 2, 4, 8, 22, 225–237, 270
Software patents, 230
Solve Intelligence, 143
Sonova, 89
Sony, 104, 183, 190, 260
South Africa, 241, 271
South Korea, 18, 42
Spain, 18, 291
Speech processing, 245
Speedel, 106
Spin-off, 105, 114, 130–133
Spin-out, 114
Spin-up, 113
Standard essential patents (SEPs), 102, 186, 191, 193
Standardization, 11, 81, 102, 168
  technology strategies, 84
Standard risk-adjust 4-factor equity model, 67
Stanford University, 36, 246
Starkley, 92
Start-up ecosystem, 269
Start-ups, 9, 267–273
State of the art, 16, 90
State Street Bank, 225, 236
Stellantis, 182
Stellenbosch University, 271
St. Gallen approach to managing technologies and patents, 81
St. Gallen Innovation Culture Navigator, 260
St. Gallen Kalbsbratwurst IGP, 21
St. Gallen Patent Index (SGPI), 53
St. Gallen Patent Portfolio Management Model, 81, 86, 95
ST Microelectronics, 56
Strategic alliance, 104
Strategic impact, 86
Strategic management, 12, 13
Strategic patent committee, 134
Strategy, 27–29
  branding, 168
  complementary actions, 43
  patent generation, 177
Stripe, 263
Substitution technologies, 83
Success factors

managing a patent department, 122
Sum-of-the-parts method, 78
Sun Microsystems, 190, 228, 229
Supplementary protection certificates (SPCs), 16, 17, 159
Sustainable innovation, 103
Swatch, 56
Sweden, 46, 198
Swiss Re, 258
Swisscom, 39
Swissreg, 287
Switch, 21
Switzerland, 2, 18, 19, 21, 22, 29, 34, 39, 42, 45, 46, 48, 210, 241, 269, 270, 291
Synthesis, 141

T

Tacitness, 47
Tactics, 30, 47
Taiwan, 42, 293
TAP, 158
Taxation, 66
Taxify, 109
Tax regimes, 290–292
Technicality, 145, 238
Technion, 271
Technologies, 2, 15, 206
AI, 237–251
biotechnology, 8, 242
blockchain, 147–155
climate, 270
cloud computing, 200
data security, 196
DLT, 147–155
fuel cell, 103
ICT, 2, 270
machine learning, 241
quantum, 242
software, 2, 4, 8, 22, 225–237, 270
sustainable, 103
Technology cycle, 267
Technology factor, 73
Technology maturity, 14
Technology portfolio, 84, 109
Technology stewardship agreement, 163
Technology transfer office (TTO), 271
TechSearch, 111
Teflon, 260
Telecommunications, 4, 35, 39, 112
TenCent, 3
TensorFlow, 245
Territoriality principle, 40
Territorial scope, 66
Tesafilm, 260
Tesla, 49, 110, 182, 185
Tête de Moine AOP, 21
Text summarization, 141
Textile industry, 12
Thaler, Stephen, 145, 241
Thermo Fisher Scientific, 164
Thomson Reuters, 216
3G, 193
3M, 92, 215, 260
ThyssenKrupp, 172
Time to market, 43, 47
Time Warner, 228
TMView, 153
Tobin's q, 67
Tomato EPO ruling, 162
Top-level domains, 22
Topography, 16, 19, 20
Toy industry, 4
Toyoda Gosei, 31
Toyota, 56, 94, 182
Tracleer, 105
Trade dress, 16, 22, 225
Trademarks, 6, 16, 20, 289
Trade secrets, 7, 16, 23, 47, 108, 244, 273, 277
Traditional knowledge, 208
Transaction, 62, 116
Transaction-cost approach, 124
Transfer price, 63
Transport and logistics, 198–200
Trivariate patent evaluation, 59
TRIZ, 135
TUM, 271
20th Century Studios, 20
25%-rule, 72
2-Click-online-shoppping, 226
Two-hurdle approach, 238

U

Uber, 107
UBS, 195
Ujo Music, 147
UK Intellectual Property Office (UKIPO), 43
Ukraine, 109
Unified Patent Court (UPC), 290
Unilever, 167
Unisys, 229
Universal mobile telecommunications service (UMTS), 189, 192
Unitary patent, 289–290
United Nations (UN), 272

United States Copyright Office, 22
United States Patent and Trademark Office (USPTO), 281
United States Postal Service, 199
Unit license rights (ULRs), 104
University of Berkeley, 211
University of California, 235
University of St. Gallen (HSG), 81, 114
University of Vienna, 211
Unwired Planet, 191
UPS, 199
US 10,097,344 B2 ('Mastercard'), 196
US 10,266,850 B2 ('CRISPR-Berkeley-Vienna'), 211
US 2012/0303537 A1 ('IP Index'), 53
US 2012/61736527 P ('CRISPR-prio'), 212
US 2013/0246301 A1 ('Uber II'), 107
US 2018/065749 A1 ('Bee drones'), 171
US 2018/065749 A1 ('Walmart'), 171
US 2018/081375 A1 ('Drone assistance'), 171
US 2018/082051 A1 ('Wristband'), 171
US 2018/082249 A1 ('Anti-theft system'), 171
US 2018/082279 A1 ('Shopping cart'), 171
US 2022/0079325 A1 ('L'Oréal'), 239
US 2023/230185 A1 ('IPwe'), 153
US 2025/0103708 A1 ('Visa'), 196
US 4,136,202 ('Nespresso Capsule'), 167
US 4,736,866 ('Harvard Mouse'/'Oncomouse'), 210
US 5,786,748 ('MTel'), 199
US 5,960,411 ('1-Click / Amazon'), 226
US 6,175,824 ('1790 Analytics'), 53
US 6,269,361 ('GoTo.com'), 36
US 6,556,992 ('Ocean Tomo'), 53
US 7,441,196 B2 ('EMG Technology'), 191
US 8,697,359 B1 ('CRISPR-Cambridge'), 211
US 9,959,512 B2 ('Uber I'), 107
USA, 1, 3, 13, 14, 17–19, 30, 34, 35, 37, 40, 42, 49, 94, 101, 111, 139, 159, 162, 199, 210, 225, 227, 235–238, 241, 245, 270, 291, 292
U.S. Bancorp, 195
35 U.S.C. §§ 155, 156, 17
35 U.S.C. §101, 238
US D504,889 S ('Apple iPad'), 19
USPatfull, 35
Utility models, 16, 18
Utilization, 70

V

Valeo, 182
Validity, 45
Valser, 21
Valuation, 12, 51, 61, 178
Valuation methods
  additional methods, 72
  cost-oriented, 64
  income-oriented, 68
  market-oriented, 66
Valuation procedures
  additional profit, 70
  analogy method, 66
  asset-based, 76
  backward valuation, 76
  bayesian method, 67
  Berkus, 75
  book value, 76
  business valuation, 75
  checklist, 76
  decision-tree analysis, 74
  direct cash flow forecast, 69
  First Chicago, 76
  future valuation multiple, 77
  historical costs, 64
  licensing price analogy, 69
  market price, 66
  Monte Carlo, 74
  precedent transactions, 77
  profit share, 72
  public comps, 77
  real options, 73
  relief from royalty, 69
  reproduction costs, 65
  residual value, 71
  risk-adjustment, 67
  risk factor summation, 77
  scorecard, 78
  sum-of-the-parts, 78
  technology factor, 73
  tobin's q, 67
  25%-rule, 72
  VC benchmark multiples, 78
  venture capital, 78
Value
  value capture, 4
  value creation, 1
Value creation, 113, 270
Value of patents
  exposure, 56
  legal, 59
  market, 59
  meaning, 62
  patent position, 60
  price, 62
  quality, 61
  technology, 60
  transaction, 62

VC benchmark multiples method, 78
Venture capital method, 78
Versata, 227
Vidal, 145
Visa, 196
Vision, 81
Vital few actions, 93
Volkswagen, 103, 182
Volvo, 186
Vorwerk, 49
VUCA, 257

W
Wall Street Journal, 2, 225
Walmart, 169, 170
Wanhua, 160
Warsaw, Rand, 235
Watch industry, 12
Watson AI Lab, 245
Watson, Thomas, 261
Waymo, 108
Wealth Fund, 108
Web of Science, 216
WeChat, 3
Weighted average cost of capital (WACC), 72
Wells Fargo, 195
Western Group, 276
Widex, 92
Wiko, 181
Wisconsin Alumni Foundation, 166
WO 2014/093712 A1 ('CRISPR'), 212
World intellectual property day, 294
World Intellectual Property Organization (WIPO), 20, 294
WPIDS, 35

X
Xerox, 215, 229

Y
Yahoo!, 36
Yandex, 109
Yescarta, 159

Z
Zara, 5
Zero Barriers, 263
ZF Friedrichshafen, 182
Zhang, Feng, 211
Zip2, 185
ZTE, 190, 191, 223

MIX
Papier aus verantwortungsvollen Quellen
Paper from responsible sources
FSC® C105338

If you have any concerns about our products,
you can contact us on
ProductSafety@springernature.com

In case Publisher is established outside the EU,
the EU authorized representative is:
Springer Nature Customer Service Center GmbH
Europaplatz 3, 69115 Heidelberg, Germany

Printed by Libri Plureos GmbH
in Hamburg, Germany